PERVERSION

Lacan's psychoanalytic take on what makes a pervert perverse is not the fact of habitually engaging in specific "abnormal" or transgressive sexual acts, but of occupying a particular structural position in relation to the Other. Perversion is one of Lacan's three main ontological diagnostic structures, structures that indicate fundamentally different ways of solving the problems of alienation, separation from the primary caregiver, and castration, or having limits set by the law on one's jouissance. The perverse subject has undergone alienation but disavowed castration, suffering from excessive jouissance and a core belief that the law and social norms are fraudulent at worst and weak at best.

In *Perversion*, Stephanie Swales provides a close reading (a qualitative hermeneutic reading) of what Lacan said about perversion and its substructures (i.e., fetishism, voyeurism, exhibitionism, sadism, and masochism). Lacanian theory is carefully explained in accessible language, and perversion is elucidated in terms of its etiology, characteristics, symptoms, and fundamental fantasy. Referring to sex offenders as a sample, she offers clinicians a guide to making differential diagnoses between psychotic, neurotic, and perverse patients, and provides a treatment model for working with perversion versus neurosis. Two detailed qualitative clinical case studies are presented—one of a neurotic sex offender and the other of a perverse sex offender—highlighting crucial differences in the transference relation and subsequent treatment recommendations for both forensic and private practice contexts.

Perversion offers a fresh psychoanalytic approach to the subject and will be of great interest to scholars and clinicians in the fields of psychoanalysis, psychology, forensic science, cultural studies, and philosophy.

Stephanie S. Swales received her Ph.D. in Clinical Psychology from Duquesne University. Working from a Lacanian orientation, she maintains a private practice conducting work both in-person and by phone.

PERVERSION

A Lacanian Psychoanalytic
Approach to the Subject

Stephanie S. Swales

Routledge
Taylor & Francis Group

NEW YORK AND LONDON

First published 2012
by Routledge
711 Third Avenue, New York, NY 10017

Simultaneously published in the UK
by Routledge
27 Church Road, Hove, East Sussex BN3 2FA

Routledge is an imprint of the Taylor & Francis Group, an informa business

© 2012 Taylor & Francis

Library of Congress Cataloging in Publication Data
Swales, Stephanie S.
    Perversion : a Lacanian psychoanalytic approach to the subject / Stephanie S. Swales.
    p. cm.
    Includes bibliographical references and index.
    1. Psychosexual disorders. 2. Sexual desire disorders. I. Title.
    RC556.S88 2012
    616.85'83—dc23
    2012000034

ISBN: 978-0-415-50128-6 (hbk)
ISBN: 978-0-415-50129-3 (pbk)
ISBN: 978-0-203-12186-3 (ebk)

Typeset in Garamond
by EvS Communication Networx, Inc.

DEDICATED TO MY PARENTS,
WITH GRATITUDE FOR THEIR LOVE
WHICH BROUGHT ME HERE.

CONTENTS

ACKNOWLEDGMENTS

I give my thanks to the great many people who, through their teaching, mentorship, support, and encouragement, helped me complete this book. First of all, I would like to thank my editor, Kristopher Spring, and Routledge for publishing this book.

I owe my profound thanks to the patients about whom I wrote in this book. They trusted me to assist them in their brave explorations of their psyches, and I hope that they found their participation in the psychotherapeutic process made a lasting positive impact on their lives. I hope that they have continued the sometimes difficult but ultimately immeasurably rewarding process of psychotherapy.

Dr. Bruce Fink directed my doctoral dissertation upon which this book is based. He did so with enthusiasm, careful attention to detail, and his vast knowledge of Lacanian theory and its clinical applications. In his various roles as my dissertation director, clinical supervisor, professor, mentor, and author of numerous excellent books, Dr. Fink has profoundly influenced my understanding of Lacan's oeuvre, my clinical work, and my ways of thinking about human life and psychopathology. What is more, Dr. Fink encouraged my own style of thinking, writing, and working with patients. I also thank Dr. Fink for having translated into English the excerpts from Lacan's work quoted in this book.

Dr. Robert Coufal, who served as a committee member for my dissertation, has also had a significant impact on my clinical work and interests. With his tireless commitment to individualized clinical care, he showed me that forensic clinicians can make an impact both on the lives of forensic patients and on the forensic system as a whole. Dr. Coufal's humanistic, existential-phenomenological, and psychodynamic perspectives on forensic psychotherapeutic work impressed and inspired me. I am lucky to have had such a kind, supportive, thought-provoking, and ethically sensitive clinical supervisor and dissertation reader.

Dr. Jessie Goicoechea not only contributed to this book as a committee member for my dissertation, but also as a professor and clinical supervisor responsible for orienting my introduction to clinical work. Through her teaching, Dr. Goicoechea passed on her compassion and respect for those who undergo psychotherapy. I am grateful to Dr. Goicoechea for having supported my growth as a clinician and having taught me her nuanced understandings of using reflexivity as a clinical tool.

Dr. Frank Scalambrino, my fiancé, has contributed much to this book and to my growth as a clinician and thinker through his support, encouragement, love, inspiring conversations, and research assistance.

I am thankful to Duquesne's McAnulty College and Graduate School of Liberal Arts for having provided partial funding for this project in the form of their 2009–2010 Dissertation Fellowship Award.

Dr. Constance Fischer has been, from the beginning of my graduate studies, a major influence on my growth as a person and as a provider of psychotherapy and collaborative assessments. Dr. Fischer touched me with her kindness, moral courage, unflagging encouragement, and wisdom. That which Dr. Fischer brings to humanistic and existential-phenomenological approaches to clinical work makes her one of the great psychologists of our day. I am thankful for her mentorship and for her useful comments on an early version of my book.

I owe my gratitude to the members of Affiliated Psychoanalytic Workgroups who provided helpful comments on an early version of Chapter 6 of my book. In particular, I would like to thank Dr. Michael J. Miller, Dr. Dany Nobus, Dr. Rolf Flor, Dr. Barry O'Donnell, Dr. Lynn Harper, Dr. Katerina Daniel, and Dr. Lawrence Wetzler.

INTRODUCTION

That is the paradox of the perverse analysand: He is someone who has a sure answer but is nevertheless perplexed.

Miller (1996b, p. 310)

[The structure of perversion], strictly speaking, is an inverted effect of fantasy. It is the subject who determines himself as an object, in his encounter with subjective division.

Lacan (1973/1998a, p. 185, translation modified)[1]

The aim of my teaching has been and still is the training of analysts.

Lacan (1973/1998a, p. 230)

This book is about perversion from a Lacanian viewpoint and it addresses many of the points of contention regarding the theory and clinical treatment of perversion. The subject of perversion poses a challenge to our "traditional" and well-established notions of ethics, logic, authority, the nature of suffering, analytic neutrality, clinical technique, and the possible outcomes of clinical work. Indeed, in the face of these challenges to our habitual ways of conceptualizing the subject and the direction of the treatment, some have said that "true" analysis with perverts is impossible.

By listening instead of turning a deaf ear to the perplexing and often disconcerting discourse of the pervert, the typically Lacanian solution to the seeming impossibility of analytic work with perverts appears: The theory and technique of psychoanalytic work with perverts must be reconceptualized in accordance with the ontological structure of perversion. Correspondingly, in this book I not only strove to illuminate the perverse

---

1   All citations from the English translations of Lacan's seminars will use the English pagination, whereas all citations from the *Écrits* will use the French pagination.

subject but also to pose the question of how the process of clinical work with a pervert must differ from that with a neurotic.

Jacques Lacan's psychoanalytic take on what makes a pervert perverse is not the fact of habitually engaging in specific "abnormal" or transgressive sexual acts, but of occupying a particular structural position in relation to the Other. Lacan's diagnostic structure of perversion, therefore, remedies the frequent conceptual confusion—even in psychoanalytic literature on perversion—between neurotics and psychotics who have "perverse" sexual preferences and those who are structurally perverse. The perverse subject is he who has undergone alienation but disavowed castration, suffering from excessive jouissance, and a core belief that the law and social norms are fraudulent at worst and weak at best.

In this book, I have sought to provide both theoretical and clinical contributions to the study of perversion. Drawing from my qualitative hermeneutic (i.e., close) reading of what Lacan said about perversion as well as my clinical work with perverts, I elucidate perversion and its sub-structures (i.e., fetishism, voyeurism, exhibitionism, sadism, and masochism) in terms of etiology, characteristics, symptoms, and fundamental fantasy. This book offers clinicians a guide to making differential diagnoses between psychotic, neurotic, and perverse patients and provides a treatment model for working with perversion versus neurosis. Two detailed qualitative clinical case studies are presented—one of a neurotic sex offender and the other of a perverse sex offender—highlighting crucial differences in the transference relation and subsequent treatment recommendations for both forensic and private practice contexts.

Lacanian Diagnosis in Brief

> [T]he perversions, such as we believe we discern them in neurosis, are not that at all. Neurosis consists in dreaming, not perverse acts. Neurotics have none of the characteristics of perverts. They simply dream of being perverts, which is quite natural, for how else could they attain their partner?
>
> Lacan (1975/1998b, p. 80)

Unlike descriptively-based diagnoses, Lacan's diagnostic system provides strong recommendations for the direction of the treatment. This is because Lacan's understanding of human suffering is *ontological*—that is, it concerns the types of beings people are in relation to language, others in the world, and enjoyment. Lacan provided us with three main diagnoses, all of which involve a certain ontological subjective position in relation to the symbolic Other. The "Other" with a capital "O" always refers to Lacan's symbolic order, and manifestations of the Other include the law, language, and any person who is perceived as radically different than the self—oftentimes parents, educators, and people in positions of authority are related to at this level. The three diagnoses are neurosis, perversion, and psychosis, and, rather than being descriptive names referring to particular symptoms, they represent *structural positions* that indicate particular ways of moving about in the languaged world with others. Roughly speaking, all three diagnostic structures indicate fundamentally different ways of solving the problems of alienation, separation from the primary caregiver, and of castration, or having limits set by the law on one's jouissance.

Jouissance is a French word and Lacanian term that is difficult to translate into English. The closest literal translation is "enjoyment," but that misses the sexual connotations of the word, which can also mean "orgasm." Furthermore, jouissance is not pure pleasure, but a combination of pleasure and pain. It is sometimes felt by the individual as unsettling, boundary-breaking, anxiety-ridden, and too much to bear. In colloquial terminology, "getting off" is a rough approximation.

As Lacan said in Seminar III (1981/1997a), each structure is constituted by a defining and causative "mechanism," or form of negation: neurosis by repression (*Verdrängung*), perversion by disavowal (*Verleugnung*),[2] and psychosis by foreclosure (*Verwerfung*). These might be understood as three primary defense mechanisms, and although psychoanalysis has focused on a dozen or so more—including, to name a few, "reaction formation" and "splitting"—those other defense mechanisms are derivative with respect to the three forms of negation that are involved in the structuring of a subject. For the most part, the field of psychoanalysis has focused on repression and foreclosure to the exclusion of disavowal.[3] In disavowal, the thought related to the perception of something is put out of mind, while the person develops symptoms that indicate the perception was actually registered and stored in memory. A famous example is Little Hans and his phobic symptom alongside his belief that his sister has a penis, despite evidence to the contrary. Disavowal, then, operates according to a kind of both/and logic: At the conscious level of intellect, Hans might say, "Of course she does not have a penis," *and* nevertheless be unable to stop himself from believing that she does have a penis. Each structure is formed in childhood, so that an adult person cannot change from one structure to another. However, this structural fixity does not exclude the possibility of substantive transformation within that structure.

An individual comes to occupy one of these three structural positions early in life in relation to the degree of instatement of the paternal

---

2 *Verleugnung* is usually translated in English as "disavowal" and in French as *désaveu*. In his later works, Lacan preferred the French term *déni* for *Verleugnung*, which means "denial."

3 This could be viewed as a consequence of the fact that fewer perverts request psychoanalytic treatment than do neurotics and psychotics.

function.[4] The paternal function has two movements. The first movement corresponds to alienation, or primal repression, whereby the person's psychical processes are split into conscious and unconscious. In it, the father, or someone representing an authority outside of the mother, pronounces a prohibition of the jouissance the child obtains from its physical connection with its mother. Once the father (or other authority) has pronounced this prohibition, which has a partial separating effect, the child is constituted as the object by which the mOther as Other obtains satisfaction. Alienation, this first movement of the paternal function, does not occur completely for the psychotic, but is firmly instated for both the pervert and the neurotic.

In the second movement, which corresponds to separation, or secondary repression, the mOther symbolizes, usually in language, her desire and lack, which are enigmatic and are not fixated upon one specific object. It is enough, though, for the mother to name a few specific objects that sometimes capture her desire, such as the father or her career. Once the mOther has symbolized her desire for something or someone other than the child, it opens up a symbolic space for the child to move into his or her own subject position, with his or her own desires. It is after this movement that the paternal function has been firmly and irrevocably instated, and the individual can be said to be neurotic. For the pervert, however, separation does not occur, and he is stuck identifying with being the actual object of the Other's jouissance. Most perverts are male, and so they identify with the penis as the actual object of the mOther's desire.

The pervert's structural position is defined by his unknowingly constituting himself as the object that causes the Other's jouissance. As a result, in the context of the clinic the pervert is a master at evoking strong feelings of countertransference. The jouissance the pervert aims to cause in the analyst can take the forms of anxiety, laughter, annoyance, frustration, horror, self-satisfaction, and surprise. As a result, if the clinician does not orient her techniques to correspond to the treatment needs of the perverse structure, the analysis for the pervert can become little more than another medium in which to get off. This is one of the primary problems encountered by clinicians in their work with perverts.

The obvious psychoanalytic answer to this particular danger is that the clinician should remain as neutral as possible and to that end manage her countertransference. While managing countertransference is crucial, it alone does not suffice to prevent the perverse analysand from playing the object-cause of the Other's jouissance as the pervert (consciously or not) is an expert at upping the ante and will invariably try, try again if he

---

4   What follows in the next two paragraphs is an extremely abbreviated and rough sketch of the theoretical elaborations I will describe in chapters 2 and 3.

fails at evoking the clinician's response. For example, the pervert might use the analyst's neutrality to his advantage and engage in dangerous or criminal acts—thus making an accomplice out of his analyst with all the emotions that might be expected to result from such a position. It follows that the pervert can make it very difficult for the analyst to avoid taking either a moralizing stance (i.e., playing the role of the pervert's insufficient superego and thus being more of a teacher or a preacher than an analyst) or the role of an impotent voyeur.

Another related result of the pervert's position as object *a* (i.e., the object-cause of the Other's jouissance) is that the pervert does not generally see himself as lacking and thus does not begin treatment in the same manner as does a neurotic analysand. A neurotic analysand in the beginning stage of treatment typically views herself as lacking both in jouissance and in knowledge about her suffering, and this provides the impetus for her to address her speech to the analyst whom she hopes will have the answers. In order for the pervert to approach the process of analysis from a position of questioning instead of a position of jouissance-causing, the analyst must find a way to get the pervert to view himself as lacking. The ways in which the analyst can go about doing so depend upon understanding the differences between the jouissance and the desire of the pervert—a differentiation which will be explained in this book.

In the chapters that follow, my explication of the perverse structure, clinical case studies, and treatment recommendations serve to show how and why the analyst's—and especially the psychotherapist's—usual approaches to the problems encountered in work with perverts fall short of the mark, and, indeed, are sometimes aimed at the wrong target entirely. On the other hand, because the pervert is a subject in the symbolic order, I will show that clinical work with perverts should bear more resemblance to work with neurotics than it does to work with psychotics. Dreams, fantasies, free association, parapraxes, repetition, and talking about the past are the fundamentals of psychodynamic psychotherapy with both neurotic and perverse analysands.

The Evolution of Perversion in Lacanian Thought

In this book, I am privileging the later work of Lacan (1964–1981) over his earlier work. This is for two main reasons. The first is that 1964 (Seminar XI) was the year that Lacan explained the two movements of the paternal metaphor, the operations of alienation and separation. These operations provide a useful framework not only for explaining the etiology of neurosis and perversion, but also for clearly differentiating between the two. Before that time, neither Freud nor Lacan had succeeded in elaborating a logically sound qualitative distinction between the two structures. The second main reason is that Lacan's emphasis during that time period on the order of the real allowed him to arrive at more nuanced under-standings of human suffering, structural positions, and the practice of psychoanalysis—understandings which take the unsayable into account. And perversion, even more so than neurosis, has to do with real order jouissance and its management. Because I am privileging Lacan's later work, much of the *Écrits* and Seminars I through X, when referenced, will be considered in light of Lacan's later conceptual understandings. For instance, even though Lacan speaks at some length about perversion in Seminar IV, he did so before having formulated his concept of split subject—a concept that is crucial to understanding and treating perver-sion. Furthermore, although Seminar VIII will be valuable in this book for its discussion of perversion in combination with the real-order object *a*, it will be necessary to interpret Seminar VIII in light of later works, such as Seminar XI, and later concepts, such as the sinthome.

Throughout his career, Lacan consistently maintained that perver-sion is most likely a structural diagnosis reserved for masculine subjects (1960/2006a, p. 823; 1973/1998a, p. 192, 1975/1998b, p. 87; 1994, p. 154). Because a consideration of the accuracy of this claim is beyond the scope of this book, Lacan's hypotheses in this regard will be briefly expli-cated, but not contested. Therefore, I will henceforth use the masculine pronoun when referring to an individual with a perverse structure.

Finally, there are many Lacans and just as many ways to conceptual-ize perversion—even though Lacan himself did not take up the study of perversion at every stage in his career. In this book, I take up a number of possible perspectives on perversion as well as of clinical work with perver-sion, but by no means is my book meant to provide an exhaustive account of all possible Lacanian perspectives on the subject.

In Lacanian fashion, let me propel us forward into the chapters of the book by formulating some questions on the subject of perversion. How does a perverse subject attain his structural position? What are the per-vert's ways of viewing life, himself, and the Other? What is the pervert asking for when he requests psychoanalysis or psychotherapy? Should the clinician give him what he wants? How can a clinician get the pervert to relinquish the position of object *a* in the session room? What are perverse symptoms? How can a clinician diagnose perversion on the basis of speech and transference? How should the clinician direct the treatment? What is the role of sublimation in perversion? What are the possible final out-comes of analysis for a perverse analysand?

1

THEORETICAL AND CASE STUDY CONTRIBUTIONS

Brief and Selective History of the Term *Perversion*

Our conceptions and practices of sexuality are discursively mediated and shift historically as different discourses and power relations emerge. In the past three centuries, the key institutional discourses that have shaped sexuality include religion, medicine, psychiatry, education, and criminal justice (Foucault, 1976/1990). Correspondingly, the term *perversion* has undergone several major shifts in meaning.[1] Perversion is derived from the Latin *pervertere*, which means "to turn around." Whatever contextual definition of perversion may be used, it always implies the transgression of a moral, social, or legal norm or value; norms and values, of course, are culturally and historically contextual. Even contemporary progressive theorists of perversion, such as psychoanalysts Joyce McDougall (1995) and Robert Stoller (1991), failed in their quest to create value-free definitions of perversion.[2]

Michel Foucault (1976/1990) pointed out that in the 18th century, religious discourse was dominant. The corresponding idea of perversion was that of sinful sexual behaviors that warranted repentance and punishment. Thus perverse acts were transgressions of religious moral norms that were often punishable by the law. An important shift occurred in the 19th century: The focus was no longer on perverse *acts* but on perverse *individuals*. In that vein, Foucault noted that the Catholic confessional shifted "the most important moment of transgression from the act itself to the stirrings—so difficult to perceive and formulate—of desire" (p. 19). A

---

1   In this section, I am not referring to Lacan's structural diagnosis of perversion, but to the other ways in which the term *perversion* has been used in the past few centuries.

2   McDougall (1995), for instance, in *The Many Faces of Eros*, tried to avoid the pejorative connotations of the "perversions" by renaming them "neosexualities" (p. 174); however, she made great use of the term *deviant* in her theories on the neosexualities. Likewise, Stoller (1991), in looking for alternative terms that would not amount to name-calling, found himself obliged to use words that hardly solved the problem, including *"aberration," "variant,"* and *"sin"* (p. 37).

person, then, was told by the power forces at play in Catholicism at large and by the priest in front of him that he must speak—again and again—about his desires, which were sinful, in order to transform *himself* into a good Christian once more. This shifted the sin from the level of a behavior to the level of the being of the subject himself.

A parallel shift occurred in other institutional sites, such as criminal justice and psychiatry. The danger of sex, though, was no longer constituted in terms of specific forbidden sexual acts, but in terms of individuals whose constitution is imbued with the will to commit forbidden sexual acts. The example Foucault gave is of the shift from the act of sodomy to the identification of the homosexual.[3] According to Foucault (1976/1990), "The nineteenth-century homosexual became a personage, a past, a case history, and a childhood, in addition to being a type of life, a life form, and a morphology, with an indiscreet anatomy and possibly a mysterious physiology" (p. 43). We focused our scientific gaze on the "perverse" homosexual individual, shifting from the practice of the act to "a kind of interior androgyny, a hermaphrodism of the soul" (p. 43). Scientific and medical discourses set about a large-scale effort to classify all of the perverse sexualities, to constitute subjects as fitting a particular type of sexuality. In this classification process, each name and type of sexuality assigned to the individual made these sexualities appear as part of reality.

The perverse became a new category in the field of sexuality, one concerned with a science of health and sickness. In medical psychiatric discourse, sinners were relabeled as perverse patients in need of some kind of medical treatment. This discourse implies a natural biological and therefore fixed norm. Richard von Krafft-Ebing's seminal book on perversion, *Psychopathia Sexualis*, which was first published in 1886, is one major representation of the medicalization of the norms of sexuality—norms which still retain clear vestiges of religious morality.[4] In his book, Krafft-Ebing spoke of a human sexual instinct, the aim of which is reproduction. However, even at that time, researchers were aware that sexual behaviors

---

3   It should be noted that homosexuality is not one of the substructures of the Lacanian diagnostic category of perversion, but that Lacan maintained in numerous places in his work (e.g., Seminar VIII) that male—and not female—homosexuality is indicative of the perverse structure. A full discussion of whether or not male homosexuality meets criteria for the structural diagnosis of perversion is beyond the scope of this book.

4   Interestingly, Krafft-Ebing was so intent upon restricting his audience to scientific and medical audiences that he wrote many sections of *Psychopathia Sexualis* in Latin so lay readers would be unable to read it. In spite of his efforts, his book became very popular among the general public. Not only did his book have 12 editions published during his lifetime, but some publishers translated the Latin sections into the languages spoken by the public. This speaks to the intense interest of the public in matters of sexuality—particularly matters of supposedly abnormal sexuality.

that did not aim toward reproduction were commonplace. Consequently, Krafft-Ebing differentiated between two kinds of perverts: one whose sexual instinct is always misdirected toward non-reproductive sexual activities and one who enjoys adding perverse behaviors to his coital activity.

Similarly, Freud, in his *Three Essays on Sexuality* (1905/1953a; 1905/1953b), tentatively perpetuated a belief in "the normal sexual aim … of copulation" (1905/1953a, p. 149) when he differentiated between people who engage in non-reproductive sexual behaviors en route to (as in kissing) or "merely *alongside* the normal sexual aim and object" (p. 161) and pathological people whose non-reproductive sexual activities have "the characteristics of exclusiveness and fixation" (p. 161). In this, Freud's first theory of perversion,[5] pathological perversion amounts to a developmental disorder, in which the person has a fixation to a certain non-reproductive sexual activity (or partial drive) that gets in the way of the "normal" adult genital sexual relationship. This type of clinical differentiation between normal and pathological perversion has persisted until the present day in some medical, psychiatric, and forensic discourses. Freud, presumably addressing Krafft-Ebing and the other sexologists of the time,[6] added that "[n]o healthy person, it appears, can fail to make some addition that might be called perverse to the normal sexual aim; and the universality of this finding is in itself enough to show how inappropriate it is to use the word perversion as a term of reproach" (p. 160). In this sense, the vast majority of people are perverse.

Given his abovementioned focus on heterosexual coitus, Freud seemed to shrink from his most radical argument in the *Three Essays on Sexuality*: We are all born with a polymorphously perverse disposition (1905/1953b, p. 191), and socialization (largely by way of the successful resolution of the Oedipal complex) is responsible for what we call "normal" sexuality. With this argument, Freud debunked completely the idea that there is an innate sexual instinct that draws people together for heterosexual reproductive-oriented intercourse to the exclusion of all other types of sexual enjoyment. "[T]he sexual instinct and the sexual object are merely soldered together" (1905/1953a, p. 148). To translate the German *Trieb* into "drive" instead of "instinct"—which has biological deterministic connotations—is truer to Freud's conception of human sexuality here. Furthermore, Freud argued that the sexual drive is not a unified one, but is fundamentally a partial

---

5   I elucidate Freud's second theory of perversion, based on the concept of castration anxiety, in chapter 3 of this book.

6   At the beginning of the paragraph from which the quote that follows was taken, Freud spoke of the "medical men, who first studied perversions in outstanding examples and under special conditions" (Freud, 1905/1975a, p. 160), indicating that they were understandably mistaken about perversions.

drive following the dictates of the polymorphously perverse disposition. In other words, the drives are partial and multiple because they have to do with certain pleasurable zones of the body, such as the anal zone, rather than the body in its entirety.

Accordingly, if we assume a polymorphously perverse disposition, then perversion is nothing but an uninhibited enactment of the normal human sexual drives. Perversity, then, is no longer a problematic to be investigated. As Dany Nobus (2006) said, "the real Freudian question would be 'Why and how does anyone ever become sexually normal?'" (p. 9). Freud and his followers, however, largely concerned themselves with "the (much less radical) issue of why and how a pervert remains entrenched in the original mechanisms of polymorphous perversity" (p. 9).

Although Freud and Krafft-Ebing had already indicated that most people do not fit completely into the medical norm of reproduction-oriented heterosexual intercourse, the medical and psychiatric discourses about sexual norms did not become substantially dismantled until Alfred Kinsey published his influential *Sexual Behavior in the Human Male* (1948/1998). The Kinsey report, which had a large sample size, empirically demonstrated that the vast majority of people deviate from the medical sexual norm. The widespread academic and societal attention the Kinsey report drew influenced the educational and moral discourses of the time. Correspondingly, the dominant discourses about sexuality and perversion shifted from religion and medicine to sociology and psychology. Since then, ideas of normal sexuality have become very relative. The term *perverse* has become taboo in favor of the more politically correct *paraphilia*—although the two mean roughly the same thing.[7] Sexologist John Money (1988) has even created "Normophilia: a condition of being erotosexually in conformity with the standard as dictated by customary, religious, or legal authority" (p. 214).

In the past several centuries, then, people themselves and peoples' experiences of their selves have been altered by the proliferation of (often scientific) discourses about sex. Foucault (1976/1990), commenting on the current discourses, said that the result is that "[m]odern society is perverse ... in actual fact" (p. 47) such that there are a considerable number of different things that turn people on, a kind of sexual mosaic. "These polymorphous behaviors" (p. 47, translation modified), according to Foucault, are an "implantation of perversions" effected by "multifarious power

---

7 Psychotherapist Wilhelm Stekel (1924/1964) coined the term *paraphilia* in 1924. Etymologically, paraphilia is derived from the Greek *para*, meaning "near," "beside," or "beyond" and the Greek *philos*, meaning "love." So, paraphilia can be literally translated as the love of something beyond the norm. Vernon Rosario (1997) said that paraphilia can be translated as "love of the perverse."

apparatuses" (p. 48, translation modified). Institutions such as psychiatry and pornography have economic interests in perpetuating, revealing, and rigidifying sexualities. Whether or not we agree with Foucault that "these polymorphous behaviors" began to be commonplace in the 19th century, and began at that time for the abovementioned reasons, it seems clear that contemporary sexual norms are very permissive in the Western world.

Verhaeghe (2001a) called the current sexual norm the norm of informed consent, "meaning that everything is allowed, on condition that both partners agree ... As a consequence, the field of perversion has narrowed down to sexual harassment and to paedophilia and incest, that is, to those cases where informed consent is lacking" (p. 62). In the present day, perversion, or paraphilia,[8] as the case may be, is therefore largely restricted to the forensic field. Consequently, rather than focusing on underlying psychological meanings, the forensic diagnoses are based on illegal behaviors, such as rape or voyeurism, and the treatment is oriented toward preventing future occurrences of those behaviors. Interestingly, according to the *DSM-IV-TR*, the paraphiliae that transgress the norm of informed consent—including voyeurism, sexual sadism, pedophilia, exhibitionism, and frotteurism—can be diagnosed if the person has acted upon his paraphilic sexual urges *or* if the person experiences marked distress related to his paraphilic urges, whereas the paraphiliae that do not transgress the

---

8   As it stands, the *DSM*-legitimated clinical phenomena that come closest to Lacan's diagnosis of perversion are the Paraphiliae. These include Sexual Sadism, Sexual Masochism, Voyeurism, Pedophilia, Exhibitionism, Fetishism, Transvestic Fetishism, Frotteurism, and Paraphilia Not Otherwise Specified. The Paraphiliae are primarily behaviorally-based diagnoses, corresponding to what are considered to be abnormal or unhealthy sexual activities. They clearly do not refer to specific structural positions; the *DSM-IV-TR* states, "[n]ot uncommonly, individuals have more than one Paraphilia" (APA, 2000, p. 567). A Paraphilia, then, is just a sexual preference that could be one among many. In addition, Paraphilia Not Otherwise Specified is a category that includes sexual preferences for "abnormal" objects not included in the other categories: "Examples include, but are not limited to, telephone scatologia (obscene phone calls), necrophilia (corpses), partialism (exclusive focus on part of body), zoophilia (animals), coprophilia (feces), klismaphilia (enemas), and urophilia (urine)" (p. 576).
    A Lacanian critique of the Paraphiliae is that these diagnoses simply name a number of particular things that arouse people's sexual desire, and they are therefore relatively unhelpful for the direction of the treatment. In contrast, perversion, neurosis, and psychosis are clinically useful diagnoses, indicating the stance the therapist should take in order to be most helpful. In practice, treatment professionals often assume that all paraphilic individuals are neurotic, rather than psychotic or "schizophrenic." From a Lacanian perspective, a paraphilic individual could be structured by any of Lacan's three diagnoses; if society considers a sexual preference to be "perverted," that does not necessarily mean that an individual who has that preference is perversely structured. Because the substructures of perversion are identified with particular perverse scenarios and preferences, however, there is likely some overlap in the two diagnostic systems. Certainly, the *DSM-IV-TR* and Lacanian diagnostic frameworks are not mutually exclusive; because the *DSM-IV-TR* is descriptively-based, a practitioner may choose to use both diagnostic systems.

norm of informed consent—including fetishism, transvestic fetishism, and sexual masochism—cannot be diagnosed solely on the basis of having acted on one's urges but are diagnosed only if the paraphilic sexual urges cause the individual marked distress.[9] Consequently, the *DSM-IV-TR* deems the informed-consent-transgressing-paraphiliae as pathological if the person commits acts of paraphilia whether or not he is distressed by them, but the same is not true for the paraphiliae that do not transgress the norm of informed consent. In other words, if there is a victim, the person is a pathological perpetrator who may be subject to mandated psychotherapeutic treatment. This is evidence that psychiatric diagnosis is sometimes based solely on the presence or absence of transgressions of existing civil law.

Lacan's structural ontological approach makes it clear that the Lacanian diagnosis of perversion is not synonymous with or reducible to behavioral transgressions of the law. In Lacanian diagnosis, the person's structural position in relation to the Other is considered first, and (sometimes illegal) sexual behaviors are taken into account secondarily, but in context and with regard to underlying psychological motives. All the same, the forensic clinic remains a privileged locus of study even for Lacanian perversion because the perverse act is often one that violates the ethical boundaries of the contextual situation and therefore one that sometimes elicits the intervention of the law. In the Lacanian framework, perversion implies a turning around of the "usual" structural neurotic position in relation to the Other and castration.

For several years, I worked at an outpatient forensic psychotherapy office, conducting psychological assessments, individual, and group psychotherapy for male "sexual offenders" (or sex offenders). Most of these sexual offenders had been diagnosed, according to *DSM* criteria, with a Paraphilia. Out of the population of sexual offenders, though, I hypothesize that only a small portion are perversely structured. Even so, I suspect that the proportion of perverts in the population of sexual offenders is much higher than in the general population. That being said, forensic clinicians in particular would do well to differentiate perversion from neurosis and psychosis.

---

9 Since the Internet became widely used, there have been a large number of sexual offenders so classified because they were in "possession" of or traded or sold illegal pornography of minors. A large number of those offenders have never committed a "hands-on" offense and therefore would not be classified as pedophilic unless they described distress related to their pedophilic inclinations. In this case, the definitions of informed consent and acting upon paraphilic urges are debatable. Some professionals see the minors depicted in the pornography as unconsenting victims—victims who were created both by the makers of the pornography and by those creating the demand for the pornography.

Therefore, if it is the case that forensic psychotherapists are treating perverse individuals as if they were neurotic[10]—forensic treatment tends to be one-size-fits-all, with neurosis as its presumed basis—then a Lacanian analytic framework would have much to offer the mainstream in terms of why certain interventions fail or even exacerbate the "offensive" sexual behavior. Both a Lacanian psychoanalytic and a forensic approach to treatment aim to reduce the victimizing activities of the pervert, although the former would do so indirectly, through the process of analysis. It follows that, if we knew how to do effective psychotherapeutic work with perverse individuals, we would not only benefit the patients themselves, but society at large. (However, permit me to highlight that not all perverts are sex offenders and that many perverts do not pose a threat to society. On the contrary, perverts often have considerable gifts for creating art. Perverts famous for their contributions to the arts include, to name a few, the author André Gide, shoe designer Manolo Blahnik, and fashion designers Yves Saint Laurent and Valentino Garavani.)

Review of Relevant Quantitative and Qualitative Research

Blind Spots in Sex Offender Treatment

Successful treatment, in the context of sex offender treatment, is solely measured by the extinction of the illegal behavior.[11] Hanson and Morton-Bourgon (2005), in their meta-analysis of recidivism studies, note the following: "A review of the core treatment targets of sexual offender treatment programs suggests that most programs direct considerable resources toward characteristics that have little or no relationship with recidivism (e.g., offense responsibility, victim awareness, and empathy)" (p. 1159).

It is interesting both that recidivism has no relationship with empathy for a victim, offense responsibility, or victim awareness, and that

---

10 I have been unable to find any forensic literature concerning how to conduct the treatment of sexual offenders differently in cases of psychosis.

11 By and large, most efficacy studies of psychological treatment for sexual offenders have found that treatment has a small to modest effect on preventing future sexual or other criminal offenses (Hall, 1995; Hanson et al., 2002). It is easy to find well-designed studies, however, that find no statistically significant effect for treatment (e.g., Marques, Wiederanders, Day, Nelson, & van Ommeren, 2005). For instance, Proctor (1996) used a cohort design that compared all the sex offenders (including rapists, exhibitionists, and hands-on child molesters) who started a community treatment program between 1989 and 1992 with a matched group from the same jurisdiction released between 1986 and 1989 when no treatment was available. After a fixed 5-year follow-up period (the same for both groups), the sexual reconviction rate was 5.6% for the treatment group compared to 13.0% for the comparison group. Even though the difference might be considered clinically significant, it was not statistically significant because of the small sample size.

most sex offender treatment professionals spend time attempting to build those characteristics. This kind of treatment aims to teach, preach, and condition the patient into developing a "higher functioning" superego. Basically, therapists are trying to appeal to a patient's sense of guilt and empathy to make a case for why his sex offense was wrong and why he should not re-offend; the hope is that, by making him feel bad for hurting someone, he will not commit the same sexual offense again. This logic relies on the belief that the man would not have committed the crime had he been fully aware (in the "moment" and the preceding moments) of the weight and impact of his sin on himself and others. This reasoning is obviously fallacious. Certainly, a thin "moral fiber" might have something to do with why the person was able to follow through with the offense, but this leaves out the multitude of possible reasons why the man was motivated to commit the sexual offense. What of the jouissance he gained in fantasizing about or engaging in the act? What about the individual's personal history, family context, and cultural context, in which the sexual offense has particular meanings? If the symptom is treated as a wart that can be removed if it is known to be ugly, then the symptom as a meaning-ful signifier will persist.

Rubbing a sex offender's nose in his mess might, if done artfully, result in his being more motivated to defecate in the toilet instead of in a public hallway, but the question that arises is the following: To what degree can a therapist successfully use the techniques of a priest or a school principal? The literature that Hanson and Morton-Bourgon (2005) reviewed sug-gested that playing priest in the therapy room is ineffective. We can only wonder what motivations or what meaningful personal signifying rela-tions underpin the therapist's masquerade as priest.

One might argue here that there were studies of psychotherapy with sex offenders that evaded Hanson and Morton-Bourgon's (2005) meta-analytic review that utilized moralizing techniques with at least somewhat more efficacy. That might lead us to pose the question: In what instances, and with what kinds of sexual offenders, are moralizing techniques effec-tive or ineffective? I hypothesize that moralizing works better with neu-rotic sexual offenders than it does with perverse sexual offenders. Perverts, compared to neurotics, have a very small capacity for guilt because the Other or the moral law exists only shakily for them. Guilt is a hallmark of a neurotic structure that corresponds to inhibition of impulses related to the firm instatement of the paternal function and symbolic order. A thera-pist, then, is mostly wasting his time in trying to appeal to the pervert's mostly absent sense of guilt.

Along those lines, Hanson and Morton-Bourgon (2005) also found that the two strongest predictive factors of sexual recidivism were sexual devi-ancy ($d.$ = .30) and antisocial orientation ($d.$ = .23)—the latter of which refers to Antisocial Personality Disorder as diagnosed by the Psychopathy

Checklist-Revised (PCL-R) (Hare, 2003), antisocial traits, and a history of rule violation.[12] Among the strongest individual predictors of any recidivism (sexual or non-sexual) were general problems with self-regulation ($d.$ = .75, 6 studies, which included measures of impulsivity, lifestyle instability, and Factor 2 of the Psychopathy Checklist Revised) or a history of nonviolent crime ($d.$ = .68, 9 studies), Psychopathy (PCL-R total scores; $d.$ = .67, 9 studies), and a history of nonsexual crime ($d.$ = .63, 8 studies). So, people with antisocial traits have the greatest risk of re-offending. Correspondingly, I propose that Psychopathy, as a somewhat personality-based diagnosis, is a diagnosis which closely resembles the Lacanian structure of sadistic perversion, and that the connection between the two warrant further study (see Willemsen & Verhaeghe, 2009). (In addition, James Masterson's structural diagnosis Antisocial Personality Disorder bears numerous close resemblances to Lacan's perverse structure, including the antisocial person's tendency to "provoke" the Other.) I hypothesize that, less frequently, psychopaths might be psychotically structured. It follows that Hanson and Morton-Bourgon's results could be understood as support for hypothesizing that sex offenders with a perverse structure are more likely to reoffend than those with a neurotic structure, and that diagnosing along Lacanian lines could be a very helpful component to sex offender risk assessment (and criminal risk assessment in general). This question of risk assessment, however, is beyond the scope of this book.

By far the most common model of sexual offender treatment is the relapse prevention approach, which was first developed for treating people with addictions (Marlatt & Gordon, 1985) and was then adapted for treating sexual offenders (Pithers, Marques, Gibat, & Marlatt, 1983). The relapse prevention model uses cognitive-behavioral techniques to identify situations, moods, and cognitions that are potential "triggers" for re-offending. Then, practitioners focus on teaching offenders self-management skills so that they can use more effective coping strategies than committing sexual offenses. Most treatment programs also teach the aforementioned empathy or victim-awareness skills and attempt to restructure the supposed cognitive distortions that contributed to the offensive behavior. One main problem of this treatment model is that it is one-size-fits-all. It assumes

---

12 It should be noted that Antisocial Personality Disorder (APD), which "exists" according to the *DSM-IV-TR*, is different from Psychopathy, which is not legitimated in the *DSM-IV-TR*. Robert Hare, the author of the PCL-R, suggests that APD can almost be reduced to criminality. Because, diagnostically, it is almost entirely based on behaviors, Hare estimated that between 80% and 85% of incarcerated criminals meet the required criteria of APD, whereas only about 20% of them would qualify for a diagnosis of Hare's Psychopathy. Psychopathy is a more "personality based" diagnosis. Psychopathy refers to a particular relationship of the patient to the law—one of being above the law or seeing through the law—and avoids accentuating sexually transgressive behaviors more than other potential effects of the patient's relation to the law.

that all sexual offenders offend for the same reasons and will respond to the same type of treatment. The relapse prevention approach assumes that all sexual offenders commit sexual offenses because of low self-esteem, stressful life events, deficits in coping skills, and being in bad moods.

Only very recently has a forensic treatment approach for sexual offenders attempted to correct this one-size-fits-all treatment modality. *The Self-Regulation Model of the Offense and Relapse Process* (Ward et al., 2004) differentiates between pathways to offending, "taking into account different types of goals (e.g., approach versus avoidance goals), varying affective states (both initial and ongoing) and different types of planning" (p. 12). The self-regulation model involves four major different pathways to offending: avoidant-passive, avoidant-active, approach-automatic, and approach-explicit. Those within the two avoidant categories wish to avoid sexual offending, but lack the coping skills necessary to prevent its occurrence. Those within the two approach categories have goals, values, and beliefs that make sexual offending a positive, enjoyable experience that they strive to repeat. The approach-automatic type is someone who impulsively takes up opportunities for committing sexual offenses, and the approach-explicit type is someone who makes "use of careful planning to execute offenses" (p. 38).

Both the self-regulation model and the relapse prevention model view prevention of re-offending as their treatment goal. However, with the approach types, the self-regulation model takes into account something that the relapse prevention model does not: Some offenders view their sexual offenses ego-syntonically. That is, the self-regulation model is, in part, an attempt to explain and recommend treatment for sexual offenders who feel entitled to "have what they want, when they want it" or "'relish' their sexual deviance, living in a world of their own because 'no one understands them'" (Ward et al., 2004, p. 41). The developers of the self-regulation model, however, see their four types as somewhat fluid, such that it is a common occurrence for an avoidant offender to become an approach offender, and vice versa. This fluidity exemplifies the self-regulation model's lack of a structural approach.[13]

Treatment for the approach-automatic offenders focuses on improving their deficits in "meta-cognitive control" (Ward et al., 2004, p. 75) by teaching "appropriate self-regulation strategies" (p. 75). Furthermore, their "significant sense of entitlement" (p. 77) is intervened with via "the

---

13 One might counter my argument for the superiority of structural diagnosis by the claim that the "phenomena" of categories—in this case approach and avoidant—are more relevant to diagnosis and treatment. However, the categories themselves lack validity insofar as their criteria are arbitrary, and it is unlikely that a sex offender would always fit neatly into one category before jumping completely to another category.

usual interventions such as cognitive restructuring for dysfunctional cognitions together with techniques designed to ameliorate empathy deficits"
(p. 77). In contrast, the approach-explicit type does not have deficits in
meta-cognitive control, and so treatment is oriented toward the alteration
of his "core beliefs" concerning sexual offenses (p. 78) through cognitive
psychotherapeutic methods such as Aaron Beck's. Treatment is the most
difficult with the approach-explicit offender group (Hudson & Ward,
2000), and I hypothesize that this is the category that perverts are most
likely to fall under, although perversion is far from synonymous with the
approach-explicit type. Because the self-regulation model is relatively new,
there has not been very much empirical research on its efficacy. There have
been no studies of treatment efficacy of the self-regulation model that
include recidivism data.

One study (Bickley & Beech, 2003) found that treatment of approach
types succeeded in significantly reducing their pre-treatment statements
that minors were able to consent to sexual activity with adults. However,
they retained the belief that minors were unharmed by sexual activity
with adults. It seems to me that any changes in the "core beliefs" of sexual
offenders in the course of forensic treatment might simply be the result
of "faking good" to the treatment providers so that they could terminate
treatment and avoid other consequences of appearing to persist in their so-
called cognitive and empathy distortions—including heckling from fellow
group members or increased incarceration time. Both the self-regulation
and the relapse prevention model rely heavily upon descriptive nosology
and cognitive-behavioral methods of change. In sum, the self-regulation
model represents only a small improvement in diagnosis and treatment
methods over those of the relapse prevention model. In both models of
sexual offender diagnosis and treatment, there is a subset of individuals
identified as treatment resistant; it is my hypothesis that many of these
individuals have a perverse structure, and that Lacan's ontological structural framework will reveal why the existing methods of treatment fail.

A recent meta-analytic study by Michael C. Seto, R. Karl Hanson,
and Kelly M. Babchishin (2011) focused on recidivism rates for online
sex offenders. Interestingly, they found that "online offenders rarely go on
to commit detected contact sexual offenses. During the follow-up period
(up to 6 years), less than 5% of the online offenders were caught for a new
sexual or violent offense. Two studies found no sexual recidivists" (p. 136).
What is more, many of the 24 studies included in their analyses reported
that the majority of online offenders had no prior "contact" sex offense
history and often "no prior criminal history of any kind" (p. 125). These
findings support my hypothesis that online sex offenders with no history
of contact offenses are very likely to be neurotic rather than perverse. In
this vein, the case study that comprises chapter 7 is of a neurotic online
sex offender.

From a natural science perspective, then, those who buy into the truth of the existence of the disorder called Paraphilia seek to investigate the phenomena using corresponding methods: quantitative studies using behaviors and cognitions as criteria. The normal scenario of natural scientific studies of paraphilic sexual offenders is the following: A quantitative study is conducted on the efficacy of cognitive-behavioral methods with paraphilic sexual offenders. The study defines treatment success as the removal of the symptomatic act from the paraphilic's life. The "data say" that there is either a small effect or no statistically significant effect of treatment on the symptom. The researcher-experts find various ways of throwing up their hands, including the conclusion that certain people are simply resistant to treatment. The researchers might say the resistance is due to "personality factors" or a "personality disorder,"[14] such as "Antisocial Personality Disorder." I propose that one of the reasons for those treatment failures or "treatment resistant" patients is that clinicians misrecognize a perverse personality as a neurotic personality. In other words, Paraphilia is a theoretical construction that falls short, and perversion is a better theoretical construction. Lacan's conception of the subject and of diagnosis is a superior alternative, not a companion, to the *DSM-IV-TR*.

From a Lacanian point of view, *the centrality of the goal of relapse prevention in forensic treatment not only sometimes sabotages the possibility of such success but also comes at the cost of other treatment aims that are more closely linked to the individual's complaints and his structural diagnosis.* For the sex offender pervert, Verhaeghe (2004) notes that "[f]ocusing exclusively on relapse prevention means one removes the perverse subject's attempt at solution without addressing the underlying problem. To the extent that relapses do stop, this must occur as a result of the treatment, not as the primary goal" (pp. 426–427). When a potential victim's well-being is at stake, however, it can be difficult to push relapse prevention into the background. One of the aims of my book is to explore this tension between forensic and psychotherapeutic goals and methods.

Existing Cases Studies of Perversion

In the process of doing research for this book, I searched high and low for existing case studies (or even short descriptions of case work in a book or

---

14 The *DSM-IV-TR* (2000) defines a "Personality Disorder [as] an enduring pattern of inner experience and behavior that deviates markedly from the expectations of the individual's culture, is pervasive and inflexible, has an onset in adolescence or early adulthood, is stable over time, and leads to distress or impairment" (p. 684). A personality disorder, especially one like Antisocial Personality Disorder, is thought to be very resistant to treatment. For psychotherapists, this logic serves as a defense, in which treatment failures are attributed to the patient's nature being inherently and permanently difficult.

paper on a particular topic) of (Lacanian) perversion, and 90% of the few case descriptions I found of masochism and sadism were not, after looking closely at them, perversely structured but were instead neurotically structured with perverse traits. About a third of the case descriptions of fetishists, exhibitionists, and voyeurs I found were perversely structured. Let this serve as a warning that when a patient is referred to as a "pervert," "pervert" can mean a great many things.

After having searched extensively for existing full-length case reports of work with perversely structured patients, I found only six—two of which were avowedly Lacanian. One, entitled "Fetishishization of a Phobic Object," was written by René Tostain (1993), a Lacanian analyst.[15] The other Lacanian case study was written by Bruce Fink, "The Use of Lacanian Psychoanalysis in a Case of Fetishism" (2003). The four case studies published by non-Lacanian psychoanalysts include Henry Lihn's (1970) case of fetishism, James Glover's (1927) case of fetishism, Sándor Ferenczi's (1916) case of childhood sadism (i.e., "A Little Chanticleer"), and Juan Pablo Jiménez's (1993) case of voyeurism; I discuss the last three in chapter 5, Lihn's case study in chapter 4, and Fink's case study in chapter 3. Clearly, like with fetishism itself, there is a lack in the literature around which little has been constructed. Although perversion is not as common as neurosis, it is common enough that more clinical case reports should be made available for the purposes of better clinical diagnosis and treatment of perverts.

In literature on perversion, there are a plethora of definitions of the diagnosis—most of which have little overlap with the structural diagnosis elaborated by Lacan. One such case report, written by Michael Good (2000), called "Perverse Defenses: A Clinical Vignette," does differentiate between neurosis and what he calls "frank or obligatory perversion" (p. 199). Good did not do a very good job of frankly defining "frank or obligatory perversion"; he seems to suggest that it is a long-standing fixation on using "perverse defenses," which make frankly perverse patients difficult to work with in analysis. Good's definition of perverse defenses has little to do with Lacan's three forms of negation. Good's perverse defenses "protect against both the experience of psychological deadness and early, regressive, and dependent themes and their associated affects, including intense shame. They can include defenses against external reality, the patient's own conflicts, and relationships with others; they involve affect intolerance, difficulties with analytic collaboration, and analytic impasse" (p. 199). It follows that Good's perverse defenses, whatever they are, exactly, do pretty much everything under the sun. The case vignette

---

15 Fink commented on Tostain's case study in his 1997 book, *A Clinical Introduction to Lacanian Psychoanalysis: Theory and Technique.*

Good gave in the article does nothing to clarify these so-called defenses or make them into anything more than ambiguously difficult human experiences. Furthermore, of his definition of perversion, Good said, "When we call someone perverse (a judgment), we refer to how that person seems provocatively to refuse to be reasonable and to act in accordance with acceptable norms in such a way as to evoke a countertransference response (at least a feeling) of judgment, criticism, or attack" (p. 200). It follows that a perverse patient is someone who is unreasonable, abnormal, and who is often subject to the therapist's criticism or attack.

There is another case report that provides a somewhat detailed account—only five pages—of analytic treatment with an individual who might meet Lacan's diagnostic criteria for perversion. It is by Arthur Leonoff (1997), and it is entitled "Destruo Ergo Sum: Towards a Psychoanalytic Understanding of Sadism." Although Leonoff treated sadism as a defensive structure and a habitual way of relating to others, he was unclear on the ontological structure of sadism. For instance, he used the rather vague differentiation of "serious" sadism versus "commonly seen" sadism. Leonoff's "Mr. X" seems to fit the latter category, perhaps in part because his sadism is mostly restricted to the realm of fantasy. A more detailed case report, with more of the patient's own speech, would be necessary to determine whether or not Mr. X fit Lacanian criteria for sadism.

A Method Suited to Madness

The unconscious is the chapter of my history that is marked by a blank or occupied by a lie: It is the censored chapter.

Lacan (1953/2006a, p. 259)

The existing body of qualitative research has, both in method and interpretation, largely ignored the unconscious (as Lacan understands it). This avoidance is particularly striking within the qualitative research of clinical psychology, because most psychologists attribute some importance to the unconscious in human existence. As a corrective to research methodologies that only reflect the conscious ego, I propose that Lacanian analysis (or psychotherapy) is ideally situated to fill in the blanks and expose the censored chapter of the unconscious—which is itself a kind of knowledge. I argue that psychoanalysis in general and Lacanian analysis in particular is already a valid method of inquiry; in some cases, the psychoanalytic interview is preferable to an interview conducted for research purposes. Finally, I argue for a Lacanian qualitative clinical case study as the research method for this book.

As Steinar Kvale (2003) pointed out in his excellent chapter, "The Psychoanalytical Interview as Inspiration for Qualitative Research,"[16] the practice of psychoanalysis has produced a wealth of important knowledge—acknowledged or not. The method by which Sigmund Freud, Jacques Lacan, Carl Jung, and others have obtained the knowledge reflected in their books on human experience and the theory and practice of therapy has been, of course, what I will refer to as the psychoanalytic interview. Our mainstream psychological textbooks are filled with knowledge gained by psychoanalytic inquiry, and yet, paradoxically, those same textbooks deny the psychoanalytic interview as a valid form of research. Insofar as psychoanalysts are interested in human experience and therapeutic change, why should we privilege what quantitative data "say" over what human beings say? Furthermore, why pretend we are sociologists and use a qualitative method, like conversation analysis, that eschews intrapsychic meanings? As an alternative to trying to squeeze a square peg into a round hole, psychoanalysts should stick to their own trade rather than borrowing methods from other disciplines.

The practice of psychoanalysis, then, although its principal aim is therapeutic change, also generates significant knowledge. Freud (1912/1958) himself noted that "[o]ne of the claims of psycho-analysis to distinction is, no doubt, that in its execution research and treatment coincide" (p. 114). The analytic interview is a qualitative method of understanding that exists outside of natural science conceptions that seek objective knowledge in the form of quantifiable, unequivocal data. Instead, psychoanalysis inquires in an open manner into the conscious and unconscious experience of a particular analysand by encouraging the analysand to speak and wonder about herself.[17] Psychoanalysis therefore involves an open qualitative interview method that does not use set questions, which would assign predetermined limits to the analysand's speech.

A psychoanalytic session employs an interpretive method, seeking in the interview itself as well as afterward to interpret the multiple, sometimes conflicting meanings of the analysand's speech. Unlike other methods, which view ambiguity and inconsistency as problems to be eliminated, psychoanalysis embraces the complexities of discourse as accurate reflections of what is means to be human. In fact, an analyst listens not only to the intended face value of the analysand's speech, but also to what the analysand said but did not want to say. The analyst's ear is tuned in to verbal and affective manifestations of the unconscious such as slips of the tongue, tales of bungled actions, surprise, overemphasis, unfinished

---

16 Kvale's chapter inspired many of the ideas in this section.
17 For simplicity's sake, I will refer throughout this section to the patient as a woman and the analyst as a man.

sentences, equivocal word usage, negation, and unprovoked denials—all of which indicate a multiplicity of meanings. The method of interpretation employed in psychoanalysis could consequently be considered a form of depth hermeneutics or a hermeneutics of suspicion (Habermas, 1972).

A skilled psychoanalyst listens to the analysand's speech with an open mind, in a manner akin to Freud's (1912/1958) notion of "evenly-suspended attention" (p. 111). He views all of the analysand's speech as significant. This is reminiscent of Clifford Geertz's (1977) painstaking notation of all of his thoughts and experiences during his ethnomethodological studies. In this way, Geertz and an analyst strive to ensure that they see as much as possible during the "data collection phase" so that their interpretations are based on as much of the whole as possible. In listening and in writing case notes (after the session) and case formulations, an analyst seeks to minimize that which is left out or avoided. Much like what the analysand leaves, consciously or unconsciously, out of her account, omitted details often have something to say which might shift the bedrock of what we thought we comprehended.

Furthermore, in contrast to listening for ways to fit the analysand's discourse into quantifiable research categories, the analyst attempts to be open to the particularities of the individual's being in the world. The analyst uses theory as a malleable entity, keeping in mind that theory helps him see some things but blinds him to others. Regular analytic supervision helps loosen up the analyst's perspective, preventing him from falling into the sometimes attractive delusion that we possess masterful complete understandings.

The type of listening practiced in a Lacanian psychoanalytic interview is anything but free-floating, aimless, or neutral.[18] The analyst must be attuned to certain phenomena, such as previously unavowed desire, in order to move the analysis therapeutically forward. A Lacanian analyst encourages the analysand to say whatever comes to mind, with as little censorship as possible, no matter how senseless or distasteful her thoughts may seem to her. Furthermore, the analyst makes it clear, via punctuation and scansion, that he is particularly interested in her dreams, fantasies, parapraxes, ambiguous phrasings, and contradictions; in short, the analyst is more interested in what her unconscious has to say than what her conscious, egoic self has to say. After all, her conscious attempts to alleviate her suffering have succeeded only in her eventual seeking of therapy. This way of speaking and being listened to contrasts starkly with what an

---

18 I doubt very much that an analyst practicing any form of psychoanalysis listens in an aimless manner. Each theoretical orientation recommends paying particular attention to certain phenomena with the belief that those phenomena fashion keys that will open doors in the therapeutic progression of analysis.

analysand is used to, and it takes her time to become more comfortable with it.

The usual qualitative research interview is a situation in which the subject speaks more or less as she usually speaks. She assumes—often correctly—that the interviewer wants to hear a coherent story about the research topic that makes sense, whether or not the interviewer asks open-ended questions. Also, the subject might censor her speech in order to fit her standards of social desirability more than if she were speaking to an analyst. Her speech, of course, will frame the possible interpretations. The unconscious is almost always left out of a qualitative interview inquiry; the subject and interviewer both collude in fitting the subject's experience into the realm of the conscious self, ignoring parapraxes and ambiguous phrasings. So it follows that the context of the interview as well as the interviewer's manner of listening and speaking highly influence the subject's speech and thus the knowledge produced by the inquiry. Insofar as an analyst or clinical psychologist is interested in the kind of human being that has an unconscious, his method of inquiry must allow for what research methods have avoided to date.

Another aspect of psychoanalysis as a qualitative research method is that it provides in-depth case studies. The analyst, rather than interviewing someone a few times as would other qualitative interviewers, often speaks with a patient multiple times a week for a number of years. The psychoanalyst, then, gets much more than a brief snapshot of a person's experience from which to formulate interpretations and explore psychopathology and the process of therapeutic change. Finally, a Lacanian analyst works with a theory that enables him to be attuned to the cultural realm of his patients. When a Lacanian analyst is situated as an Other in the symbolic order, he can, via transference projections, for instance, lay bare the analysand's stances toward the various cultural Others such as the parental Other and the educational Other.

As Lacan reminded us, attaining absolute objectivity and truth is an impossibility—something that natural scientific methods do not acknowledge. However, there are some senses in human science research in which objectivity of method is desirable. As Kvale (2003) pointed out, the practice of psychoanalysis, perhaps surprisingly, meets criteria for research objectivity in four key senses: freedom from partisan bias, intersubjective agreement,[19] the method's ability to reflect the nature of the research object, and allowing the object to object.

Regarding the fourth criterion of objectivity that the analytic interview satisfies, the analysand in analysis, of course, does sometimes object to

---

19 For Lacan, the notion of intersubjectivity itself is problematic, because all communication is miscommunication.

interpretations made by the analyst. This brings up an interesting and oft-posed question: Because an analyst refrains from immediately taking at face value the analysand's "yes" or "no," can an analysand "really" object? When an analysand rejects the analyst's interpretation, the possibilities are as follows: She is resisting acknowledging some unconscious phenomena, the interpretation was off the mark, or the patient refused the truth value of the interpretation because she wished to displease the analyst.[20] Freud (1912/1958) recommended solving this dilemma through the practice of a more indirect form of validation: The analyst should carefully observe how his interpretation affects the analysis, seeking to notice alterations in the analysand's symptoms, free associations, dreams, and fantasies. Kvale (2003) called this practice "pragmatic validation" (p. 292). The practice of psychoanalysis itself is thus already a sound qualitative research method.[21]

The Lacanian psychoanalytic interview, like any clinical or research practice, has certain epistemological and ontological assumptions. Like discourse analysis, which is social constructionist, Lacanian analysis is epistemologically relativistic. This means that there are no objective truths, because human experience is shaped by language and by particular social, historical, and political conditions. Analysis' medium of healing and of gaining knowledge is speech. Lacanian analysis involves a certain structure and set of techniques that allow the analysand to articulate herself in a way that is therapeutically transformative. In the process of analysis, an analysand's knowledge of herself shifts as she becomes curious about what her unconscious has to say. The analysand sheds much of her egoic-realm knowledge as half-truths, and, in the process of grappling with the unsaid and the unknowable, paradoxically produces knowledge.

Ontologically speaking, Lacan (1973/1998a) said that being is constituted in the act of speaking. According to Lacan, we are situated in language in a way that is amenable to the previous discussion of Lacanian

---

20 In the practice of Lacanian analysis, however, the patient's manifest acceptance or refusal of an interpretation is likely to be aimed at only one meaning of the interpretation, because Lacanian interpretations are polyvalent rather than unequivocal.

21 There are, of course, numerous ethical questions to consider in using the psychoanalytic interview as a qualitative research method. One such question is whether or not to audio- or video-tape sessions—with the analysand's consent, of course. The presence of recording equipment in the room will serve as a constant reminder to the analysand that her words are being listened to for some other purpose outside of the therapeutic aim of analysis. We must recall that most of the knowledge gained from the practice of analysis has not involved the use of recording devices, and so there is no need for the analyst to jump unthinkingly into the world of verbatim transcripts in the name of scientific method. Detailed case reports, including excerpts from the analyst's notes of the analysand's speech, are sufficient to compile a text from which the reader can critically evaluate the knowledge claims made. In this book, I used detailed case reports rather than audio- or visual recordings, and the subjects involved gave their informed consent. Furthermore, Duquesne University's Institutional Review Board approved my study.

analysis as qualitative inquiry. Neurotic and perverse speech provides polyvalent meanings—both on the conscious, intended level, and on the unconscious, unintended level. As Lacan told us, the unconscious is structured like a language, the unconscious being the Other's discourse. Through the study of an analysand's speech, we can come to know about being, separation, alienation, cultural Otherness, the repressed, and how all of these manifest themselves differently according to a particular cultural context. Therefore, epistemologically speaking, the best way to go about studying the kind of speaking being that can be neurotic, psychotic, or perverse is through a study of the process of Lacanian psychoanalysis itself.

Consequently, in this book my primary method involved providing two Lacanian qualitative clinical case studies of work with my former patients, written using process notes. One was a perversely structured exhibitionist and the other a neurotically structured obsessive. Both were legally considered sexual offenders, were supervised under state parole or Federal Probation, and had been diagnosed with a Paraphilia. All identifying information has been disguised, and all participants gave their informed consent. My other main method for this book was a qualitative hermeneutic reading of Lacan's published work dealing with perversion.

In the chapter that follows, I briefly outline only those Lacanian concepts that are necessary to understanding the remainder of the book. Experienced Lacanians may wish to jump ahead to chapter 3.

2

BUTTON TIES OF LACANIAN THEORY

The Paternal Metaphor, Subjectivity, and the Remainder

Speech and Language

[S]ymptoms can be entirely resolved in an analysis of language, because a symptom is itself structured like a language: A symptom is language from which speech must be delivered.

Lacan (1953/2006a, p. 269)

Yet, it will never be mine, this language, the only one I am thus destined to speak ... And, truth to tell, it never was.

Derrida (1996/1998, p. 2)

Speech is a powerful force; it creates the meanings that structure our experience.[22] Our thoughts, behaviors, and desires are shaped by the words we speak and hear spoken by others. Psychoanalysis seeks to discursively translate symptoms, as phenomena that "insist" or disrupt the life of the person requesting to begin analysis, into meaning. In his later years, Lacan posited that there is a kernel of the symptom that resists being made into meaning.[23] Although his ideas about that kernel substantially altered his teachings and will be explored in what follows in this book, what remained essential and incontrovertible was that putting the symptom

---

22 My assumption in this book is that the reader already has a workable knowledge of basic Lacanian concepts, such that this chapter is not meant to introduce the novice to Lacanian theory and practice but instead to highlight the essential Lacanian theory for what follows in this book. To those unfamiliar with Lacan, I recommend reading any one of the following introductory books on the practice of Lacanian clinical work prior to continuing to read this book: Bruce Fink's (1997) *A Clinical Introduction to Lacanian Psychoanalysis: Theory and Practice*, Michael J. Miller's (2011) *Lacanian Psychotherapy: Theory and Practical Applications*, and Raul Moncayo's (2008) *Evolving Lacanian Perspectives for Clinical Psychoanalysis: On Narcissism, Sexuation, and the Phases/Faces of Analysis in Contemporary Culture*.

23 This kernel of the symptom is of the real order, the order whose contents have not been symbolized and even resist symbolization.

into words transforms the symptom. Many of Lacan's contributions result from his emphasizing the importance of speech and language in psycho-analytic practice as well as in the development of the subject.

Lacan is famous for having said that "the unconscious is structured like a language" (1973/1998a, p. 149). Lacan's hypothesis is partly based on the work of Freud, who showed that the linguistic processes of condensation and displacement are the two major mechanisms evident in dreams, and thus in unconscious processes in general. Lacan also drew from the work of structuralist linguists Ferdinand de Saussure (1916/2005) and Roman Jakobson (Jakobson & Halle, 1956/1971), who, each in their own way, showed that the processes of metaphor and metonymy[24] are fundamental to language. Utilizing these three thinkers, Lacan identified displacement and condensation as the primary operations of the unconscious and equated displacement with metonymy and condensation with metaphor. It follows that the unconscious (or the symbolic order) consists of letters, phonemes, and relationships between its elements that allow for metaphor and metonymy and thus the production of signification or meaning. Correspondingly, metaphor and metonymy are ways of understanding phenomena that have to do with the symbolic order: symptoms, dreams, parapraxes, subjectivity, desire, and love.

Importantly for Lacan, "desire *is* a metonymy" (1957/2006a, p. 528) because desire is subject to the same process of perpetual deferral, desire always being "desire for something else" (p. 518). Just as desire is a metonymy, "the symptom *is* a metaphor" (p. 528). Specifically, repression results from a metaphorical process. The signifier (i.e., a word) "below the principal bar, in the denominator" is "the signifier that has disappeared [and become] the repressed signifier" (1973/1998a, p. 249). Although many psychoanalysts and psychotherapists today assume that affects are what are repressed, what Freud in fact said was that what is repressed are the "*Vorstellungrepräsentanzen*" (p. 217), which is usually translated into English as "ideational representatives." Correspondingly, Lacan said that the signifier is what is repressed, or the "representative of the representation" (p. 218). When repression occurs, then, a signifier (or several signifiers) becomes the hidden term in a metaphor. The repressed signifier is available to conscious reflection, but it functions differently as a result

---

24 A more traditional definition of metonymy than that of Lacan (1957/2006a, p. 515) is the use of one concept, person, or object to refer to another to which it is related. Synecdoche is a common form of metonymy, whereby a part of something is used in order to refer to the whole. For instance, "All hands on deck" is a synecdoche in which "hands" metonymically refers to "sailors." The nature of desire is metonymic in this way, because the object of demand refers to a part of desire.

of its repression, connecting to other repressed signifiers in the signifying chain.[25] The affect related to the signifier is displaced, not repressed. Although Lacan's conception of the symptom gained in complexity in the 1970s, there remained an aspect of it that was a metaphor, and thereby able to be dissolved through speech.

Lacan, Jacques Derrida, and others used Saussure's *Course in General Linguistics* (1916/2005) to show that the history of metaphysics, which can be seen as a search for an ultimate fixed meaning, a transcendental signified, or universal truth, is doomed to failure. Both Lacan and Derrida remarked that people desire to believe in a transcendental signified, because that belief would allow a view of themselves and the world as complete and essentially meaningful. Correspondingly, people prefer to pretend that they are masters of their own domain—that they can control their thoughts, speech, and actions. The structure of language prevents this mastery from being a possibility. On the one hand, there is no signifier that completely represents anything, in this case a human experience. This is reflected in the common complaint that one's words of expression—of love, for instance—are inadequate. On the other hand, meaning is always ambiguous. When we speak about something to someone, it is the listener who decides what s/he has heard, and s/he might choose to assign a different meaning to the speaker's words than that which the speaker intended. As a result, Lacan held that all communication is miscommunication.

There are always multiple ways to read a statement. The statement might include a word or phrase that has numerous meanings, might have been uttered in a spirit of sarcasm, might be doubted as to its sincerity, and depends upon context. As an example, not only does "the primacy of the signifier over the signified" (Lacan, 1956/2006a, p. 467) mean that the signifier has more influence than the signified (the concept represented by the signifier) in determining the meaning of the sign, but it can also mean that the signifier uttered has primacy over what was intended by the speaker. In that regard, slips of the tongue are excellent examples of the primacy of the signifier. If a man buying fish at a seafood store said, "I'd like a little ass" instead of "I'd like a little bass," we should take him at his word, privileging what he actually said over what he meant to say.[26] With parapraxes, then, the accidental signification, which points to Other, unconscious meanings, is privileged over the consciously intended mean-

---

25 From 1957 on, Lacan often referred to what he called the "signifying chain" (1957/2006a, p. 502), which refers to a series of signifiers that are linked together and depend upon each other for the construction of meaning. Lacan described the signifying chain as "links by which a necklace firmly hooks onto a link of another necklace made of links" (1973/1998a, p. 502).

26 Of course, "I'd like a little ass" can signify several possible wishes on the part of the man: that he have sexual relations with someone, that he lose weight and reduce the size of his buttocks, or that he own or even eat a donkey.

ing. Consequently, Lacan called the primacy of the signifier an "utterly disconcerting" (p. 467) idea. Our unconscious, as that which we would prefer not to reveal to ourselves and others, often speaks through us without our consent. A Lacanian analyst listens to the letter of the analysand's speech and punctuates certain ambiguous phrases, slips of the tongue, and other common manifestations of the unconscious both to show the patient that his imaginary identifications are only the tip of the iceberg and to help the patient decipher his own unconscious.[27]

The Real

Of course, as it is said, the letter kills while the spirit gives life.

Lacan (1957/2006a, p. 509)

The "real," along with the symbolic and the imaginary, is one of Lacan's three orders of experience. Although Lacan introduced the real as one of three orders as early as 1953, my focus in this book will be on his formulations of the real after 1964, which marks the beginning of what Miller designated as Lacan's second phase of teaching. (The third phase begins in 1974 and ends with Lacan's death in 1981.) The real does not refer to

---

27 Within the structure of language, meaning is determined according to the temporality of the signifying chain. "For the signifier, by its very nature, always anticipates meaning by deploying its dimension in some sense before it. As is seen at the level of the sentence when the latter is interrupted before the significant term: 'I'll never ...,' 'The fact remains ...,' 'Still perhaps ...' Such sentences nevertheless make sense, and that sense is all the more oppressive in that it is content to make us wait for it" (Lacan, 1957/2006a, p. 502).

The signifying chain, then, has a dual temporality that is both anticipation and retroaction. While someone is speaking words such as "The fact remains ...," the listener anticipates the sentence's conclusion, which is the moment at which s/he can grasp the meaning of the speaker's words. When the speaker has completed the sentence with the words "that many facts are dubious," for instance, the meaning of the sentence is retroactively constituted, such that the previous speech takes on new meaning. "Whence we can say it is in the chain of the signifier that meaning *insists*, but that none of the chain's elements *consists* in the signification it can provide at that very moment" (p. 502). The temporality of the signifier and of meaning is not, then, in the moment of the instant. Meaning is either about to arrive or has already arrived.

The dual temporality of the signifying chain structures the way in which we assign meaning to phenomena. Meaning is constructed after the fact. In psychoanalysis, an analysand has the opportunity to use the temporality of the signifying chain, which is also the temporality of the (Lacanian) subject, to her utmost advantage. Through speaking about herself and listening to her speech in a new way, she changes who she "is" by creating new meanings about who she was. The analytic subject is never static, however, because she is always in a process of becoming, always both anticipating and retroactively constituting herself. It is inaccurate to say that the analysand recalls her past experiences, both because her memories are not perfectly preserved, accurate representations of her past, and because her speech in the analytic context reconstructs and rewrites her history.

"reality"—a concept which is rooted in the social construction of meaning. Instead, the real refers to what is radically non-discursive—to what cannot be translated into thought or words. Of the real, Lacan said that it is "the domain of that which subsists outside of symbolization" (1954/2006a, p. 388). Consequently, the real is "the impossible" (1973/1998a, p. 167). It is akin to the Kantian thing-in-itself, as that which is unknowable insofar as we cannot say anything about it.

Lacan maintained that the real suggests its presence in that which does not work in the symbolic. As Fink (1995) put it, "Lacan's position here is that something anomalous *always* shows up in language, something unaccountable, unexplainable: an aporia. These aporias point to the presence within or influence on the symbolic of the real. I refer to them as *kinks in the symbolic order*" (p. 30). These kinks can be said to appear because the lack of a transcendental signified makes the set of language intrinsically incomplete. Somewhere, then, there is something that does not mean anything. Lack of meaning is one way in which the real manifests itself. An example of a kink in the symbolic order is object *a*—a Lacanian concept that will be explained later in this chapter and will figure centrally in this book.

Miller (2009b) taught that Lacan *conceived* of a first real, R_1, a real before the letter, and a second real, R_2, a real after the letter. In Lacanian terminology, existence is caused by the "letter" or the symbolic. Something can be said to exist when it is put into words because speech is what constitutes social reality. Because the real is non-discursive, it cannot be said to exist. Instead, the real "ex-sists." In the notes to his translation of Seminar XX, Fink said that Lacan borrowed "ex-sistence" from Heidegger, and employed it to convey something "that stands apart, which insists as it were from the outside, something not included on the inside" (Lacan, 1975/1998b, p. 22). The real, as something that is outside of the symbolic, reveals its ex-sistence through the kinks in the symbolic.

"There is no absence in the real" (Lacan, 1978/1991b, p. 313) and "[t]he real is without fissure" (p. 97). Therefore, the real is an order defined by presence, fullness, and lack of differentiation. We are born with a certain amount of what might be called real or bodily jouissance, which is a "substance" (Lacan, 1975/1998b, p. 26) similar to Freud's libido. Correspondingly, the infant's experience is of a fullness of jouissance, such that we might even say that the infant's entire body is an erogenous zone.

The Imaginary Order

Initially, the infant does not differentiate between her body and the outside world. The infant develops a sense of self (i.e., an ego) by beginning to differentiate her experience. Whereas before there was only a unified fullness, now there are objects and the self, and therefore rudimentary, nebulous distinctions between inside and outside. At this point, the infant has developed her *imaginary* order. Contrary to an English connotation of the word *imaginary*, the imaginary order does not refer to a realm of fantasy, but rather to the visual images we have of ourselves, others, and the world. In addition, the imaginary realm refers to the other ways in which we perceive the world through our senses. The imaginary order is closely tied to similarity and imitation—to development by imitating others—and therefore also to ethology and animal psychology. Correspondingly, the imaginary order has to do with our comparisons of ourselves with others such that *aggression and rivalry are hallmarks of imaginary order relations* (Fink, 1997, p. 32).

The infant's imaginary order predates what Lacan called the "mirror stage." The mirror stage is the process by which the infant develops a solid sense of self (i.e., an ego and an ego-ideal) and enters into the symbolic order. In the mirror stage, the infant's mirror image[28] is captivating to her because it allows her to see herself as unified and physically mature long before she actually reaches that state of maturity. Her identification is thus a jouissance-invested misidentification. This enjoyable fiction is at the root of the ego, because the infant's enjoyment motivates her to identify with her mirror image. At the foundations of the ego, then, is an alienation; she is not who she thinks she is. As Nobus (1999) put it, "the nucleus of a human being's self-image is a mirage, no matter how familiar it may seem" (p. 117). The imaginary order therefore has the connotations of deception and lure.

The Symbolic Order and the Mirror Stage

The ego becomes stabilized by the instituting of the symbolic order that occurs by way of the mirror stage. Lacan described the infant's birth into subjectivity in his 1961 reformulation of the mirror stage (1961/2006a, pp. 647–684), found in "Remarks on Daniel Lagache's Presentation: 'Psychoanalysis and Personality Structure.'" In this article, Lacan emphasized the effects on the child of the presence of the parental Other, the Other

---

28 The infant's mirror image is the first representation of the *ideal ego* (written in Lacanian algebra as $i(a)$). The ideal ego, an imaginary order projection, is an illusory and beautiful self-image. This ideal self-image is precious to the child, and she will defend it as a prized possession, passionately contesting anything that implies that she is not as perfect as she believes. The analytic subject may therefore respond with aggression when an analytic intervention exposes the mirages of the ideal ego or the ego (Lacan, 1953/2006a). The ideal ego changes over time, because the child's conception of the perfect self is an evolving one. Therefore, the ideal ego is impossible to achieve, and "will only asymptotically approach the subject's becoming" (Lacan, 1949/2006a, p. 94). "Man's ideal unity... is never attained as such and escapes him at every moment" (Lacan, 1978/1991b, p. 166) although he is unfailing in his attempts to catch up to it.

in which the child first encounters discourse, who is holding the child up to the mirror.

> It would be a mistake to think that the Other (with a capital *O*) of discourse can be absent from any distance that the subject achieves in his relationship with the other, the other (with a lowercase *o*) of the imaginary dyad … For the Other where discourse is situated, which is always latent in the triangulation that consecrates this distance, is not latent as long as it extends all the way to the purest moment of the specular relation: to the gesture by which the child at the mirror turns toward the person who is carrying him and appeals with a look to this witness; the latter decants the child's recognition of the image, by verifying it, from the jubilant assumption in which *it* [elle] certainly *already was*. (p. 678)

It is the child's relationship with the Other that facilitates his jubilant assumption of his mirror image in a very important way—a way that allows him to become a subject. Lacan posited that every human being wants to see himself as having a special place in the world, and becoming a subject is one method by which the child can achieve that self-image.[29]

In the mirror stage, the child's relationship to the other of the imaginary dyad is assured, but what is not assured is the triangulation with the Other. Lacan's conception of the advent of the subject takes into account the failure involved in "what is known as 'hospitalism,' in which mothering attentions are clearly seen to have no other deficiency than the *anonymity* with which they are meted out" (1961/2006a, p. 679). In order for the child to have an encounter with the Other where discourse is situated—the parental Other—the child must see and hear himself as having a symbolic space in the desire of the parental Other. In other words, the child must believe himself to be of special importance to the Other in order for the Other's response, in speech and gaze, to have a structural impact on him, shaping how he sees himself and desires to see himself.

The child "appeals with a look to this witness" (Lacan, 1961/2006a, p. 678), wanting his recognition of his mirror image to be verified by an approving parental Other. The delighted parental figure might say "Yes! That's you, isn't it! Look at what a handsome boy you are!" The child internalizes his mirror image and invests it with libido because of his

---

29 The other method is used by the psychotic. Roughly speaking, the psychotic's delusional system provides him with a special place of importance. In his delusions, for example, he might be the special target of the surveillance of the Martians.

caretaker's gesture[30] or words of approval. The loving Other's ratification enables the child to identify with the Other of discourse, and this is a *symbolic* identification, not an imaginary one. This amounts to an incorporation of the symbolic order, such that the Other full of signifiers becomes the child's unconscious.

The infant's enjoyment of the loving caretaker's approval motivates him to orient his future identifications according to his interpretation of his caretaker's ideals, goals, and admired qualities. Accordingly, the child may want to be a "good boy" or "smart" or a "fighter." In this way, the child makes symbolic identifications with the Other, adding layers of misidentification to his ego matrix. Each time he internalizes an admired aspect of an Other (caretakers, teachers, famous people, etc.), recognizing himself as having his father's wit—much admired by his mother, for instance—he becomes further alienated by the symbolic order. Through this process, the child's perception of the ideals and tastes of his caretaker(s) become introjected in the "form" of his *ego-ideal* (written as I(A)) such that he comes to judge himself on the basis of his interpretation of the perspective of his caretakers. "The point of the ego ideal is that from which the subject will see himself, as one says, *as others see him*—which will enable him to support himself in a dual situation that is satisfactory for him from the point of view of love" (Lacan, 1973/1998a, p. 268); "The ego-ideal is a formation that … is based on the ego's unconscious coordinates" (1961/2006a, p. 677). The ego-ideal, as the child's internalization of his caretakers' view of him, allows him to see himself as lovable. The ego-ideal, then, is a symbolic introjection whereas the ideal ego is an imaginary projection. The ego-ideal solidifies the foundation of the ego, establishing firm boundaries between self and other and self and objects. The creation of the ego-ideal and the unconscious that occurs in the completion of the mirror stage marks the child's alienation by the Other of discourse and his transition into subjectivity.

The Imaginary and the Real after the
Letter: An Alienating Narrative

When the child incorporates the symbolic order, the symbolic subordinates, rewrites, and restructures the imaginary and the real. Having achieved a stable ego and an ego-ideal, the subject has fewer occasions to experience the aggression and competition tied to imaginary order relationships. In other words, now that the child has a permanent identity that serves to firmly differentiate *Innenwelt* (i.e., inside) and *Umwelt* (i.e.,

---

30 Even if the caretaker only smiles or nods, those are gestures that have already been associated with the caretaker's frequently uttered words of approval and recognition.

outside) and to give him a special place in the world, he no longer needs to fight for his identity and its corresponding perks. Instead, the stable ego becomes the new vantage point from which the child experiences jealousy and aggression. After "the letter," what is at stake in imaginary relations are things of discursive importance.

Lacan believed that "the letter kills" (2006a, p. 848), which is to say that a child's entrance into the symbolic realm of language necessarily entails a loss of being itself. In the process of becoming a subject, the child suffers a loss of being that leaves him with a basic, irrevocable lack that Lacan called "*manque à être*" (1973/1998a, p. 29)—translated as "want-to-be" or "lack of being." Much of the real before the letter is annihilated by the symbolic order, being drawn into the signifiers used to describe it. There is always a residue or "supplement,"[31] however, of the real that can never be eradicated by symbolic overwriting. However, the real after the letter is not simply the remainder of the first real, because the symbolic changes its structure. Whereas the real before the letter was full and unbroken, the real after the letter marks and divides the body into distinct erogenous zones.

In the process of socialization, caretakers express demands to the child that involve and have effects on his body—for instance, "go to the bathroom now" and "don't touch that!" The body is discursively mediated, becoming alienated from the body of the living being.[32] As Fink (1995) put it, "[i]n the course of socialization, the body is progressively over-written with signifiers; pleasure is localized in certain zones, while other zones are neutralized by the word and coaxed into compliance with social, behavioral norms" (p. 24). Different parts of the body take on meanings determined by the parental and social Others. Our bodily pleasures and pains are therefore all tied to our relationship to the Other.

Another way to talk about the symbolic order's effects on the real is to focus on the child's loss of some of its jouissance of the pure living being. Lacan therefore agreed with this aspect of Freud's Oedipal Complex, in which the child must relinquish a "piece of instinctual satisfaction" (1905/1953b, pp. 186-187) or must give something up in order to enter into society. Referring to Marxist theory, Lacan, in Seminar XVII, called jouissance a "surplus" that has no use-value for society. Lacan referred to the process of relinquishing jouissance in exchange for pursuing the

---

31 I do intend the allusion to Derrida's *différance* or supplementarity.

32 The term *living being* applies to the infant before he learns to speak and to living beings of the non-human order. Psychotics, who can speak but who have not incorporated the structure of language, are also referred to as living beings.

symbolic achievements one desires as "castration."[33] The jouissance that remains after the encounter with the Other is shaped and limited by the symbolic. And, roughly speaking, the neurotic undergoes a significantly more extensive process of castration than does the pervert.

The real after the letter is characterized by everything that is excluded from the chain of signification. Accordingly, Fink (1995) said that the "real is perhaps best understood as that which has not yet been symbolized, remains to be symbolized, or even resists symbolization; and it may perfectly well exist 'alongside' and in spite of a speaker's considerable linguistic capabilities" (p. 25). As part of the second real, we can think of trauma as being an event that presented the analysand with such difficulty that he was not able to put his experience of it into words. Trauma, along with other unsymbolized phenomena, manifests itself as fixation. The subject is stuck on something, and this blockage manifests itself in that which the analysand's speech circles around, but does not enunciate. It might be a word for which the analysand can come up with no associations, that signifier having no connection to a signifying chain. In general, the real is evident in things about which the analysand claims to have no memory or knowledge. In Lacan's words, the real "appears in relations of resistance without transference—to extend the metaphor I used earlier, I would say, like a punctuation without a text" (1954/2006a, p. 388). The analyst, by listening for these gaps in the analysand's knowledge, begins to have a clear sense of what is missing. Symbolization implies dialectical movement, and so one aim of psychoanalysis is to make interpretations that get the analysand to symbolize the traumatic aspects of the second real, thus loosening his fixations and relieving some of his suffering.

The Paternal Metaphor

> For, if the symbolic context requires it, paternity will nevertheless be attributed to the woman's encounter with a spirit at such and such a fountain or at a certain rock in which he is supposed to dwell. This is clearly what demonstrates that the attribution of procreation to the father can only be the effect of a pure signifier, of a recognition, not of the real father, but of what religion has taught us to invoke as the Name-of-the-Father.
>
> Lacan (1959/2006a, p. 556)

Lacan's paternal metaphor (or paternal function), with its corresponding operations of alienation and separation, is the metaphor by which Lacan

---

33 The concept of jouissance provides one entry point into Lacanian diagnostics, because each structural position involves a different way of experiencing and managing jouissance. Very simply put, of the three structures, the psychotic retains the most bodily jouissance and the neurotic retains the least.

explains the creation of the subject out of the living being. The Name-of-the-Father, instated by the paternal metaphor, serves as an authority beyond the primary caretaker that partially separates the child from that caretaker. This separation gives the child as living being the symbolic space necessary to become a subject.

Despite the connotations of its name, the paternal function is simply a metaphor or a role—albeit a very specific and significant one. Not only does its success not depend upon the presence of an actual father, but it also can be carried out by a person of any gendered identity. Lacan called this metaphor "paternal" for two reasons. The first has to do with the concept of paternity; the Name-of-the-Father is responsible for the birth of the subject into the symbolic order. Without an authority beyond that of the mother, there would be no subject, but only a living being. Because of the absence or failure of the paternal metaphor (and the mirror stage), the psychotic is someone who never becomes a subject. The second reason is that it is most often a father who carries out this symbolic role of prohibition in our current cultural context.

Furthermore, in French, the Name-of-the-Father, or *Nom-du-Père*, suggests multiple meanings applicable to the paternal function. *Nom* means "noun" as well as "name," and so the *Nom-du-Père* evokes a noun such as "father" used in the mother's speech. The mother's discourse has the power of endorsing or denying the authority of the *Nom-du-Père* or father. *Nom* as name refers to the parts of the father figure's full proper name; he usually gives his child his last name. *Nom* also suggests the function of the name as designating someone or something, alive or dead, present or absent, who is made present and important by way of the mother's discourse. In addition, *Nom* is pronounced like *non* ("No" in English), and so *Nom-du-Père* also calls to mind the father's prohibition (of the mother-child near unity).

For Lacan, what provokes anxiety is not so much the child's separation from her caretaker,[34] but rather the mother's overproximity. Assuming the infant is at least to some extent wanted and cared for by her mother, her first status (at least from her perspective) is of being nearly one with her mother. Through the mother's breast and her loving words, touch, and gaze, the infant derives jouissance. At the same time, however, Lacan theorizes that the baby perceives—whether accurately or not—her mOther's desire for her as threatening and potentially smothering.

Anxiety as defined here is caused by the lack of lack or the lack of a gap between the mother and the child. The child experiences anxiety at the prospect of being no more than an extension of her mother. The

---

34 The concept of separation anxiety is an extremely commonly referenced form of childhood anxiety in psychoanalytic literature today.

smothering mother might be no more than a perception of the child's. (Even if the mother were not smothering from a so-called objective view of reality, what psychoanalysis takes to be its concern is the subjective reality of the individual, and of how and why her subjective reality came to be as such.) Nevertheless, some mothers do have a tendency to use their children as their primary sources of jouissance, being relatively uninterested in the satisfactions that other people and other pursuits have to offer.

Even though we might think of the mother's desire for her child as being innocuous and even necessary, the mother's desire becomes dangerous when she does not respect her child as a separate person. In analysis, psychotics sometimes describe their mothers as possessive and invasive. These mothers were perceived to act as if there were no law or legitimate restrictions on their desires, so that they treated their children as property with which they could do as they pleased.

> The mother's desire is not something that is bearable just like that, that you are indifferent to. It will always wreak havoc. A huge crocodile in whose jaws you are—that's the mother. One never knows what might suddenly come over her and make her shut her trap. That's what the mother's desire is. Thus, I have tried to explain that there was something that was reassuring ... There is a roller, made out of stone of course, which is there, potentially, at the level of her trap, and it acts as a restraint, as a wedge. It's what is called the phallus. It's the roller that shelters you, if, all of a sudden, she closes it. (Lacan, 1991/2007, p. 112)

Although this quote from Lacan's Seminar XVII might be interpreted as demonizing the mother, making her into a crocodile who wishes to consume her child, it may also be read as a dramatic portrayal of the dangers of lacking a symbolic space of one's own. It is only when the stone roller of the paternal function separates the child from her mother that she develops an ego-ideal that anchors and stabilizes her sense of self. As evidenced by psychotic breaks, a destabilized ego and a lack of differentiation between inside and outside can be terrifying. The phallus[35] or Name-of-the-Father, then, protects the child from *le désir de la mère*, which can be translated as both the child's desire for the mother and the mother's desire. The paternal function serves to block both the child's attempt to remain at one with her mother—after all, the mother is her primary source of jouissance—and the mother's attempt to keep her child as close as possible.

---

35 In the late 1960s, Lacan began using the term *phallus* to refer to the Name-of-the-Father. The phallus is a signifier that has its own importance, however, which will be explicated in chapter 3.

There are two other perspectives from which we can understand the living being's anxiety. The first of these perspectives has to do with the fact that anxiety is the only affect that indicates a connection to the real (Lacan, 2004). The psychotic is a living being who suffers anxiety because she has an unmanageable amount of real jouissance. In Seminar XXII, Lacan remarked that anxiety is caused when the body is overwhelmed or permeated by jouissance (1975, p. 104). This conception of anxiety is similar to Freud's first theory of anxiety, in which anxiety results from excessive quantities of libido that cannot be discharged. The symbolic order sets limits to or drains away much of the living being's jouissance and organizes that which remains, such that the pervert and the neurotic have less jouissance and therefore less anxiety.[36] The power of the word neutralizes the real, and so there is no neutralization for the living being who has not undergone alienation. "[T]he ultimate real ... [is] something faced with which all words cease and all categories fail, the object of anxiety *par excellence*" (1978/1991b, p. 164).

The second perspective has to do with the living being's relationship to language. When the child first encounters signifiers, it is as a swarm of nonsense signifiers, or S_1s, that are undifferentiated. Cooing and baby talk are the stuff of this swarm. The child's immersion in the swarm of signifiers marks the child's first encounter with the mother as Other, but the child assumes that they are unified. When the child develops an imaginary order but has not yet incorporated the symbolic order, the child cultivates very *tenuous* imaginary distinctions between self and other—meaning that the swarm of signifiers is made into a collection. The confusion between self and others (including the Other of discourse) persists, but the imaginary order facilitates a temporary reduction of that confusion. Through the interdiction wrought by the paternal metaphor, the swarm of signifiers is permanently and firmly collectivized, creating a clear sense of differentiation between self and other. Consequently, neurotics and perverts have the general sense that they use language like a tool rather than that they are a tool for language.

In psychosis, the foreclosure of the paternal function results in the psychotic's sense of being "inhabited, possessed, by language" (Lacan, 1981/1997a, p. 284), as if some external force planted it in her. The feeling of not being in control of language arouses the psychotic's anxiety. Likewise, psychotic individuals relate to signifiers as if they were things rather than representations of meanings (Fink, 1997, p. 95). The successful operation of alienation results in what Lacan called a *"point de capiton"* (1981/1997a, p. 303), which has been translated as a "button tie" or a

---

36 Specifically, desire and the law, two main aspects of the symbolic order, put limits on jouissance, thereby decreasing anxiety.

"quilting point" (p. 303), and button ties permanently link signifiers to signifieds, creating a number of anchoring points or stable meanings in the collection of signifiers. The living being lacks these button ties, and so his world of meanings is structured by way of imaginary mimicry. The instability of meanings, of the connection between signifiers and signifieds, also subjects the living being to anxiety.

Ways of describing that which provokes anxiety in the living being:

1. The lack of a symbolic gap between child and mother;
2. Fragility of the ego and of the differentiation between inside and outside;
3. An excess of unorganized jouissance;
4. Being inhabited by language, as if it were an external force;
5. Fragility of meanings because of the lack of button ties.

Alienation

What must be stressed at the outset is that a signifier is that which represents a subject for another signifier.

Lacan (1973/1998a, p. 207)

All that subsists here is the being whose advent can only be grasped by no longer being.

Lacan (1961/2006, p. 678)

Alienation (along with separation) is a developmental process that occurs in a time that Lacan described as a "logical moment."[37] That is, alienation occurs neither in a single instant, as if at the push of a button, nor by way of a steady, chronological growth. Instead, alienation is a moment that, logically speaking, must have occurred in order for the subject to have achieved his present structure. Alienation represents the moment when the living being incorporates the Other of discourse and becomes a subject who has a place in the symbolic order—a subject who is split or divided by language.

In alienation, the first operation of the paternal function, there are three roles. The child plays the first role, as a living being who chooses either to accept (*Bejahung*) or foreclose the symbolic order. The first Other plays the second role, which is that of someone who has a primary part in loving and nurturing the child. The third role, that of the second Other

---

37 The explications of alienation and separation that follow are mostly based on Lacan's treatment of those operations in his Seminar XI.

or the Name-of-the-Father, may be played by the person who is the first Other or by a second person. The second Other is someone who represents a consistent authority or Law beyond the desires of the first Other. An actual father is someone who may *represent* the symbolic Name-of-the-Father; the person of the father is strictly differentiated from the symbolic role he may play. The stereotypical occupants of the roles of first and second Other are the mother and the father, respectively.

In alienation, the father comes between the mother and the child and partially separates the two, allowing the child to have a sense of himself (or herself) as a person separate from his mother. The child often associates the father with the mother's absences, for instance hearing the father and mother talking after being put to bed, and so the father is experienced as someone who obstructs access to the mother. In the child's view, the father imposes limitations on the jouissance the child can achieve with the mother. For example, the father might say, "You're too old to be hanging onto your mother like that!" or "It's time for you to start sleeping in your own room like a big boy so I can have some time with your mother." The father functions to prohibit jouissance.

$$\frac{\text{The Father's Prohibition}}{\text{The Mother as a Source of Jouissance}}$$

The first moment of the paternal function, then, has the structure of a metaphor, in which the term above the bar replaces the term below the bar. In this case, the prohibitive father cancels out the mother as a source of jouissance. This kind of father believes that there is something wrong with the mother-child dyad, and he puts himself in the position of master by doing and saying something to prohibit the jouissance of the mother-child relationship. He might not see the need to justify his reasons, instead referring to his name as an indicator of his authority: "You'll do it because I said so!" The father need not have any special or superior qualities of judgment in order to be given the position of master. Even today, many fathers are granted positions of authority by their family members simply because they, as fathers, are traditionally expected to take on that role. In this sense, the father is a *semblant*; he has the appearance, at least, of someone with authority. Some men gladly assume this position of unquestioned authority, believing in their own semblance.

Lacan emphasized that "we should concern ourselves ... with the importance [the mother] attributes to [the father's] speech—in a word, to his authority—in other words, with the place she reserves for the Name-of-the-Father in the promotion of the law" (1959/2006a, p. 579). It is not enough to consider only the smothering mother or the powerless father in relation to the child; the child, mother, and father must be taken into account as a triad in terms of the place the mother's speech gives to the authority of the father. The mother's discourse, then, serves either to give weight to the father's authority or to undercut it. As examples of the former, the mother might say, "Your father will give you a spanking if you keep doing that!" or "What would your father say about this?" or "Go ask your father if you can have that." Using this kind of discourse, the mother sets up the father as an authority beyond herself—the father is the one who gives punishment and whose judgment should be respected and feared. The father's name or *Nom* becomes associated with a prohibitive "No!" The Name-of-the-Father is a function that is sustained by numerous statements he makes and that are said about him by the mother. These statements are linked to the father's name, such that the paternal function can be instated by the father's name or any one of its related statements. In this regard, Miller (2006b) said that "the Name-of-the-Father is only the name of a function that one must write NP (x), where the x in parentheses designates the variable and questions in each clinical case what role the Name-of-the-Father plays" (p. 70).[38] Although alienation, generally speaking, metaphorizes or bars the jouissance of the mother, it also has specific effects in each individual case.

If the mother's discourse systematically undermines the authority of the father, the paternal function may fail. The mother may ignore or argue with the father's opinions and commands, never giving credence to his words and acting only according to her own wishes. She may often say to her child, "We can do whatever we want," or "Your father doesn't know what he's talking about!" Her derision of the father's authority must generally be almost total in order to prevent alienation. Even in families in which the mother presides over the father, the father still may have enough authority to balance the mother's rule. The mother's complaints about her husband, for instance, suggest that he has a certain strength in hampering her ability to do as she pleases.

In other cases, the father's (or second Other's) relation to the Law itself is to blame. Lacan said that failures of the paternal function

> are found with particular frequency in cases where the father really functions as a legislator or boasts that he does—whether he is, in fact, one of the people who makes the laws or presents himself as a pillar of faith, as a paragon of integrity or devotion,

---

38 "Names-of-the-Father" was the name Lacan assigned to his aborted seminar of 1963. Because Lacan only delivered the first lecture and subsequently refused to elaborate on his intended topic, we are left to conjecture as to the meanings of the Names-of-the-Father. Miller, in his article, "The Names-of-the-Father" (2006b) guessed that the plural means not only that there are multiple possible signifiers that function as the Name-of-the-Father but also that there is no privileged, correct Name-of-the-Father (p. 69).

as virtuous or a virtuoso, as serving a charitable cause whatever the object or lack thereof that is at stake, as serving the nation or birth rate, safety or salubrity, legacy or law, the pure, the lowest of the low, or the empire. These are all ideals that provide him with all too many opportunities to seem to be at fault, to fall short, and even to be fraudulent—in short, to exclude the Name-of-the-Father from its position in the signifier. (1959/2006a, p. 579)

Accordingly, the paternal function fails even in less extreme cases when a father (or second Other) is found inadequate or fraudulent in his relation to the Law. A father might make so many exceptions to the rules he sets for himself and his child that the exception becomes the rule—his actions guided by the arbitrariness of his whims. For instance, a father says that stealing is wrong but then brings home office supplies he stole from work, justifying that he earned them or that his workplace has an overabundance of them. In addition, parents often set limits for their children that depend solely on their moods or convenience, and then lift those restrictions whenever it suits them. The child notices this and other hypocrisies, and, with enough of them, may learn by imitation to become his own law rather than accept the authority of a law beyond his own wishes. This kind of parent shows the child that he does not obey any laws above those governed by his own desires.

In other instances, the paternal function fails because the father sets himself up as a rival to the child, speaking and acting toward the child solely on the imaginary plane. This type of father is a character marked by "unbridled ambition or authoritarianism" (Lacan, 1981/1997a, p. 204) whose unlimited demands on the son make him seem "monstrous" (p. 204). He is a father who cannot be pleased, and he punishes his child (who is often a son—fathers sometimes seeing less need to compete with a girl) without respecting ideas like "fairness." This father "manifests himself simply in the order of strength and not in that of the pact, [and so] a relation of rivalry, aggressiveness, fear, etc. appear" (p. 205). The father who manifests himself in the symbolic pact, on the other hand, tells his child, "This is mine, but you may have that instead" or "You will do your chores, but then you will have some free time to spend as you choose." A father who incarnates the Law in the manner of the pact appeals to a distributive justice that puts limits on his demands.

Fink (1997) gave an example of his work with a psychotic patient whose father relentlessly competed with him.

> One of my patients said that his father wanted a girl, not a boy, and competed with his son in many areas: when there was cake, the father would take it all, and the mother would be forced to "split things half and half between them"; when my patient went

to college, his father decided to enroll in the same academic program as his son. The mother's symbolic interventions were not
sufficient to counter the father's rivalrous relationship with his
son, and the latter began having psychotic episodes in his twen-
ties. (p. 251)

When the ego-ideal does not form and the first movement of the paternal
function fails, psychosis results. A child becomes psychotically structured
by way of the mechanism that Lacan translated from Freud's *Verwerfung*
as "foreclosure" (1981/1997a, p. 321). Psychosis is the result of the foreclosure of the Name-of-the-Father. Foreclosure, then, is the radical rejection
or exclusion of a key signifier that would ground the child in the symbolic
order by serving as the primordial button tie between signifier and signified. On the other hand, the child's acceptance of the Name-of-the-Father
through primal repression is constitutive; repression allows the child to
become a subject with an unconscious. The foreclosure of the Name-of-
the-Father makes subjectivity and the unconscious impossibilities for the
child. Unlike the linguistic mechanism of repression, foreclosure operates
outside of the symbolic register, such that foreclosed phenomena "return"
seemingly from the outside of the psychotic by way of imaginary processes including delusions and hallucinations. Foreclosure indicates that
the child has some degree of "choice" as to whether or not to accept the
symbolic order, although it is easier to conceive of the failure of the paternal function in terms of the first and second Others.

As previously stated, the paternal function can be successful in any
possible family constellation, although arguably some assemblages lend
themselves more easily to the instatement of the Name-of-the-Father. In
the case of a family with a mother and a father, the usual course of events
is that the mother is the first Other and the father is the second Other. A
mother is equally capable of respecting a law beyond her own desires, but
she nevertheless tends to only play the role of first Other. One reason for
this may be that it is easier for the child to perceive the two different functions (of acting according to one's own desires and of putting limits on
jouissance according to a principle) when they are embodied by two separate people. Another reason may be that mothers and fathers, like most
people, are more likely to criticize each other's violations of the Law than
to criticize their own. If the father is the primary caretaker and first Other,
then the mother may very well be called upon to act as second Other, the
father also having difficulty playing both roles.

The paternal function, as previously stated, has the structure of a metaphor, and insofar as metaphor is what creates meaning, the paternal function is the metaphor that anchors the entire symbolic realm. The subject's
incorporation of the paternal metaphor therefore amounts to the incorporation of the structure of language, allowing him to create meaning by

way of metaphor and metonymy. In alienation, the Name-of-the-Father as a prohibitive forceful signifier cancels out or replaces the (smothering) mother as source of jouissance. The first movement of the paternal metaphor results in primal repression, in which the child's psychical processes are split into conscious and unconscious. What becomes repressed and therefore pushed into the unconscious is the child's desire for what the Name-of-the-Father forbade: a certain jouissance with his mother. The child, having made his first symbolic identification with the Name-of-the-Father, is now a split subject—a subject who irrevocably lacks being and jouissance.

Lacan held that prohibition creates desire. It is only after the child's access to the mother is restricted that the subject realizes that he longs for what he is now lacking. According to the time of the signifier, all linguistic meanings are determined by difference and deferral, such that the meaning of an event is constituted after the event's occurrence (when a comparison between at least two different states can be made). When the metaphor of alienation is achieved, a meaning is created regarding the child's former relationship to his mother: Desiring the former, lost relationship to the mother is wrong. After the fact, the subject judges his separation from his mother and his corresponding loss of jouissance to have been traumatic, even if it was also a great relief.

The meaning (a signified), "my desire for my mother is wrong" becomes permanently affixed to the words (signifiers) associated with the Name-of-the-Father. A kind of knot is thereby woven in the fundamental gap between the signifier and the signified. Button ties are necessary in order to make meanings by temporarily halting the "incessant sliding of the signified under the signifier" (Lacan, 1957/2006a, p. 502). Using Freudian terminology, we might say that a button tie ties together the "word-presentation" (*Wortvorstellungen*) or signifier and the thing-presentation (*Sachvorstellungen*) or the culturally constituted meaning. Rather than creating an unbreakable false "essential" meaning, a button tie allows the culturally constituted literal meaning(s) of a signifier to be compared to its figurative meaning(s). "[T]he 'button tie' [*point de capiton*], by which the signifier stops the otherwise indefinite sliding of signification" (Lacan, 1960/2006a, p. 805) provides the necessary illusion of a fixed ultimate meaning. ("[T]he sliding of the signified under the signifier [is nevertheless] always happening (unconsciously, let us note) in discourse" (Lacan, 1957/2006a, p. 511).)

The Vel of Alienation: Your Money, or Your Life!

"Your money or your life!" If I choose the money, I lose both. If I choose life, I have life without the money, namely, a life deprived of something.

Lacan (1973/1998a, p. 212)

Alienation consists in this *vel*, which—if you do not object to the word *condemned*, I will use it—condemns the subject to appearing only in that division which, it seems to me, I have just articulated sufficiently by saying that, if it appears on the one side as meaning, produced by the signifier, it appears on the other as *aphanisis*.

Lacan (1973/1998a, p. 210)

The child as living being is faced with a *vel*, or an either/or choice, in which he is forced to lose something. The child must chose to lose either his place in the symbolic order or his being. The mugger's threat, "Your money or your life!" exemplifies the *vel* of alienation, insofar as it is clear that you are going to lose your money whatever you choose; the prudent choice is to give the mugger your money and hope that he will let you keep your life. In the child's encounter with the Other of language, his choosing subjectivity means electing to lose his being. In permitting a signifier to represent him, the subject disappears beneath the bar, losing his being and becoming a subject divided by language.

$$\frac{S_1}{\$}$$

In other words, there is a part of the subject that exists outside of the set of meaning, and that is the unconscious. S_1, as a first master signifier that is cut off from the signifying chain, is pure nonsense.

Lacan said that the subject's representation by S_1 causes *Urverdrängung*, or primal repression, which is "the necessary fall of this first signifier" (1973/1998a, p. 251). Importantly, the nonsense master signifier (S_1) also corresponds to the symbolic unary trait that produces the ego-ideal by way of introjection. The kernel of the ego-ideal, Lacan said, "is not in the first field of narcissistic identification" (1973/1998a, p. 256) but is in the field of the symbolic Other.

The [unary trait], in so far as the subject clings to it, is in the field of desire, which cannot in any sense be constituted other than in the reign of the signifier, other than at the level in which there is a relation of the subject to the Other. It is the field of the Other that determines the function of the [unary trait], in so far as it is from it that a major stage of identification is established in the topography then developed by Freud—namely, idealization, the ego ideal. (p. 256)

The ego-ideal is the vantage point from which subject sees himself as ideal ego and correspondingly feels complete and loved by the Other.[39]

Although Lacan talked about the operation of alienation prior to Seminar XI, what Lacan adds in that seminar is crucial to his later theorizations of subjectivity: "It is in this living being, called to subjectivity, that the drive is essentially manifested" (1973/1998a, p. 203). The child's entrance into the symbolic order is the condition for the possibility of the creation of the partial drives and of object *a*. In order to explain the drives and object *a*, I will first introduce the operation of separation—an operation that plays a major part in their formation.

---

39 Lacan said that the non-meaning of the master signifier (S_1) or unary trait has an important "direct implication" (1973/1998a, p. 212) on the aim of interpretation (for those subjects who have undergone alienation). "Interpretation is directed not so much at the meaning as towards reducing the non-meaning of signifiers, so that we may rediscover the determinants of the subject's entire behavior" (p. 212). Put a different way, Lacan also said, "it is not the effect of meaning that is operative in interpretation, but rather the articulation in the symptom of signifiers (without any meaning at all) that have gotten caught up in it" (1966/2006a, p. 842). What does it mean to say that analysts should direct interpretations toward non-meaning?

Lacan's recommendation suggests that interpretations should be aimed at revealing a subject's master signifiers. Those repressed signifiers are a main part of what constitutes the symptom of the subject. Each unary signifier represents an alienating identification with the Other. For example, "smart" may be a master signifier for a subject, who introjected it when her father said, "You are so smart! Just like your mother!"—indicating that the father loves the child and the mother because they are smart. The subject who incorporated the unary trait "smart" then continuously made efforts to try to appear smart to Others so that she may feel lovable.

Of course, "smart," is a meaningful signifier insofar as it is a signifier in the Other of discourse. However, for this subject, "smart" is repressed, and therefore a part of the non-meaning of her particular unconscious. Master signifiers, in their locus in the unconscious, do not become meaningful until they are dialectized through interpretation—until they rise above the bar, making connections with signifiers in the conscious signifying chain. When interpretation reveals a master signifier, the revelation is experienced by the subject as a jubilant one (paradoxically connected to the jubilation she felt at initially incorporating the alienating signifier), because she feels as though she has mastered a previously insistent, inexplicable determinant of her behavior by gaining some knowledge about it. When a master signifier is dialectized, the subject knows something about why she originally admired the quality the S_1 represented and for whom she incorporated the unary trait into herself. Furthermore, dialectizing the master signifier may be understood to reduce to nothingness the problematic meaning of the S_1, relieving the subject's associated suffering.

We may also say that the master signifier is part of the real after the letter, insofar as it is a signifier that resists symbolization. The following quote from Lacan's "The Subversion of the Subject and the Dialectic of Desire" provides support for this perspective: "The cut made by the signifying chain is the only cut that verifies the structure of the subject as a discontinuity in the real. If linguistics enables us to see the signifier as the determinant of the signified, analysis reveals the truth of this relationship by making holes in meaning the determinants of its discourse" (1966/2006a, p. 801). In other words, the subject, who is an effect of the symbolic order, is the cut that forms the R_2 out of the unbroken R_1. The subject is represented by the irruptions of the real in discourse as that which does not make sense, but nevertheless structure the subject and her discourse.

Separation

Separare, to separate—I would point out at once the equivocation of the *se parare*, of the *se parer*, in all the fluctuating meanings it has in French. It means not only to dress oneself, but also to defend oneself, to provide oneself with what one needs to be on one's guard, and I will go further still, and Latinists will bear me out, to the *se parere*, the *s'engendrer*, the *to be engendered*, which is involved here.

Lacan (1973/1998a, p. 214)

Whereas alienation entails the subject's encounter with the Other of language, separation entails the subject's encounter with the Other of desire. Language and desire are two different aspects of the Other. The Other full of signifiers is one part, and the Other of desire is the other part. When put into words, the Other's desire may be represented by the phallus, which is the signifier of desire and jouissance, or by S($\mathexist$), which is the signifier of the lack in the Other.[40]

In separation, the second operation of the paternal metaphor, there are three roles: child, first Other, and second Other. The first Other plays almost the same role in separation as s/he did in alienation. The first Other still has a primary part in loving and nurturing the child, but the child perceives the first Other differently according to his newly acquired symbolic viewpoint. For the subject, the first Other is now someone who is clearly differentiated from him, and he has repressed his desire to return to the jouissance-full unity he imagines they had prior to alienation. In addition, the subject as a separate being wants the Other to love him and gain jouissance from his presence. At the same time, the child's proximity to the first Other continues to be a source of anxiety—although his anxiety is less than that of the living being. The child, then, plays the role of the subject who chooses either to accept or reject a further split from the first Other. The third role, that of the second Other, lawgiving Other, or Name-of-the-Father, may again be enacted by the person who is the first Other or by a second person. In separation, however, compared to alienation, it is much more common for the first Other to function as both first and second Other. This is because in separation what is at stake is the symbolization of the first Other's desire. The role of the second Other is none other than putting the desire of the first Other into words.

Whereas psychosis is associated with certainty, subjectivity is associated with doubt. "[D]oubt, doubting we know who we are and know who the Other is, is born and enabled by alienation" (Lacan, 1973/1998a, p. 264).

---

40 Insofar, however, as desire springs from what was lost in castration, the phallus is also the signifier of lack.

The living being does not wonder or doubt who he is. The subject, on the other hand, is lacking in being and unknown to himself. The subject is an unknown X. The subject, unlike the living being, has an ego-ideal, and the ego-ideal is what ties his subjectivity to an alienating Otherness, so that he no longer knows himself. The subject as *manque à être* wants to find his being, and so he asks the question "Who am I?" Because a meaningful answer can only reside in the Other of meaning, the subject looks to the Other to provide an answer. The subject's ego-ideal discloses that his search has to do with his being lovable in the eyes of the Other. In the search for being, the child attempts to be loved by the Other. In love, the subject finds a temporary fullness of being, because love connects the subject with the Other, sometimes providing the illusion of oneness that the child unconsciously desires with his mOther.

The subject asks "Who am I?" and "What does the Other want?"

The first object he proposes for this parental desire whose object is unknown is his own loss—*Can he [afford to] lose me?* The phantasy of one's death, of one's disappearance, is the first object that the subject has to bring into play in this dialectic. (Lacan, 1973/1998a, p. 214)

The subject who arrives at the unusual conclusion that his first Other asks for or *demands* nothing but him—that he *is* the Other's object *a*—is a perverse subject. (I elaborate upon the causes of perverse subjectivity in chapter 3.) At this stage, object *a* is the object-cause of the Other's jouissance. More commonly, what the first Other wants is eventually symbolized as *desire* for something or someone other than the subject, resulting in neurosis by way of secondary repression. Secondary repression constitutes object *a* as the object-cause of the Other's desire. In other words, prior to separation the Other's lack is perceived in terms of jouissance, whereas after separation it is perceived in terms of desire.

After alienation, the Other is no longer seen as complete, but is now seen as lacking something. Initially, the subject encounters the post-alienation Other as the Other of demand, and these demands rewrite the child's real and imaginary orders in particular ways. "In a way, S_1—S_2 is a representation of the Other's demand ... The subject is defined through the signifier of the Other's demand" (Brousse, 1995, p. 109). The lack implicit in demand is one that has a counterpart that can plug it up; although demand permanently overwrites need, demand remains something that calls for a specific object of satiation. Consequently, if the child believes himself to be the object that will fill the lack of the Other of demand— that is, satisfying the demanding Other—the child feels joined at the hip to the Other. "[H]is mother is constantly on his back" (Lacan, 2004, p.

67). This lack of symbolic space causes the child anxiety. Desire, on the other hand, has no perfect complement, and so the child's encounter with the Other of desire enables him to further separate from the Other. The child cannot understand the first Other to be desiring, however, until her desire is put into words. In Fink's (1997) words, once the first Other's lack, or desire,

> has been named, the weight of her demands (her real, physically unavoidable demands regarding the child's bodily functions, for example) lifts, and a space of desire opens up—a space in which her desire is articulated and moves, and in which her child can model his desire on hers. (p. 177)

The child's encounter with the Other of desire opens up a symbolic space for the child to move into his own subject position, with his "own" desires.

The articulation of the mOther's desire enables the child to further separate from his mOther because of the nature of desire. Desire has no perfect counterpart, and it therefore corresponds with an eternal lack. Desire seeks its satisfaction but by definition is essentially unsatisfied. Desire "is caught in the rails of metonymy, eternally extending toward the *desire for something else*" (Lacan, 1957/2006a, p. 518). Desire never ceases and only seeks its own continuation. Because there is no object that completely satisfies desire, it is impossible for the child to be his mOther's sole object of desire. Once the child perceives the desire of his mOther, he realizes that he can no longer be the be-all and end-all of her existence, and perhaps that he never was.

The Name-of-the-Father in separation functions as the first signifier(s) of the mOther's desire. In the child's perception, the mOther's demand for him has been replaced or neutralized to some extent by the signifier of the mOther's desire.

$$\frac{\text{Child's Name}}{\text{Signifiers of Mother's Demand}}$$

$$\downarrow$$

$$\frac{\text{Name-of-the-Father, Phallus, or S(\cancel{A})}}{\text{Mother's Desire}}$$

The Name-of-the-Father might, for instance, be "work" inasmuch as someone has said that the first Other "wants to go back to work now that the baby is old enough for daycare." This someone must be a person that the child grants a particular authority in terms of possessing knowledge about his first Other. Therefore it is most often the first Other herself or another immediate family member given authority in the mOther's discourse who successfully signifies the desire of the first Other. If the first Other seems to want nothing other than her child and a father signifies her desire for something other than the child, the child will likely discount the father's words if the first Other has discounted the father's authority. The Name-of-the-Father must be credible.

The subject has a choice in accepting or rejecting the symbolization of the mOther's desire. The subject's degree of freedom in this regard is unknown. The subject's acceptance of the Name-of-the-Father amounts to a castration or a loss of jouissance that corresponds to separation from the mOther. (In Lacanian algebra, what is lost in castration is represented by $-\varphi$.) The subject, then, may be motivated to disavow his initial perception of the mOther's desire so that he may retain his jouissance and his unquestionably special place in the mOther's world. It is more likely, though, as exemplified in the case of Little Hans, that the subject prefers to be "forced" to submit to castration so that he may gain his own symbolic space—one that is relatively devoid of anxiety. Hans consciously fears that his father is angry with him for being so close to his mother just as he fears that his mother will go away. Inasmuch as fears betray an unconscious desire, it is more correct to say that what Hans wants is for his mother to go away and for his father to force separation. (I speak more about the case of Little Hans and perverse disavowal in chapter 3.) For the mOther's desire to be successfully symbolized, the second Other of the Law must have forcefully demanded the separation of the mother-child dyad. The Name-of-the-Father is the vehicle of the Law that regulates the desire of the first Other and the child.

What is repressed in secondary repression has to do with the child's desire to be the object of his mother's jouissance and also with the child's drive-related desires (wanting to masturbate in public, for instance). Accordingly, secondary repression involves a further rewriting of the imaginary and the real by the symbolic. One consequence of this rewriting is that more jouissance is drained from the body, and the remainder is concentrated in the genital zones. Secondary repression therefore has to do with castration, because the neurotic subject has given up jouissance in the form of his remaining satisfactions at being the object of his mother's jouissance. In exchange for his castration, the neurotic subject now has the symbolic space to be able to pursue symbolic satisfactions. He wants to make symbolic achievements in the world, and for the Other to hold him in high regard. Nevertheless, the neurotic is left with the sense that he got a bum deal; his substitute satisfactions, derived from abiding by the law and gaining love and recognition from the Other, do not measure up to what he feels he has lost. Although the neurotic has the freedom to pursue his desires, he is often unaware of what he wants (because of repression) or is inhibited in pursuing it (because of the further rewriting of the drives and loss of jouissance). Neurotics, in contrast to psychotics and perverts, are blocked to a large degree from pursuing their desires because of inhibitions, anxieties, fear, guilt, and revulsion.

At the point of separation, once the first Other's desire has been put into words, the child generally asks "Who am I in the desire of my mOther?" and "Who am I in the desire of my second Other?"[41] *These questions will continue throughout the subject's life, and psychoanalysis may be seen as the process of answering them.* The subject's desire to be the object of the Other's desire replaces the subject's wish to be the object of the Other's jouissance. The subject's encounter with the lack in the Other enables him to read Other meanings into the Other's discourse—Other meanings that reveal the Other's desire rather than the Other's demand.

> In the intervals of the Other's discourse, the child experiences something that is radically mappable, namely, *He is saying this to me, but what does he want?...* It is [in metonymy] that what we call desire crawls, slips, escapes, like the ferret. The Other's desire is apprehended by the subject in what does not work, in the gaps in the Other's discourse, and all the child's *whys* reveal not so much an avidity for the reason of things, as a testing of the adult, a *Why are you telling me this?* ever-resuscitated from its base, which is the enigma of the adult's desire. (Lacan, 1973/1998a, p. 214, translation modified by Bruce Fink)

The child, in his quest to become more lovable and desirable to the Other, attempts to decipher the enigma of the Other's desire so that he can try to perfect himself accordingly. The child pays great attention to the Other's speech and behavior in his attempt to ascertain the irreducible quality possessed by the phallus (Φ) that incites her desire.

The subject as *manque à être* searches for his lost being by asking the question "Who am I in the desire of the Other?" "Whereas the first phase [alienation] is based on the substructure of union, the second [phase of separation] is based on the substructure that is called intersection" (Lacan, 1973/1998a, p. 213, translation modified by Bruce Fink). Separation is an intersection defined by what is *lacking* in both the set of the subject and the set of the Other. At this intersection, "[o]ne lack is superimposed upon the other ... It is a lack engendered from the previous time that serves to reply to the lack raised by the following time" (p. 215). In other words, the subject's lack in being—that was engendered by alienation—serves to reply to the lack in desire or the Other's desire. Put yet another way, the subject

---

41 In this case, the second Other refers to a person other than the first Other.

answers the enigma of the Other's desire ("What does the Other desire?") with his being ("Who am I?"). In this way, the subject invents himself as that which the Other desires (object *a* as the desired object). In embodying what he concludes the Other desires, the subject hopes to regain being and return to his imagined former state of wholeness.

The processes of alienation and separation enable us to understand Lacan's famous dictum: *"Le désir de l'homme, c'est le désir de l'Autre,"* (1973/1998a, p. 38). According to Fink, (1997, p. 238), this can be translated either as "Man's desire is for the Other to desire him" or as "Man's desire is the same as the Other's desire." The meaning of the former translation is suggested by the child's desire to be important to and loved by the parental Other. The meaning of the latter translation is evident in the child's incorporation of the desire of the parental Other into his unconscious, such that the Other's desires become his desires. If the Other desires to be at the top of her field, so too might the subject desire to make a name for himself in his career—his choice of career also being shaped by the desire of the Other. More importantly, though, what causes the subject's desire is not the Other's desire for any particular object but the Other's desirousness as such. The Other's desire as pure desirousness (object *a* as the object-cause of desire), as a desire that cannot be extinguished by any object, is what elicits the subject's desire.

The following diagram is the illustration suggested by Miller to represent separation, which I use here because Lacan did not provide any such depiction.

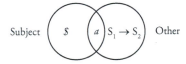

In this diagram, it is clear that object *a*, in separation, is situated at the intersection of the lack in the subject and the lack in the Other. In Seminar XI, object *a* is defined as the remainder left behind by the intersection of the symbolic with the real. Object *a* is one of Lacan's most important concepts, and it plays a key role in the operation of separation insofar as the subject identifies with object *a*. Object *a* is consequently the last

> remainder of the hypothetical mother-child unity to which the subject clings in fantasy to achieve a sense of wholeness, as the Other's desire, as the jouissance object, as that 'part' of the mOther the child takes with it in separation, and as the foreign, fateful cause of the subject's existence that he or she must become or subjectify in analysis. (Fink, 1995, p. 83)

Object *a*: The Vital Remainder

The power of pure loss emerges from the residue of an obliteration.

Lacan (1958/2006a, p. 691)

Out of all his concepts, Lacan's object *a* is not only one of the most central but is also one of the most frequently revised. Although I shall not attempt a comprehensive account of object *a*'s many usages, I will discuss those that are central to this book. From the early 1950s until Seminar VII, Lacan's object *a* was a strictly imaginary object equated with the ego. In Seminar VII (1959–1960), Lacan's discussion of object *a* as *das Ding* was the inauguration of its subsequent usage as an object in the real— that is, an object that defies articulation in language. Because it is in the real, object *a* is an object associated with jouissance, being, and desire.[42] After Lacan began referring to object *a* as an object in the real, however, he sometimes used object *a* to refer to an imaginary order semblance or façade of the real order object *a*.

I have so far touched upon the concept of object *a* as representing the object that causes jouissance, the object of jouissance (or the object that is enjoyed), the object that causes desire, the object that is desired, and as the subject's being (as represented in the symbolic). Object *a* is the result of the birth of the child into subjectivity, and it plays a key role in both perversion and neurosis because it structures the subject's drives and desires. Because the psychotic possesses an ego, albeit an unstable one, the psychotic can be said to possess object *a* in a certain sense, however the discussion that follows here will be restricted to the objects *a* of the pervert and the neurotic.

Object *a* may be helpfully considered to be the real remainder of the process of alienation. The child's partial separation from the Other produces object *a* as a remnant of the hypothetical mother-child unity. Consequently, object *a* is a symbol indicating both a lack in being and the "object" to which the subject clings to ignore her lack in being. The subject as *manque à être* attempts to regain her lost being along with her supposed sense of unity through her relationship with object *a*. Likewise, the subject's relation to object *a* is Lacan's definition of fantasy. Lacan represents fantasy by the matheme $ \$ \lozenge a $: the split subject in relation to object *a*.[43]

---

42 Although desire is commonly associated with the symbolic order, desire actually springs from the lack in the Other. That lack in the symbolic is the real.

43 The lozenge may also mean "desire for" such that the formula for fantasy may be read, "the split subject who desires object *a*." This reading of the lozenge, however, loses the important connotation that the split subject has a particular relationship to object *a* that is defined by her history.

The subject's fantasy or particular relation to object *a* reflects the way she wants to be positioned with respect to the Other's desire. One of the meanings of object *a*, as previously mentioned, is the Other's desire; the Other's desire serves as the cause of the subject's desire. In her fantasy, the subject obtains jouissance for herself by orchestrating object *a* in the scenario in accordance with what is most exciting to her. Jouissance, as exciting satisfaction, may be consciously associated with any number of types of pleasurable or painful feelings. In fantasy, the subject simultaneously connects herself to the Other and clings to the real. The subject's fantasy and resulting jouissance provide her with an illusory sense of wholeness.

Correspondingly, one major way in which Lacan formulates object *a* is as the lost object. Although Lacan is indebted to Freud for this conceptualization, Lacan, in typical form, significantly revised Freud's notion of the lost object (1986/1997b, p. 222). For Freud, the lost object before it became lost was first an object passively encountered by the infant that provided satisfaction, such as the mother's breast. After the infant's initial experience with the breast, he recalls the memory of his experience of satisfaction and attempts to refind the now lost object either by way of a primary process (such as hallucination) or by way of a secondary process (seeking it out in the world). Once the child reaches the genital stage, his sexual object-choice is a repetition or an actual refinding of the lost object.

In contrast, Lacan's object *a* as lost object was never fully present; it was never an actual object, but was only constituted as an object by way of fantasy once the infant could differentiate between herself and objects. In other words, because the infant initially knows no separation or distinction between herself and the *Umwelt*, an object such as the breast cannot yet be said to exist for the infant. The breast and its meaning as the lost object of satisfaction is only constituted after the advent of the ego. In addition, the infant's repeated experiences of the absence of the breast and hence of the absence of satisfaction lead her to constitute the breast as an object separate from her that she cannot control. Once the child develops her sense of self as separate from the *Umwelt*, she becomes irreversibly separated from her initial object of satisfaction.

From the very advent of object *a*, the object is always already lost. "It is in its nature that the object as such is lost" (Lacan, 1986/1997b, p. 52). The child can never refind the breast as she imagines she experienced it the first time—as something connected to and not separate from herself. The lost object is therefore a fantasmatic construction, and so any actual breast the child encounters fails to measure up to the breast as object *a*. Object *a* as fundamentally lost is the cause of desire and plays a central role in fantasies.

Another meaning of Lacan's object *a* is that of *das Ding* ("the Thing," in English), a concept loosely based on "neuron *a*" from Freud's *Project for a Scientific Psychology* (1895/1950). As part of the perceptual system, Freud's neuron *a* is an "unchanging apparatus" (Lacan, 1986/1997b, p. 51) in relation to the variable "neuron *b*" that forms links with other neuron *b*s. Lacan "translated" Freud's *Project for a Scientific Psychology* such that neuron *b*s became signifiers and *Bahnungen* ("breaches," in English) became the connections linking signifiers together (p. 39). Neuron *a*, now *das Ding*, is the element that is "excluded" (p. 71) from the signifying chain, although the chain revolves around it. In other words, *das Ding* is "the beyond-of-the-signified" (p. 54), an object that ex-sists in the real.

Furthermore, *das Ding* serves "a primordial function" (Lacan, 1986/1997b, p. 62): "It is then in relation to the original *Ding* that the first orientation, the first choice, the first seat of subjective orientation takes place ..." (p. 54). *Das Ding* has a role in the birth of the subject. Lacan said, "[i]t is as a function of this beyond-of-the-signified and of an emotional relationship to it that the subject keeps its distance and is constituted in a kind of relationship characterized by primary affect, prior to any repression" (p. 54). "[P]rior to any repression" (p. 54), or prior to the child's incorporation of the symbolic order, the child encounters *das Ding* or object *a* in its relations with the first Other. In the initial encounter with *das Ding*, which Lacan called the "primal scene" (1973/1998a, p. 69), the child experiences a primary, highly jouissance-laden affect. The child therefore wants to remain in a proximal relationship with *das Ding*, but because getting too close to it results in strong anxiety, "the subject keeps its distance" (1986/1997b, p. 54). The primary affect leads to the constitution of a particular primal position—corresponding to a structural subjective position—with respect to *das Ding*; the hysteric's relation to *das Ding* is one of disgust, unpleasure, or aversion (pp. 5–54), and the obsessive, who experiences an "excess, too much pleasure" (p. 54) in relation to *das Ding*, feels guilty afterward and adopts a strategy of avoidance (p. 54). Another way of accounting for the child's birth into subjectivity, then, is as a defense against the jouissance associated with *das Ding* (Fink, 1995, p. 95).

Lacan, following Freud, said that "one goal of the specific action which aims for the experience of satisfaction is to reproduce the initial state, to find *das Ding*, the object" (1986/1997b, p. 53). "The pleasure principle governs the search for the object and imposes the detours which maintain the distance in relation to its end" (p. 58). As a lost object in the real, object *a* is, of course, impossible to find. Nevertheless, the subject searches for and finds approximations of object *a*—often in romantic relationships. The subject's fundamental stance toward object *a* can often be surmised by the clinician on the basis of what her analysand tells her about his sexual experiences—particularly the early ones.[44] The observation that those who react to *das Ding* with guilt and aversion are obsessive and that those who react to *das Ding* with disgust are hysterical is one of great diagnostic importance. I will discuss the pervert's primary relation to *das Ding* in chapter 4.

Object *a* is the fantasmatic substitute for the being lost in castration (-φ), such that object *a* is both behind and ahead of the subject. Object *a* represents both what was lost and what the subject wishes to refind. In Seminar VIII Lacan said, "It was a find, that of the fundamentally partial nature of the object insofar as it is the pivot, center, key of human desire" (Lacan, 2001, pp. 176–177). Object *a*'s intimate connection to the subject's *manque à être* is at the root of its function as the object-cause of desire.

Because object *a* is part of the real, it is invisible and unspeakable. How, then, does object *a* manifest its presence? When the subject approaches something or someone that embodies her object *a,* she experiences jouissance in the form of an affect such as disgust, elation, guilt, or anxiety. In addition, the evidence of object *a*'s presence in fantasy is the jouissance the subject derives from her fantasies. Object *a* often plays a visual role in the subject's fantasies, and it generally appears in a veiled or dressed up form. Lacan designates a visual form of object *a* by the formula $i(a)$, meaning an image of *a*.

Many of the objects *a* that Lacan discusses *seem* to be produced by a bodily organ. Lacan's list of objects *a* includes "the [breast], the feces, the phallus (as an imaginary object), and the urinary flow. (An unthinkable list, unless we add, as I do, the phoneme, the gaze, the voice ... and the nothing.)" (1966/2006a, p. 817). The eye, for instance, seems to produce the gaze (object *a* in the scopic field). But the gaze, as part of the real, is not an actual object at all. The seeming nothingness of the gaze as object *a* is what is represented by the signifiers (including "eye") associated with object *a*. Perversion, as I will explain in chapter 4, has a special relationship to the gaze and the voice.

Objects *a* were forged by a number of what Lacan called "the cut" (1966/2006a, p. 817) during the child's process of socialization. The cut is a signifier inscribed on the body at the place where object *a* seems to be affixed to an organ. Cuts are marks of castration, indicating the loss of jouissance resulting from the child's birth into subjectivity. Lacan said,

> The very delimitation of the "erogenous zone" that the drive isolates from the function's metabolism (the act of devouring involves

---

44 My definition of "sexual" here is a very broad one: sexual experiences are those in which a subject experiences jouissance in relation to object *a*.

organs other than the mouth—just ask Pavlov's dog) is the result of a cut that takes advantage of the anatomical characteristic of a margin or border: the lips, "the enclosure of the teeth," the rim of the anus, the penile groove, the vagina, and the slit formed by the eyelids, not to mention the hollow of the ear. (p. 817)

The cuts of castration are formed through the child's relation to the Other. The mOther makes demands that the child eat (oral zone), listen (aural zone), look (scopic zone), go to the bathroom (anal zone), and so on, and the child's interpretation of these demands result in the formation of his drives. The subject identifies with the cuts of castration, and her identifications involve unary traits.

The Partial Drives

Object *a* is intimately connected to the drive; the drives circle around objects *a*. Translating Freud's *Trieb* as "drive" rather than "instinct" (Lacan, 1973/1998a, p. 49) as James Strachey did in the *Standard Edition*, Lacan said that the concept of the drives was one of Freud's "fundamental concepts" (p. 12). Freud distinguished between *Instinkt* ("instinct"), which is a purely biological function at the level of the living being, and *Trieb*, which is linked to instinct but is structured by the symbolic and is particular to each subject. The drives are formed through the child's process of socialization by way of the Other's demands—demands which often have to do with the child's body. Lacan's matheme for the drive is $ \mathcal{S} \lozenge D$ (1966/2006a, p. 817). It may be read: The split subject in relation to demand. As in the case of fantasy, the subject has a certain relation to the drive that mirrors the way she wants to be positioned with respect to the Other's demand.

The drives unceasingly revolve around objects *a* (Lacan, 1973/1998a, p. 257), never reaching a goal but finding satisfaction in their repetitive circular path. The drive is "indifferent" (p. 168) to the attainment of an object insofar as the oral drive, for example, does not stop once the individual has eaten. "Thus any object can be adopted as the drive object, though the drive object is not just any old object. The Other's demand determines which object is adopted" (Brousse, 1995, p. 112).

According to Miller (2009b), the drive is "the final transformation of need, and at the same time, it's the final transformation of demand beyond desire and love" (pp. 41–42). Just as demand overwrites the needs of the living being, so too desire, love, and the drive have their effects on the subject. Miller notes that need, demand, desire, love, and the drive all imply different ways of pursuing satisfaction. Of the satisfaction of the drive, Lacan said the following:

Between these two terms—drive and satisfaction—there is set up an extreme antinomy that reminds us that the use of the function of the drive has for me no other purpose than to put in question what is meant by satisfaction … [The satisfaction of the drive] is paradoxical … For if one distinguishes, at the outset of the dialectic of the drive, *Not* from *Bedürfnis*, need from the pressure of the drive—it is precisely because no object of any *Not*, need, can satisfy the drive. Even when you stuff the mouth—the mouth that opens in the register of the drive—it is not the food that satisfies it, it is, as one says, the pleasure of the mouth. (1973/1998a, pp. 166–167)

The paradox of the drive is that it does not, like a need, have a specific, delimited, material object that would satisfy its search, but that it obtains satisfaction nevertheless—in the repetitive movement of its circuit. At the same time, the subject has instantaneous impulses for something. Consequently, the "temporal structure of the drive's satisfaction is the instant" (Soler, 1995, p. 52) as opposed to the temporal structure of the signifier, which is a dialectic between anticipation and retroaction. Nevertheless, the constant pressure exerted by the drive differentiates its temporal structure from that of need, which is periodic.

The drives are the only "pathway by which the impact of sexuality is manifested in the subject" (Lacan, 1966/2006a, p. 849). By circling around their objects, the drives bring sexuality as part of the real into the symbolic and imaginary orders (1973/1998a, p. 168). Freud, in his essay "The Sexual Aberrations" (1905/1953a), wrote that sexuality consists of *Partieltriebe* or partial drives which correspond to different erogenous zones. For instance, the anal drive corresponds to the anus and the oral drive corresponds to the mouth. Freud argued that the drives of children are partial, but that proper development at the latency phase affords the genital organs priority over the partial drives such that the drives fuse together.

Lacan rejected the idea that the partial drives could ever fuse to form a complete drive. Lacan said, "A drive, insofar as it represents sexuality in the unconscious, is never anything but a partial drive. This is the essential failing [*carence*]—namely, the absence [*carence*] of anything that could represent in the subject the mode of what is male or female in his being" (1966/2006a, p. 849). A drive is partial insofar as it "*merely* represents, and partially at that, the curve of fulfillment of sexuality in the living being" (1973/1998a, p. 177). The drives are only translations and modifications of sexuality in the living being.

Lacan also emphasized the drive's relation to death. "[T]he drive, the partial drive, is profoundly a death drive and represents in itself the portion of death in the [sexual] living being" (1973/1998a, p. 205). There are four reasons for the drive's relation to death. One is that the drive, as the subject's sexuality, is linked to sexual reproduction and thus to the cycle of birth and death. "So you see, the link between sex and death, sex and the death of the individual, is fundamental" (p. 150). Another reason is that the drive attempts to go beyond the limits of the pleasure principle and obtain an excess of jouissance.[45] Yet another reason is that every drive, in its circuit, pursues its own extinction. The final reason is that the drive, like Freud's death drive (*Thanatos*), involves repetition.

It is important for clinicians to note that the subject's question regarding her identity is partially answered at the level of the drives. For Lacan, there is a "subject in the real" (1966/2006a, p. 835)—which might also be called the subject of jouissance or the subject of the drives. The subject of jouissance is caused by the signifier (p. 835) insofar as the symbolic order structures the drives. Psychoanalysis allows the subject to "discover something about his or her unconscious as knowledge, but also [to] learn something about him or herself as a libidinal subject" (Soler, 1995, p. 53). Jouissance is a substance (Lacan, 1975/1998b, p. 26) that is separate from the Other (although it can ex-sist in the Other), and so the subject's identity at the level of jouissance has more solidity than at the level of the sliding signifier. The successful completion of a psychoanalysis is contingent upon the analysand's subjectification of her identity as subject of jouissance as well as subject of the symbolic.

As I have said, Lacanian psychoanalysis may be seen as the process of answering the questions "Who am I?" and "What does the Other want?" (Lacan, 1973/1998a, p. 214). When the neurotic analysand engages this enigma in terms of the Other's desire, her curiosity propels her along the process of discovering and dismantling each of her misidentifications. The enigma of this persistent question of identity at the level of being drives the analysis forward in the case of a neurotic analysand. Where, then, does that leave the possibility of practicing analysis as we know it with a pervert, lacking as he does a persistent question of identity at the level of being? In other words, since the pervert has a clear answer to this question—he *is* the Other's object *a*, why would he seek out analysis in the first place, and, if mandated to engage in psychotherapy, what outcomes and transference relations are possible? These are some of the crucial questions that serve as driving force for the remainder of this book.

---

45 "What is at issue in the drive is finally revealed here—the course of the drive is the only form of transgression that is permitted to the subject in relation to the pleasure principle" (Lacan, 1973/1998a, p. 183).

3

THE ETIOLOGY OF PERVERSION

The whole problem of the perversions consists in conceiving how the child, in its relationship with its mother—a relationship that is constituted in analysis not by the child's biological dependence, but by its dependence on her love, that is, by its desire for her desire—identifies with the imaginary object of her desire insofar as the mother herself symbolizes it in the phallus.

Lacan (1959/2006a, p. 554)

Perversion And Its Etiology

A pervert, as I have said, is a subject who has undergone alienation, but who has disavowed separation. The perverse structure is, like all three structures, fundamentally a solution to a problem. The pervert's problem ultimately stems from the inadequacy of the paternal function.[46] His problem is that he experiences an unmanageable amount of anxiety or jouissance in his relation to the Other because he lacks a signifier for the Other's desire, $S(\bar{A})$. Without being put into words, the lack of the Other seems unbearable and horrible. In lieu of a better solution ($S(\bar{A})$), the pervert "identifies with the imaginary object of [the mother's] desire insofar as the mother herself symbolizes it in the phallus" (Lacan, 1959/2006a, p. 554). As object a, the object-cause of jouissance, the pervert plugs up the hole in the Other by providing the Other with jouissance and temporarily squelching the Other's desire. Consequently, unlike for the neurotic, for the pervert there is no persistent question of identity at the level of being. The question "Who am I?" has a clear answer for the pervert; he *is* the object that completes the mOther.

Perversion is a strategy for increasing the power of the paternal function and thereby setting limits to jouissance. By way of disavowal, the

---

46 I agree with Fink that perversion is due to the inadequacy of the paternal function, such that the pervert undergoes alienation but not separation. In addition, I follow the lead of Fink, Miller, Tostain, and others in highlighting the role of disavowal in perversion.

pervert creates a substitute for the insufficient Other of the Law—one that has the power and the will to separate him from his first Other and to force him to give up the jouissance associated with the first Other. This substitute is neither permanent nor sufficient, however, and so the pervert continues to suffer from an excess of jouissance and a lack of subjective space of his own.

After the child has successfully undergone alienation, the child's transformation into a neurotic subject—instead of into a perverse subject—depends upon two related processes involved in the logical moment of separation: the child's acceptance (instead of disavowal) of castration and of the Law and his perception of the Other's lack in terms of desire (instead of in terms of jouissance).[47] A minority of subjects become perverse, and the topic of this chapter is to explore the phenomena that impede or prevent the processes of separation from occurring.

Key Aspects of Perversion
1. The paternal function is inadequate.
   a. The subject disavows separation.
   b. The subject refuses or is denied castration, and so he suffers from an excess of jouissance.
   c. The subject encounters the lack in the Other only in terms of jouissance and not in terms of desire.
2. Perverse fantasy = $a \lozenge \$$. He is the instrument of the Other's jouissance.
   a. The pervert has a limited ability to desire. His identity is determined by being the actual object of jouissance of the Other.
3. The lawgiving Other exists, but only precariously; the pervert fervently tries to make the Other whole and to give it a stable existence.
4. The pervert has an especially close relation to the gaze and the voice.

Castration and the Phallus: Giving Up φ for Φ

Castration means that jouissance has to be refused in order to be attained on the inverse scale of the Law of desire.

Lacan (1960/2006a, p. 827)

For Lacan, castration, generally speaking, is the renunciation of jouissance for the substitute satisfactions the individual obtains in subjectivity. Castration plays a key role in both alienation and separation. In alienation, the child sacrifices some jouissance in order to become a subject in the symbolic order. In separation, the subject gives up some jouissance derived

---

47 These two processes should be understood as I have elaborated them in chapter 2.

from the drives when his fantasy changes from $\$ \lozenge D$, or the split subject in relation to the Other's demand, to $\$ \lozenge a$, or the split subject in relation to the object-cause of the Other's desire. The perverse subject does not undergo the castration involved in separation.

A neurotic subject position is acquired when the first Other (often the mOther)'s desire is named and the subject perceives the mOther's lack in terms of desire. Correspondingly, the neurotic subject's renunciation of some of the pleasure of the drives results from this shift in how he perceives the Other and his relation to the Other. Post-separation, the subject no longer constitutes himself solely as the object of his mOther's demands—demands which are tied to the jouissance of the partial drives. Instead, the subject attempts to become object a, the object-cause of the Other's desire.[48] By giving up his position as object-cause of the Other's jouissance in favor of the position of object-cause of the Other's desire, the subject sacrifices some jouissance associated with the Other's proximity and with the drives, which are structured by the Other's demand. The neurotic subject, having given up some of the jouissance of the drives, gains satisfactions in the order of desire, by pursuing "his" desires, modeled as they are after the Other's desire.

It is important to note that becoming neurotic involves a transformation of the fantasy object. *Prior to separation, the object that supports the fantasy $\$ \lozenge D$ is an actual object, a presence. After separation, the object that supports the fantasy $\$ \lozenge a$ is a real-order object, an absence, or a lack.* The perverse fantasy, resulting from refusing or thwarting separation, is one in which the object that fuels it is a presence. The perverse fantasy is $a \lozenge \$$ (Lacan, 1962/2006a, p. 774), and will be discussed at length in the next chapter. For now, it will suffice to say that the pervert places himself in the position of the object, and that this object is not the object-cause of the Other's desire, but the object-cause of the Other's jouissance.

Our understandings of the etiology and structure of perversion rest upon our interpretation of the phallus. Even though Freud makes a distinction between the penis and the phallus as a symbol of male desire (and of female desire), he often equates the two. The same is true of Lacan—particularly in his work in the 1950s. Because the distinction is an important one, I strive to make it clearly in this book.

The image of the erect penis, and not a flaccid one, serves—in our current societal context—to symbolize desire. The phallus as an imaginary object (rather than as a signifier), unlike the organ of the penis, is always erect. The imaginary phallus (φ), therefore, is distinct from the penis as a biological organ. Furthermore, because it is an imaginary order phenomenon, the imaginary phallus refers to the role that the penis plays in the

---

48 It is structurally impossible for the subject to fill the lack in the Other of desire.

child's fantasy and it represents the boy's narcissistic attachment to his penis and the pleasures it affords him.

At the level of the symbolic, the phallus as a signifier (Φ) is the signifier of desire, of the Other's lack. Its imaginary counterpart, according to both Freud and Lacan, is the image of the erect penis (the imaginary phallus). Its existence in the real is designated by object a, although it, as real, is the unspeakable cause of the Other's desire, and is not a signifier.

Why is the signifier of desire represented in the imaginary by the erect penis? The erect penis[49] is able to provide a universal visual symbol of male sexual desire insofar as an erection is generally associated with male sexual desire. If a man does not have an erection in a sexual encounter, his partner might very well feel undesired by him. Every man's sexual desire can be represented by the imaginary phallus (although this does not exclude a particular man's desire from also being represented by something else). The phallus is a culturally and historically contextual signifier; it is possible that some other signifier—such as one associated with female genitalia—may serve or may have served as the signifier of desire.

However, there is no signifier of desire in widespread use that corresponds to female sexual desire, probably because female sexual desire is extremely difficult to clearly represent. There is no one visible physiological sign of a woman's arousal that is present in the majority of sexual encounters. In this sense, the set of women cannot be totalized in the same way as can the set of men, and this fact has numerous consequences for Lacan's theory on gender. Because female sexual desire lacks an unambiguous and universal symbol, it too is represented by the imaginary phallus.[50] This is likely what often causes women to have difficulty understanding and describing their sexuality in something other than in masculine terms. [51]

---

49 In the clinic as well as in everyday discourse, subjects often speak about objects that metonymically represent the imaginary phallus for them. For instance, objects such as skyscrapers, cigars, and tall, thin cacti sometimes play phallic roles in dreams, jokes, literature, and movies.

50 It is from this observation that Freud concluded that masculine libido is the only type of libido. Even though Lacan agrees with Freud that there is only one symbolizable form of libido (Lacan calls it phallic jouissance), Lacan theorized (with the help of clinical evidence and support from literature) that there is an Other jouissance that is not representable within the symbolic order. Women have access not only to phallic jouissance, but to this unsayable Other jouissance as well. Men are restricted to the experience of phallic jouissance.

51 Luce Irigaray, in her chapter "Desire" from *This Sex Which Is Not One* (1977), protests against the representation of female desire in masculine terms, and argues, against Lacan, that it is possible to signify femininity and female desire in strictly feminine terms. Irigaray recommends, as a starting point, that we change the way we speak of female genitalia. Instead of talking about female genitalia in visual terms, Irigaray says we would talk about it in tactile terms, because she believes that the essence of femininity has to do with the primacy of touch. Furthermore, Irigaray equates femininity with infinity and multiplicity, versus masculine finitude and singularity. Correspondingly, Irigaray says "woman 'touches herself' all the time, and ... her genitals

There is yet another reason why the signifier of lack is represented by the image of an erect penis. In "The Subversion of the Subject and the Dialectic of Desire," Lacan says that the phallus is the signifier of the sacrifice of jouissance in the castration complex, thus making the phallus the signifier of lack. The imaginary phallus, Lacan says,

> that is, the image of the penis—is negativized where it is situated in the specular image. That is what predestines the phallus to give body to jouissance in the dialectic of desire ... It is thus that the erectile organ—not as itself, or even as an image, but as a part that is missing in the desired image—comes to symbolize the place of jouissance. (1960/2006a, p. 822)

Although this passage, in typical Lacanian fashion, resists easy interpretation, its meanings are highly relevant to the topic at hand in this chapter. What is key to understand here is that Lacan is referring both to castration (as the logical moment of separation) and to the subject's interpretation of its specular mirror image according to the Other's desire.

Even though parents do, even in the present day, make literal castration threats,[52] what functions more commonly for the child as a "castration threat" are the parents' demands that she or he give up jouissance associated with masturbation. The parents' demands "Don't touch that" or "Don't do that in front of company" are interpreted by the child to mean that all of her or his masturbatory pleasures are prohibited by the Other. In the child's mirror image of her- or himself as desirable to her

---

are formed of two lips in continuous contact. Thus, within herself, she is already two—but not divisible into one(s)—that caress each other" (p. 354). Later, Irigaray describes the vagina and the labia as an "incompleteness of form which allows [a woman's] organ to touch itself over and over again, indefinitely, by itself" (p. 355). Therefore, Irigaray does not come up with one signifier which would serve as alternative to the phallus, but instead recommends a multiplicity of metaphors and phrases.

Despite wide readership and interest in Irigaray's solution, it is now 33 years since the publication of her chapter and evidence points to the fact that her signifiers of feminine desire have failed to take root. The reason for this likely has to do with the necessity for a signifier of feminine desire that has a clear and universal imaginary counterpart. Furthermore, Lacan theorizes that there is something essential about language that renders impossible putting the essence of femininity into words. Someone with a feminine structure, according to Lacan, is defined by the presence of real order Other jouissance in addition to symbolic order phallic jouissance. Although it may be said to be unfair that the phallus signifies feminine desire, it may also be said to be unfair that individuals with a masculine structure are limited to experiences of phallic jouissance.

52 For example, "I will cut off your penis if you do that again" or "I will cut off your hand if you keep touching yourself with it."

or his parental Other, then, the imaginary phallus "is negativized" and "missing" (Lacan, 1960/2006a, p. 822) insofar as the genitals are seen as negative and undesirable.

Lacan emphasizes that the imaginary phallus is particularly suited to this function of negativization because "its position as a 'pointy extremity' in the form predisposes it to the fantasy of it falling off—in which its exclusion from the specular image is completed as is the prototype it constitutes for the world of objects" (1960/2006a, p. 822). Therefore, it is the obvious visibility of the erect penis that lends itself to the fantasy of it falling off or being cut off. This fantasy is set in motion by the child perceiving that his genitalia are a liability, as being subject to or having already been lost. Correspondingly, Lacan symbolizes the negativization of the genitals by $-\varphi$, or negative phi, indicating that the image of the erect penis is always threatened with loss. The imaginary phallus, being threatened with loss, is perceived by the child to provide such a precarious source of jouissance that the "decision"[53] to give up φ for Φ almost naturally follows.

Although Lacan did not explicitly mention how girls undergo the process of castration in "The Subversion of the Subject and the Dialectic of Desire," he did so in other articles, for instance in his article "On Freud's 'Trieb' and the Psychoanalyst's Desire."

> (It is the fact that a woman must go through the same dialectic [of castration], whereas nothing seems to oblige her to do so—she must lose what she does not have—which tips us off, allowing us to articulate that it is the phallus by default that constitutes the amount of the symbolic debt: a debit account when one has it, a disputed credit when one does not). (1960/2006a, pp. 852–853)

It follows that Lacan maintained that girls too give up jouissance and undergo castration. Furthermore, the process of castration for girls has just as much to do with the phallus and with the penis (that she does not have), although clearly they are not forced to give up their jouissance in exactly the same fashion as boys.

Returning to the issue of the negativization of the imaginary phallus in "The Subversion of the Subject and the Dialectic of Desire," we may here assume that this process of negativization and castration (of giving up a narcissistic attachment to one's genitalia) is easier for girls than for

---

53 The word *decision* connotes, in our culture, a conscious choice. To what degree the child's choice is conscious or unconscious is a matter of debate, but it not one that has dramatic consequences for the theory behind working with neurosis and perversion.

boys.[54] This is because the mirror image of a girl already reflects the lack of a "pointy extremity" (Lacan, 1960/2006a, p. 822), so a girl can fantasize that her imaginary phallus has already fallen off or been cut off. There is no use in protesting a loss that has already occurred. Perhaps this is one way we can understand Lacan's statement in this article that "the male sex [is] the weaker sex with regard to perversion" (p. 823).

Furthermore, castration threats also commonly fall under the category of demands intended to separate the child from the primary caregiver. A child's eroticism is related to the mOther insofar as it was her words, touch, care, and attention that invested the child's erogenous zones with jouissance in the first place. A child's masturbatory behavior and corresponding fantasies are therefore always connected to the mOther. Accordingly, castration is considered to involve a relinquishing of jouissance related both to the imaginary phallus and to the primary caregiver.

Resolving the Castration Complex

[P]erversion may be spoken of as fear of castration, fear of the Other's castration essentially.

Miller (1996b, p. 317)

Typically, especially in Freud's work, the child is said to fear castration because of the loss of jouissance it entails. Following the psychoanalytic rule that a fear often betrays a wish, it might be, however, that the child to some degree wishes for castration for that very reason; too much jouissance is difficult to bear. Whether the child accepts castration out of fear, hope, or both, the child overcomes the castration complex and becomes neurotic by renouncing his narcissistic attachment to his imaginary phallus and its associated drive-related jouissance in favor of the symbolic phallus and the opportunity to gain substitute satisfactions through pursuing activities and personal qualities valued by the parental Other. The neurotic here takes his cues from the Other, and displaces some of the jouissance formerly associated with the imaginary phallus—thought to be undesirable by the Other—to pursuits desired by the Other. *It is through castration, in the shift from imaginary to the symbolic, that the value that the child assigned to a physically present object (the genitalia) is transferred to the intangible object* a. The symbolic phallus (Φ) signifies "the place of jouissance" (Lacan, 1960/2006a, p. 822) and is "the signifier of jouissance" (p.

---

54 Lacan did not equate biological sex with gender identity. Instead, in Seminar XX Lacan explained the etiology and differences between masculine and feminine *structures*, which do not necessarily follow from the presence of male or female (or something outside of those two categories) genitalia.

823) insofar as it represents the determinants of the Other's jouissance and desire. Often, Lacan called the phallus (Φ) "the signifier of the Other's desire" (1958/2006a, p. 694). The neurotic subject achieves a further separation from the Other through the process of castration which gives him the freedom to come into being as a desiring subject, although he models his desire and jouissance on that of the Other.

According to Lacan and Freud, the pervert does not give up φ for Φ, and therefore retains his jouissance and his position as the instrument of the Other's jouissance. What causes the perverse response to the castration complex? Lacan said very little in the way of direct hypotheses as to the causes of perversion. However, Lacan's detailed elaborations of separation, castration, the phallus, and object *a* provide ample theoretical material from which to make such hypotheses. In general, *the perverse solution to the castration complex is due to the inadequacy of the paternal function.* Several aspects of the inadequacy of the paternal function will be explored in this chapter.

One contributing factor in the "choice" to retain jouissance may be that *the pervert's imaginary phallus fails to become negativized.* If the child's imaginary phallus does not undergo negativization, there is no motivating force influencing the child to give up some of the jouissance associated with it and the drives. The minimal conditions for the imaginary phallus to be negativized are that the child (as split subject, post-alienation and pre-separation) sufficiently respects the second Other, the lawgiving Other, and that the person representing the lawgiving Other utters demands interpreted by the child as castration threats. Frequently, what prevents these two conditions from being met is the great value the first Other places on the child's imaginary phallus, an unusually close relationship between the first Other and the child, and the first Other's derision of the lawgiving Other. At a minimum, two people must make the appropriate contribution for this condition to be met: the child and at least one parental figure. I will define the qualifier "sufficiently" in the paragraphs that follow the chart.

Reasons for the Failure of the Negativization of the Imaginary Phallus
1. The second Other (the lawgiving Other) is not sufficiently respected by the child
   a. because of the child's refusal to sufficiently respect the second Other;
   b. because the first Other does not sufficiently respect the second Other (as reflected in the first Other's discourse);
   c. because of both of the above.

2. The child never attributes castration threats[55] to the second Other
    a. because of the child's refusal to interpret any of the second Other's statements as castration threats (owing to Condition 1a, the child's refusal to sufficiently respect the second Other);
    b. because the child is unable to interpret any of the second Other's statements as castration threats (owing to Condition 1b, the inadequacy of the second Other as reflected in the discourse of the first Other);
    c. because the parental figure embodying the second Other never uttered castration threats.
3. The child perceives the parental figure who plays the role of first Other to approve of and/or derive jouissance from the child's penis, giving the imaginary phallus a positive symbolic value that resists negativization.
4. The child perceives himself to be the be-all and end-all of the existence of the first Other.

All of these conditions relate to what was earlier referred to as the inadequacy of the paternal function. Regarding Condition 1, it follows that if the second Other is not sufficiently respected by the child, any castration threats made will fall flat, having no effect on the child's perception of its desirable mirror image. Conditions 2a and 2b logically follow from the fulfillment of Condition 1. The child either will not or cannot interpret any of the second Other's statements as castration threats because the child believes statements made by the second Other are fraudulent, empty, and impotent. Condition 2c is probably rare, owing not only to the wide variety of statements that could logically be interpreted as castration threats, but also to the widespread social convention that it is inappropriate to touch or show one's genitalia to others. In the event that Condition 2c is met but Condition 1 is not met, we might still say that that 2c is related to a partial failure of the paternal metaphor, insofar as its function at the stage of separation is to force the child to relinquish imaginary satisfactions (φ) for symbolic ones (Φ).

If the lawgiving Other is not *sufficiently* given credence by the child, then, the child will become perverse rather than neurotic. The child as split subject has successfully undergone alienation, and so he has to some degree recognized and accepted the second Other. At this in-between stage, *the future pervert is the child who comes to see the lawgiving Other as nothing but a façade.* The most likely—as well as the most frequently clini-

---

55 The reader should remember that the term *castration threats* covers a wide variety of statements, including the common requests that the child refrain from touching his genitals when there is company present or that the child be less attached to his mother.

cally reported—way in which the child attains this position with respect to the second Other is through the second Other's position in the discourse of the first Other.

The first Other, often a mother, having superficially recognized the Name-of-the-Father and thus having enabled the child's alienation by language, subsequently reduces the symbolic authority of the Law to a mere system of social conventions. According to her, the Law is a façade that needs to be respected only for the sake of keeping up appearances. Frequently, the lawgiving Other is represented by the father. In such cases (such as in the clinical case presented in chapter 6), the mOther, with her child as audience, peristently pokes fun at the authority of the father, revealing the emptiness beneath the surface of its tricks. Although the child recognizes the lawgiving Other, the mOther's derision of it results in the child seeing it as without consequence. Any demands uttered in the Name-of-the-Father only gain significance if they are convenient for the mOther. The Law of the father is demonstrated to be insubstantial in the face of the mOther's whims.

In the perverse Oedipal constellation, then, the lawgiving Other is found to be seriously lacking in credibility. Consequently, any castration threats uttered in the Name-of-the-Father either will not or cannot be taken seriously by the child, thus preventing the negativization of the imaginary phallus. The child goes on thinking and acting as if no threat had been uttered. There is no Other who can force the child to relinquish his jouissance and undergo castration. Nor is there an Other who can convince the child that symbolic pursuits are a superior alternative to imaginary jouissance. There is only the child, the first Other, and a second Other whose existence is tenuous. This structure binds the child closely to the first Other.

A common factor supporting the perverse Oedipal constellation is the first Other's interest, enjoyment, or pride in the child's penis (Condition 3). The manner and quantity of attention the first Other pays to the child's penis affects the localization of jouissance. If a first Other attaches great value to the child's penis, the child will probably develop a large narcissistic investment in his imaginary phallus. This narcissistic investment, however, should be understood in terms of the child's erotic relation to the first Other. The jouissance the child attaches to his imaginary phallus is always associated with the first Other, such that the two different types of castration threats[56] function in the same way and cause the same effects—regardless of whether one, the other, or both types of threats are uttered to

---

56 One general type is the demand that the child cease masturbating, and the other type is the demand that the child maintain a greater distance from the first Other and not be so tied to the first Other's "apron strings."

the child. A child whose first Other places immense value on the child's penis will most likely strongly resist either type of castration threat.

Condition 4 is closely related to Condition 3—so much so that I have not yet encountered a clinical case of perversion (either in print or in clinical experience) in which only one condition was met. It is statistically and clinically quite normal for a first Other to consciously or unconsciously use the child to cover up her symbolic lack of jouissance (rather than simply acting upon a child-rearing instinct or upon unselfish love). When a parent chooses to have a child, she or he is doing so out of a certain desire or lack that she or he hopes the child, as a source of satisfactions, will fill. Correspondingly, in Seminar IV Lacan (1994) said, "A mother always requires her child to have (or be) the phallus, which the child symbolizes or realizes more or less" (p. 56).

The first Other of a pervert has such a strong and seemingly exclusive interest in the child that the pervert never comes to understand that he only "more or less" (Lacan, 1994, p. 56) resembles the lack in the Other.[57] In other words, the pervert never interprets the symbolic phallus (as the signifier of the lack in the Other) as the signifier of the Other's metonymic, ever sliding desire—which he could never hope to satisfy. Instead, so perfectly does he seem to resemble what the Other wants that he believes the Other lacks something which is present in the world (namely, him) rather than something which is absent.

In our society, it is a statistical fact that mothers are most often in the role of primary caregiver (or first Other). Moreover, it is a clinical fact that a mother is more apt to take a son than a daughter as her perfect complement, and it is likely that this has to do with the mother's culturally formed notions concerning the biological sex of the son. In Fink's (1997) words,

> Insofar as mothers do not often take their daughters as their complement to the same extent, look to them for such intense satisfaction in life, or take such great interest in their genitals, the mother-daughter relationship is rarely eroticized to the same degree, jouissance is not usually symbolically localized for females in the same way, and the struggle with the father over separation from the mother generally does not come to a head in the same way or focus on a specific organ. (pp. 172–173)

---

57 One might think, as in Tostain's (1993) case of John, that a boy who is an only child is more likely to become a pervert than a boy who has siblings (especially siblings who live in the same home with himself and his mother). However, in all of the cases of perversion that I have encountered in my clinical work, the pervert had at least two other siblings.

This clinical fact supports Lacan's supposition that "the male sex [is] the weaker sex with regard to perversion" (1960/2006a, p. 823).

Estela Welldon (1988/1992) spoke at length on the perverse mother-child relation, emphasizing that the mother treats her child as a narcissistic extension of her own body and derives sexual gratification from their contact. In her words, "the opportunity that maternity offers to have complete control of a situation creates the right pre-conditions for certain women ... to exploit and abuse their children. This is how the mothers of maltreated children, transsexuals, and—especially—sexually perverted men are constituted" (p. 91). Other notable authors who wrote on perversion have observed similar relational phenomena, including McDougall (1972), Bak (1968), and Rosen (1996). For instance, one patient was told by his aunt that his "mother used to play with his penis to stop him from crying; another [recalled] how, even at school-going age, he used to lie in bed with his mother fondling her bare breasts; another ... that this mother still bathes him at the age of 22" (Rosen, 1996, p. 290).

As another example of a perverse mother-child relationship, Lihn's (1970) provided a case study of a fetishist who

clearly remembered the baths and the thorough scrubbings his mother gave him, especially in the region of the buttocks and genitals. Her zealous efforts to keep him clean and well also including squeezing his blackheads and the frequent administration of enemas [until he was 12]. He had easy access to the bathroom whenever his mother used it for any reason. Also outside the bathroom nudity was commonplace in childhood. Even now when the patient visited at home he often found his mother dressed only in panties and bra. (p. 352)

These events show an eroticized mother-child relation lacking in privacy and modesty. The mother's intrusive overstepping of the physical boundaries between herself and her child is quite evident.

The inadequacy of the paternal function is what allows the too-close mother-son bond to form in the first place. In support of this, Lacan said, "But Freud reveals to us that it is thanks to the Name-of-the-Father that man does not remain bound [attaché] to the sexual service of his mother" (1960/2006a, p. 852). If the Name-of-the-Father is inadequate, then, the son "remain[s] bound to the sexual service of his mother" (p. 852). "[S]exual service" does not necessarily imply what our society might consider to be sexual abuse, but instead implies an eroticized, jouissance-laden relationship between the mother and son in which the son is constituted solely as the object of the mother's demand. The child cannot fully function as a subject in the symbolic order if he remains bound to his mother as the object-cause of her jouissance. Echoing Winnicott, we might say

65

that the "good-enough" lawgiving Other functions to separate the child from the first Other—a separation which irrevocably alters the relationship between child and Other from one of jouissance to one (primarily) of desire.[58]

There are numerous possible reasons why the second (lawgiving) Other might be inadequate at the logical time of separation. For instance, the person playing the role of second Other (often a father figure) may have become absent from the child's life after the time of alienation, the first Other did not perpetuate his role through her discourse, and no other person assumed the role of second Other. Alternatively, the father might be glad that the mother is giving so many of her attentions to the child because this enables him more freedom, and thus he does not want to separate his son from his wife. As another example, the father may be confused or ambivalent about his role as symbolic separator, shying away from making a demand such as the traditional incest prohibition: "Your mother is mine, but you can have any other woman." On the other hand, the father's castration threats might simply be lacking in force when compared to the will of the mother and her ability to undermine an authority beyond herself.

Desire or Jouissance? Naming the Lack in the Other

If the Name-of-the-Father were to speak, it would say, "You are not the phallus!"

Miller, "Donc" (June 29, 1994)

As I explained in detail in chapter 2 the second major process involved in accepting the operation of separation (the first is castration) is perceiving the lack in the Other in terms of desire. Post-alienation, the child, now split subject—unlike the living being/psychotic—knows he has a special place in the Other. The child knows he is wanted and loved by the Other, and therefore he knows that there is a lack in the Other. The child's next transformation will depend upon whether he will interpret the Other's lack (the symbolic phallus or the S(Ⱥ)) in terms of demand and jouissance (the pervert's interpretation) or in terms of desire (the neurotic's interpretation).

---

58 Perversion cannot be considered a "stage" in development that neurotics pass through because it is likely that many neurotics did not have such eroticized relationships with their mothers or encounter the Law as a façade. Furthermore, perversion results only after the operation of disavowal of castration, and the symptoms and relation to the Other which follow cannot be said to have been there prior to disavowal. The neurotic does not disavow castration, but accepts it and represses his desire for the mOther.

The minimal conditions which must be present for the child to realize that the symbolic phallus signifies desire are that (1) there be a reputable authority concerning the mOther (2) who convincingly puts the mOther's desire into words. The conditions supporting the prevention of this realization are essentially the same as those responsible for the failure of the negativization of the imaginary phallus,[59] with the modification of Condition 2.

Obstacles to Interpreting the Symbolic Phallus as the Signifier of Desire

1. The second Other (the lawgiving Other) is not sufficiently "respected" by the child. "Respect," in this case, requires both love and the child's sense that the second Other makes demands of him not arbitrarily but in his "best interest."
   a. because of the child's refusal to sufficiently "respect" the second Other;
   b. because the first Other does not sufficiently "respect" the second Other (as reflected in the first Other's discourse);
   c. because of both of the above.
2. The child never hears a convincing signifier of the Other's desire
   a. because of the child's refusal to interpret any of the first or second Other's statements as signifiers of the first Other's desire ;
   b. because the child is unable to interpret any of the first or second Other's statements as signifiers of the first Other's desire (owing to the lack of credibility of the first and second Other);
   c. because neither the first or second Other utters a signifier of the first Other's desire (either in the child's presence or as told to the child by a reputable authority, such as a therapist).
3. The child perceives the parental figure who plays the role of first Other to approve of and/or derive jouissance from the child's penis, giving the imaginary phallus a positive symbolic value that resists negativization.
4. The child perceives himself to be the be-all and end-all of the existence of the first Other.

Even if the mOther's desire is put into words for the child, the child will be likely to disbelieve or possibly *disavow* those words if the person who says them lacks credibility. For example, if the child does not "respect" the lawgiving Other (Condition 1), the person representing the Other of the Law will not have the power to name the mOther's desire. In addition

---

59 The failure of the negativization of the imaginary phallus, as we have seen, signifies not only the failure to place a negative value on the masturbatory pleasures of the penis, but also the failure to place a prohibition on a too-close relation between first Other and child.

(if through experience and the mOther's speech), the child has concluded that he is the perfect complement to the mOther (Condition 4) and that he gives the mOther a great deal of jouissance (Condition 3), he may discredit the mOther's own statements concerning the objects of her desires (for things other than the child).

The Positivizing Function of the Symbolic Phallus

As we have seen, the symbolic phallus represents the related processes of castration and the naming of the Other's desire. Of the shift from the imaginary to the symbolic, Lacan said,

> The shift of $(-\varphi)$ (lowercase phi) as phallic image from one side to the other of the equation between the imaginary and the symbolic renders it positive in any case, even if it fills a lack. Although it props up (-1), it becomes Φ (capital phi) there, the symbolic phallus that cannot be negativized. (1960/2006a, p. 823)

Lacan thus said that when the symbolic phallus is born, it is "positivized," suggesting three related meanings. The first is that the symbolic phallus, as signifier (in contrast to the image of the phallus), is unable to be destroyed or "negativized." The second suggested meaning is that the symbolic phallus is associated with the qualities and pursuits deemed positive or desirable by the Other. Finally, when the phallus signifies the imagined loss of jouissance, it both brings the loss into existence and neutralizes the negative value of the loss to some extent, as is often the case when something painful is put into words. Consequently, the symbolic phallus signifies language's function of positivization, which amounts to the process of signification itself.[60]

The child cannot understand his mOther to be a desiring being until her desire is put into words. At the same time, the signification of the mOther's desire both brings the Other's desire into existence for the child and alleviates the child's anxiety about his mOther's lack. The naming of the mOther's desire enables the child to undergo a second separation from his mother. This further shift into the symbolic realm drains more jouissance from the child's body as his ability to desire is increased.

---

60 "For [the phallus] is the signifier that is destined to designate meaning effects as a whole, insofar as the signifier conditions them by its presence as signifier" (Lacan, 1958/2006a, p. 690).

Fetishism, Disavowal, and the Maternal Phallus

Related to the importance of putting words to the mOther's desire is the importance of assigning different names to male and female genitalia. The fetishist is the child who, unable to assign a signifier to the mother's genitalia, *disavows* the perception of what seems to him the *absence* of a penis and maintains side by side two pieces of contradicting knowledge: The knowledge that his mother has a penis is held alongside the knowledge that she does not have a penis. In the realm of belief, one piece of knowledge is favored: the pervert possesses a strong belief that women have penises. A brief digression into Freud's second theory of perversion will help elucidate the fetishist's disavowal of the mother's lack of a penis.

Freud, in his paper "Fetishism" (1927/1961), opined that the moment of the child's discovery of female genitalia is a traumatic one that has potentially symptomatic consequences. Freud said,

> Probably no male human being is spared the fright of castration at the sight of a female genital. Why some people become homosexual as a consequence of that impression, while others fend it off by creating a fetish, and the great majority surmount it, we are frankly not able to explain. (p. 154)

In Freud's theory, a boy experiences castration anxiety at his first sight of his mother's genitalia, having previously assumed that she had a penis and now believing that his father must have castrated her, just as he could castrate him. "The great majority surmount" (p. 154) castration anxiety by giving up masturbation and the infantile object choice—the mother—because the child believes these to be his father's demands.

The fetishist, in order to ward off castration anxiety, disavows his mother's castration (her literal lack of a penis). Freud said that the child's perception of his mother's genitalia is put out of mind (via disavowal) because it provides evidence that the father is capable of castrating him if he does not relinquish his libidinal investment in his mother. The child interprets the sight of his mother's genitalia to mean that the father has already castrated his mother, and that his father might very well do the same to him if he does not obey his father's will. By disavowing his perception of his mother's genitalia, the child is able to avoid feeling castration anxiety and to refuse to give up his mother.

At the same time, the mechanism of disavowal both stems from and results in "the divided attitude of fetishists to the question of the castration of women. In very subtle instances both the disavowal and the affirmation of the castration have found their way into the construction of the fetish itself" (Freud, 1927/1961, p. 156). Correspondingly, the fetishist experiences both "[a]ffection and hostility" (p. 157) toward his fetish, "mixed in unequal proportions in different cases, so that the one or the other is more clearly recognizable" (p. 157). Consequently, the child's fetishistic solution to castration anxiety is only a partial solution; some castration anxiety remains and is manifest in the fetishist's relation to the fetish.

Disavowal, according to Freud, involves a *Spaltung* or split, in which two pieces of *knowledge* are maintained side by side even though they contradict each other. The child may learn to repeat only what others say ("Of course women don't have penises") for the sake of saving face, but nevertheless at some level he maintains the knowledge that women do have penises. Alongside these pieces of knowledge is the absolute conviction that the child's mother has a penis. This conviction is a belief so prized that it is defended at all costs and against any evidence to the contrary. The fetish is a libido-invested object that serves as substitute for the penis of the mother, and it maintains the disavowal and split in the child's ego.

Freud's second theory of perversion was an improvement on his developmental model of perversion (in which perversion was defined by the quantitative factors of fixation on the sexual object and exclusiveness of the sexual aim) because disavowal served as a qualitative criterion of (fetishistic) perversion. Nevertheless, his theory is criticized for indiscriminance owing to his 1940 article "Splitting of the Ego in the Process of Defence" in which he generalized *Spaltung* to neurotics. Furthermore, Freud did not explicate the mechanism of disavowal of castration in cases of other types of perversion. In addition, Freud does not explain the causes of the fetishist's solutions of disavowal and the fetish; what makes a child "choose" disavowal over repression? Finally, numerous theorists, including Serge André (2006, p. 112, p. 116) and Verhaeghe (2001a, p. 67), are not convinced by Freud's emphasis on the penis and on a fear of actual castration.

Lacan made use of Freud's second theory of perversion and solved some of its problems. In Seminar VI (1959), Lacan first formulated a differentiation between perversion and neurosis (p. 325) that would persist until the end of his career: in the neurotic fantasy ($\$ \Diamond a$) the accent is on the split subject, whereas in the perverse fantasy ($a \Diamond \$$) the accent is on object *a*. Thus, "[t]he structure of desire in neurosis is of a quite different nature than the structure of desire in perversion and, after all, these two structures are [diametrically] opposed" (p. 479).

In Seminar XI, Lacan further distinguished perversion as a separate structural category by beginning to make use of disavowal: Object *a*, in perversion, "is the foundation of an identification disavowed by the subject" (1973/1998a, p. 186). Whereas, in causal explanations of (fetishistic) perversion, Freud attributed the pervert's disavowal exclusively to the disavowal of the maternal phallus, Lacan extended the notion of disavowal as cause of (all substructures of) perversion to the Other of the Law and to the child's narcissistic attachment to his penis. For Lacan, disavowal is a creative attempt to prop up the paternal function.[61] In addition, because Lacan's theoretical framework focuses on the child's relation to the Other, to the Other's desire and Law, to the drives, and to his primary caregiver, this framework allows for suppositions regarding the etiology of perversion that may be significant improvements upon our being "frankly not able to explain" (Freud, 1927/1961, p. 154) the "choice" of perversion.[62] For instance, whereas Freud's description of the child's discovery of his mother's genitalia depicted a largely imaginary order event (in which the child's perception of his mother's genitalia in contrast to his own and his father's took center stage), Lacan's theory (see, for instance, Seminars IV and VIII) emphasized the crucial symbolic determinants of the child's disavowal of female genitalia.

A Lacanian interpretation of Freud's "Fetishism" (1927/1961) might state that the fetishist desires to preserve his belief in the "maternal phallus" because that would mean that his mother does not wish to take possession of his penis because she already has one of her own. What is more, Lacanian understandings of fetishism focus on the signifiers constituting each person's fetish and how the fetish serves to prop up the paternal function. For Lacan, the fetish is thus a symbolically determined symptom, one that does not simply represent the "missing" penis of the mother. Lacan, then, addressed a weakness in Freud's theory of fetishism—that it focused too much on the imaginary determinants of the fetish. Freud's theory of fetishism relies on the supposition that every child sees his mother's (or another female's) genitalia and that it is that sight which allows the child to either accept or disavow his mother's lack of a penis. In contrast, Lacan's theory of fetishism is grounded in the importance of the subject's relation to the Other and of symbolizing sexual difference in language.[63]

---

61 Beginning on page 78, I explain how disavowal attempts to prop up the paternal function.

62 On the other hand, as Nobus (2000) points out, there is something compelling in Lacan's 1946 idea of an "unfathomable decision of being." Although this idea applies to the decision between psychosis and neurosis, it could arguably be extended to perversion.

63 Janine Chasseguet-Smirgel (1978) pointed out, in her own way, the pervert's lack of a signifier for sexual difference by saying that perverts engage in a negation of the difference between the sexes as well as the difference between the generations (p. 27). Jiménez's (2004) case of the voyeur, Matías, exemplifies this double-denial: "Matías's relationship with his mother was enormously ambivalent. On the one hand, he claimed to hate her because she was intrusive and domineering; on the other, he said that he communicated with his mother wordlessly, felt extremely close to her and knew her as well as he knew himself. When he was small, his mother, a seamstress, used to dress him in girl's clothing to show the styles to her clients. He would describe a mother who guessed his desires, intentions and most intimate fantasies, and who used this knowledge to dominate and subjugate him" (p. 75).

Fink's Case of Fetishism

Fink's (2003) case of the fetishist "W" is one of the richest case histories of fetishism, and it provides good examples of disavowal and of belief in the "maternal phallus." Furthermore, because neither of W's parents provided a name for the female genitalia that significantly differed from that for male genitalia, for W there was a lack of difference between the sexes. Lacking the signifier for sexual difference, W engaged in many homosexual acts and fantasies and struggled to create a gendered identity for himself—often preferring the socially determined feminine role over the masculine one.

W, like most children, was curious about the difference between the sexes and about the origin of babies. His mother informed him that babies came out of a "special opening" (p. 52), and W concluded that the special opening must be a "butt" because the women in his family had larger butts than did the men. Two neighborhood girls also explained to him that "boys and girls were different because 'boys have one thumb and girls have two thumbs'" (p. 52). Neither of these explanations of sexual difference utilize different signifiers for male and female genitalia, and neither explanation provides a firm distinction between the sexes. The difference between the sexes, as explained to W, amounted to a quantitative, rather than a qualitative difference.

When W was 5, his mother discovered that his father had never divorced one of his previous wives, thus reducing the symbolic value of their marriage and of the last Name-of-the-Father given to W and his mother. W's mother began complaining about her husband in front of W, and W subsequently adopted a derisive attitude toward his father. W, who had already had a close relationship with his mother, became even closer to her, and seemed to share his mother's opinion that his father was not a "real man." Most often, the child needs to experience an intruding force coming between himself and his mOther in order to effect separation; the other factors supporting separation are usually not enough in and of themselves.[64] In cases such as that of W, in which W's mother behaved and spoke in a way that showed she thought of W as her possession, the force of the second Other must be even stronger in order to separate the child from the mother. In W's case, his mother's altered attitude and discourse about his father prevented his father from having the power necessary to effect the operation of separation.

Amongst W's symptoms were impotence with his sexual partners and difficulty masturbating. Through the process of analysis, W came to relate

---

64 It is therefore most common that, in separation, one parental figure plays the role of second Other and another parental figure plays the role of first Other.

these symptoms to feeling as though his mother had claimed his penis as her own. For example, W recalled an incident in which he, as an adolescent, was masturbating for one of the first times and his mother walked into the room. She put his hand on his erect penis and then walked out of the room. W "was unable to finish masturbating and felt unable to masturbate thereafter for a long time. It was as if she had claimed his organ as her own, he said. It had 'died' and was 'rotting'" (p. 57). More generally speaking, W's mother tried to prevent him from having enjoyment and desires that did not have to do with her; if he said, for example, that he wanted to go to the park, it was certain that she would not allow him to go there (p. 59).

W, then, came to believe that he and his penis were the objects of his mOther's demand. Because W also lacked a signifier for his mOther's desire and lacked a signifier for sexual difference, W felt a great deal of anxiety related to his position of object-cause of his mOther's jouissance. Because of the inadequacy of the paternal function, W's solution to this problem was fetishism. The fetishistic solution involves both a fetish and a belief in the "maternal phallus."

Lacking a signifier for sexual difference, and not having seen female genitalia, as a child W formed a lasting belief that his mother had a penis. In analysis, W said, "'Why would she cover herself up with a towel in coming out of the bath if she didn't have one to hide?'" (p. 54). "[E]ven in his 20s he did not think women had pubic hair, associating such hair with men, not women" (p. 54).

W developed a boot fetish. This fetish, like any other symptom, was overdetermined and thus constituted by numerous signifiers and by particular memories. Essentially, the boot served two main functions: to serve as a substitute for himself and his penis, such that W could reason that it was not him that his mother wanted, but something associated with boots, and to stand in for the ambiguity around sexual difference. In terms of the former function, the boot, by serving as a Name-of-the-Father, a signifier of something W's mOther wanted beyond himself, temporarily propped up W's paternal function. According to Fink,

[W] perhaps reasoned as follows: "What she wants is not my penis, but something associated with fathers, something which is a sign of their power—boots." Boots were, after all, a representative of his mother's own father, whom she considered to be a real man and in whose boots W masturbated for the first time. (In masturbating, he was perhaps symbolically "giving her the boot(s)" while he took back his penis.) The boot was also associated with his own father, who had a thing about black boots, and with his father's last name. The boot could thus be understood as an attempt to insert a father substitute between himself and his mother, as if to say "it isn't me that she wants, it's him." (p. 66)

Consequently, the boot fetish can be said to prop up the paternal function by way of a metaphorical substitution. As I have described, the paternal function, also called the paternal metaphor, has the structure of a metaphor. The boot fetish works because it plays a role in fueling the metaphorical operation of separation.

The boot fetish also represented the ambiguity concerning sexual difference. The boot was related to signifiers representing masculinity and femininity for W, such as "butt," "thumb," "tube," "booty," "boob," and "root." W first saw female genitalia when he was 6 years of age, but because no one had provided him with a name for what his sister had, W was only able to understand this sight in terms of the penis—for which he did have a name. As a result, the meaning W ascribed to his perception of female genitalia was that girls lack a penis. Following Freud, we can say that W's interpretation elicited castration anxiety because his next thought was that his sister had been castrated and that he might also be castrated. Fink said,

> The fetish would thus appear as a solution to this anxiety, for the term *boot* preserves a *both/and* structure of things by bringing both female and male characteristics with it, according to W. A boot has an opening, making it vagina-like, but it also has a shaft and a shine, making it penis-like. In other words, the fetish can be understood as creating a space for both lack (an opening) and its possible filling, for both emptiness and fullness, thereby eliminating W's anxiety. (p. 67)

Fink's explanation here of the function of the fetish (and its dependence upon the mechanism of disavowal) is an excellent one. The fetishist's solution to castration anxiety, then, is not so much defensive as it is creative; the fetish, by balancing lack with presence, creates a symbolic space for the pervert that reaches outside of the grasp of the mOther.

In the course of W's analysis, his symptoms—including his aforementioned impotence and difficulty masturbating dissolved. W's depression abated, and he reported improvements in all areas of his life. W's analysis enabled him to gradually reclaim his body from the Other (p. 57).

Fundamental Fetishism?

Regarding the criticism of Freud that his example of disavowal of castration was restricted to fetishism, Lacan maintained that there is a "fundamental fetish in every perversion as an object perceived in the signifier's cut" (1961/2006a, p. 610). This implies that object *a* as fetish is present at the foundations of every perversion. If we accept this claim, the necessity to describe the mechanism of disavowal at work in each type of perversion is thus diminished, though not erased. That being said, Lacan does not, in fact, describe the disavowal of castration in any instances of perversion except fetishism and male homosexuality[65]—either in case material or in theoretical explanation. His discussions of the etiology of voyeurism, exhibitionism, sadism, and masochism are restricted to the drives and to the relation to the Other.

It is clear from the case material of fetishists—including Fink's (2003) W, René Tostain's (1993) John, and Freud's (1909/1955) Little Hans— that fetishists, do, as a rule, disavow their mother's genitalia. The fetish, as symptom, results from that disavowal and includes, via the overdetermination typical of symptoms, signifiers and desires relating both to the father figure and the primary caregiver. Fetishists, then, lack a signifier for sexual difference.

There are at least two valid ways of interpreting Lacan's claim that there is a "fundamental fetish in every perversion as an object perceived in the signifier's cut" (1961/2006a, p. 610). The first, as I have mentioned, is that every pervert became perverse by way of a fetish—such that sadism, for instance, is considered secondary to the fetish. The second is that object *a* as actual presence, like the fetish, versus absence, is common to all the perversions. The pervert, in contrast to the neurotic, identifies with an object *a* that is tangibly present, that being the object-cause of jouissance. The Other's lack, for the pervert, can be plugged up by an object, and that object is himself. The Other's lack, for the neurotic, is understood to be structurally without a complement, because the neurotic knows the Other has *desires* which do not concern himself.

When the Other's desire is not named (as in the case of perversion), the child experiences a great deal of anxiety in the face of this nameless, unsignified lack. *This constitutes the problem to which the structure of perversion provides a solution. The pervert's solution to the anxiety caused by the namelessness of the lack in the Other is to become the object that plugs the lack in the Other by giving the Other jouissance.* On occasions upon which the pervert is confronted with the lack in the Other, he experiences anxiety and quickly attempts to fill the Other's lack. At the same time, the fetish functions to symbolically take the place of the pervert, so that his sacrifice to the Other is not total. By "reasoning" that what the mOther wants is not himself but his penis, some part of his body and subjectivity remain his own.

---

65 Lacan did not consider female homosexuality to indicate a perverse structure.

"[P]erversion may be spoken of as fear of castration, fear of the Other's castration essentially" (Miller, 1996b, p. 317). Take, for example, the Marquis de Sade in his relation to the limits of the Other of language. Sade's vehement negation of God functions to negate the limits of language and of reason. The limits and lack of the Other are experienced by the pervert as intolerable. (This aspect of perversion will be further discussed in chapter 4.)

Pousse-à-la-femme: Perverse Traits in Psychosis

It is sometimes difficult to make a differential diagnosis. One such problem the therapist might encounter in her or his initial sessions with a male patient is differentiating between psychosis and perversion. The reason for this is that both psychotics and perverts lack the signifier for sexual difference, and so, as a result, both tend toward homo- or bisexuality and a lack of understanding of the difference between the sexes. Correspondingly, in Lacan's "On a Question Prior to Any Possible Treatment of Psychosis," he described the features of psychosis in the following manner: "The first is that of a transsexualist practice, not at all unworthy of being related to 'perversion'" (1959/2006a, p. 568). In order to clarify the difference between the lack of the signifier for sexual difference in perversion and psychosis, I will first turn to psychosis.

Freud (1911/1958) explained psychosis by way of a repressed passive homosexual relationship to the father. In contrast, Lacan said that a homosexual identification is an effect rather than a cause of psychosis. Lacan provided two explanations for this—one early and one late in his career. Both explanations, however, hinge upon the "foreclosure of the Name-of-the-Father in the place of the Other—and the failure of the paternal metaphor that I designate as the defect that gives psychosis its essential condition" (1959/2006a, p. 575). In psychosis, a part of the symbolic is foreclosed and returns in the real. In other words, what Lacan more accurately called "transsexual" phenomena in psychosis result from the failure of the paternal function.

In Seminar III and "On a Question Prior to Any Possible Treatment of Psychosis," he maintained that transsexual phenomena in male psychotics is the result of the presence of a father figure who established an imaginary order rivalrous and erotically charged relationship with his son rather than a symbolic one. "No triangulated Oedipal relation can form, and the child assumes a feminine position in relation to the domineering, monstrous father—the imaginary father" (Fink, 1997, p. 99). "Interestingly enough, the psychotic may also describe himself as in a [stereotypically] feminine or passive relation to language itself, passively submitting to it, invaded by it, or possessed by it" (p. 99). When a male psychotic's imaginary order is stabilized, his feminine position can sometimes remain hidden on account of his imaginary order identifications with his male peers. On the other hand, some male psychotics report experiencing themselves as a woman since their early childhood, and these individuals are likely to desire sex change operations.

In describing psychotic feminization, Lacan later formulated the term "*pousse-à-la-femme*" which, according to Fink (1997) "literally means 'budding into a woman' or 'growing into womanhood/womanliness'; less literally, 'a surge to become like a woman'" (p. 251). When a man has a psychotic break, his imaginary order identifications collapse and he is subjected to the process of *pousse-à-la-femme*. In the case of Schreber, for example, he believed that he must be transformed into a woman and become the wife of God in order to repopulate the world with new beings and thereby redeem the world. Schreber reportedly had "a feeling that enormous numbers of 'female nerves' [had] already passed over into his body" (Freud, 1911/1958, p. 17), invading his body with jouissance. In addition, Schreber dressed himself in women's clothes and adornments.

In his later work, Lacan suggested that the male psychotic does not necessarily require an erotically charged rivalrous relationship with a monstrous father in order to undergo *pousse-à-la-femme*. Instead, because the male psychotic is missing the paternal function, he does not attain a masculine structural position and is therefore subjected to *pousse-à-la-femme* and to an invasive and enduring experience of the "Other jouissance" which is characteristic—albeit more occasionally—of feminine structure. (See Fink, 1995, and Swales, 2011, for further elaboration of the masculine and feminine structures.) In brief, the symbolic father who imposes limits on the male child is a necessary condition for the child to attain a masculine subject position.

In contrast, *pousse-à-la-femme* does not describe the effects of the absence of the signifier for sexual difference in perversion. Unlike the psychotic, the pervert is not subject to invasions of Other jouissance or to psychotic breaks. Because he underwent alienation and is a subject in the symbolic order, his perception of his female genitalia, although disavowed, was registered in the symbolic. What is more, because the pervert is permanently a subject in the symbolic order, his identifications as a masculine subject are not subject to collapse—the symbolic order preventing the imaginary order from collapsing as in a psychotic break.

In addition, the pervert, and not the psychotic, maintains a belief in the maternal phallus. Because the psychotic foreclosed the Name-of-the-Father and did not incorporate structure of language, the signifier for sexual difference and the signification of lack ($S(\cancel{A})$) are not at issue for him. Consequently, he had no motivation or ability to disavow his perception of female genitalia.

What is unclear in Lacan's works is whether or not perverts can attain a masculine subject position. In Seminar XX, Lacan said that the successful operation of the "phallic function," or the alienation brought about by language, is the condition for the possibility of attaining a masculine (or feminine, for that matter) subject position. Masculinity and femininity are therefore different ways of being alienated within the symbolic order. Perverts, of course, are split subjects, and thus would seem to also be masculine or feminine subjects. However, only neurotic men and women are defined in Lacan's formulas of sexuation, and Lacan never addressed the question of the sexuation (or lack thereof) of perverse subjects.

Disavowal

The mechanism of disavowal should be understood as a defense, not against the lawgiving Other's demand that the child sacrifice jouissance, but against the inadequacy of the lawgiving Other. *Disavowal is a creative attempt to prop up the Law and to set limits to the excess in jouissance experienced due to the child's problematic relation to the first Other.* The disavowal of the lawgiving Other might be described in the following terms: "I know very well that my father [or father figure] hasn't forced me to give up my mother and my corresponding jouissance, but I'm going to make believe that the force of Law exists with someone or something that represents my father."

The mechanism of disavowal, as I have said, involves the maintenance of two contradictory pieces of knowledge together with a strongly held belief that one of the two pieces of knowledge is true. In matters of superstition—in which a belief is held despite evidence to the contrary—therefore, disavowal is often pertinent. For example, "I know very well that if, in one breath, I blow out all the flames of the candles on my birthday cake, my wish won't really come true, but nevertheless I believe it's true. Consequently, I make a wish every year and try my best to blow out all the candles with one breath." The superstitious person, like the pervert, so fervently wants the "but all the same" or "nevertheless" clause to be true that she or he believes it strongly despite evidence to the contrary. This belief presupposes the existence of the Other. In this example, the superstitious person believes in some Other that hears her silently made wish and has the power to grant it. Once the belief is formed through the process of disavowal, the person's belief in the Other is correspondingly strengthened.

Little Hans and Little Widdlers

In order to further elucidate the mechanism of disavowal and the structure of perversion, I will now briefly explicate Freud's case of Little Hans (1909/1955) from a Lacanian perspective. Freud's case study, which follows Hans beginning at the time at which he was almost three and ending when Hans was almost five years old, provides ample material from which to understand the etiology of perversion. This is not only due to the young age of Hans but also due to his father's extensive reports of his discourse, symptoms, and daily life. A Lacanian reading of the case of Little Hans allows us to see that Hans' father is incapable of separating Hans from his mother, so that Hans' father may be said to inadequately represent the lawgiving Other. Correspondingly, in Seminar IV Lacan suggests that the only signifier that serves a paternal function for Hans is "horse." Toward the end of Seminar IV, Lacan suggests that he considers Hans' horse phobia to be but a temporary Name-of-the-Father, such that his structural position is that of a fetishistic pervert rather than a phobic neurotic. Hans, then, undergoes alienation, but not separation.

In 1906, one year after the publication of Freud's *Three Essays on Sexuality*, Freud asked his followers to send him observations of children that might corroborate his theory of infantile sexuality.[66] Mr. Graf consequently sent Freud detailed reports concerning his son, Hans, and Freud not only corresponded with Mr. Graf about the case but also met with Hans and Mr. Graf on one occasion. Freud said that Hans' "parents were both among [his] closest adherents" (1909/1955, p. 6).

Hans, at ages two and three, had "a quite peculiarly lively interest" (Freud, 1909/1955, p. 7) in his penis, which he described as his "*wiwimacher*" or "widdler." Correspondingly, Hans and his mother had the following exchange:

Hans: "Mummy, have you got a widdler too?"
Mother: "Of course. Why?"
Hans: "I was only just thinking." (p. 7)

Hans also said to his mother, "I thought you were so big you'd have a widdler like a horse" (p. 10). Hans thus came to believe that everyone, whether male or female, had a penis, and he wanted to see the penis of every person and animal. Consequently, Hans was unable to understand sexual difference; for him, there was only one sex.

When Hans was three and a half years old, "his mother found him with his hand on his penis" (Freud, 1909/1955, p. 7) and she proceeded to literally threaten him with castration. She said, "If you do that, I shall send for Dr. A to cut off your widdler" (pp. 7–8). Hans, however, remained unconcerned, neither indicating anxiety nor giving up the pleasure of touching his penis. In the same vein, about a half year later,

---

66 Clearly, Freud's research was methodologically flawed. Nevertheless, there is no reason to doubt the reports of Hans' speech and behaviors described in this case.

his mother asked: "Do you put your hand to your widdler?" and he answered: "Yes. Every evening, when I'm in bed." The next day, January 9th, he was warned, before his afternoon sleep, not to put his hand to his widdler. When he woke up he was asked about it, and he said he had put it there for a short while all the same. (p. 23)

Hans, then, continued to masturbate even though his mother asked him to refrain from doing so.

When Hans was three and a half years old, Hans' little sister Hanna was born. Soon after, Hans saw Hanna being bathed, and he said, "'But her widdler's still quite small'... and then added, as though by way of consolation: 'When she grows up it'll get bigger all right'" (Freud, 1909/1955, p. 11). Hans thus believed, contrary to his perception of female genitalia, that Hanna had a penis, and that it only appeared to be different because she was young and small. His disavowal was enabled by his mother's repeated assertions that every living animal and human had a penis. Had his mother explained sexual difference and given female genitalia a name that differed from "widdler," then it is likely that he would not have disavowed the absence of Hanna's penis. Hans' disavowal, then, was a disavowal of sexual difference.

When Hans' parents finally explained sexual difference to him, he was four and a half years old and Hans did not throw out his old belief in the universality of widdlers in favor of the new information; the information came too late and was too contrary to his previous experiences. In addition, Hans and his parents still referred to female genitalia as "widdlers," although his parents maintained that female genitalia differed somehow from male genitalia. By the end of his treatment, Hans still believed that girls and women had penises. Hans also believed that boys and men could have children. Hans said he wanted to have children, and he played with his imaginary children. On one such occasion, his father said to him, "'but you know quite well that boys can't have children.' [Hans responded,] 'Well, yes. But I believe they can, all the same.'" (Freud, 1909/1955, p. 95). Hans' disavowal of the knowledge that girls do not have penises and that boys cannot have children resulted in his unshakable belief to the contrary.

The Inadequacy of the Paternal Function

Hans had an unusually close relationship with his mother, who clearly derived a great deal of jouissance from his presence. She was lacking in what today are called "boundaries" with Hans, as shown by her giving Hans a daily bath and afterwards drying and powdering him (Freud, 1909/1955, p. 19), often taking him into the bathroom with her (p. 57), letting him get into bed with her despite protests from her husband (p. 39), and giving Hans a guilt trip when he expressed a desire to separate from her (p. 17).[67] Correspondingly, Hans experienced a general state of anxiety prior to the solidification of the horse phobia that occurred after Freud began overseeing the case. Rather than understanding Hans' anxiety as resulting from separation from his mother, we should understand it as the result of his overproximity to his mother.[68]

In this vein, "Hans (aged four and three-quarters) woke up one morning in tears. Asked why he was crying, he said to his mother: 'When I was asleep I thought you were gone and I had no Mummy to coax [his expression for 'to caress'] with'" (Freud, 1909/1955, p. 23). Hans' fear that he articulated by way of the dream revealed a wish; at some level, Hans wished that his mother *would* go away. Correspondingly, Hans' father noticed that when Hans

> was in bed in the evening [at Gmunden in the summer] Hans was usually in a very sentimental state. Once he made a remark to this effect: "Suppose I was to have no Mummy," or "Suppose you were to go away," or something of the sort; I cannot remember the exact words. Unfortunately, when he got into an elegiac mood of that kind, his mother used always to take him into bed with her. (p. 23)

Hans' remarks were wishes that his mother would go away and let him have symbolic space of his own. In typical fashion, his mother responded

---

67 In contrast, Hans' mother beat Hanna (Freud, 1909/1955, p. 72, p. 79). My patient Ray, an exhibitionist, had a similar experience. Ray's mother beat and threw things at his older sisters, whereas she never did so with him, paying instead special attention to him. These clinical observations support the hypothesis that mothers take sons to be their complements in life more often than they do so with daughters.

68 Numerous psychoanalytic (non-Lacanian) clinicians (Chasseguet-Smirgel, 1974; Glasser, 1996; Greenacre, 1968; McDougall, 1970; Stoller, 1976) have noted that perverts display an ambivalent attitude toward intimate closeness with another person. On the one hand, they wish to merge with the Other, and on the other hand, they experience an "annihilation anxiety" (Glasser, 1996, p. 285) that proximity to the Other carries with it a "loss of self, a disappearance of his existence as a separate, independent individual" (p. 284). According to Mervin Glasser, the pervert responds to annihilatory anxiety through a defensive reaction such as "flight from the object, retreating emotionally to a 'safe distance' ... This is expressed in such attitudes as placing a premium on independence and self-sufficiency. In therapy, it may be encountered as a wish to terminate treatment, as a constant argumentativeness or negativism, as the development of an intellectual detachment, and so on" (p. 285). Although Glasser notes that the wish for and anxiety about unity with the Other is common to non-perverse subjects, he emphasizes that annihilation anxiety is particularly strong with perverts.

to his remarks by taking him into bed with her and thus reasserting their especially close relationship.

Hans' close relationship with his mother may not have formed in the first place had his father more strongly asserted his role as second Other. The castration threats made all come from Hans' mother rather than his father, and it is plain that Hans' mother's qualities as first Other prevent her from being an effective medium for the second Other. Hans himself seemed to believe that his symptoms were related to his not having been forced to give up masturbation. Hans said of his anxiety, "'it's so bad because I still put my hand to my widdler every night'" (Freud, 1909/1955, p. 30).

A dream or fantasy—it is unclear which—of Hans' figures centrally in the case, and exemplifies his problematic position within his family: *"In the night there was a big giraffe in the room and a crumpled one; and the big one called out because I took the crumpled one away from it. Then it stopped calling out; and then I sat down on top of the crumpled one"* (Freud, 1909/1955, p. 37). Although symbolic productions should be interpreted in light of the patient's own associations, we have little opportunity to do so because Hans' father did not give Hans the chance to associate to his fantasy, but only asked him to give further details and to explain its logic (as if such phenomena were supposed to follow everyday logic!).

That being said, the description provided by Hans' father of their recent family life is instructive.

> The whole thing is a reproduction of a scene which has been gone through almost every morning for the last few days. Hans always comes in to us in the early morning, and my wife cannot resist taking him into bed with her for a few minutes. Thereupon I always begin to warn her not to take him into bed with her ("the big one called out because I'd taken the crumpled one away from it"); and she answers now and then, rather irritated, no doubt, that it's all nonsense, that after all one minute is of no importance, and so on. Then Hans stays with her a little while. ("Then the big giraffe stopped calling out; and then I sat down on top of the crumpled one"). (Freud, 1909/1955, p. 39)

It is notable that their family name, Graf, is nearly a homonym of the word for "giraffe" (*giraf*). It is but a short interpretive stretch, then, to say that the big giraffe is Mr. Graf and the crumpled giraffe is Mrs. Graf. In the scenario, Mr. Graf, the big giraffe, protests weakly, calling out in anger when Hans takes Mr. Graf's place. Hans takes possession of Mrs. Graf, the crumpled giraffe. The daily scene in which Hans gets into bed with Mrs. Graf suggests that Mrs. Graf's will is stronger than that of Mr. Graf and that Mrs. Graf prefers Hans to her husband. Mr. and Mrs. Graf, in fact, obtained a divorce some years later.

Freud based his interpretations and recommended interventions on the faulty assumption that Hans' pre-phobic anxiety-related symptoms were caused by his fear of his father. In his estimation, were Mr. Graf to appear to Hans to be still less fearsome and angry, Hans' fears would abate. On the contrary, Hans is unafraid of his father and afraid of his mother. *She* is the one that he would like to beat (Freud, 1909/1955, p. 81). Hans would have been better off if his father had forcefully played the role of symbolic separator, and indeed the case study provides us with numerous instances in which Hans tried to believe that his father was angry with him on account of Hans' close relationship with his mother. Unfortunately, in each instance Mr. Graf denied that he was angry with Hans.

Freud's central intervention in the case was also marked by the downplay of Mr. Graf's symbolic role. Consider the following scene from Freud's consulting room, at which Freud, Mr. Graf, and Hans were all present.

> I then disclosed to him that he was afraid of his father, precisely because he was so fond of his mother. It must be, I told him, that he thought his father was angry with him on that account, but this was not so, his father fond of him in spite of it, and he might admit everything to him without any fear. Long before he was in the world, I went on, I had known that a little Hans would come who would be so fond of his mother that he would be bound to feel afraid of his father because of it; and I had told his father this. "But why do you think I'm angry with you?" his father interrupted me at this point; "have I ever scolded you or hit you?" Hans corrected him: "Oh yes! You have hit me." "That's not true. When was it, anyhow?" "This morning," answered the little boy; and his father recollected that Hans had quite unexpectedly butted his head into his stomach, so that he had given him as it were a reflex blow with his hand. (p. 42)

Mr. Graf is anxious to be loved and not feared by Hans—so much so that he not only never hits or scolds Hans but he also interrupts Freud to correct Hans' perception that he is angry with him. Hans, on the other hand, wants his father to be angry with him such that he imbued intentionality to an accidental strike of his father's hand. Freud, from a rather god-like perspective of omniscience, educates Hans about the situation by making an Oedipal interpretation.

Hans saw Freud as a knowledgeable authority above and beyond his father, as he hoped that the "professor" would put an end to Hans' "nonsense" when all the facts of the matter were communicated to Freud

(1909/1955, pp. 42–43, p. 48, p. 61). The positive effects of Freud's interpretation are likely due to two things: his depiction of the father as someone to be feared and his having drawn attention to the signifiers connecting the father and the feared horses. In terms of the former, prior to Freud's interpretation it had not consciously occurred to Hans that he should be afraid of his father. Hans had seen his father not as a forceful representative of the Law but as a weak bystander (in the giraffe fantasy) and even as Hans' accomplice in breaking and then getting punished by the Law (pp. 39–40). After Freud's interpretation, Hans often insisted that his father must be angry with him. Take, for example, the following exchange between Hans and his father.

I: "What do I really scold you for?"
He: "I don't know." (!!)
I: "Why?"
He: "Because you're cross."
I: "But that's not true."
Hans: "Yes, it is true. You're cross. I know you are. It must be true."
(Freud, 1909/1955, pp. 82–83)

Freud's mistake lay in his assumption that Hans was already afraid of his father, and that this fear, if decreased, would correspondingly decrease Hans' symptoms of anxiety. Freud might have succeeded in making Hans neurotic, rather than perverse, had he emphasized Mr. Graf's anger and instructed Mr. Graf to play his proper part.

Nevertheless, the meeting with Freud had some therapeutic effect because Freud also revealed the connection between the kind of horse of which Hans was afraid and Mr. Graf. Even though Mr. Graf was unable to take up his role as symbolic separator, the horse was sufficiently convincing in that role. Hans subsequently adopted "horse" as a substitute for the Name-of-the-Father, and this marked the development of his horse phobia. Consequently, Hans experienced a sharp decrease in anxiety. Phobia, then, is a strategy that bolsters an inadequate paternal function. In Seminar IV, Lacan said that the phobic object is the phallic signifier (Φ), "a phallus that takes on the value of all signifiers, that of the father if need be" (1957/1994, p. 425). In the *Écrits*, Lacan defined the phobic object as "an all-purpose signifier to make up for [*suppléer*] the Other's lack" (1961/2006a, p. 610). In an individual with a phobic (neurotic) structure, the phobic object functions to instigate secondary repression. The phobic's solution to the inadequacy of the paternal function is thus permanent and successful. In contrast, Hans' paternal function was propped up only as long as his horse phobia remained. Hans, by way of disavowal, attained a structural position of perversion.

Hans' horse phobia, or "nonsense" [*Unsinn*], as he called it, began forming when he went on a walk with his mother and saw a big heavy black bus horse fall down. The horse gave Hans "'a fright *because it made a row with its feet*'" (Freud, 1909/1955, p. 50). Of the incident, Hans said to his mother, "I was afraid a horse would bite me" (p. 24). Hans henceforth became afraid that a horse similar in type to the bus horse would fall down and bite him.

The phrase "it made a row with its feet" had another important signification for Hans. Hans himself was in the habit of kicking or making a row with his feet when he was angry or when he had to do "number two" "and would rather play" (Freud, 1909/1955, p. 54). Hans thus associated making a row with one's feet with being angry and wanting to have one's own way. In associating to horses biting, Hans said, "There's a white horse at Gmunden that bites. If you hold your finger to it it bites." (p. 29). It is perhaps significant that Hans said "finger" instead of "hand," as "finger" might easily represent "penis."

While Hans was alone with his mother on the walk, then, a horse (which represented his father) fell down and made a row with its feet. Hans understood the horse's row with its feet as expressing anger towards him as well asserting the force of its own will. Hans became afraid that the horse would bite him, and his fear may be read psychoanalytically as expressing a wish. Hans wished for castration. He wished to be forced to relinquish his mother and cease masturbating. Hans experienced castration anxiety when he saw such horses, and he consequently was temporarily separated from his mother.

After the development of his horse phobia, Hans continued to try to bolster Mr. Graf's symbolic position in relation to himself, as Mr. Graf's claim on him was unclear to Hans. In various ways, Hans asked his father, "I belong not only to Mummy but also to you?" (Freud, 1909/1955, p. 87, p. 100) and Hans never received a satisfying answer. For instance, when Mr. Graf explained to Hans where babies come from—and thus the story of how Hans came to be—he said that children grow inside their mother and are then born into the world by being pressed out of her. On two other occasions, Mr. Graf gives Hans explanations in which God makes the decision to create a baby (p. 87, 91). The father has no place in any of these stories.

Finally, Hans sides with his mother. According to Hans, "'Mummy said if Mummy didn't want [another baby], God didn't want one either. If Mummy doesn't want one she won't have one'" (Freud, 1909/1955, p. 91). Correspondingly, in Hans' understanding, himself, his father, and even God are at the mercy of his mother's whims.

Disavowal in *No Country for Old Men*

The following description of the operation of disavowal in a case of sadism is derived from the movie *No Country for Old Men* (2007). Consequently, it should be considered less as a clinically valid case study and more as a clear and instructive example of speech and behavior indicative of disavowal. (Even so, the subfields of psychoanalytic film and literary theory are based upon the assumption that it is valid to apply psychoanalytic theory to film and literature.)

The perverse sadistic villain in *No Country for Old Men* props up his paternal function by way of a coin toss. Chigurgh, the villain, is chasing a man named Moss because he knows Moss is in possession of a suitcase full of money that Moss took from the scene of a cocaine deal gone wrong. Chirgurgh, seeing through the façade of the Law,[69] has constructed his own law or moral code by which to live. He murders, steals, and destroys property when he "needs" to do so in order to get the money and remain free. For instance, when he lacks a vehicle or wants a new one, he tricks someone into stopping to help him[70] and then murders the person and steals his car.

When Chigurgh encounters someone when he is not in need and who is not obstructing his hunt for the money, he appeals to his law, which might be called the law of fate or of chance, to decide whether or not the person will be killed. Chigurgh takes a coin from his pocket and instructs the other person to "call it." If the person chooses correctly, then Chigurgh lets him live. Although a coin toss operates according to the principle of chance, such that there is an equal chance of winning or losing, Chigurgh's law might also be said to involve fate for the following reasons. On the one hand, Chigurgh sets the stakes (life or death), and he sets them so high that the choice could be fatal. He is playing with the fate of his victims. On the other hand, Chigurgh insists that the other person "call it" rather than he, which raises the meaning of the coin toss from chance, in which the chance would be the same no matter which party "called it," to an event of fate in which the potential victim makes a choice and tests whether or not fate is on his side. Demonstrating his perverse and

---

69 This is evidenced by Chirgurgh's serial murdering as well as by what he says to Wells—a man who has been trying to apprehend Chirgurgh for years—before he kills Wells: "If the rule you followed brought you to this, of what use is the rule?" Wells responds, "Do you have any idea how goddamn crazy you are?" Although Wells is not a representative of law enforcement, he, as a neurotic subject who desires to stop Chigurgh from committing murder, is firmly rooted in the symbolic order of Law, and defines craziness as thinking, acting, and being outside of Law. Chigurgh's question served to deride the logic and existence of the Law. Chigurgh prefers his own law, as discussed in the text.

70 Chigurgh's lure thus involves appealing to the widely held moral law to help one's neighbor.

particular sense of moral law, Chigurgh says to one potential victim, "You need to call it. I can't call it for you. It wouldn't be fair. It wouldn't even be right." Chigurgh interprets the results of the coin toss as fate, as determining what *must* be done.

Chigurgh's role in the coin toss is that of the enactor of the Other's will (the god of fate). When his victims protest, saying, "You don't have to do this"—referring either to the coin toss or committing murder—Chigurgh remarks that they all say the same thing, and remains unconvinced by their argument. When Chigurgh gives his final victim in the movie the opportunity to "call it," she refuses to "call it." He insists, becoming visibly upset. She refuses again, remarking, "the coin don't have no say. It's just you." He replies, "I got here the same way the coin did." In the absence of the Other of the Law, Chigurgh wants the Other of fate to exist; he wants there to be a law governing his actions and which makes sense of the world. He does not want to see his actions as a series of free choices devoid of any guiding principle. Chigurgh becomes anxious when his final victim refuses to play her role in his scenario because she exposes the tenuous existence of the Other. Were she to have played her role, *she*, as split subject, would have been the one to experience a moment of anxiety prior to learning whether she would live or die. Chigurgh's role, as the one who elicited the victim's anxiety, would have been that of the instrument of the Other's jouissance. Chigurgh's disavowal, related to the Other of fate, might be phrased as follows: "I know very well that it's my choice whether or not to kill this person, but all the same, maybe it's fate."

After one of Chigurgh's potential victims wins the coin toss, Chigurgh tells him to keep it because it's his "lucky quarter," but not to keep it in his pocket, "or it'll get mixed in with the others and become just a coin. Which it is." Because it follows the logic of disavowal, this kind of magical or superstitious thinking is often produced by perversely structured individuals. The disavowal here might be expressed as follows: "I know very well that it's just a coin like all the rest, but all the same, I prefer to believe it's lucky and special and to treat it as such."

Concluding Remarks on Diagnosis

In this chapter, I have elaborated a number of aspects of perversion which should aid clinicians in making differential diagnoses. These include, but are not limited to, the operation of disavowal, the "family" roles that correspond to the structure of perversion, the fetish, and a belief in the maternal "phallus." The chapters that follow will serve to further elaborate clinical signs of perversion.

4

PERVERSE RELATION TO THE OTHER
Fundamental Fantasy, Language, and the Drives

Only my formula for fantasy allows us to bring out the fact that the subject here makes himself the instrument of the Other's jouissance.

Lacan (1960/2006a, p. 823)

Perversion ... is a response [to] the jouissance of the Other. It's not a question about its desire, but a response about ... what to do to ensure its jouissance.

Miller (2009b, p. 48)

Fundamental Fantasy

Perversion, like neurosis, is a strategy in relation to the Other with respect to jouissance. Perversion, said Lacan, involves "a recuperation of φ that would scarcely seem original if it did not concern the Other as such in a very particular way. Only my formula for fantasy allows us to bring out the fact that the subject here makes himself the instrument of the Other's jouissance" (1960/2006a, p. 823). In this passage from "The Subversion of the Subject and the Dialectic of Desire," Lacan said that both perverse and neurotic subjects (having undergone alienation) have lost some jouissance (-φ) and attempt to recover or recuperate it. The fantasized and impossible end result of obtaining that lost jouissance is restoration of the subjective fullness of complete unity with the Other. Lacan highlighted that the difference between the perverse and the neurotic subject's attempts at recuperation is the "very particular way" (p. 823) in which the pervert's attempt involves the Other. The pervert's subjective position in relation to the Other—as the "instrument of the Other's jouissance" (p. 823)—stands in stark contrast to that of the obsessive neurotic. *While the obsessive negates the Other in the effort to regain lost jouissance, the Other is necessary for the pervert. This difference provides a main criterion for making a differential diagnosis between obsession and perversion.* An explication of the fundamental fantasies of the obsessive and the pervert will elucidate the bases for this criterion and the differences between the two structural positions.

But first, what is a fundamental fantasy and how is it different from a fantasy? Lacan defined fantasy as "an image set to work in the signifying structure" (1961/2006a, p. 637). In other words, fantasy is comprised of imaginary and symbolic order elements. Structured by a jouissance-producing relation to the Other and to object *a*, fantasy functions to maintain and support the subject's desire. Lacan's conception of fantasy thus also involves real order phenomena such as jouissance and the traumatic real manifested in repetition. In this respect, fantasy is an attempt to bind jouissance into the symbolic. As defined in chapters 2 and 3, a fantasy is the subject's attempt to achieve a sense of wholeness by inscribing a certain place for himself in relation to the Other—as object-cause of desire, for instance.

The fundamental fantasy is a way of representing the subject's myriad fantasies in "lowest terms."[71] Miller (1996a) offered the following definition:

> Analysis really is a process of simplification—you call it "shrinking." I find it marvelous that analysts are called "shrinks," because analysis involves the shrinking of the libido and the progressive construction of the fundamental fantasy from various fantasies, the construction of the subject's fundamental maxim, to use Kant's term ... That is, the fundamental fantasy is essentially a formula that says, "Act in such a way that your will always obeys the formula." (p. 224)

The fundamental fantasy is not something that exists prior to the process of psychoanalysis but something that is constructed within analysis. Correspondingly, the fundamental fantasy is not rigid and impossible to modify. In fact, one of the ways in which Lacan spoke of the outcome of a successful analysis was as a traversing of the fundamental fantasy (see Seminar XI, pp. 273–274). Essentially, the fundamental fantasy refers to the subject's way of imagining himself in relation to the Other's desire (object *a*).

Perverse versus Obsessive Fundamental Fantasy

Lacan's general formula for the neurotic fundamental fantasy ($ \lozenge a$) best applies to the obsessive, who is most often male. The obsessive thus tries to overcome separation (and recover his lost jouissance) by constituting

---

71 *Lowest terms* is a mathematical term referring to the form of a fraction in which the numerator and the denominator have no factor in common except 1. A fraction in lowest terms is therefore the simplest form of a fraction, and the easiest with which to work.

himself in relation to the lost object *a*; at the level of fantasy, unity is restored to the split subject when he regains the lost object. It is diagnostically important to note that the obsessive refuses to acknowledge that object *a* is related to the Other. The obsessive seeks to deny his dependence on the Other, preferring to see himself as a complete or unbarred subject (S) rather than as a split subject ($). In the obsessive's relation to object *a*, he tries to annihilate the Other's desire and the Other's very existence. This partially explains his penchant for masturbation and drug use. Another common obsessive strategy for negating the Other involves thinking of someone or something other than his partner when he is having sexual intercourse. In this sense, the obsessive's fundamental fantasy might be more correctly rendered as (S ◊ *a*).

In Seminar VIII, Lacan wrote the following matheme for obsession: Å ◊ φ (*a, a', a'', a''', ...*) (2001, p. 299, 301). The obsessive subject is represented by Å here because of his "never being at the place at which he seems to designate himself at any moment" (p. 301). For example, the obsessive says, "I'm a lawyer, but I'm really an artist." According to Lacan, "[t]he formulation of the second term of the obsessive's fantasy very precisely alludes to the fact that the objects are for him, as objects of desire, situated as a function [*mis en function*] of certain erotic equivalences" (p. 302). In other words, the imaginary function of castration has the effect of making equivalent all of the objects of the obsessive's desire. Each object *a* is fungible for another "in the permanent metonymy for which the obsessive's symptomatology is the perfect example" (p. 302). By viewing the cause of desire as an object detachable from an actual human partner, the obsessive refuses to recognize the existence of the Other.

Another common obsessive strategy to annihilate the Other's desire involves the obsessive's close connection to the anal drive and to the Other's demand. Concerning the Other's demand, Lacan said, "the anal level is the locus of metaphor—one object for another, give the faeces in place of the phallus. This shows you why the anal drive is the domain of oblation, of the gift" (1973/1998a, p. 104, translation modified). The obsessive attempts to neutralize the Other's desire by meeting all of the Other's demands. He hopes that his abundant gifts will leave the Other with nothing left to desire. "'Everything for the other person,' the obsessive neurotic says, and that is indeed what he does, for being caught up in the perpetual whirlwind of destroying the other, he can never do enough to ensure that the other remains in existence" (2001, pp. 245–246).

In general, desire is maintained by keeping the object that causes it, object *a*, at a certain distance. The obsessive, however, sustains his desire not so much by avoiding object *a* as by maintaining his distance from the Other's desire. Lacan said the obsessional's desire flickers, vacillates and vanishes to the degree that he approaches [the Other's desire] ... That desire was approached as something to be destroyed because, first of all, the Other's desire as a reaction was presented to him as his rival, as something that immediately bore the mark to which he reacted with the style of destructive reaction that is the reaction underlying the relationship of the subject to the image of the subject as such, to this image of the other insofar as it dispossesses and ruins him. This mark remains in the approach by the obsessional to his desire which ensures that every step toward it makes it vanish. (Seminar VI, June 18, 1958)

Elsewhere, Lacan more simply said the subject is "eclipsed at the precise point where the object *a* attains its greatest value" (1977, p. 29). In other words, the obsessive attempts to avoid that which has to do with the cause of his desire because the closer he gets to realizing the object of his desire, the more the Other (and the Other's desire) eclipses him as a subject—making him feel as though he does not exist. The proximity of the Other threatens the obsessive with what Lacan—and Ernest Jones before him—called *aphanisis*: the fading or disappearance of the subject (1973/1998a, p. 207).

Because of the obsessive's difficulty tolerating moments of *aphanisis*, he sets out to avoid the presence of the Other by making his desires *impossible* (Lacan, 2001, p. 291). The obsessive typically constructs situations in which "the object of his desire becomes the signifier of this impossibility" (1977, p. 36). For instance, he falls in love with women who are or seem to be completely unapproachable. In response to his fear of the Other's desire, *obsession is characterized by impossible desires.*

The obsessive dislikes manifestations of his own desire not only because it threatens him with *aphanisis* but also because it is a sign that he, having lost jouissance, is already a subject lacking in being ($). The obsessive grapples with the question of being by formulating the primary question as "Am I dead or alive?" Demonstrations of his subjective division, including desire and manifestations of the unconscious, arouse anxiety in him, making him feel as though he does not exist; the obsessive equates existence with conscious thought. The obsessive, therefore, uses conscious thought and the destruction of the Other's desire to create the semblance of control and complete independence that allows him to feel aware of his constant existence.

In contrast, the pervert does not seek to negate the existence of the Other. The obsessive's negation of the Other is allowed by the fact that, for him, the Other permanently exists. In perversion, the Other must be made to exist. The perverse fundamental fantasy, then, reflects the pervert's commitment to making the Other exist by plugging up the lack in the Other. In "Kant with Sade" (1963/2006a), Lacan provides a matheme for perversion that is the inverse of the structure of neurotic fantasy: $a \lozenge \$$ (p. 774). The pervert occupies the role of object a in relation to the split subject.

This matheme for the perverse fundamental fantasy is best understood when considered in the context of the schema in which it was introduced (Lacan, 1963/2006a, p. 774):

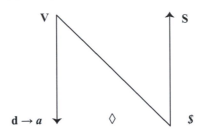

"The lower line accounts for the order of fantasy insofar as it props up the utopia of desire" (p. 775); "d" represents desire, and the pervert's particular relation to $\$$ fuels his desire. "The curvy line depicts the chain" (p. 775) that begins at a, the place occupied by the perverse subject, and first links the pervert with V, which stands for *volonté-de-jouissance* (p. 775) or the will-to-jouissance. Lacan said that this V or will-to-jouissance, "occupying the place of honor here, seems to impose the will [*volonté*] that dominates the whole" (p. 775) chain. This will is not that of the pervert but instead is his interpretation of the Other's will.

This schema portrays how the pervert puts himself in the position of object a so that he can approach his partner on behalf of the Other's will-to-jouissance. The effect of his approach is that he reveals the lack in his partner (as a lack in jouissance), such that his partner's identity as a split subject ($\$$) is obvious. The pervert brings out and then plugs up the lack in the Other. At the end of the chain is S, indicating that the pervert's fundamental fantasy results in the emergence of "the brute subject of pleasure (the 'pathological' subject)" (Lacan, 1963/2006a, p. 775).

The role of jouissance is paramount in the perverse fundamental fantasy. The perverse subject, occupying the role of object a, does not play the role of object-cause of the Other's desire, as in hysteria, but instead plays the role of object-cause of the will-to-jouissance (V) or of the Other's jouissance. He locates himself as the object of the [Other's] drive (Lacan, 1973/1998a, p. 185). The pervert, according to Lacan, "is the subject reconstituted through alienation at the cost of being nothing but the instrument of jouissance" (1963/2006a, p. 775). The pervert believes that what the Other lacks and thus wants is jouissance, and he sets out to bring jouissance to the Other and thereby make the Other exist through being complete. Through his endeavors to plug up the lack in the Other, the pervert, as instrument, gains jouissance for himself.

Whereas the obsessive attempts to eradicate the effects of *separation* on the *subject*, the pervert attempts to eradicate the effects of *alienation* on the *Other*.[72] It is for this reason that, in lieu of considering the entire schema Lacan provides in "Kant with Sade," the perverse fundamental fantasy is better written as $a \lozenge \text{\AA}$, or the object-cause of jouissance in relation to the Other. In contrast to the obsessive's negation of the Other, shown by the omission of the Other from $\$ \lozenge a$, this formula ($a \lozenge \text{\AA}$) emphasizes the pervert's necessity to prop up his relation to the Other. Furthermore, just as the obsessive does everything in his power to deny his own lack, such that his fundamental fantasy might be written $S \lozenge a$ instead of $\$ \lozenge a$, so too does the pervert make every effort to cancel out the lack in the Other, such that his fundamental fantasy might be written $a \lozenge A$ instead of $a \lozenge \text{\AA}$.

It might be difficult to read or listen to an example of a fantasy and determine whether it was produced by a neurotic or a perverse individual. The crucial difference between the fantasy structure of the two diagnoses has little to do with the content of an individual fantasy and much to do with the way the subject relates to the fantasy. In André's (2006) words,

> Whereas the neurotic remains silent about the fantasy, or only "confesses" to it with a high degree of reticence, in this way bearing witness to the division he experiences between his position as a subject and the position he tends to occupy in the fantasy, the pervert pronounces his fantasy, claims the right to it, even forces the Other to listen to it when he does not succeed in convincing him through so-called perverse behaviors alone. (pp. 123–124)

Indeed, perverse patients are remarkably quick to make full use of the rule of free association in psychoanalytically-oriented treatment. It is often that in the first session a pervert (who has no prior experience with psychotherapy) will say whatever comes to his mind with little concern, shame, or anxiety in the face of the possibility that he may provoke the therapist's judgments; inhibitions regarding following the rule of free association are a hallmark of neurosis, and the lack thereof indicate perversion.

According to André (2006), the pervert's use of his fantasy is distinguished by his "aim of including an Other into it":

> Whereas the fantasy is a private matter for the neurotic, for the pervert it serves to attract an Other, either to persuade this Other that this fantasy is also his, or to corrupt him in such a way that

---

72 The operation of separation and its consequences are not in the pervert's vocabulary, so to speak.

he is willing to act out the fantasy with him. Hence, in his relationship with his fantasy, the pervert is not alone. (p. 124)

The pervert, unlike the neurotic, needs to make the Other exist. It follows that the pervert seeks out someone to play the role of Other and either enact his fantasy with him or bear witness to his fantasy.

Perverse Versus Hysteric Fundamental Fantasy

The final formula for perversion ($a \Diamond A$) may be compared to a formula for hysteria ($a \Diamond Ȧ$) in a way that usefully illustrates the similarities and differences between the hysteric and the pervert.[73] The two main differences are as follows. First, even though both the hysteric and the pervert occupy the role of object a in relation to the Other, the hysteric positions herself as the object-cause of the Other's *desire* while the pervert positions himself as the object-cause of the Other's *jouissance*. Second, despite the fact that both the hysteric and the pervert take as their partner an Other who is lacking—a desiring Other in the hysteric's case and an Other lacking in jouissance in the pervert's case—the hysteric aims to sustain the Other's lack whereas the pervert aims to transform the lacking Other into the complete Other (Ȧ into A).

In terms of a major similarity between the two structures, the hysteric's fundamental fantasy involves an Other who is at first glance the one who desires, just as the pervert's fundamental fantasy involves an Other who is at first glance the one who experiences jouissance. Beneath the surface of the fantasy structure lies the fact that the hysteric and the pervert actively author the entire scenario. The hysteric, for her part, brings the Other to desire in the fashion of her choosing, and she identifies with the Other and desires as if she were the Other. Likewise, the pervert causes the Other to experience jouissance in a manner of his choosing, and he controls and chooses the jouissance he reserves for himself.[74] For instance,

---

73 See Fink (1997, pp. 257–258) for a clear social-psychological explanation of why obsessives are often men and hysterics often females. Essentially, Fink points out evidence that mothers in our cultural-historical epoch tend to nurture their male children more generously than their female children, and that this gives boys the sense that they are lacking in something which must be plugged up (by object a) and girls the sense that their mothers are lacking in something and that they, as objects a, should mend the lack in their mothers. In chapters 2 and 3, I made it clear that the pervert had a relationship with his mother that was similar in this respect to that of an hysteric. The crucial difference is that the hysteric tries to overcome separation by making herself the object of the Other's desire, and that the pervert tries to overcome alienation by making himself the object of the Other's jouissance.

74 Identification with the Other is perhaps a primary feature only in sadism, which will be discussed in the section reserved for the discussion of sadism in chapter 5.

the masochist demands that his partner punish him and "force" him to do certain things—things which are particular to the coordinates of desire of the individual masochist and thus elicit his own jouissance.

Although it is true that the pervert gains jouissance from his relation to the Other, it is more valid to emphasize that the pervert induces the Other to limit the pervert's jouissance. *Perversion is ultimately a strategy for setting limits to jouissance.* In the masochistic scenario, for example, the masochist causes the Other to experience jouissance in the form of a great anxiety about what is happening, such that the Other feels that s/he cannot tolerate it any longer and consequently forcefully commands the masochist to stop (and perhaps to do something else). The masochist's partner thus becomes the lawgiving Other, voicing her or his will-to-stop-jouissance. The fundamental fantasy is the (neurotic or perverse) subject's way of supporting the circuit of desire, and, as Lacan said, *"desire is a defense, a defense against going beyond a limit in jouissance"* (1960/2006a, p. 825). While the hysteric desires and makes the Other desire in accordance with the Law, in relation to what is prohibited, the pervert, as a subject for whom the Law exists only precariously, must propagate his desire and thus limit his jouissance by making *a* law be pronounced and come into being. The perverse strategies to setting limits to jouissance differ according to the substructure of perversion involved; these various strategies are discussed in the sections of chapter 5 devoted to the different substructures of perversion.

Continuing the comparison between the fundamental fantasies of hysteria and perversion, the hysteric's partner is a masterful Other who has knowledge or power and thus seems to her to possess jouissance that she lacks. Believing the Other to unjustly possess a surplus of jouissance,[75] the hysteric strives to recover her lost jouissance through arousing the Other's desire for her. Transforming herself into an enticing object for the Other, the hysteric causes the Other's desire and gains jouissance in the process. However, *the hysteric (and the neurotic in general) staunchly refuses to be the instrument of the Other's jouissance.* Corresponding to her primal relation to *das Ding*, the hysteric finds the Other's jouissance repulsive, and so she develops strategies to avoid or deny being the object of the Other's jouissance. When she is engaging in sexual acts with a man, she might remove herself, in thought, from the position of object-cause of his jouissance—imagining, for instance, that she is someone else. Another such strategy is that of keeping the Other's desire unsatisfied so as to assure that she will maintain her role as desired object. Rather than aiming at an unbarred Other as does the pervert, the hysteric strives to perpetuate the Other's

---

75 As I noted in chapter 2, through the processes of alienation and separation jouissance is drained from the neurotic and, in some fashion, is transferred to the Other's account.

status as lacking and thus desiring. In fact, the hysteric herself is characterized by her *desire for unsatisfied desires* (Lacan, 2001, p. 425).

In analysis, an hysteric frequently talks and complains about her relationships with various types of Others in her life, such as her boss or husband. She might say that no matter how hard she tries to be the best employee or the most desirable wife, she is continually undervalued and taken advantage of. No one desires her enough or in the way in which she wants to be desired, and everyone seems to use her as an object for his own satisfaction. For example, her husband loves her, but uses her as a sex object and still desires other women. Essentially, her complaints boil down to her difficulty in maintaining her position as object-cause of desire while fending off being the instrument of the Other's jouissance.[76] It follows that, although the hysteric and the pervert have similar fundamental fantasies, the hysteric aims at the Other's castration and seeks to be the object-cause of the Other's desire while the pervert aims at a cancellation of the Other's castration and seeks to be the object-cause of the Other's jouissance.

What is more, the hysteric and the pervert seek out different types of Others. The hysteric's partner is "at first"[77] a masterful unbarred Other (A) in whom she then endeavors to inscribe lack in the form of the Other's desire for her. The pervert, in contrast, "at first" takes as his partner a barred Other (Å) for whom he then endeavors to fill its lack in the form of himself as instrument of the Other's jouissance. Beyond appearing to be lacking in jouissance, who or what embodies the Other for the pervert? To a large degree, the pervert's Other is particular to the individual and his relationship with his childhood caregiver(s). There are, however, a few very general patterns as to the type of person who embodies the Other—when the type of Other in question is the pervert's sexual and/or romantic partner and/or partner/victim in his perverse act—for the pervert. One such trend is that the pervert's Other is often a woman. Another such trend, upon which I will first elaborate, is that the pervert's partner who plays

---

76 The descriptions provided here of the problematic relations to the Other, object *a*, and desire experienced by the hysteric, obsessive, and pervert are found in reality in varying degrees of pathology and are largely amenable to psychotherapeutic or psychoanalytic treatment.

77 I have enclosed "at first" in quotation marks here in order to show that the temporality involved should not be understood in a strict sequential sense. Although a possibility, it is not necessarily the case that the hysteric's interest in an Other is first sparked by her recognizing in him some qualities that represent the Other for her and that she only afterward attempts to inscribe a place for herself in the locus of his desire. It is also possible that a man's desire for her sparked her interest in him, and that she subsequently found qualities in him to assign him to the place of Other such that she would continue to attempt to be the object-cause of his desire. Alternatively, the sequence of events might simply be unclear. What is more important than temporality here is that the hysteric strives to create a lack in the Other, a lack that is uniquely and enduringly suited to her.

the role of Other is often as fungible and as short-term as is the obsessive's object a.

The reasons why the partner the pervert chooses as his Other is often fungible and short-term have to do with the fact that the pervert is the object-cause of jouissance rather than desire. Because the Other, having been castrated, is in reality always lacking in jouissance, the pervert's task of restoring jouissance to the Other, of making the barred Other complete, is structurally impossible. The most the pervert can achieve is to create moments at which the Other's intense jouissance *temporarily* causes the Other to seem complete. This, in turn, *temporarily* fortifies the existence of the lawgiving Other when the Other pronounces a law and sets limits to the pervert's jouissance. The hysteric, as the instrument of the Other's *desire*, is able to perpetuate in the long-term her own desire and her position in relation to a particular Other who goes on desiring her. Founded upon desire, a relationship between an hysteric and an individual Other can often last—with waxings and wanings of desire—long enough to fit socially constructed ideas of a long-term relationship. On the other hand, founded upon jouissance, the relation between a pervert and an individual Other more often than not measures its duration in terms of hours, minutes, or even seconds (in the case of the exhibitionist).[78]

In this vein, something of interest about what is called the perverse act or scenario is that, like the obsessive ($\text{\AA} \lozenge \varphi$ (a, a', a'', a''', …)) in his search for objects a, the pervert seeks out an endless chain of metonymic Others.[79] Although it is possible (usually through love—and perverts do fall in love) for a pervert to form a long-term relation or relationship, in which he would repeatedly incite intense jouissance in a particular Other, he usually is unable to or avoids doing so in favor of shorter-term relations. Once the exhibitionist, for instance, exposes himself to a woman walking around a deserted street corner, he does not run after that woman and expose himself to her again. He does not stalk her and expose himself only to her for months on end nor does he attempt to date her. Indeed, there is often very little about her that appeals to the exhibitionist other than the fact that she is a woman; one woman victim is as good as another. She does not have to have a certain hair color or a certain build or style of dress. There are important exceptions to this, however, such as the common exclusion of prepubescent girls and old women from the set of possible female victims. These exceptions could be explained by social taboos, but

---

78 In contrast, neurotic and perverse relationships to an Other that have their bedrock in the register of symbolic love can last a lifetime.

79 The fetishist is a notable exception to this. While certainly it is possible for him to daily find a new partner who embodies the Other for him, he does so more rarely than do the other four substructures of perversion.

because a significant number (though perhaps not a majority) of perverts do not lend much credence to social conceptions of morality, it is more likely that prepubescent girls and old women do not embody the Other for the pervert because they are not as strongly associated with feminine sexuality or the mOther. As I have established, the pervert's first Other is almost always a woman; it is also the case that victims of perverse acts tend to be women (Cavendish, 2009, p. 220).

Why do the pervert's relations with the Other in his perverse scenario tend to be so short-lived? One reason, already mentioned, is that the specifications for embodying the Other—being a woman—are so general that there is little reason for a pervert to expend the effort involved in maintaining a longer-term relation with a particular woman. Another possibility is that pursuing a particular woman (enacting the perverse scenario with one woman on multiple occasions) may, in cases of sadism, voyeurism, and exhibitionism in particular, substantially increase the pervert's likelihood of getting apprehended by the police. Even though being arrested and charged with a crime such as indecent exposure is one way of propping up the paternal function,[80] it seems—from the frequency with which perverts get caught by law enforcement—as though the perverse solution relies less upon an actual intervention of the law than upon an Other who enunciates the law. A third possible reason for the short-term nature of the pervert's relation to an Other is that, in cases of sadism and masochism, the Other may initially have given her consent but retracted it at some point during or after her encounter with the pervert, deciding afterwards to avoid the pervert.

A fourth reason may be that the longer a pervert knows an Other, the more she seems to be just an other like himself. As fleeting victim, a woman is able to embody the radical Otherness that connects him to her. If the pervert gives himself a chance to see her difference and individuality, then his desire to enact his perverse scenario with her dissipates. Related

---

80 The following is an excellent example of the pervert's desire for limits to be set to his excessive jouissance:

A man aged forty-one wrote a self-referral letter: "I'm in complete despair over my compulsive behavior in which I feel compelled to exhibit my genitals to women and to obtain a response from them which frees me from awful states of anxiety. I became aware of this at the age of eleven and since then I have been able to perform these actions with much care and premeditation which have prevented my detection. However, in the last few months I've noticed that I take more and more risks, as for example, doing these at the train station near my home, at the same time and even to the same woman, or from my car, all situations in which I could be easily identified. I'm forty-one, married, with four children and with a very responsible job. I'm aware that all my personal and professional achievements are in jeopardy but I feel unable to stop myself from this irrational behavior, the more dangers I encounter the more sexual pleasure I get out of it. Please help me." (Cordess & Cox, 1996, p. 276)

to this fourth reason is yet another possibility: The Other is defiled by the jouissance she experiences in the perverse scenario, such that her status is reduced to that of an imaginary other and the pervert loses his interest in her. This possibility relies upon the assumptions that the pervert seeks out an Other whom he can degrade and that, once degraded, she is no longer appealing to him. (This fifth claim will be justified and explicated in the next chapter.) The above first, fourth, and fifth reasons may be considered "internal" or structural to the pervert, while the other reasons have more to do with the world and with the reactions of the partner.

A sixth possible reason is that, when enacting his perverse scenario, the pervert wants to provide jouissance to an Other who does not want it—or at least who does not want it in that particular form or to such an excessive degree, as sometimes occurs in sadistic and masochistic scenarios. This often means that the pervert surprises the Other and that the Other is nonconsenting. When the Other is nonconsenting, it is easier for the pervert to transgress the pleasure principle and cause an excess in jouissance. So too is it easier to provoke the Other to pronounce the law. A woman who seems to be asking for jouissance cannot appear to be the Other sorely lacking in jouissance that the pervert requires nor will she protest and call forth the lawgiving Other. For example, Ray, the exhibitionist discussed in chapter 6, began to commit indecent exposure to a woman whom he subsequently identified as a prostitute. By way of reaction to his exposure, she walked closer to him and asked, "Do you want any help with that?" At that point, Ray lost his erection and drove off.

Plugging Up the Lack in the Other

Lacan's schema for and commentary on the structure of perversion that he provided in "Kant with Sade" and in Seminar X (January 16, 1963) shows that the pervert is committed to filling the lack in the Other by offering up himself as object-cause of jouissance. The Other is seen as castrated, as an entity lacking in jouissance. The pervert becomes anxious in the face of the Other's lack, and his solution is to bring something to the Other that can mask the Other's defects. Perverts attempt to fill the lack in the Other in a variety of different ways and registers. One fundamental register is that of desire, concerning which the pervert identifies with the imaginary object of desire (the imaginary phallus, φ). Another fundamental register is that of jouissance, which involves the pervert's being object a—the object-cause of the Other's jouissance. A third fundamental register—overlapping with both desire and jouissance—is that of speech.

It is in the register of jouissance that the pervert directs the bulk of his energy. Jouissance is the pervert's realm of expertise. According to Lacanian analyst Jean Clavreul (1980), "[the pervert's] knowledge about eroticism [makes him feel] assured of obtaining the other's jouissance under any circumstances" (p. 224). The pervert, then, is an expert at exposing the lack in the Other and in divining how to bring about "a recuperation of φ" (Lacan, 1960/2006a, p. 823) in the Other. The perverse scenario is not the only way in which the pervert brings jouissance to the Other. For example, Chris, an exhibitionist involved in one of the sexual offenders groups I co-facilitated, always complimented a woman on her physical appearance before sexually exposing himself to her. Chris held it to be true that women are lacking in jouissance and that they, more so than men, experience jouissance when complimented on their appearance. As another example, Ray, an exhibitionist whose case study makes up chapter 6, caused the jouissance of the Other in group psychotherapy by often joking, making outlandish statements, and encouraging—by word and example—the other group participants to speak in detail about their sexual fantasies and behaviors.

I now turn to a discussion of how a pervert attempts to plug up the lack in the Other in the register of speech and language.

Perversion and the Letter as Fetish

The Other of language, as I emphasized in chapter 2, is fundamentally incomplete and in transformative flux, there being no transcendental signified, "no such thing as a metalanguage" (Lacan, Seminar XIV, November 23, 1966), "no language being able to say the truth about truth" (1965/2006a, p. 868). As Lacan discussed in his essay "Science and Truth" (1965/2006a, pp. 855–877), there are limits to knowledge and to language. That being said, because the perverse subject is a slave to maintaining the fiction that the Other is complete, *the pervert refuses to acknowledge that there is something that cannot be said or known.* Just as the pervert experienced horror at the nameless lack of his mOther, so too does the lack in the Other of language arouse his anxiety. Confronted with a failure of language, the pervert is motivated to negate—often by way of disavowal—those limits. Nevertheless, in order to negate the lack in the Other the pervert must first have perceived that the lack ex-sists.

Ray, for example, was initially opposed to the idea of the unconscious for reasons that differ from those of the typical obsessive. While the obsessive denies the existence of the unconscious in the effort to see himself as a complete *subject* with control over his thoughts and actions, the pervert negates the idea of the unconscious in order to see the *Other* as unbarred. The concept of the unconscious introduces to the pervert the unsettling idea that the Other is not as she or he appears, but is instead permanently and structurally divided into two: conscious and unconscious.

The concept of the unconscious challenges the pervert's *near certainty* that everything can be said or known about the Other. The pervert, as a subject in the symbolic order, never has the complete certainty of the psychotic; having incorporated the structure of language into his being, the pervert perceives at some level that language and the Other is fundamentally incomplete. Through the process of Ray's psychotherapy, including interpreting his dreams, Ray soon came to see that the unconscious operates with a logic not unlike that of language. Once Ray realized that there was a successful method of interpreting manifestations of the unconscious, the concept of the unconscious ceased to present a threat to his belief in the unbarred Other.

The pervert, of course, is also devoted to maintaining the fiction of the Other's completion in the register of jouissance. The pervert specializes in finding ways to temporarily fill the lack in the Other with jouissance. As an example, Ray became distressed when the neurotic participants in his sexual offenders psychotherapy group negated their relation to their own jouissance. Consequently, the fabric of Ray's symbolic world threatened to tear at the seams in the face of the Other's denials of a will-to-jouissance and the temporary sense of subjective fullness gained by experiencing jouissance. Taking on a fetishistic function, the words that Ray used in such moments to plug up this lack in the Other had to do with "responsibility." Ray protested against every occasion when another participant evaded responsibility for his actions or denied deriving jouissance from his illegal behavior, effectively saying, "Take some responsibility! You did what you wanted to do!" Ray frequently encouraged the other participants to speak about the jouissance they gained from their behaviors, whether legal or not.

A perverse subject desires to see any lack in the Other as one which can be filled. Concerning the Other of knowledge, André (2006) said,

> It is precisely against [the limits of reason] that the pervert protests, by upholding in many instances, be it only in the peculiar relationship entertained with fantasy, the challenge of saying everything. This challenge of saying everything is a constant factor, for example, in the works of Sade and Céline, and it also explains the frequency of mania among perverts. It is this challenge, which perverse disavowal addresses at S($\bar{A}$), that explains Sade's virulent atheism. The negation of God in Sade's work operates as a negation of the limits of reason. (p. 119, translation modified)

Sade negates God, who is a metonymy for the limits of the Other of knowledge, by way of disavowal.

André referred to Annie Le Brun's book, *Sade: A Sudden Abyss* (1990), in his discussion of the function of Sade's negation of God. André (2006) concluded that Sade's "proliferation of blasphemy" (p. 120) functions to fill the "gaping hole that God, as signifier, leaves in reason" (p. 120). From this conclusion it is apparent that Sade's words of blasphemy function as a fetish to plug the lack in the Other.

According to Miller (2009a), "the Lacanian fetish is an image projected on the veil that hides the lack in being" (p. 62). Along these lines, André (2006) noted that

> Sade sees in the notion of God a revolting lack of being (*manque d'être*) that generates an even more revolting "deficiency of human being," a genuine "want-to-be" [*manque à être*]. In his relationship to language, the type of speech that Sade proposes in order to fill this lack of being plays exactly the same role as the imaginary phallus with regard to the mother's castration. (p. 120, translation modified)

Given the fact that Sade goes to great lengths to blaspheme God, another interpretation is probable. Rather than representing the hole in the Other of reason, God represents the barred Other who, according to Sade in his poem, "*La Vérité* [Truth]," has a "tenuous existence [*ta frêle existence*]." In order to make the Other's/God's existence less tenuous, Sade becomes the instrument of the Other's jouissance by bringing jouissance to God in the form of blasphemy. In Sade's view, God, in his sacred purity, is an Other severely lacking in jouissance. God's lack of jouissance is what makes God so "vile" and "horror"-inspiring to Sade. At the very least, the lack in the Other arouses Sade's anxiety.

Sade's disavowal of God could be expressed in the following phrase: "I know perfectly well that God does not exist, but all the same I can't help but go to great lengths to blaspheme God." Sade's belief in God is solidified in his fetishistic acts of blasphemy, which must be repeated to excess. Why would Sade bother to blaspheme an entity that truly did not exist for him? The truth revealed in "*La Vérité*," then, is that Sade's blasphemy functions not as a negation of God but as a fetish which serves to make God exist. Sade needs God.

As a pervert, Sade's place in the symbolic order is dependent upon the existence of the Other. In this regard, Lacan said, "I will ask you to look at my article '*Kant avec Sade*,' where you will see that the sadist himself occupies the place of the object, but without knowing it, to the benefit of another, for whose *jouissance* he exercises his action as sadistic pervert" (1973/1998a, p. 185). Unbeknown to himself, Sade spent his life as the instrument of God's jouissance. As Lacan said, the sadist's position as object-cause of the Other's jouissance is "the foundation of an identification disavowed by the subject" (p. 186).

The pervert's ignorance of his position as object *a* is clearly illustrated in the schemae for neurosis and perversion that Lacan gave in Seminar X (2004, p. 62) as follows:

The "A" above the line or wall represents *Autre* (Other, in English) such that, for each schema, the side of the subject is to the left of the wall and the side of the Other is to the right of the wall. The side of the Other is the only side that is visible to the subject. Correspondingly, the side of the subject is marked by ignorance, and so Sade, as a perverse subject, is blind to the fact that he occupies the position of the object *a*.

Sade's ethical philosophy takes a surplus of jouissance as its guiding principle. In his notes to "*La Vérité*," for example, he says, "Give ourselves indiscriminately to all that our passions inspire, and we will always be happy." For the neurotic, lack organizes desire and discourse. In contrast, Sade's life and discourse is structured by an excess in jouissance—by fetishistic presence rather than lack. For Sade, then, "excess is itself a metaphor for the momentum of desire" (Le Brun, 1990, p. 181). In André's (2006) opinion,

> The beyond of satisfaction, which the Sadean master turns into the maxim governing his relationship to desire is, in this way, first of all an excess of language, and only subsequently a sexual excess. That the challenge of saying everything is doomed to fail is beyond doubt and this is perfectly illustrated by the end of *The 120 Days of Sodom*, where one can see the fall-out of the manic symptom. (p. 121)

The pervert's excess in jouissance often manifests itself in such excesses of language.

The pervert devotes himself to the attempt to say everything. Correspondingly, *the oral drive often manifests itself as a major clinical feature of perversion*.[81] In speech and writing, perverts are often verbose and pay great attention to detail. (Many perverts successfully use writing to sublimate their desires for perverse acts.) What is more, just as neurotic speech

---

81 The importance of the oral drive in understanding perversion will be further elaborated in the following chapter.

frequently involves negation indicative of repression, perverse speech frequently reveals the operation of disavowal.

Consider the case of Chris, an exhibitionist who regularly attended one of the weekly psychotherapy groups for sexual offenders that I co-facilitated. Chris was the only exhibitionist in a group comprised mostly of neurotic men. Over the course of several years of group involvement, Chris was consistently the most verbose group participant. Chris chose to speak at length about himself at numerous group sessions, going into such great detail that he sometimes bored the other participants. In addition, when the group focused on other participants, Chris often commented exhaustively on their life situations, sometimes relating their situations to some of his own, other times giving advice, and still other times making empathic comments. More important to the present discussion, however, than the content of Chris' words, is how his speech indicates his relation to the Other. Chris did indeed seem to be attempting to say everything, to see the Other of language as complete.

Although the pervert is permanently a subject in the symbolic order, his seat in the symbolic order is neither as solid nor as ornate as that of the neurotic. Compared to the neurotic, the pervert's identity, desire, and jouissance are more restricted and dependent upon the Other. Consequently, Lacan said that, like the psychotic, the pervert may attempt to solidify his special place in the symbolic by including himself in some kind of linguistic network of his own creation. For example, in Seminar IX (February 28, 1962), Lacan suggested that the marks made by the Marquis de Sade on his bedpost functioned to inscribe Sade's jouissance in a writing system in which he could grant himself a special place.

Along these lines, Chris' main hobby, to which he devoted time several days a week, was compiling, organizing, and writing a family history. In this effort, Chris visited libraries and read articles on microfilm. Chris regularly attended family reunions, and hoped to connect there with members of his family unknown to him (for the ostensible purpose of gathering information from them about their lives) as well as to reconnect with family members with whom he was already well acquainted. Chris wanted to make their family history as complete as possible; he had already been working on it for years, and no end date was in sight. In this way, as the writer of their family history, Chris attempted to carve out a special place for himself in the family tree. In a symbolic world of his own authorship, he was more than just his mOther's son.

Consider another example of the pervert's relation to the letter, that of the trial testimony of the infamous 15th-century sadist Gilles de Rais. Gilles was a wealthy and powerful French nobleman who was executed at the stake following the testimonies of dozens of witnesses who claim that the members of Gilles's entourage kidnapped, over a period of about eight years, more than a hundred adolescent and preadolescent children, almost exclusively boys, whom Gilles then submitted to disturbing rituals of erotic torture, then summarily murdered by strangulation, decapitation, or dismemberment. (Penney, 2003, p. 126)

In a well-explicated article, James Penney (2003) pointed out numerous characteristics of Gilles' testimony that are indicative of a perverse relation to the Other.

Penney said that, prior to the beginning of his public trial, Gilles' attitude changed with regard to the church's authority over his indictment after the Inquisition threatened him with excommunication. Gilles greatly feared "the consequences of being jettisoned from the community of God and so deprived of a chance for salvation" (Penney, 2003, p. 130). Gilles, a believer in God, may have been afraid of eternal damnation, but he may also have been afraid of having no relationship to the Other, for who would he be without the Other?

After the threat of excommunication, Gilles "desired to repeat his out of court confession in the public confines of the trial 'to remedy its faults in the event that he had omitted anything, and to make more thorough declarations of the points develped summarily in the … articles [of indictment]'" (Penney, 2003, p. 130). In his trial, Gilles set about confessing his "sins" in so much explicit detail that he even confessed to more "sins" than those for which he was charged. Gilles, then, tried to say everything possible on the subject of his guilt. "Oddly, however, Gilles did not consider the description of his crimes as grounds for the potential reinstitution of the excommunication. Indeed, Gilles thought that his chances at absolution increased in proportion to the morbid completeness of his confession" (p. 130). This strange way of thinking may be expressed in terms of disavowal: "I know very well that the more detail I provide of my crimes, the more likely I am to be severely punished, but all the same I am *certain* that God in his divine clemency will forgive me all the more easily."

Gilles is certain that God's desire is to forgive sinners like himself. Gilles is certain of this knowledge because, as Miller (2006a) says, "certitude is always more on the side of *jouissance*" [than on the side of the authority of the Name-of-the-Father] (p. 23). Because a pervert has more jouissance than does a neurotic, the pervert has less doubt (which, as I said in chapter 2, is a hallmark of neurosis) and more certainty. Gilles does not doubt that he knows what the Other wants. Gilles, as object-cause of the Other's jouissance, became the greatest of sinners so that he might have

the most spectacular acts of contrition, [and would] best con-
form to the divine will to grant the grace of salvation. Far from
perverting the theological position on grace in late medieval
Christianity, Gilles's confession uncovers the authentically perverse kernel of forms of Christian casuistry that safeguard a
realm of illicit taboo by granting divine pardon to the believer
in advance ... In a theological framework that allows for certainty with respect to the content of the final judgment, the subject acquires divine forgiveness and favor by means of the very
transgression of the terms of the covenant. (Penney, 2003, pp.
149–150)

Gilles attained certainty of his role as instrument of God's jouissance—
God gaining jouissance in granting His forgiveness—by engaging in such
obviously sinful behavior and then confessing and asking for divine pardon. Gilles went about fulfilling God's will-to-jouissance by committing
crimes and then begging for forgiveness. To Gilles' mind, the severity of
his transgressions ensured that "he will be *especially* forgiven for his particularly scandalous crimes" (p. 150). Through Gilles' horrible crimes and
detailed confession, he gained for himself a special position in relation to
the Other: the instrument of the Other's jouissance.[82]

Certainty as Magical Thinking

As I explained in chapter 2, psychosis is associated with certainty and
subjectivity is associated with doubt. The pervert is less plagued by doubt
and more plagued by certainty than is the neurotic, because the pervert,
as the instrument of the Other's jouissance, lacks a persistent question of
identity at the level of being. The pervert's certainty relates to matters of
jouissance. He is certain that his role is to plug up the lack in the Other
with jouissance. In Clavreul's (1980) words,

The pervert's knowledge is equally a knowledge that refuses to
recognize its insertion in a "not-knowing" that precedes it: it is a
knowledge that is given as truth ... In the end, this knowledge is
rigid and implacable; it cannot be revised in the face of facts that

---

82 According to Penney, a neurotic relation to God and to sin in 15th-century France would have
    been different in the following way: "While the neurotic subject indulges in crime as a result of
    an irrational, pathological motivation beyond its conscious control, and then chastises itself as a
    means of both intensifying the enjoyment of transgression and reconstituting the contours of its
    symbolic universe, the pervert commits the crime in order retroactively to present himself as the
    object-cause of redemption. The pervert, in short, must commit the sin with reference to which
    he will subsequently rationalize his innocence" (2003, p. 151).

belie it. This knowledge about eroticism feels assured of obtaining the other's jouissance under any circumstances. (p. 224, translation modified)

Perverse certainty is evident in the second phrase in each disavowal; the claim attached to "but all the same" is the one that the pervert believes to be true despite evidence to the contrary. The pervert's certainty bears resemblance to what has often been called "magical thinking" with regard to children. For example, "I know very well that my stuffed animals are not alive, but I can't help but believe that they are only pretending and that, at night or when I am not looking, they move and talk just as I do." Such a child might consequently arrange his stuffed animals carefully so that they are comfortable and can breathe.

Perverse certainty and the operation of disavowal in perversion is more likely to have to do with the lawgiving Other or the maternal phallus. Consider the following example. In a session toward the end of our psychotherapeutic work—which was by no means a complete analysis—Ray said that when he was driving to his appointment and was close to the office building, he was stopped at a light and saw what he thought might have been my car behind him. Then, he saw a woman crossing the street and he thought to himself, "Don't even look at her because if that's Stephanie, Stephanie will see and will wonder what I was thinking." Ray said that he knew that I was probably not in the car behind him and he knew that I could neither see his gaze (from my vantage point) nor read his mind, but all the same he could not help but believe that I was there and would know if he thought about exposing himself to the woman crossing the street. Despite what Ray knew about my limitations, he nevertheless preferred to believe that I would know were he to look at and consider exposing himself to a woman. This belief, facilitated by disavowal, enabled him to prop up the paternal function. In this scenario, and, indeed, throughout much of our analytic work, Ray saw me as the lawgiving Other in addition to the subject-supposed-to-know. Ray believed—without me ever having confirmed, denied, or supported his belief—that I would know if were he to commit an act of indecent exposure and that I would turn him in to law enforcement officials.

The Force of the Imaginary Order and the Drives

The pervert's certainty is but one of the numerous phenomena linked with the pervert's excess in jouissance. In general, the pervert's imaginary order processes and drives are stronger and less under the control of the symbolic than are those of the neurotic. Consequently, *aggression and rivalry (related to the imaginary order) and impulsivity (related to the drives) are*

usually notable features of perversion, with symbolic success often being less
important to perverts than to neurotics.

It should be emphasized that, just as neurotics vary widely in their levels of "impulse control" and "drive inhibition" due to factors such as family and social contexts (for example, the difference between neurotic teenagers who drink alcohol, do drugs, and take part in fights related to street gangs and neurotic teenagers who refrain from doing such things altogether and delay their gratification for symbolic achievements), so too do perverts vary widely on those levels. Criminals such as Gilles de Rais are extremely rare exceptions even among perverse subjects. The paternal function can be propped up without transgressing an ethical boundary, as shown, for instance, in my example of Ray at the stoplight.

The pervert's excess of jouissance, while it may appear desirable from the standpoint of the neurotic, is actually at the root of a good deal of his suffering. The pervert is far from being a carefree sensualist. Instead, the perverse subject is fundamentally lacking in freedom. The pervert's jouissance is either fixated to a fetish or he is compulsively driven to enact an almost invariable scenario; the pervert manages his jouissance through these compulsions, but he afterward often suffers from shame and may experience social, occupational, or legal consequences.

Just as psychotic suffering is expressed in terms of "phenomena" (e.g., delusions or message phenomena) instead of "symptoms," perverse suffering is often expressed in terms of perverse enactment rather than by perverse symptoms. Nevertheless, when perverse individuals do experience symptoms, they frequently manifest themselves as forms of anxiety (e.g., mania), depression, or psychosomatic symptoms (e.g., impotence or prolonged childhood enuresis). The fetish is impossible to dissolve owing to its structural permanence and importance, but discovering and elaborating upon the signifying relations that constitute it can go a long way toward relieving the pervert's symptoms and improving the quality of his life.

Perversion and the Drives

Perversion does not appear as the pure and simple manifestation of a drive, but it turns out to be related to a dialectical context which is as subtle, as composite, as rich in compromise, as ambiguous as a neurosis.

Lacan (1957–1958, pp. 230–231)

It is the [perverse] subject who determines himself as an object, in his encounter with subjective division.

Lacan (1973/1998a, p. 185, translation modified)

What is at issue in the drive is finally revealed here—the course of the drive is the only form of transgression that is permitted to the subject in relation to the pleasure principle.

Lacan (1973/1998a, p. 183)

Like the neurotic subject, the perverse subject has a particular way of situating himself in relation to the drive. In perversion, the subject locates himself as the object of the Other's drive. The perverse subject brings jouissance to the Other by making himself the object of the Other's drive. In exhibitionism and voyeurism, the pervert locates himself as the object of the scopic drive (Lacan, 1973/1998a, pp. 182–183). In sadism and masochism, the pervert locates himself as the object of the invocatory drive (2006b, p. 257).[83] Lacan does not discuss fetishism in terms of a predominant drive. From what Lacan does say about fetishism, however, paired with the available case studies, I offer an hypothesis: fetishism has to do with the scopic drive. This hypothesis will be explored below.

Using the example of Alcibiades, Lacan said the pervert is he "who pursues jouissance as far as possible" (1960/2006a, p. 826). The pervert's means of doing so is the drive, as "the course of the drive is the only form of transgression that is permitted to the subject in relation to the pleasure principle" (1973/1998a, p. 183). Before further explicating the pervert's relation to the drive, it will be necessary to explore the course of the drive in more detail.

The drive, which is structured by the child's relation to the Other, is a demand that is paradoxically always satisfied. The purpose of the drive is not to reach a goal but to follow its aim or path. And it is the perpetual and repetitive circuit of the drive around its object *a* that allows the drive to produce its own satisfaction. Therefore, the drive might usefully be considered as a linguistic program (Miller, 1996b, p. 316).

In Seminar XI, Lacan elaborated his theory of the circuit of the drive. In so doing, he referred to Freud's concept of the drive as a montage composed of vicissitudes: the source (*Quelle*), the object (*Objekt*), the thrust (*Drang*), and the *Ziel*. Lacan translated *Ziel* into two different English words, "*aim*" and "*goal*" (1973/1998a, p. 179)—both of which are relevant to the circuit of the drive. "The *aim* is the way taken" (p. 179) while the goal is the completion of the circuit. Lacan provided the following diagram to illustrate the drive's circuit (p. 178):

---

83 The object *a* of the invocatory drive is the voice. The invocatory drive involves jouissance in seeing. It is explained in more detail below.

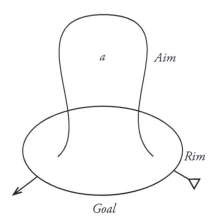

In the drive's circuit, the drive originates in the source, or what Lacan calls the "rim" (1973/1998a, p. 179) and which is essentially the erogenous zone.[84] The pressure of the drive moves it along its path or "*aim*" (p. 179) of circling around the object *a* and returning to the erogenous zone and thus achieving its "*goal*" (p. 179). The drive's circuit is structured by three grammatical voices: active, reflexive, and passive (p. 177). Take, for example, *Schaulust*,[85] or the scopic drive.

Stage 1: active = to see
Stage 2: reflexive = to see oneself
Stage 3: passive = to be seen

Ultimately, "what is involved in the drive is *getting oneself seen (se faire voir)*. The activity of the drive is concentrated in this *getting oneself (se faire)*" (p. 195, translation modified). This is why Lacan emphasized that the drive is fundamentally active (p. 200). As he said, "it is obvious that, even in its supposedly passive phase, the exercise of a drive, a masochistic drive, for example, requires that the masochist give himself, if I may be permitted to put it in this way, a devil of a job" (p. 200, translation modified). Lacan

---

84 The erogenous zones have a rim-like structure. "The very delimitation of the 'erogenous zone' that the drive isolates from the function's metabolism—the act of devouring involves organs other than the mouth—just ask Pavlov's dog—is the result of a cut that takes advantage of a margin or border: the lips, 'the enclosure of the teeth,' the rim of the anus, the penile groove, the vagina, and the slit formed by the eyelids, not to mention the hollow of the ear" (Lacan, 1966/2006a, p. 817).

85 Freud's term *Schaulust* combines the German word *lust* (translated in English as "pleasure") with the word rendered in English as "looking" or "seeing." *Schaulust* could therefore be translated into Lacanian terminology as "jouissance in seeing." The activity of the scopic drive may thus be particularly apparent in moments when a subject watches something with intense curiosity or fascination, and her jouissance is subjectively experienced as pleasure, shame, anxiety, or disgust.

concluded that each of the three grammatical stages "with which Freud articulates each drive must be replaced by the formula of *getting oneself seen, heard* and the rest of the list" (p. 200, translation modified) of partial drives given by Lacan.

Another way of writing the three grammatical stages is the following: he sees, he sees it (himself), and it (he) is seen by the Other. "He" is the subject, "sees" is the verb, and "it" is the object of the drive. Consequently, it is apparent that the subject is reduced to an object in the course of the drive's satisfaction. Because the pervert's position is that of object-cause of the Other's jouissance, the pervert is the person in whom the structure of the drive is most clearly revealed. In Lacan's words,

> I have also shown that, in the profound relation of the drive, what is essential is that the movement by which the arrow that sets out towards the target fulfills its function only by really re-emerging from it, and returning on to the subject. In this sense, the pervert is he who, in short circuit, more directly than any other, succeeds in his aim, by integrating in the most profound way his function as subject with his existence as desire. (1973/1998a, p. 206)[86]

Consider also the following passage:

> *The object, here, is the gaze—the gaze that is the subject,* which attains it, which hits the bull's eye in target-shooting. I have only to remind you what I said of Sartre's analysis. Although this analysis brings out the agency of the gaze, it is not at the level of the other whose gaze surprises the subject looking through the keyhole. It is that the other surprises him, the subject, as entirely hidden gaze. (p. 182, emphasis added)

Paradoxically, the object of the drive is, at the same time, the subject of the drive.

This subject of the drive affords a kind of acephalous subjectivity in the real, as contrasted with the subject of the unconscious. The subject as drive is that which pursues jouissance. In the neurotic, the subject as drive is "prior to analysis, hemmed in, kept down, and silenced as much as possible by the ego and the superego, by desire as it forms in language on the basis of the Other's discourse, which transmits the Other's desires, values, and ideals" (Fink, 1997, p. 208). The pervert is less dominated than

---

86 It is also possible to interpret this passage to mean that the neurotic's aim is more indirect than that of the pervert because she aims to be not the drive-object of jouissance but the object of desire, which requires her to go beyond the circuit of the drive to achieve her aim.

the neurotic by the Other's desire, and so the pervert's subjectivity at the level of the drive, manifested in the perverse act, sticks out and obscenely disrupts the neurotic's symbolic world, arousing her anxiety.

The Gaze, the Voice, and Perversion

The gaze and the scopic drive figure prominently in the structure of perversion, particularly with regard to exhibitionism, voyeurism, and fetishism. What is the gaze, exactly? "The *objet a* in the field of the visible is the gaze" (Lacan, 1973/1998a, p. 105). Seminar XI marked Lacan's invention of the gaze as object *a*, which Lacan credited to the influence of Maurice Merleau-Ponty's posthumous book *The Visible and the Invisible* (1968).[87] The gaze is *a priori* and subjectless. We experience this gaze as if we were being looked at by the world; it is empty, indeterminate, invisible, and impossible but nevertheless keenly experienced.

> Let us recall the archetypal scene from Hitchcock: a heroine (Lilah in *Psycho*, Melanie in *The Birds*) is approaching a mysterious, allegedly empty house; she is looking at it, yet what makes a scene so disturbing is that we, the spectators, cannot get rid of the vague impression that the object she is looking at is somehow *returning the gaze*. (Žižek, 1996, p. 90)

In this experience of the gaze, we feel looked at by some presence that we know is not there. We feel anxiety at the overproximity of the object at times when the object is unveiled and disrupts the consistency of our reality.

---

87 In Seminar XI, Lacan added both the gaze and the voice to the list of psychoanalytic objects *a*. Whereas the oral and anal drives have been supposed to correspond to chronological stages of psycho-social-biological development, and have thus played major roles in stage theories of development for over a century, the scopic and invocatory drives did not appear in psychoanalysis until Lacan applied his structuralist and linguistic viewpoint to the topic of the drives, focusing on the development of the linguistic subject. That said, the rudiments of the scopic drive did appear in Freud's conception of *Schaulust*, and in that sense Lacan expanded and clarified *Schaulust* according to his ontological framework. According to Miller (2007), Lacan added the gaze and the voice to the Freudian list of objects *a* because of his clinical experience working with psychosis. "It is a clinical experience in which gaze and voice manifest themselves in separate forms, clearly characterized by their exteriority with regard to the subject … Lacan extracted the scopic object from the delusion of surveillance because this delusion renders manifest the *separate* and *external* presence of a gaze under which the subject falls. In a similar way, it is from the phenomena of mental automatism … that Lacan extracted the object voice. Here one speaks of voices, although these voices are all immaterial—they are nevertheless perfectly real to the subject. They are even what he cannot doubt, despite the fact that nobody can record them. Their sonorous materiality is not what would be at the fore here" (p. 140).

The presence of object *a*, of course, can also produce desire. In Freud's (1927/1961) article "Fetishism," Freud described the case of an analysand who had lived in England for some of his early childhood before moving to Germany, and who subsequently developed a fetish for women with "a shine on the nose" (*Glanz auf der Nase*) resulting from the homonymic relation between *Glanz* (translated as "shine" in English) and "glance." The *Glanz auf der Nase* represented the gaze, making the fetishist feel gazed at and evoking his desire. As a general rule, the subject's desire is produced when object *a* is veiled[88] or disguised, and the subject's anxiety is provoked when object *a* lacks the veil's adornment and is experienced in its nakedness as overproximate. The fetishist analysand identified with the gaze, and as such he was the object of the scopic drive in his relation to the Other. The fetishist's jouissance was permanently fixated to his fetish and to the scopic drive.[89]

The gaze represented an important correction to Lacan's treatment of the scopic field in his theory of the mirror stage. In the mirror stage, the mirror and the scopic self-observation ("I see myself seeing myself") prop up the materialization of the image and imaginary identifications. In so doing, the mirror stage obscures the distinction between vision—made possible by the eyes and the brain—and the gaze as object *a*, in which "the subject sustain[s] himself in a function of desire" (Lacan, 1973/1998a, p. 85). What is more, unlike the oral and anal drives, which operate at the level of demand, the scopic and invocatory drives operate at the level of desire, "of the desire of the Other" (p. 104).

Although Lacan cited Jean-Paul Sartre's concept of the gaze in chapter 7 of Seminar XI (1973/1998a, p. 84), it was largely to differentiate Lacan's concept of the gaze as apprehended in the field of desire from Sartre's gaze as apprehended in the gaze of others. For Sartre,

> The gaze is seen [*se voit*, which might also be translated as "sees itself"]—to be precise, the gaze of which Sartre speaks, the gaze

---

88 In Lacan's terminology, the veil is a type of semblance, and a semblance is something that functions to mask nothingness. The "maternal phallus" is such a semblance.

89 As a more recent example, the fetishist Lihn (1970) described had traits of voyeurism and exhibitionism—rather than of sadism or masochism which imply a relation to the invocatory drive—and had the following fetishistic ritual: "to put on a pair of his mother's panties, conceal his penis between his thighs, and with them apply pressure to his penis while looking at himself in the bathroom mirror, imagining himself to be a woman with a penis. He preferred to leave the bathroom door open so that while masturbating he could hear his mother singing and moving about the house. The closer she came, the more excitement the patient experienced; and he would not shut the door until his mother was almost close enough to see him ... [He also engaged in] masturbation on the beach in a manner in which he could almost be seen by other bathers while wearing the [swim trunks] his mother made for him" (pp. 352–353).

that surprises me and reduces me to shame, since this is the feeling [Sartre] regards as the most dominant. (Lacan, 1973/1998a, p. 84)

For Lacan, however,

> The gaze ... is not a seen gaze, but a gaze imagined by me in the field of the Other ... If one does not stress the dialectic of desire one does not understand why the gaze of others would disorganize the field of perception. It is because the subject in question is not that of reflexive consciousness, but that of desire. (1973/1998a, p. 84, 89, translation modified)

Prior to the gaze of others, then, is a fundamental subjectless gaze in the field of desire. The scopic drive indicates that there is an invisible gaze which aims at the subject.

All objects *a*, as objects in the real, are intangible and invisible. The gaze, we might say, is veiled, hidden, or cloaked by elements of the imaginary order.

> Generally speaking, the relation between the gaze and what one wishes to see involves a lure. The subject is presented as other than he is, and what one shows him is not what he wishes to see. It is in this way that the eye may function as *objet a*, that is to say, at the level of lack (-φ). (Lacan, 1973/1998a, p. 104, translation modified)

Lacan's matheme *i(a)*, the image of object *a*, implies an image or a person that dresses up the object *a* that it hides. Object *a*, as an object in the real, has nothing to do with aesthetic beauty, but it sometimes takes on the quality of beauty when veiled by a beautiful image. The veil comes between the subject and the object *a*.

When the imaginary order fails or is disrupted, the object *a* as real distorts the appearance of reality and arouses the subject's anxiety. As Slavoj Žižek pointed out in his foreword to Henry Bond's *Lacan at the Scene* (2009), an excellent example of this failure may be found in Marcel Proust's *The Guermantes Way* (1952), when the narrator uses the telephone for the first time, calling his beloved grandmother.

> After a few seconds of silence, suddenly I heard that voice which I supposed myself, mistakenly, to know so well; for always until then, every time that my grandmother had talked to me, I had been accustomed to follow what she was saying on the open score of her face, in which the eyes figured so largely; but her voice itself I was hearing this afternoon for the first time. And because that

114

voice appeared to me to have altered in its proportions from the moment that it was a whole, and reached me in this way alone and without the accompaniment of her face and features, I discovered for the first time how sweet that voice was ... but also how sad it was; then, too, having it alone beside me, seen, without the mask of her face, I noticed for the first time the sorrows that had scarred it in the course of a lifetime.

The voice, object *a* of the invocatory drive, is described by the narrator in its unveiled state. His grandmother's voice, a real-order object detached from its veil (previously always accompanying image of his grandmother's face), unsettled the narrator's sense of reality and altered his perceptions of his grandmother.

A real presence indeed that voice so near—in actual separation. But a premonition also of an eternal separation!... I have known the anxiety that was one day to wring my heart when a voice should thus return (alone, and attached no longer to a body which I was never more to see).

The narrator's anxiety is the result of the voice as object *a* appearing in reality. The voice appeared to the narrator in "an obscene overproximity, a presence more intimate, more penetrating, than that of an external body in front of us" (Bond, 2009, p. xi).

The Veil, Fetishism, and the Gaze

We return to the interpretation of the scene where the young child discovers the absence of the penis in his mother, since we must elucidate the very important question ... *with what eye does the mother see her child, who looks at her?"*... But here there is no response, there is only a question. The look and the eye retain their mystery. And it is thus that for the pervert the eye will have a problematic place that neurotic and normal subjects reserve for the phallus and the loved object ... Is the eye there to see, to look, to *jouir*, or better yet, to seduce?

Clavreul (1980, p. 226)

In Seminar IV (1994, p. 156), Lacan provided the "schema of the veil" (p. 156), which he said represented the structure of fetishism.

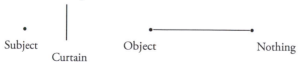

Subject   Object   Nothing
Curtain

Referring to this schema, Lacan said, "This is the subject, this is the object, and this over here is the nothing, which is also the symbol, or the phallus in as much as the woman doesn't have it" (p. 156). For Freud, the nothing is the mother's lack of a penis, and the fetish object is, by way of metonymy, a substitute for the missing penis (p. 157). For Lacan, the nothing is the fundamental lack in being.

In an intermediary position between the subject and the object, the veil functions to disguise the fact that, behind the object ex-sists the Other's lack in being. In other words, this schema shows how the fetish is an image projected onto a veil that conceals a lack in being. This image is not fundamentally in the visual field but in the field of the scopic drive; Freud's analysand was probably the only one to notice the shine on women's noses. Because the fetish is permanent, we can say that the veil is what allows the image to be permanently inscribed.

As previously stated, the fetish includes imaginary, symbolic, and real order determinants. In other words, as in Fink's (2003) case of W, the boot corresponds to the image of a boot, to signifiers such as "boot," "butt," and "thumb," and to the gaze as object a.[90] In fetishism, the fetish object is comprised of a mixture of elements having to do with the subject, the ambiguity around sexual difference, and the second Other.[91] Therefore in fetishism, unlike in voyeurism and exhibitionism, the gaze cannot be located *either* on the side of the subject *or* on the side of the Other, but instead is located in object a on the side of both the Other and the subject. For the fetishist, the gaze is primary insofar as the mOther's gaze was focused on him, the apple of her eye, and on his penis, and also insofar as he, like little Hans, focused his gaze on the place where his mOther's penis should have been. It was in his mOther's gaze that the fetishist took up his symbolic position.

The Voice and the Invocatory Drive

At the scopic level, we are no longer at the level of demand, but of desire, of the desire of the Other. It is the same at the level of the invocatory drive, which is the closest to the experience of the unconscious.

Lacan (1973/1998a, p. 104)

The voice and the invocatory drive are the object and drive that predominate in masochism and sadism (Lacan, 2006b, p. 257). Just as the gaze as object a has little to do with vision, so too is it the case that

---

90 Fink himself, however, does not highlight the gaze or the scopic drive in his case study of W.

91 In the case of W, for instance, the boot fetish functioned as a Name-of-the-Father or second Other. Boots were a signifier of W's mOther's desire and were associated with a law outside of herself. The boot also served as a substitute for W and his penis.

the voice as object *a* does not in the least belong to the sonorous register ... [Consequently, we must consider] the function of the voice as *a-phonic* [*a-phone*], if I may say so. This is probably a paradox, a paradox that has to do with the fact that the objects called *a* are tuned to the subject of the signifier only if they lose all substantiality, that is, only on condition that they are centered by a void, that of castration. (Miller, 2007, p. 139)

It is because of the emptiness of the voice that Miller went on to define the voice as the unspeakable (p. 145).

Lacan said that the invocatory drive "is the closest to the experience of the unconscious" (1973/1998a, p. 104) because of the voice's fundamental relation to speech and language. (Recall that "the unconscious is structured like a language"; p. 149.) According to Miller (2007), the voice is "everything in the signifier that does not partake in the effect of signification" (p. 141). "Speech knots signified—or rather the 'to be signified,' what is to be signified—and signifier to one another; and this knotting always entails a third term, that of the voice" (p. 141). In other words, the voice is what ties the signifier to the signified. Consequently, the Lacanian voice cannot be said to be something we utilize; instead, "the voice inhabits language, it haunts it. It is enough to speak for the menace to emerge that what cannot be said could come to light" (p. 145).

In Seminar X on Anxiety, Lacan (2004) designated the voice as the superego (p. 341). The superego, "in its intimate imperative, is indeed 'the voice of conscience,' that is, a voice first and foremost, a vocal one at that, and without any authority other than that of being a loud voice" (1961/2006a, p. 684). This voice of conscience appears either to lack an identity or to be the subject's own voice. The voice of the superego is the voice of the drives.[92]

Whereas the ideal ego is the imaginary order idealized self-image and the ego-ideal is the symbolic introjection of the Other's ideals and tastes, the superego is the real order counterpart to the ego-ideal. The "obscene, ferocious figure of the superego" (Lacan, 1961/2006a, p. 619) insatiably bombards the subject with impossible demands that stem from the ego-ideal. The more a subject tries (and inevitably fails) to meet the unreasonable demands of the superego, the more the subject feels guilty and "bad." This cycle, with its production of excessive guilt, leads us to raise the question of if and how this cycle can be stopped.

In Seminar VII, Lacan (1997b) suggests "a reconsideration of ethics ... of a kind that gives this question the force of a Last Judgment: Have you

---

92 Lacan (2004) said, "there cannot be a valid analytic conception of the superego which forgets that at its most profound phase the voice is one of the forms of object *a*" (p. 342).

acted in conformity with the desire that is in you?" (p. 314). This law of desire is a kind of fourth agency (along with the id, ego, and superego)—one which tells the subject to act in conformity with her desire.

> Opposed to this pole of desire is traditional ethics ... [which involves] the cleaning up of desire, modesty, temperateness, that is to say the middle path we see articulated so remarkably in Aristotle ... [which] is wholly founded on an order that is no doubt a tidied-up, ideal order. (pp. 314–315)

The law of desire is opposed to traditional ethics, which is associated with the ego-ideal—with the internalized socio-symbolic ideals and norms that seem "good," "mature," and "reasonable." Seen within this framework, the superego is an agency that bullies the subject on account of her betrayal of the law of desire in favor of the seemingly good ego-ideal. When the cruel ferocity of the superego increases, it confronts the subject with her guilt; it must be said, however, that Lacanian guilt is not defined in relation to the subject's failure to live up to her ego-ideal. Instead, "the only thing one can be guilty of is of giving up on one's desire" (1997b, p. 321, translation modified). This conception is similar to that of bad faith in Sartre.

It is in this sense that a pervert experiences less guilt than does a neurotic. The pervert's greater access to jouissance and comparative lack of drive inhibition naturally results in the pursuit of desires. Furthermore, although there is a symbolic place for the Law in the world of the pervert, the lawgiving Other is seen as a constructor of façades. Because the pervert rejects the authority and validity of the lawgiving Other, his ego-ideal is markedly different than that of the neurotic. The pervert's ego-ideal is lawless. Nevertheless, it remains comprised of the desires, ideals, and socio-cultural norms followed by the primary Others in his life. As such, the pervert's ego-ideal does include its own kind of moral codes. The pervert does introject commonly shared symbolic values and ideals. Furthermore, the pervert, by way of identification and imitation, assembles his own makeshift moral "laws."

Nonetheless, insofar as the superego is the real order counterpart to the ego-ideal, the pervert may be considered to have an "inferior" superego to the extent to which he has not accepted castration. Even so, this is not to say that the pervert lacks in moral conscience but rather that there is a qualitative and quantitative difference between the superegos of neurotics and perverts. Correspondingly, and contrary to popular psychoanalytic thought, Lacan emphasized that the superego can neither be equated with the Law nor with moral conscience.

> [T]he interiorization of the Law has nothing to do with the Law ... It is possible that the superego serves as a support for the moral

conscience, but everyone knows that it has nothing to do with the moral conscience as far as its most obligatory demands are concerned. What the superego demands has nothing to do with that which we would be right in making the universal rule of our actions. (1997b, p. 310)

The superego is best considered as a particular function or operation instead of as a set of specific contents. Moral conscience and the introjected Law are contents that are taken up by the function of the superego. The superego as "a voice first and foremost" (1961/2006a, p. 684) is the process of making an imperative: "You must...!" The more the subject renounces jouissance in the name of sociocultural ideals or moral conscience, the more jouissance is available to fuel the sadistic superego's imperative. And there is always some jouissance experienced in the enactment of the moral law. In Freudian terms, the id refuses to be stifled. The pervert, having refused castration, does not easily fall victim to the vicious cycle of the superego. The pervert gives relatively free reign to his id. This difference has major implications for making differential diagnoses between neurosis and perversion.

Perversion and Sublimation

Somewhat paradoxically, even though the pervert is he "who pursues jouissance as far as possible" (Lacan, 1960/2006a, p. 826), the pervert has a great capacity for sublimation. Miller (1996b) said,

> There is a question in psychoanalysis as to the connection between sublimation and perversion, and not a few true perverts have enormously contributed to human sublimation—no other clinical structure involves as many literary references as perversion. The point is not to either confuse or distinguish sublimation from perversion conceptually, but to see that they stem from the same question: satisfaction from activities other than fucking. (p. 312)

The pervert devotes great stores of jouissance toward making the Other exist, and this process can take on the form of sublimation. Creating literature is just one of the methods at the pervert's disposal to prop up the paternal function by way of sublimation instead of by acting out a perverse scenario. The enthusiasm with which Chris energetically devoted himself to researching his family history indicates one such alternative sublimation. It follows that when treating a perverse patient the analyst should keep in mind the pervert's strong capacity for sublimation, and when the pervert speaks in a session about his sublimation activities it may be beneficial to punctuate or highlight them. *Clinical work with perverts should aim to assist the pervert in the creative (and impermanent) process of propping up his paternal function, and toward this aim to call the pervert's attention to the importance and functions of his sublimation.*

The Quaternary Schema of Perversion

Incidentally, how can one say, just like that, as Freud goes on to do, that exhibitionism is the contrary of voyeurism, or that masochism is the contrary of sadism? He posits this simply for grammatical reasons, for reasons concerning the inversion of the subject and the object, as if the grammatical object and subject were real functions. It is easy to show that this is not the case, and we have only to refer to our structure of language for this deduction to become impossible.

Lacan (1973/1998a, p. 170)

Lacan repeatedly insisted that, contrary to the opinions of Freud and Krafft-Ebing, masochism is not the opposite of sadism and exhibitionism is not the opposite of voyeurism.[93] Furthermore, Lacan held that a subject cannot alternate back and forth between masochism and sadism or exhibitionism and voyeurism. Instead, Lacan established a non-symmetrical relationship (based on the gaze) between exhibitionism and voyeurism which is parallel to the non-symmetrical relationship (based on the voice) between masochism and sadism (Miller, 2006c, p. 26). Based on his reading of what Lacan said about perversion in Seminar XVI, Miller (p. 27) provided the following "quaternary schema":

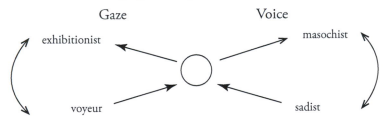

This quaternary schema shows that the exhibitionist and the masochist situate themselves in relation to object *a* in the same manner: Taking up the ostensibly passive grammatical voice of the drive, they make the object *a* as gaze or voice appear in "the field of the [O]ther as deserted by jouissance" (Lacan, 2006b, p. 254).

---

93 Lacan (2004) said, "Sadism is not the inverse of masochism … The structure is more complex" (p. 207).

Referring to the exhibitionist, Lacan (2006b) said, "The essential part is, properly and above all, to make the gaze appear in the field of the Other" (p. 254). Then, referring to the masochist, he added,

> In the way in which we have seen the exhibitionist *jouit*, the axis of gravity of the masochist revolves around the level of the Other and giving the voice back to him as a supplement, not without the possibility of a certain derision, which appears in the margins of masochistic functioning. (p. 258)

Essentially, the exhibitionist (in being gazed at by the Other, in making his erect penis be gazed at by the Other) and masochist (in being spoken to or commanded by the Other) plug up the lack in the Other by offering up themselves as the object of the Other's drive.

In addition, as the schema shows, the voyeur and the sadist also situate themselves in relation to object *a* in the same manner: Taking up the active grammatical voice of the drive, they bring their own object *a* to the field of the Other and make the Other whole by their act. The voyeur gazes, and the sadist speaks. The sadist, for instance, tries "to complete the Other by removing speech from him and by imposing his own voice, but in general this misfires" (Lacan, 2006b, pp. 258–259).

The quaternary schema and the roles of the gaze and the voice in each of the substructures of perversion will be discussed in more detail in chapter 5. In this chapter I have attempted to illustrate the multitudinous yet structurally specific ways in which the pervert's relation to the Other may be represented by the matheme $a \lozenge \$$ (Lacan, 1963/2006a, p. 774).

5

THE PERVERSE ACT AND
SUBSTRUCTURES OF PERVERSION

The perverse subject loyally offers himself up to the Other's jouissance.

Lacan (2004, p. 62)

The Perverse Act and Woman as Other

It is necessary to radically distinguish the perverse act from the neurotic act. The perverse act is situated at the level of the question concerning jouissance. The neurotic act, even if it refers to the model of the perverse act, has no other goal than to sustain that which has nothing to do with the question of the sexual act, namely, the effect of desire.

Lacan (Seminar XIV, June 7, 1967)

As I have elaborated, the pervert's first Other is almost always a woman. What is more, the perverse subject always has a problematic relationship with his mOther; she is a subject who claims his subjectivity for her own, using him as the instrument of her jouissance rather than allowing him the subjective space necessary to have a desire of his "own." Although the "blame" may also be assigned to the second Other and to the subject himself, *aggression toward the mOther is a very common feature of perversion.* Contrary to the common psychoanalytic conception of the son's Oedipal aggression toward the father, perversion is an instance in which the subject's aggressive feelings are more frequently and substantially directed toward the mother. It should come as no surprise that the pervert expresses his aggression toward his mOther in the perverse act, in a scenario in which he supplies the Other with jouissance. Just as the perverse subject's mother transgressed his ethical "boundaries," so too is the pervert fixated on a certain method of forcing jouissance (which is often in the form of intense anxiety) on the Other.

Repetition is one of Lacan's four fundamental concepts of psychoanalysis, and the perverse act is one of the most obvious forms of repetition. Repetition is always connected to the real. In repetition, the subject reaches for the lost object and, inevitably, misses it. Of course, for perverse and neurotic subjects, the mother is the fundamental lost object. It is not so much the repetition, but the real as a "missed encounter" (Lacan, 1973/1998a, p. 55) that is important. According to Lacan, trauma was the first form of "the real as [an] encounter" (p. 55) to be noticed by Freud. Trauma frequently appears unveiled (p. 55), as can be seen in nightmares—in which the dreamer awakens the moment before her encounter with object a—and in the perverse act.

The essence of a symptom is repetition, and the perverse act is a major type of symptom found in perversion.[94] "Repetition first appears … *in an action* … As long as we speak of the relations of repetition with the real, this action will remain on our horizon" (Lacan, 1973/1998a, p. 50). An act, as a symptom, ties together components of the imaginary, symbolic, and real orders that reflect the subject's identity.[95] *"It is necessary to radically distinguish the perverse act from the neurotic act. The perverse act* is situated at the level of … *jouissance. The neurotic act* … has no other goal than to sustain … *the effect of desire"* (Lacan, Seminar XIV, June 7, 1967). *The perverse act is a way of managing and limiting jouissance* via a corrective restaging of the pervert's post-alienation relations to the first and second Others. The perverse act thus exemplifies a perverse solution to the inadequacy of the paternal function.

As such, the perverse act involves the perverse subject, someone representing the first Other, and someone representing the lawgiving Other. The perverse act, at the very least, involves the pervert and another person. This other may appropriately be called a victim because the pervert's act always transgresses the limits of consent. The victim plays the role of first Other, but may additionally embody the lawgiving Other. Alternatively, an observer may play the role of the lawgiving Other or a potential or imagined observer (such as a police officer or a religious official) may embody the lawgiving Other. In the pervert's act, the pervert himself is the instrument of the Other's jouissance, and the jouissance he brings to the field of the Other causes the lawgiving Other to put his foot down.

---

94 The evolution of the definition of *symptom* in Lacan's works is deserving of a book-length study. For our purposes, then, we shall define a symptom as follows: a symptom is a master signifier, a signifier that is not linked up to other signifiers in the symbolic order but instead is a self-referential non-sensical structure of jouissance. The symptom is a kernel of jouissance that is responsible for the production of meanings. The symptom, or sinthome, as Lacan called it in his later works, is the fourth ring of his Borromean knot and, as such, ties the imaginary, symbolic, and real together. A person's sinthome is therefore her or his core identity. "The symptom, in essence, is jouissance" (Lacan, 2004, p. 148).

95 An act is "not mere [animal] behavior" (Lacan, 1973/1998a, p. 50) because a subject is ethically bound to assume responsibility for it—even for the unconscious desires which may have been expressed in his act.

In a perverse act, the pervert elaborately stages his fantasy scene by way of a script that varies little over time. (The rigidity of the perverse act is a reliable diagnostic criterion.) Exhibitionists, voyeurs, masochists, and sadists each have their own characteristic type of perverse act. Within each substructure, there is a great degree of individual variation. The common factors are the manner in which each pervert is the instrument of the Other's jouissance and his position with respect to the gaze or the voice. An individual pervert, however, acts according to a fixed repetitive scenario made up of particular signifying elements.

The jouissance derived from the perverse act is subjectively felt to be qualitatively different than sexual intercourse and quantitatively more pleasurable. We shall focus, for the moment, on the exhibitionist. In his book *Sexual Deviation* (1996), psychoanalytic forensic practitioner Ismond Rosen noted the following:

> On exposure, the exhibitionist becomes aware of intense genital sensations and a sense of inner pleasure, in excess of anything else he has experienced, including heterosexual orgasm. There may or may not be an erection and masturbation may or may not be indulged in. The fact that neither erection nor ejaculation is necessary for the experience of specific pleasure is evidence of the hyper-libidinization of the genital area. (p. 180)

In this particular section of his chapter "Exhibitionism, scopophilia, and voyeurism," Rosen neglects the symbolic order and the pervert's relation to the Other.[96] The intense pleasure that the pervert experiences from his perverse act is dependent upon its enactment in relation to the Other.

Let us turn to an example of a perverse act—that of Chris, an exhibitionist. According to Chris, a man in his 50s, he had committed thousands of acts of indecent exposure. He was charged and convicted for less than 10. As a result of the years he spent incarcerated and on parole, paired with his wife having filed for divorce (on account of his sexual offenses), Chris decided to make the prevention of his exhibitionistic acts a priority; in that effort, Chris went beyond the stipulations of his parole and participated in once weekly individual and group psychotherapy sessions.

In his past, Chris often spent hours every day committing acts of indecent exposure. His preferred scene was a large parking lot, such as can be found by a shopping mall. Chris drove to such a parking lot, scanned the scene for police officers, and then parked his car if no police officers were in sight. He then watched for women exiting the shopping mall. When

---

96 Much of Rosen's text does, however, focus more on the symbolic and the pervert's relation to the Other.

he saw a woman who was alone walking toward her car, he followed her. Upon approaching her, he gave her a sexualized compliment of her body. Then, he pulled his penis out through his open fly and masturbated in front of her until she walked, ran, or drove away. At that point, Chris left the scene and committed indecent exposure to another woman. (While in public, Chris almost never masturbated to orgasm.)

Chris maintained that he always hoped that a woman would become aroused by his display and desire to have sexual intercourse with him; this occurred on only two occasions out of thousands. Chris did, in fact, have sex with the woman on those two occasions. In contrast to Chris' conscious avowal, his behavior manifested the opposite desire because he often refused opportunities for sexual intercourse with his wife or with women he briefly dated. In the same vein, Chris said that he wanted a woman to whom he exposed his penis to respond with approval or pleasure, but the response that he actually got from his victim was predictably one suggesting surprise, anger, disgust, or fear. Given the fact that Chris committed acts of indecent exposure so frequently and very rarely saw evidence of his consciously desired response, it is safe to suppose that his truer, unconscious desire was to provoke surprise, anger, disgust, or fear in his victims. As Fink (1997) noted, "a person's concrete actions often give us a far better sense of his or her fundamental fantasy than the fantasies of which he or she is aware, especially at the beginning of an analysis" (p. 272).

The Perverse Act as Means to Propping Up the Paternal Function

Even though the pervert's fantasies and dreams may reflect a limitless jouissance, the structure of reality puts limits on jouissance; a perverse act, therefore, is always a way to manage jouissance. In terms of time, for instance, the duration of perverse acts is limited by the pervert's bodily constraints. Some of the major bodily restrictions include fatigue, hunger, thirst, and the need to urinate or defecate.

In addition, perverse acts are ways of limiting jouissance because of the presence of a lawgiving Other—one which may be imagined or actual. For example, the imagined potential presence of a police officer at the scene of the act led Chris to stop engaging in acts of indecent exposure to prevent himself from being arrested. When a victim screamed for help or reached for her cell phone (probably to call the police), Chris left the scene. The victim's response invoked the reality of a lawgiving Other. Because perverse acts are repetitive and break social/ethical bonds, they are likely to lead to apprehension by the police. Exhibitionists and voyeurs who have been arrested for their crimes speak of feeling shame and a seemingly paradoxical sense of *relief* upon their arrest by lawgiving Others. The experience of relief in such moments is related to the temporary propping up of the paternal function and decrease in jouissance.

Bond, in his book *Lacan at the Scene* (2009), noted that perverts often target law enforcement agents or priests to be a witness to their crimes or to the aftermath of their crimes. In the words of Clavreul (1980), "insofar as he brings a look, the Other will be the partner and above all the accomplice of the perverse act" (p. 226). The presence of the Other is necessary for the pervert. Likewise, Bond (2009) pointed out that while a neurotic murderer will often try to hide the body in "some inconspicuous corner in order that the body might remain undiscovered" (p. 46), a perverse murderer will go to no such trouble. In contrast, the murder victim of a pervert "lies in the grass (staring up at the sky) in the middle of a pleasant enough garden, and in full view of a nearby house, a factor that also implies close proximity to numerous potential witnesses" (p. 46). Such actions increase a perverse murderer's chances of being apprehended by the police. In addition, a perverse murderer commits his crime in part because in so doing he provides law enforcement agents with what they want: a crime and a criminal to apprehend; a perverse murderer thus acts as the instrument of the Other's jouissance and makes the Other whole.

In cases of masochism and exhibitionism, the victim of the perverse act may herself embody the lawgiving Other. The victim of the masochist, having been brought by the masochist to a certain unbearable level of anxiety, enunciates the law in the form of a command such as "Stop!" The exhibitionist's victim may embody the lawgiving Other by alerting others or perhaps even simply by leaving the scene. In sadism, however, the sadist himself plays the role of lawgiving Other, exacting punishment and placing limits on the jouissance of his victim while at the same time identifying with him or her. The pervert, by way of his act, either himself or gets anOther to bolster the lawgiving Other through jouissance-ridden invocations or gazes of protest that substitute for enunciations of the moral law itself.

Defiling the Other in the Perverse Act

The pervert's ambivalence toward the mOther is manifested in the perverse act: he is captivated by the Other for whom he experiences both "[a]ffection and hostility" (Freud, 1927/1961, p. 157). As I mentioned in chapter 4, the victim of a perverse act is almost always a woman, and this is best accounted for by the fact that the first Other of a pervert is almost always a woman. In the perverse act, the pervert unconsciously displaces his hostility toward his mother onto his female victim. Women are for the pervert prototypical Others lacking in jouissance, and, as object *a*, he provides them with an excess of jouissance (which is often subjectively experienced by the victim as anxiety, horror, or intense shame). In stripping his victims of their consent and forcing this level of jouissance upon them, the pervert effaces the subjectivity of his victims—just as his subjectivity was disrespected by his mOther. The pervert reduces the Other to the level of jouissance.

It is instructive that the pervert's fundamental relation to the Other is to function as the instrument of the Other's jouissance insofar as that relation reveals that the pervert conceives the Other as A̸—as lacking in jouissance. According to Nobus (2000), the fantasies of the pervert are oriented toward defiling "pure and unblemished, yet deficient and disconcerted objects that are desperately in need of [jouissance]. On the level of the fantasy, the pervert does not desire lascivious and voluptuous studs (or vixens) [as the neurotic might], but ostensibly innocent, sexually deprived angels" (p. 44). In the perverse act, the pervert defiles his victims, shocking them and subverting their conventional sense of decorum and of the limits of jouissance. In Clavreul's (1980) words, "[M]ost important for the pervert is the fact that the Other be sufficiently engaged, inscribed in the social structure, notably as someone respectable, for each new experience to have the sense of a debauchery where the Other is extracted from his system in acceding to a jouissance that the pervert has mastered" (p. 227). Correspondingly, the perverse analysand, in the beginning stages of analysis, often attempts to place the analyst in the role of a "pure and unblemished" Other and to provide jouissance to the analyst.

In the perverse act, the pervert forces jouissance upon a non-consenting Other, and in so doing expresses aggression. The pervert, despite what he may consciously believe, actively orchestrates his role as object-cause of the Other's jouissance. As Verhaeghe suggested (2001b), *the pervert's activity is a type of corrective restaging of the "trauma"*[97] *he experienced "passively" as a child at the hands of his mOther.* In the perverse act, the mOther is forced to play a passive role to the pervert who actively constructs the scenario. Nevertheless, the perverse act in all other respects maintains the roles of the pervert and the mOther.

Because the pervert's existence is permeated more by the level of demand and the imaginary order than by the level of desire and the symbolic order, he is subjected to concerns related to power, control, aggression, and rivalry more so than is the neurotic. Verhaeghe (2001b) suggested conceptualizing the future pervert's relationship with his mOther as one in which he was victimized. As an adult, the pervert reverses these roles by taking an active stance and pushing the Other into the position of victim.

---

97 The term trauma should here be understood as a broad term encompassing a wide variety and degree of subjectively felt pain rather than what might legally qualify as sexual or physical abuse.

> The clinical descriptions demonstrate time and again that the perverse scenario comes down to the installation of a relationship of power; the other has to be mastered. Even the masochist pulls the strings from start to finish; he or she dictates what the other has to do ... [A]dult perverse behavior ... [shows] the necessity of taking the active position in order to control the other. (pp. 84, 87)

Just as neurotic (usually hysteric) individuals who mutilate their bodies are often "actively" repeating and inscribing a past physical or psychological trauma, so too do perverse individuals reenact a traumatic relation to the mOther with the proviso that they are the ones pulling the strings.

We should remember, however, that Lacan said the pervert's position as object-cause of the Other's jouissance is "the foundation of an identification disavowed by the subject" (1973/1998a, p. 186). In other words, the pervert disavows his role in a perverse act, believing himself to be the one in control when it is more true at anOther level to say that he is a passive object (-cause of the Other's jouissance) than an active subject. Some of the pervert's anxiety is relieved by his belief in this enjoyable fiction.

Because the pervert's original traumatic relation to his mOther involved his mOther's excess of power and control in relation to him, the pervert in his act and in his relationships defensively avoids putting himself in interpersonal situations that run the risk of stripping him of his power and control. In the case of masochism, this may at first seem counter-intuitive, but the masochist's total subjection to the will of his partner is nothing but a façade. *The perverse act, then, involves five key relational dynamics: immodesty/shame, jouissance/anxiety, control, a breach of consent, and the invocation of a temporarily powerful lawgiving Other.*

A perverse act is fundamentally related to either the scopic or the invocatory drive. As exemplified in the case of Chris, who gets himself seen by a female victim, "[t]he dialectic of the drive is profoundly different both from that which belongs to the order of love and from that which belongs to the well-being of the subject" (Lacan, 1973/1998a, p. 206). Clearly, for Chris, being a slave to the scopic drive (by committing perverse acts) does nothing to increase his well-being and has nothing to do with love.

Jouissance and the Pervert's Fundamental Relation to the Other

Perverts suffer from an excess of jouissance. Correspondingly, there are four major paths by which they strive to manage their jouissance. The first two were mentioned above, and may be achieved—amongst other ways—through a perverse act. The first major path is by staging a situation in which the paternal function is bolstered. Because this path most directly links up with the causative problem of the perverse structure, this is the most effective way that the pervert has at his disposal of managing his jouissance. This path includes instances of sublimation. Second, the pervert, in his role as object a in relation to the Other, can manage his jouissance by taking "active" control, holding the reins.

Third is the pathway of desire. As I mentioned in previous chapters, desire sets limits to jouissance. Because the state of being in love is characterized by desirousness, when a pervert falls in love or loves his children his excessive jouissance is temporarily reduced. In Lacan's (2004) words, "only love allows jouissance to condescend to desire" (p. 209). Given that a pervert is restricted in his subjectivity and in his ability to desire, his desire fails to "do the job" of limiting his excessive jouissance. Nevertheless, just as a neurotic's desire can be fixated or repressed, so too can the desire of a pervert be fixated and repressed. (This is clearly shown in Fink's 2003 case of W, a fetishist who became more in touch with his desires as the analysis progressed.) Therefore, the process of psychoanalysis, which aims to set free and increase one's ability to desire, may aid a pervert in the quest to manage jouissance. Lacanian analysis works on behalf of the analysand's Eros.

Fourth, drugs—whether prescription or not—that slow down the central nervous system or reduce his sexual hormone levels can reduce the amount of jouissance experienced by the pervert. This fourth path brings up a much-debated treatment question concerning whether or not it is clinically advantageous or ethical to prescribe psychotropic medication to analysands. I will discuss this question in a bit more detail in chapter 8.

Each substructure of perversion has its own particular fashion of solving the problems caused by the inadequacy of the paternal function. Each substructure has a particularly strong relationship to either the gaze or the voice, and so the quaternary schema (Miller, 2006c, p. 27) presented in chapter 4 is reproduced below with the addition of the fetishist to the schema. There is a non-symmetrical relationship between exhibitionism and voyeurism that is parallel to the non-symmetrical relationship between masochism and sadism. In other words, the exhibitionist and the masochist relate to object a in the same manner, and the voyeur and the sadist relate to object a in the same manner. The fetishist, on the other hand, makes the gaze appear "in" the fetish itself such that the gaze appears in the fields of both subject and Other.

Before I turn to detailed discussions of each substructure of perversion and to the primary objects a that correspond to them, it is important to note that the *superficial* traits, behaviors, and discourse associated with each substructure are not necessarily mutually exclusive with the others. In the case of a neurotic analysand, her symptoms and discourse sometimes make it initially difficult to distinguish between a diagnosis of hysteria or obsession, because it is common for a person with a substructure of obsession to have some traditionally hysteric complaints, such as psychosomatic symptoms, and vice versa. We will notice that the same is true for perversion. To use the example of Chris, while his exhibitionistic act involves both the gaze and the voice, his primary object *a* is the gaze, and his essential relation to the Other is that of the instrument of the Other's jouissance who makes the gaze appear in the field of the Other.

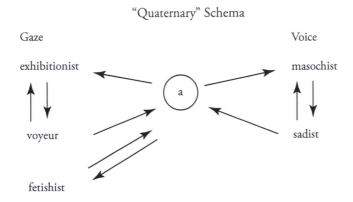

"Quaternary" Schema

Gaze   Voice

exhibitionist   masochist

voyeur   sadist

fetishist

The Gaze and Shame: Exhibitionism, Voyeurism, and Fetishism

> You grasp here the ambiguity of what is at issue when we speak of the scopic drive. The gaze is this object lost and suddenly refound in the conflagration of shame, by the introduction of the other.
>
> Lacan (1973/1998a, p. 182)

> The gaze I encounter is, not a seen gaze, but a gaze I imagine in the field of the Other.
>
> Lacan (1973/1998a, p. 84)

The gaze is intimately related to the affect of shame. As previously stated, the primary drive for the exhibitionist, the voyeur, and the fetishist is the scopic drive, and so shame plays a prominent role in these substructures. According to Lacan, the exhibitionist makes the gaze appear in the field of the Other, while the voyeur makes the gaze appear in himself in order to plug up the hole in the Other. Correspondingly, the exhibitionist's aim is to produce a feeling of shame in the Other, while the voyeur himself experiences shame. Following what Lacan says about fetishism, it is my hypothesis that the fetishist makes the gaze appear "in" the fetish, which means that the gaze appears both in the field of the subject and in the field of the Other.

It is notable that the gaze and the scopic drive of a pervert differ from those of a neurotic insofar as their ideational representatives have only been affected by primal repression and disavowal rather than by both primal and secondary repression. In effect, what this means is not only that the scopic drive (and the drives in general) of a pervert is "stronger" than that of a neurotic but also that the lawgiving Other has had little, if any, impact on his scopic drive. When considering the function of the scopic drive as it functions in perversion, then, we must take into account the kind of Other under whose influence the scopic drive was re-written.

First, the scopic drive is related to a primordial Other, to an Other prior to the one who judges. The primordial Other does not judge but "only sees or [allows to] be seen" (Miller, 2006d, p. 13). Shame is a primary affect in relation to the primordial Other. Within the realm of the scopic drive, nudity and the sight of genitalia are the first provocations of shame. Correspondingly, the importance in perversion of the image of the boy's penis has to do with the modesty and shame of both the boy and his mOther.

In contrast, "guilt is the effect on the subject of an Other that judges, thus of an Other that contains the values that the subject has supposedly transgressed … guilt is [therefore] related to desire" (Miller, 2006d, p. 13). Because perverts, in comparison with neurotics, have less desire and were much less impacted by the lawgiving Other, it follows that perverts also have much less capacity for guilt. The importance of this fact should be emphasized because the current one-size-fits-all treatment for sexual offenders depends upon the success of methods that aim to appeal to and increase their feelings of guilt. Clinicians who try to make perversely structured sexual offenders feel guilty about what they have done are simply barking up the wrong tree.

In "Kant with Sade," Lacan implies that shame and modesty—antonymic terms which are reciprocally related to each other—have to do with jouissance.

> jouissance is that by which Sadean experience is modified. For it only proposes to monopolize a will after having already traversed it in order to instate itself at the inmost core of the subject whom it provokes beyond that by offending his sense of modesty [*pudeur*]. For modesty is an amboceptor with respect to the circumstances of being: between the two, the one's immodesty by itself violating the other's modesty. A connection that could justify, were such justification necessary, what I said before regarding the subject's assertion in the Other's place. (1963/2006a, pp. 771–772)

Interpreting this passage, Miller (2006d, p. 13) said that shame and modesty are related to the jouissance that "instate[s] itself at the inmost core of the subject" (Lacan, 1963/2006a, p. 771). When Lacan said, "modesty is an amboceptor with respect to the circumstances of being" (p. 771), he suggested that, within the "circumstances of being," which are constituted by the primordial relationship between the subject and the Other, modesty is attached to both the subject and the Other. When the subject is immodest, the Other's modesty is correspondingly violated, and vice versa. Jouissance is bound up in this amboceptive relationship.

And so it is that the jouissance of the exhibitionist, voyeur, and fetishist becomes fixated on the image of the genitalia, which is to say that the jouissance which perhaps most defines a pervert belonging to one of these three subtypes is an effect of his relation to the mOther mediated by the immodesty of the scopic drive. Likewise, the exhibitionist, voyeur, and fetishist often speak about embarrassment, modesty, and shame. The above quote from "Kant with Sade," of course, equally applies to masochism and sadism in relation to the invocatory drive, such that violations of modesty are integral to each of the substructures of perversion.

In perversion, the pervert tries to prop up the existence of the Other by appealing to the primordial Other, by appealing to the Other that is most firmly woven into the fabric of his symbolic world—the primordial Other of the gaze or the primordial Other of the voice. By pushing the primordial Other beyond the limits of the pleasure principle, the pervert tries to ensure that the lawgiving Other will make its presence known and intervene.

Exhibitionism[98]

[A]n exhibitionist does not expose himself only to young girls, he also sometimes does so in front of a tabernacle.

Lacan (2006b, p. 253)

---

98 Rosen (1996) co-led a psychodynamically-informed long-term process group for male exhibitionists, and he found that there were major distinctions between what he called the "simple" or "regressive" type of exhibitionist and the "phobic-impulsive" type. "The first is the simple or regressive type, where the exhibitionist act follows as the result of some rather obvious social or sexual trauma, disappointment or loss, or as an accompaniment to a severe mental or physical illness, including the vicissitudes of old age and alcoholism. These people tend to the [sic] rather reserved and shy with social and sexual inhibitions and fear, but their personalities are on the whole relatively good ones, as seen in their intimate associations and work records ... Personality disturbance is much more intense in the second group which is the phobic-impulsive type ... In this group one finds persons who regularly exhibit and become recidivists. Where the impulsive aspect predominates they are often of an amoral cast of mind, prone to other forms of character disorder and actual perversion such as transvestism and voyeurism, as well as the commission of crimes of stealing" (p. 176). This method of classification is one which can aid the clinician in differentiating between a neurotic individual who has committed an act or several acts of indecent exposure and a perverse individual who, unless very young, has committed numerous acts of indecent exposure.

> It is at the level of the field of the Other deserted by *jouissance* that the exhibitionistic act situates itself to make the gaze emerge there.
>
> Lacan (2006b, p. 254)

The Other is necessary in perversion, and this is especially obvious in the case of the exhibitionist. The exhibitionist depends upon the presence of an audience; exposing his genitals to the mirror is of no interest to him (Miller, 1996b, p. 318). Neither would the exhibitionist be interested in exposing his genitals to women at a nude beach. Instead, the exhibitionist is driven to show his genitals to a series of Others because, for the exhibitionist, "the jouissance at stake is the Other's" (Lacan, 2006b, p. 256). The exhibitionist shows his penis to a female Other "to try and produce shame in the Other, shame for not being the same. The exhibitionist tries to make Woman exist; indeed we might say that Woman doesn't exist *except* for the exhibitionist" (Miller, 1996b, p. 318). In making a show for the Other of having the penis (as a biological organ) and in getting his possession of it seen by an Other, the exhibitionist makes object *a* as the gaze appear in the field of the first Other as deserted by jouissance. (The first Other became deserted by jouissance through the process of castration in which s/he lost some of her bodily jouissance.)

In order to provide the Other with jouissance, the exhibitionist makes the Other look at his erect penis, and in so doing shows her what she lacks. During his act of indecent exposure, the exhibitionist's interest is centered upon the Other and her reaction to his display. He gazes at the expression in her eyes and on her face and also listens for a possible vocal response. The exhibitionist's aim is to provide the Other with jouissance in the form of a shock or feelings of shame, anxiety, or horror. Lacan said,

> It is not easy to define what a gaze is … People wonder what the effects of an exhibition are—namely, whether or not it frightens the witness who seems to provoke it. People ask themselves whether the exhibitionist intends to provoke the shame, fear, or echo, a ferocious or consenting reaction. But this is not the crux of the scopophilic drive, which you can characterize as you wish, as active or passive, the choice is yours—in appearance, it is passive, since it offers up something to be seen. The crux is, strictly speaking and above all, to make the gaze appear in the field of the Other. (2006b, pp. 253–254)

The epiphanic moment of the exhibitionistic act occurs when the gaze appears in the Other: The shocked, horrified, repulsed, and anxiety-filled reaction of the victim is important insofar as it is the sign that she is experiencing the gaze in herself.[99]

Furthermore, Lacan said, "It is not only the victim who is concerned in exhibitionism, it is the victim as referred to some other who is looking at him" (1973/1998a, p. 183). In addition to the gaze of the victim and the gaze of the exhibitionist, then, there is a third gaze which is the imagined gaze of third party. It is not the exhibitionist's gaze that makes the victim feel ashamed, but instead this third party's gaze. In other words, "if someone were to be watching me [the victim], what would s/he think?"

"The exhibitionist is, in effect, grabbed by the jouissance of the Other's [the victim's] watchful eye" (Miller, 2006c, p. 27). At the moment of the appearance of the gaze in the field of the Other, the exhibitionist feels strongly connected to the Other.[100] When the victim flees the scene or calls the police, the law temporarily appears and puts an end to the gaze and to the over-proximate connection between the pervert and the Other.

The setting for the exhibitionistic act is the public sphere, and the exhibitionist exposes his penis to a woman who is unknown to him.[101] Each of these common criteria for an act of indecent exposure subverts social norms of morality, going against the rules of the neurotic's lawgiving Other. This underscores the idea that the pervert's goal is to attract the attention of a lawgiving Other so that limits may be set to his jouissance. Were the pervert's act to more subtly transgress social mores, then neither would the gaze appear in the Other nor would the victim or another person be sufficiently riled to invoke the lawgiving Other.

Another diagnostically important difference between an act of exhibitionism and a "normal neurotic" sexual act is that, in the former, the gaze takes the place of touch. It is very rare that an (perverse) exhibitionist touches his victim. This highlights the importance of the gaze in

---

99 This confirms that the fundamental aim of the pervert is not to strip the victim of her subjectivity and reduce her to an object, but rather to highlight her lack of jouissance that is characteristic of subjectivity and then to attempt to fill her lack with the gaze.

100 See chapter 6, in which the case of Ray, an exhibitionist, is presented. Ray describes feeling a "little connection" with his victim at the moment of the appearance of the gaze.

101 The following is Rosen's (1996) explanation of the exhibitionist choosing a stranger for the victim of his perverse act as well as how the pervert's mother often held a puritanical attitude toward sex: "Exposing to the stranger is still dangerous but preferable to exposing to the familiar woman who stands for mother because of the greater danger inherent in the castration complex. Many patients were extremely prudish with their wives; they took care never to let each other be seen in the nude, and their pattern of sexual behavior in intercourse was rigidly conventional. There is general agreement in the literature on the puritanical attitude towards sex in the families of exhibitionists as well as in themselves. The highly inhibited and shy exhibitionists are therefore a result of the excessive reaction formations against scopophilia" (p. 186).

exhibitionism as distinct from the exhibitionist's sexual and romantic desires. What is more, the primacy of the gaze paired with the other highly controlled aspects of the exhibitionist's act (including choosing for his victim a stranger and choosing for his venue a public place where his victim's surprise is ensured), go a long way toward giving the exhibitionist a sense of "safety" and being in control.

The more the pervert (of any substructure) *feels* in control of the scenario and assured of the intervention of a lawgiving Other, the less threatening will be the Other's proximity. By choosing for his victim a stranger, the exhibitionist keeps the Other at a safe distance because a stranger is less likely to consciously remind him of his mOther than is a woman with whom he is acquainted (on account of having less available information about her to compare and contrast with his mother). The exhibitionist usually places himself at a significant physical distance from his victim, and this contributes to his sense that he will not be overwhelmed by the presence of the Other. Likewise, he avoids touching the victim, and this makes us wonder what the phenomenological experience of the exhibitionist would be were a victim to touch the exhibitionist in some fashion. Finally, the exhibitionist tries to ensure his control over the scenario by catching the Other off guard and not giving her the opportunity to consent. Instead, he "listens" to the "voice" of the Other's will-to-jouissance, viewing the Other as a subject lacking in jouissance and obeying his inner compulsion to fill her with jouissance. "[T]he jouissance at stake is the Other's" (Lacan, 2006b, p. 256), and the pervert's anxiety is relieved when he can, through a perverse act, transfer some of his surplus jouissance to the Other's account. *What the pervert disavows is his position as object-cause of the Other's jouissance; he believes himself to be a powerful Other and his victim to be reduced to an object, when in fact the truth of the matter is that it is the other way around.*

The Pervert's Ambivalent Relation to the mOther

Outside of the exhibitionistic act, the exhibitionist attempts to keep Others at a distance through similar strategies. In general, perverts have ambivalent relationships with their mOthers. Consequently, *the various conscious efforts of perverts to gain more independence from their mOthers often are foiled by their unconscious wishes to remain close to them.* In addition, the fundamental relation between the pervert and the Other is a qualitatively different relation than that of the neurotic and the Other that often appears to be a matter of quantity. In other words, it appears to our neurotic eyes that a pervert is closer to his mOther than is a neurotic, but this quantitative difference masks a more essential qualitative difference. The pervert, not having sufficiently internalized the lawgiving Other, is joined at the hip (or eyes, as the case may be) to his mOther and must make creative efforts to conjure up a temporary lawgiving Other. As a result, the pervert's efforts to bring about a permanent separation from his mOther are ultimately doomed to fail, although some temporary solutions can be quite effective and law-abiding.

Fink's (2003) case study of W provides us with an excellent example of the lack of success of the pervert's efforts to bring about further separation from the Other.

> After W had been with a woman for the first time at age 26, his mother asked if he had "entered her." He responded by yelling, "This is none of your business." When he told her of his first adult homosexual experience at age 36, she made it clear that she felt this could not possibly have been what *he* wanted, saying that "these homos have tried to recruit you." Telling her at age 46 that he had a boyfriend, she commented, "Still trying to get out from under your mother?" The tone of ownership seems quite unmistakable in many of her comments to him. (*We should not, however, overlook the fact that he continued to tell her about his love life, thereby keeping her involved in it.*) (p. 59, emphasis added)

W's anger and expressed desire for separation, evident in his yelling to his mother that his love life was none of her business, sharply contrast with the fact that W continued to tell his mother about his love life. This ambivalence is characteristic of the pervert's relationship to the mOther.

In the same vein, both Chris and Ray often spoke about their mothers and their efforts to untie themselves from their mothers' apron strings. Ray all but moved out of his parents' home as a teenager, and then quickly joined the army upon turning 18. This required that he move across the country from where his mother lived. Very similarly, Chris joined the Air Force when he graduated high school, and correspondingly moved across the country from his mother's residence. Nevertheless, their physical distance from their mothers did nothing to change their fundamental relations to the Other. Both committed acts of indecent exposure throughout their involvement with the military, and Ray was dishonorably discharged on account of it. Within a few years, both Chris and Ray moved back to their hometowns and lived in close proximity to their mothers. In another case, a sadistic analysand who was gainfully employed chose to move back in with his parents in his late 20s and was still living with them in his mid-40s with no plans or desire to move out.

In addition, the fact that Chris and Ray both enlisted in the military—strongly associated as it is with the law—is suggestive of their desires to prop up the paternal function. Indeed, it is common for perverts of all substructures to form such associations with organizations representative of the law. Other instances of which I am aware include the priesthood and practicing law.

Chris and Ray both spoke about the shame and embarrassment they caused their mothers as a result of their exhibitionism. Each of them described his mother as an Other partially devoid of jouissance, as a prudish woman who thought it improper to talk about sexuality and who was especially concerned with upholding a certain appearance of decorum to others—whether true or not. In committing and being charged with acts of indecent exposure, they shocked and embarrassed their mothers. Ray's mother went so far as to move in order to avoid the gazes of the neighbors. What is more, Ray said that he enjoyed embarrassing his mother. Exhibitionists go a step further than their mOthers in deriding the lawgiving Other because they refuse, in their acts of indecent exposure, even to put up a façade of abiding by the social mores of the lawgiving Other.

Chris and Ray each have loved only one woman thus far in their lifetimes, and each woman metonymically stood in for the mOther. Both relationships were long-term, but Chris and Ray did many things to ensure that the relationships would not be especially close ones. For example, Ray broke up with his girlfriend, Susan, at least two or three times per year, and refused to live with her until they had been dating for five years. Even then, Susan moved back in with her parents several times a year. Furthermore, Ray assented to saying "I love you" to Susan only very rarely and on his terms, not hers; if she asked him to tell her he loved her, he invariably refused. Nevertheless, Ray was dependent upon Susan. During the periods of time in which Susan and Ray were not in a relationship, Ray said that he no longer knew who he was or how to live his life.

Likewise, Chris' marriage failed after he had been incarcerated for the third time on account of his exhibitionism, and Chris ostensibly did all he could to get back together with her. Chris said he had "no identity without [his wife and kids]" and said that they were what made his life worth living. Nevertheless, he said that, even if he and his ex-wife remarried, he would never move back in with them because he liked the independence of living by himself. What is more, Chris seemed to annoy his ex-wife and even his children by helping out around their house without their consent—buying groceries and household items, embarking on home improvement projects, and re-organizing things.

Exhibitionism and the Oral Drive

As I mentioned in chapter 4, the manifestations of the oral drive are often primary features of perversion. Of the two cases discussed briefly so far, both Chris and Ray spoke easily, often, and in great detail in their group psychotherapy sessions. Chris was especially aroused by female breasts, and especially enjoyed eating. Ray, for his part, smoked at least a pack of cigarettes a day. When he tried to quit on one occasion, he bought several large bags of lollipops to serve as a substitute. Likewise, Rosen (1996) noted that

> certain exhibitionists seem to be fixated at the oral level. Thus, loquacious Dick described himself as a "mouth in trousers." The hostility of the oral phase, seen as biting and devouring, is projected on to the outside world and a similar retaliation is expected. It is the strength of this fixation which gives to later objects such as the female genitalia their hostile oral character. (p. 181)

Enuresis and Exhibitionism

It is my hypothesis that enuresis is a common feature of exhibitionism and fetishism based on the fact that both Chris and Ray wet themselves until they were teenagers, as well as on the research presented in the article "Enuresis: A Functional Equivalent of a Fetish" (Calef, Weinshel, Renik, & Lloyd Mayer, 1980). Shortly after the dissolution of their symptoms of enuresis, Chris and Ray began committing acts of indecent exposure, and so it is likely that the two symptoms are related. Ray's enuresis is described in detail in chapter 6. In perversion, enuresis is a symptom that is related to castration fears. In Ray's and Chris' lives, enuresis functioned to keep them especially close with their mothers while at the same time expressing aggression toward their mothers (because their mothers had to clean up the mess left by their uncontrolled penises).

Chris described his father as a monstrous figure who threw "temper tantrums" and whipped Chris and Chris' siblings with a belt seemingly at random and without providing a good reason as to why they deserved to be punished. When Chris saw his father take off his belt, Chris would become afraid and wet himself. Sometimes, this had the effect of disgusting his father so that Chris was able to avoid getting beaten. Chris' mother comforted him after his father became angry at him, assuring him that he had done nothing wrong.

Chris said that his father's feelings toward him seemed to be characterized either by anger or by not wanting to have anything to do with him. Chris reported that his father became angry at him and his siblings for being "normal rambunctious kids" and for trying to get his attention and love. Chris' father preferred to leave all of the child-rearing duties to his wife. Correspondingly, Chris' father adequately filled the function of the Name-of-the-Father so that Chris underwent primal repression, but he was unable to fill the role of lawgiving Other. Chris was keenly aware that his father was childish and inconsistent with his "temper tantrums" and that his father preferred to let his mother have an especially close relationship with him.

Chris' enuresis was a castration-related symptom. Chris' enuresis was one way in which he avoided getting punished at all by his father and stood up for his right to jouissance—his right to be a loud, rambunctious kid. Chris' enuresis was a message that said that Chris was a "momma's boy" even as an adolescent.

After Chris peed himself, Chris' mother washed his urine-soaked underwear, and so Chris' symptom was also a call to his mOther. In group sessions, Chris said he felt angry with his mother because she never intervened on his behalf. He felt she should have been alarmed that he was "peeing [his] pants" out of fear. Chris said he understood and empathized with his father's whipping him more than with his mother's inaction. One aspect of the above is a common formulation in perversion, in which the pervert takes the side of the father against the mother, hoping thereby to bolster the weak father function. In using the phrase "peeing [his] pants"—a phrase used to suggest that someone laughed so hard and uncontrollably that he lost control of his bladder—Chris suggested that he was not only afraid of being whipped by his father but also at some level enjoyed it. At an unconscious level, Chris did not really want his mother to wrest from him what little relationship he had with his father, but instead he wanted his mother to see that he enjoyed it. The fact that Chris knew his mother had the dirty job of washing his urine-soaked underwear corroborates the idea that Chris expressed anger at his mother through his enuresis, for which he held his mother responsible.

Case Example Excerpts of Exhibitionism Considered

Rosen (1996) provided the following example of an exhibitionist patient who met the criteria for his "phobic-impulsive" type—the type that is most likely to fall in the category of perversion. "For example, Peter, a highly intelligent patient, had constant recurring fantasies that his genitals would be bitten off by sharks in the swimming pool, bath water, and bed, which was evidence of his severe phallic castration anxiety expressed in phobic terms" (p. 176). Peter's "constant recurring *fantasies*" (p. 176, emphasis added) of getting his genitals bitten off by sharks clearly suggest that he wishes, at some Other level, to be castrated. The source of his anxiety is not so much the possible presence of genital-eating sharks but rather their absence—or the absence of an adequately forceful lawgiving Other. Notice that Peter's fantasy is that "sharks" rather than a single shark bite off his genitals. Perhaps he unconsciously reasoned that just one shark could not do the job. Instead, it would take several sharks to be able to castrate him. After all, his own father was, by himself, insufficient to instigate the process of castration. Peter's father, mother, or both of them may have contributed to the creation of the shark fantasies and to their locales in a swimming pool, a bathtub, and a bed. Correspondingly, Peter spoke about his "early memories of seeing little girls' genitals which had been, as it were, cut off" (p. 197).

Chris and the Letter or "What Happened to 'the Customer is Always Right?'"

On several occasions, Chris wrote a letter to an authority figure (representing the lawgiving Other) in which he complained about the care he received from one of that authority figure's employees (representing a mOther figure). Each time, Chris hoped that the authority figure would see that a moral law had been broken, would enforce the rules more strictly on his or her employee, and would apologize to Chris. Chris found a creative and law-abiding way to prop up his paternal function by lodging a formal complaint to someone representing a lawgiving Other against a mOther figure.

On one occasion, Chris dined at a chain restaurant where he had dined many times before and usually ordered the same dish. This time, Chris was served by a rude waiter and had a problem with his meal. The waiter argued with Chris about the problem, trying to tell Chris that the meal was fine the way it was. Chris insisted that the meal was prepared differently than it usually was, and he finally succeeded in getting the waiter to take back the meal and fix it to his liking. When the bill came, Chris found he had been charged extra for the alteration in the meal, and Chris hotly contested this with the waiter, who was unwilling to reduce the price of the meal. Chris spoke with the manager, who then took the side of the waiter against Chris. Chris paid the bill but wrote a lengthy letter of complaint to the head of the company. His letter was appropriately re-routed to the customer service department, and, about six months later, Chris received a generic response of apology, along with a gift certificate. Chris was very pleased with this victory. Nevertheless, years after the event, he still recounted his story with a considerable degree of anger.

On a similar occasion, Chris went to a chain fast food restaurant and ordered his usual meal. The cashier overcharged him by about fifteen cents, and when Chris pointed out this error to her, she disagreed with him and told him she had rung the order up correctly. Chris continued to argue with her to no avail, and so he asked to speak with the manager. The manager spoke with Chris and refunded him his fifteen cents. Chris had been sufficiently upset by this incident that he spoke about it in a group session. In exploring the importance of his having been shortchanged at the fast food restaurant, Chris found the occasion to tell the group about the previous occasion at the chain restaurant.

Group participants recalled a similar event in Chris' life, in which he wrote a letter of complaint to his psychiatrist (a woman) about the poor treatment he was receiving from her at a treatment facility for sexual offenders. The letter was well over five pages long and detailed how he felt treated like a person without dignity and a voice of his own. Chris' chief complaints were lobbed at the psychiatrist. Chris' psychiatrist read the letter and shared it with Chris' judge, with whom she was friends. (Chris knew that they were acquainted.) The psychiatrist reportedly felt "threatened" by the letter, and she succeeded in getting Chris, who was on parole, put back in prison.

I read the letter in question, and it seemed relatively innocuous to me. Although Chris' anger at his psychiatrist was emphatically stated, Chris made no threats to harm her. Instead, Chris emphasized that he thought his psychiatrist deserved to feel ashamed of the way she was running the treatment center. In the letter, Chris said that he did not think that his psychiatrist was an empathic type of person who would listen to his complaints and make efforts to change her style of working with him—although that did not stop him from writing the letter to her. Chris perhaps felt that his verbal attack on the psychiatrist went much deeper than what appeared in his letter.

In each situation, Chris was angry at someone who represented his mOther. The food service workers and the psychiatrist were all in roles in which their jobs were to give some kind of care to Chris. Chris was angry at each mOther figure not only for failing to give him adequate nurturing, but also for disrespecting him. Chris felt that his rights as a "consumer" and as a subject were violated when a mOther figure made a mistake such as "short-changing" him and then refused to listen and agree with Chris, thereby not assuming responsibility for her mistake. Chris' anger and frustration mounted when he felt that his voice and feelings did not matter to the mOther figure, and that she was going to act in accordance with her will and desires and not those of a lawgiving Other (such as the corporate rules and guidelines).

Chris became very distressed in these seemingly minimally frustrating situations because they mirrored the problems he encountered with the first Other as a young child. The other (mostly neurotic) psychotherapy group participants wondered why Chris was so significantly distressed by these scenarios. Indeed, the majority of neurotic subjects would not have become nearly as upset by these inadequacies in the provision of service as did Chris, and, in any case, would not have been upset for the same reasons.

In these scenarios, Chris got a father figure involved in his dispute with the mOther figure.[102] In so doing, Chris temporarily propped up his

---

102 One of the workers was a man, but he also functioned as a mOther figure just as male analysts often are positioned as such in the transference.

paternal function. Because the mOther figure acted as if there were no law above and beyond her own desires, Chris himself attracted the attention of the lawgiving Other and tried to enlist his help. Chris' complaint against the mOther figure was that he had not been treated fairly, had not been listened to, and had not received care that was in his best interest, but instead received care that served the interests of the mOther figure. In each instance, the father figure was professionally obligated to respond in some way to Chris' call for help.

When Chris was in the role of "consumer" in relation to a company employee, Chris had more power to make himself seen and understood than he did in his role as a child in relation to his mOther and disinterested father. Chris said he felt his anxiety and anger considerably decreased when he received an apologetic response to his letter and when the manager refunded him his fifteen cents. Interestingly, Chris said that his anxiety, but not his anger, decreased when the judge sent him back to jail. Perhaps, in Chris' case, simply being incarcerated was a way to prop up his paternal function.[103] Chris' anger remained because he thought that the judge, who was friends with his psychiatrist, had been coerced into re-incarcerating Chris by the forceful influence of the psychiatrist.

Chris and Symbolic Achievements

Chris had been receiving Social Security Disability (SSD) payments for well over a decade, and that had been his sole means of income. Chris had no physical disability but instead received SSD because of a diagnosis of major depression at the time of his application for SSD. Since then, Chris continuously received SSD checks without having to undergo another evaluation. Several of the participants in his psychotherapy group voiced that they did not believe that Chris met the criteria for mental health SSD, which amount to being unable to work because of mental health issues. However, Chris wanted to remain on SSD, having no desire to work. When defending himself to the group, Chris reasoned that, were he to get a job, he would quickly become overwhelmed with anxiety and might consequently commit an act of indecent exposure. Chris was content to spend the majority of his time at home, watching television, masturbating (he limited himself to masturbating three days a week for several hours at a time), researching his family tree, and leaving his house to visit his children and attend his individual and group psychotherapy sessions.

On a related note, Chris spoke on several occasions about an experience at a job he had a few decades ago as a cook at a restaurant. The dishwasher

---

103 This is a conjecture on my part, and I am by no means suggesting that all perverts should be incarcerated for life as a way to manage the problems inherent to the perverse structure.

quit, and Chris volunteered to take on the duties of the dishwasher, in addition to his job as a cook, until a new dishwasher could be hired. This was a great deal of extra work. Although Chris did get paid for the overtime hours he put in, he complained that never once during the half a year that he held these two job responsibilities, did his boss thank him or give him positive recognition. Feeling resentful and angry, Chris quit his job. Chris had felt similarly resentful in the military when he repeatedly got passed over for promotions. What is more, in group, Chris often complained that he was "bending over backwards" to help his ex-wife and children around the house, but that not only did they not thank him, but they often expressed annoyance at his frequent presence and his meddling in their affairs.

Chris, of course, chose to continue bending over backwards for the Other in situations in which he consistently received apathetic or negative reactions from the Other. This, therefore, is something of a masochistic position as well as a repetition compulsion. Chris, not having received his due symbolic recognition from his mOther or father as a young child (despite his best efforts, probably at doing household chores for his parents), recreated as an adult situations that mirrored his early relations to his parental Others. In addition, it is useful to consider Chris' phrase "bending over backwards" in relation to the fact that his father wanted him to bend over (forwards) to beat him. In this respect, "bending over backwards" may be Chris' way of avoiding his father's punishment.

Tom

The father of Tom, an exhibitionist in Rosen's (1996) psychodynamic psychotherapy group, was a man "who was an obsessional personality [and] a moral coward, especially during air raids, while his mother was strong and dependable. Tom identified with her and at the age of 16 he chased his father out of the house—it was at this age that his exposures started" (p. 192). On a related note, Tom talked about a fight he witnessed between his parents when he was a boy. His mother had angrily "thrown a plate on the floor or at father, who had gone out to the garden and stayed there" (p. 200). As an adult, "Tom angrily despised his father at length for his weakness" (p. 196). Clearly, Tom's interpretations of his father and mother are the ones most common to the structure of perversion.

After the group had met numerous times, Tom admitted to having exhibited himself again. He described

> how his bicycle had turned into his usual haunt, "as if of its own accord," and he had partially exhibited himself to two girls. He felt very ashamed but a new feature had appeared; he wanted to apologize and made to do so, but they ran away. This need for

apology was accepted as a hopeful sign, attributed to the work of the group. (p. 196)

Most likely due to the influence of the group, Tom wanted to take back his exhibitionistic act. It seems as though the group functioned as a stand-in lawgiving Other for Tom, especially because Tom felt inclined to admit to the group what he had done. (Ray had a very similar experience, which I describe in detail in the next chapter.)

Michael

Michael, age 19, was another exhibitionist who participated in Rosen's (1996) psychotherapy group. Michael was described as

> the most uncontrolled member of the group, like a primitive chunk of primary process ... Michael sat through the first meeting sprawled out in his raincoat and hat. He would burst into meetings late, argue firmly and inconsequentially about wage rates and hold the group's attention by his imperturbable vigor even when attacked. He settled down remarkably, came neatly dressed and showed flashes of helpful insight. He claimed to be able to control his proclivities by willpower. (p. 194)

Michael had an obsessional symptom: He had to pick up all the papers in the street before he could commit an act of indecent exposure. Michael's presentation and discourse obviously defied social standards of propriety and might be defined as a bit shocking. Rosen did not provide us with much information about Michael's life, however, which would enable us to better understand Michael's obsessional symptom.

Rosen did tell his readers, however, that Michael's parents separated when Michael was three years old and that Michael was "shuffled thereafter between relatives and boarding schools" (p. 194). Michael also knew that his father had made another woman pregnant around the time of his birth. Michael's fetish object was girls' underwear, and he "exposed himself and masturbated to girls in the dark, in cinemas, and on beaches" (p. 194).

Voyeurism

Voyeurism involves trying to see a woman as devoted to the jouissance of her own body and making her realize that, even when alone, she is being watched by another.

Miller (1996b, p. 318)

The voyeur brings in the gaze himself to plug up the hole in the Other and thereby make the Other whole.

> What occurs in voyeurism? At the moment of the act of the voyeur, where is the subject, where is the object? I have told you that the subject is not there in the sense of seeing, at the level of the scopic drive. He is there as a pervert and he is situated only at the culmination of the loop. As for the object—this is what my topology on the blackboard cannot show you, but can allow you to admit—the loop turns around itself, it is a missile, and it is with it, in perversion, that the target is reached.
>
> The object, here, is the gaze—the gaze that the subject is that hits him, that hits the bull's eye in target-shooting. I have only to remind you what I said of Sartre's analysis. Although this analysis brings out the agency of the gaze, it is not at the level of the other whose gaze surprises the subject looking through the keyhole. What is important is that the other surprises him, the subject, as entirely hidden gaze.
>
> You grasp here the ambiguity of what is at issue when we speak of the scopic drive. The gaze is this object lost and suddenly refound in the conflagration of shame, by the introduction of the other. (Lacan, 1973/1998a, p. 182)

At the moment of the voyeuristic act, the voyeur is object *a* in the form of the gaze. The pervert, recognizing himself as the gaze, experiences a conflagration of shame when his gaze obturates the hole in the Other.

The voyeur hides himself in his efforts at getting a good view of his object, and his object is always a woman. But

> what is the subject trying to see? What he is trying to see, make no mistake, is the object as absence. What the voyeur is looking for and finds is merely a shadow, a shadow behind the curtain. There he will fantasize any magic of presence, the most graceful of girls, for example, even if on the other side there is only a hairy athlete. What he is looking for is not, as one says, the phallus—but precisely its absence, hence the pre-eminence of certain forms as objects of his search. (Lacan, 1973/1998a, p. 182, translation modified)

The voyeur tries to discover the truth of femininity in gazing at a woman when she thinks she is not being seen. The voyeur is trying to see "the object as absence" (p. 182), which is to say that he wants to confirm that a woman lacks a penis.

> The object of desire of the voyeur … is very precisely what can
> only be seen there insofar as she props it up on the basis of some-
> thing ungraspable: a simple line where the phallus is lacking.
> (Lacan, 2006b, p. 254)

The voyeur's interest is provoked by "what cannot be seen in the Other"
(p. 254), by the absence of the phallus.

At the same time, by providing the gaze himself, the voyeur "will fantasize any magic of presence" (Lacan, 1973/1998a, p. 182). The voyeur

> brings the gaze to the field of the Other, except that even prior to
> that it was as if the Other, in what he spies, is already manifest
> as being seen from the point of view of his ideal—the bathing
> woman who is already made likable under a gaze that still isn't
> materialized. And in fact that is, under the ideal, so to speak,
> *plus-de-jouir*. (Miller, 2009b, pp. 49–50)

The voyeur's act is not so much about the features of a particular woman
as it is about the object as absence that is made manifest in the voyeur's
gaze. In other words, the voyeur's gaze and the presence of a woman are
the only elements required to turn the woman's lack into a "magic of presence" (1973/1998a, p. 182).

The voyeur, like all perverts, disavows his position as object *a* in the
perverse act, fooling himself into believing that he is an active subject in
control of the situation. According to Lacan, the exhibitionist is the

> one who succeeds in what he has to do, that is, bring jouissance
> to the Other, and an other [the voyeur] who is only there to plug
> the hole with his own gaze, without letting the other see even
> the slightest bit more about what he is. It is more or less the same
> thing in relation between the sadist and the masochist. (2006b,
> p. 256)

Despite being, at the moment of the voyeuristic act, equivalent to the
gaze as object *a*, the voyeur still manages to avoid recognizing himself as
object *a*.

The voyeur chooses to look at a woman who has not given her consent
and is not aware that someone is watching her. The voyeur's act occurs
exclusively in situations in which he might be caught—either by the
woman herself or some other person. Going to a strip club or looking at
pornographic pictures and videos of women who supposedly were ignorant of the fact that they were on camera are much less interesting to
the voyeur than spying on an unsuspecting woman himself (sometimes
with the aid of a hidden camera which might be discovered). The voyeur

usually desires to gaze at an unsuspecting woman who is in a partial or complete state of nudity. The voyeur is often attracted to situations in which a woman is likely to be found undressing, going to the bathroom, bathing, or engaging in sexual acts. The paternal function is temporarily propped up when the voyeur is caught in the act—when the voyeur becomes aware that someone, even the victim herself, sees him looking at the victim. The effect is strengthened and prolonged if the other person hands him over to law enforcement.

Case Examples of Voyeurism Considered

Noel: "You've Got Nothing to Look at!"

Rosen (1996) described the case of Noel, a voyeur in his mid-20s who was treated with weekly psychodynamic psychotherapy in an outpatient forensic context. Prior to the start of Noel's psychotherapy, he had eight convictions for watching women in public bathrooms, the last of which was somehow combined with theft. Noel had previously been diagnosed with "immature and unstable personality with psychopathic traits, and compulsive abnormal sexual behavior" (p. 188). Prior to his beginning psychodynamic psychotherapy, he had undergone a year of non-analytic psychotherapy along with a course of hormone therapy intended to diminish his sexual desire. Noel married at 23, at which point the hormones were no longer prescribed to him so that he might freely engage in his marital sexual life.

Much to his humiliation, Noel was bathed by his mother until he was 11 years old. After that time, Noel's mother sometimes entered the bathroom when his genitals were exposed. When Noel became angry, his mother said, "You've got nothing to look at!" (Rosen, 1996, p. 189), which led to his first acts of voyeurism in public as well as in his home. "You've got nothing to look at!" is an important phrase open to several different interpretations. One is that Noel's penis was inferior to other penises, such that Noel was inferior to other men or not a "real man." Another interpretation, one which is supported by Noel's feminine identifications, is that Noel is a girl. Alternatively, the phrase suggests that Noel's mother, by comparison, did have something worth looking at. Consequently, Noel desired to discover what it was that his mother and women had by way of genitalia that was something at which to look.

As a teenager, Noel at times tried to see his mother's genitals uncovered while she was in the bathroom, and she spanked him for spying on her. Noel associated these memories to those of discovering his "mother's soiled sanitary towels as an adolescent and as a small child, which aroused his disgust and the thought that if father only knew about these things what he would say" (Rosen, 1996, p. 189). For Noel, there was something dirty and sexually arousing about his mother, her genitalia, and the things and activities associated with her genitalia (such as her going to the bathroom and her menstrual blood). As a child, Noel reasoned to himself that his father was ignorant of Noel's sexual arousal caused by his mother and her toilet habits, and that, were his father to become aware of this, his father would disapprove and intervene. What is more, Noel assumed that his father would also become disgusted (or aroused) by his mother's soiled sanitary towels and the like, and that his father would put a stop to his mother's disgusting sexuality. By saying to himself, "If father only knew about these things, what would he say?" Noel attempted to strengthen his father's role as lawgiving Other.

The sounds associated with going to the bathroom both fascinated and disgusted Noel, and he associated his corresponding fantasies of seeing and listening to women in bathrooms with his primal scene. When Noel was four years old, he heard his parents having intercourse through the thin walls of his bedroom. "He was terrified, prayed they would stop, and later lay awake waiting for a repetition of the event, feeling left out and resentful" (Rosen, 1996, p. 189). Noel's feeling left out and profoundly lonely (p. 189) when bearing blind witness to this primal scene may have coincided with Noel's logical moment of primal repression. Also related to his primal scene was his experiencing disgust at the moment of orgasm during sexual intercourse with his wife. Noel was then "compelled to think of millions of others having intercourse at the same time, like animals" (p. 189).

Metonymically related to the sounds his mother made in the bathroom and while having sex with his father, Noel's disgust both disguised his desire to have sexual intercourse with his mother and his desire to be his mother. The noises she made in the bathroom and while having sex with Noel's father aroused Noel's curiosity and desire to see what was going on within her private sphere. Those noises must have sounded to Noel as though his mother were either enjoying herself or in pain or some combination of both. (The menstrual blood on the sanitary napkins was evidence of the latter.) *Noel desired to see his mOther's private jouissance.* In the words of Miller (1996b), "Voyeurism involves trying to see a woman as devoted to the jouissance of her own body and making her realize that, even when alone, she is being watched by another" (p. 318).

In one of his psychodynamic psychotherapy sessions, Noel reported that he had had conscious

> thoughts of intercourse with mother. He said that this was the worst kind of incest and he found such ideas quite intolerable, but that going into toilets was the next best thing to intercourse with mother. The importance of his voyeuristic acts as a defense

against his intense incestuous desires for his mother, as well as an expression of them, became clear. (Rosen, 1996, p. 189)

Importantly, Noel's acts of voyeurism were also defenses against the inadequacy of the paternal function. This is the case both because Noel was very likely to get caught in the act and punished[104] but also because they allowed Noel to express aggression toward his mOther—aggression which has a temporary effect of separation.

Noel said that spying on women while they are going to the bathroom is a way of degrading them. More specifically, Noel desired to degrade, express anger at, and hurt his mother. Through his offenses and court appearances, he succeeded in hurting his mother. In the same vein, as a boy Noel "dug tunnels in ponds and filled them with frogs, newts, eels, and adders, watched them tangling together, then would cut them to bits with a knife, or pour on oil and set them on fire" (Rosen, 1996, p. 190). Rosen did not provide any information regarding Noel's associations to these events. Perhaps their tangling together was associated in Noel's mind with the primal scene, and Noel's aggressive acts were meant to put an end to his parents' private jouissance. Alternatively, the tunnels Noel dug in ponds represented the bathtub, and the painful bloodbath Noel inflicted upon the amphibians was akin to the harm his mother inflicted upon him by bathing him until he was 11 years old. It also is quite possible that the amphibians symbolized Noel's mother, and that his torturing the amphibians reflected his taking up an active position and retaliating against his mother in kind.

Amphibians were not the only objects of Noel's aggression, however, because Noel killed his own pet rabbit. A notable exception is that Noel did not kill or hurt a bird under any circumstances, even to put an already injured bird out of its misery. Noel thought of birds as "tender" (Rosen, 1996, p. 190). What might account for this? In lieu of Noel's own associations, we might hypothesize that birds held a special place in Noel's psyche because their beaks reminded him of penises. More specifically, Noel desired to protect birds just as he protected himself from castration.[105]

The following episodes provide more examples of Noel's repressed desires to hurt his mother.

Once at school he spoiled a prize cabbage the children were growing by poking his finger through it—and when later an interpretation about his wish to damage mother's breast was given on

---

104 Noel "would frequently be caught, as it were, on purpose" (Rosen, 1996, p. 189).

105 Noel was 8–10 years of age when he "would get resentful with his mother and express this in cruelty to animals" (Rosen, 1996, p. 189).

different material, he associated back to the cabbage and said that it had to be holed exactly in the centre. This was interpreted as representing the nipple … He had thoughts of cutting a woman's breasts right off where they joined the rib cage, and added that he also had fantasies of cutting women's nipples out. He continued to describe how, when he was younger and was served mince meat and mash, he would mix it all up and make the food into a square, then make a ploughed field out of it with a fork, then cut the centre square and eat it, then a square on the left, right, north and south, then other squares, but could not finish it like this and had to gobble it all up. The interpretation was made that the squares were to take the breast shape away. (Rosen, 1996, p. 190)

It may very well be that Noel associated women's breasts and nipples with femininity and with his mOther because he lacked a more distinctive signifier for sexual difference. Alternatively, women's nipples and breasts are related to breastfeeding and maternal nurturing, and so Noel's fantasy of cutting off a woman's nipples or breasts might symbolize a wish for independence from his mOther or an angry rejection of the kind of intrusive and force-feeding care he received from his mOther (exemplified in being bathed by her until he was 11). Perhaps Noel, at some level, was the hole in the mOther, and this is the root of his compulsion to put a hole in the cabbage/woman's breast.

Rosen (1996) emphasized that "despite his nuisance value to women in toilets, the moral suffering inflicted on his family, and a single physical altercation with his father and fights with his brother, none of these oral-sadistic fantasies were acted out with women" (p. 190). A further caveat provided by Rosen is that despite Noel's strong feelings of resentment toward his mother and his complaints against his father (e.g., "[Noel] craved his father's attention and admiration, but the latter took all his exploits and excellent sporting abilities quite coolly"; p. 189), Noel's "parents [were] eminently respected in their neighborhood, and presented to legal and medical authorities as well-adjusted responsible persons who had made great personal sacrifices in order to advance their son's education" (p. 190).

Another important feature of the case of Noel was his feminine identification. For example, Noel imitated the way he had seen women go to the bathroom "by squatting and arranging his clothes" (Rosen, 1996, p. 189). Noel "had to defend himself against the wish to become like [his] mother. Thus, artistic sensitivity to poetry and music was a source of fear as this aroused a feeling of feminine identification, and was checked by his daring exploits" (p. 189). Through his being punished by the law for his acts of voyeurism, not only was his faith, as it were, in the lawgiving Other strengthened, but he could also show his masculinity to [his] mother, make up for his sense of genital inferiority, further humiliate his parents, and counter his fears of a feminine identification. He felt his parents wanted a girl instead of him, and as a child he had fantasies of being a girl. He said he would hate to be a woman, because of chaps like him frightening them in toilets, afraid of being raped or murdered. (p. 189)

Lacking a signifier for sexual difference, Noel experienced uncertainty and anxiety related to his sexual identity. Noel seemed to associate femininity with weakness and emotionality, and masculinity with daring exploits and strength. Nevertheless, all of these qualities were made evident by Noel's speech and actions, but Noel continued to think that if he could only be aggressive and reckless enough, he would rid himself of vulnerability and femininity.

According to Rosen, Noel made progress during his first six months of psychodynamic psychotherapy. During that time, Noel reported improvement in his relationships and ability to work. With "increasing insight his aberrant impulses were able to be resisted" (Rosen, 1996, p. 190) to a higher degree than prior to treatment.

During treatment at the clinic the patient re-lived much of the original feelings associated with the experiences described. He became extremely sensitive to loneliness and acted out his voyeurism when he became depressed, for example, when a social engagement with his wife suddenly could not be kept. His treatment could not be carried to a successful conclusion although he was making excellent progress as he had to be transferred to a new therapist after six months. Although the changeover was carefully handled by all concerned with his full knowledge and agreement, and he liked his new female therapist, stating he preferred her to a male doctor, this provoked a fresh burst of voyeuristic activities for which he was sentenced to prison. (pp. 190–191)

Despite the premature end to Noel's analysis, his response to treatment was positive.

Jiménez's Case of Matías: Therapeutic Responses to Disavowal

Jiménez (1993) published an excellent and instructive case study of voyeurism which has been recently reproduced in the book he edited with Moguillansky, *Clinical and Theoretical Aspects of Perversion: The Illusory Bond* (2011). Jiménez described the course of the first two years of analysis with his patient, with whom he had sessions four times weekly. Matías, a

29-year-old man, initially sought treatment because of "chronic shyness, intense erythrophobia—which occurred whenever he thought people were looking at him—and acute social anxiety, which had led him from a young age systematically to avoid situations where, for example, he had to read or speak in public" (1993, p. 489). In addition, since his adolescence Matías had prowled his neighborhood with binoculars in the hope of spotting a woman in a state of partial or complete undress. The gaze, then, was manifestly a primary feature in his voyeuristic and social anxiety symptoms.

Unusually for a man of his age and in his culture, Matías lived with his parents until after his second year of analysis. He had ambivalent feelings about gaining independence and living away from his mother, with whom he had a symbiotic relationship. On the one hand, Matías hated his mother on account of her being "possessive and domineering. On the other hand, Matías said that he and his mother understood each other without having to resort to words: he felt extremely close to her and said he knew her as well as he knew himself" (Jiménez, 1993, p. 490). Matías was bothered by his mother's conviction "that everything he did was related to her" (p. 495). Matías described his father "as reserved and schizoid," (p. 490) as a weak and often absent man who, when angry, "resorted to total silence and left the room" (p. 490).

Matías' fetish object was a woman's brassiere, which had to be stolen from a woman. Despite his usual shyness and meekness—he was reportedly even incapable of "raising his voice in public" (Jiménez, 1993, p. 490)—Matías "was capable of climbing balconies and breaking into houses, while their occupants slept, to steal brassieres. On these occasions he felt like a superman and was not afraid" (p. 490). He carried out these activities and his acts of voyeurism almost exclusively in his parents' neighborhood. In addition, Matías' perverse acts were especially likely to occur after experiences of social humiliation.

Matías hoarded his stolen brassieres in a cupboard that he called his "treasure *chest*" (Jiménez, 1993, p. 490, emphasis added). Matías

> had masturbated compulsively since the age of 7, sometimes several times a day, and had developed this into a ritual over the years. Now in order to masturbate, he had to squeeze his chest at the level of his pectoral muscles by using a cord or belt. He then fitted the resulting "breasts" into a woman's brassiere, which had to be stolen and not bought. (He had stolen his first brassiere from an aunt when he was 7, while on holiday at his grandparents' farmhouse.) He then proceeded to tie his erect penis firmly with a cord and masturbate in front of a mirror. (p. 490)

Because of the prominent role of breasts and brassieres in his masturbatory ritual, it is notable that Matías preferred to spy on women who were masturbating or stroking their breasts. It is as if he, in the act of masturbation, created exactly what he desired to see when committing an act of voyeurism.

Furthermore, Matías' masturbation ritual involved pretending he was a woman, creating a "*virtual* conviction of being a man and a woman at the same time" (Jiménez, 1993, p. 493).[106] When Matías was young, "his mother, a seamstress, used to dress him in girl's clothing to show the styles to her clients" (2004, p. 75). As further evidence that Matías lacked the signifier for sexual difference, in speaking about his group of friends he emphasized, "'We are equal in the gang, there are no sexual or other differences'" (1993, p. 489). Supporting Chasseguet-Smirgel's hypothesis, not only did Matías deny the differences between men and women but he showed, according to Jiménez, a "capability to feel, think and act ... *as if* there were no differences between human beings, men or women, children and parents, him and me, etc., although at the same time he was capable of recognising the differences at a cognitive level" (p. 493). Matías disavowed these differences; despite cognitively knowing that men and women and children and adults are different, he believed with virtual certainty that these differences did not exist.

In fact, the main difficulty Jiménez described having in his analysis with Matías had to do with the frequent occurrence of disavowal. Jiménez, however, did not seem to be familiar with the term "disavowal," instead describing occurrences of disavowal as "distortions in communication" (Jiménez, 1993, p. 491), "paranoia" (p. 491), "faulty logic" (p. 492), and a "denial of the reality of the perceptive space between [Jiménez and Matías]" (p. 492). For example, Matías had the "*virtual* conviction[s] that other people could read his thoughts and emotions through his gestures or what he said" (p. 489, emphasis added) and that he, in turn, knew the true inner meaning of someone's words or gestures. In analysis, for instance, Matías believed that he knew the meanings behind Jiménez's clearing his throat or remaining silent, "which he did not take ... as hypotheses but as incontrovertible evidence that needed no further proof" (p. 492). In Jiménez's words, "No matter what I did or did not do, whether I spoke or was silent, and whatever I interpreted, Matías would reinterpret my interpretation, movement, sound or silence, and attribute to me intentions that I usually failed to perceive myself" (p. 491).

Jiménez deduced that Matías' virtual convictions regarding mindreading that led to his social anxiety were projections, and also that Matías

---

106 Matías' "*virtual* conviction" (Jiménez, 1993, p. 493, emphasis added) does not constitute a psychotic conviction or a delusion but is instead the near-certainty that results from disavowal.

reinterpreted Jiménez's words "in the same way as when interacting with his mother" (Jiménez, 1993, p. 491). Jiménez spent over a year focusing his interventions almost exclusively on Matías' disavowal. The way in which he went about doing so, however, was misguided. Jiménez said he "avoided giving interpretations of content and instead repeated the detailed description of the vicious circles of communicative interaction in the here-and-now and, where possible, in his daily life" (p. 492). In Jiménez's words,

> I added that [Matías] did not understand that during any communication we must constantly be alert to whether we have understood what the other person has really said and, for this reason, I frequently asked him what he meant by something he had said. I told him that whenever he felt humiliated, which happened every day, he responded with immediate withdrawal, without checking whether he had really been put down or whether he merely 'believed' the other person had done so. I said that he was building a castle of suppositions that was very probably founded on false premises, although this did not rule out the possibility that his suppositions might sometimes be true. (p. 492)

In intervening in this cognitive-behavioral manner, Jiménez was trying to convince Matías that he was using faulty logic and that he would be better off if he adopted Jiménez's type of logic.

Matías responded to Jiménez's attempts to "correct one of his perceptions" (Jiménez, 1993, p. 492) by attributing "some hidden meaning to the explanation, which made it lose its value, and so on *ad infinitum*" (p. 492). Clearly, then, Jiménez failed in his attempts to stop the operation of disavowal by way of interventions that taught the merits of neurotic reasoning. The target of his interventions should not have been the strange logic of disavowal but instead the causes of its operation.[107]

Consequently, Matías' analysis was at somewhat of an impasse for the months in which Jiménez made his misguided interventions. Jiménez eventually found a different and more effective way of working with Matías' disavowal—one which targeted that which the disavowal defended against. This occurred when Jiménez realized that "Matías was almost feverishly convinced that [Jiménez] could see his face and gestures

---

107 Furthermore, Jiménez's misguided interventions functioned to negate Matías' assertions that the Other is unbarred. Matías' disavowal resulted in his belief that, by bringing his gaze to the Other, he would attain a kind of omniscient view of reality/truth. Jiménez's interventions conveyed the message that Matías does not succeed in plugging up the lack in the Other and making it whole, and so Matías' resistance to this message was one of the main reasons for his refusal of the veracity of Jiménez's interpretations.

while he was lying on the couch. [Jiménez] confronted him many times with this fact, with no result" (Jiménez, 1993, p. 492). Jiménez said that his

> concern grew, until I opted for tackling the issue in a direct way and told [Matías] how much of him I could see from my seat: only his hair and part of his forehead, but not his face. He replied that he did not believe me and claimed that I could see his face from my position behind the couch. To my surprise, in several subsequent sessions, he persisted with this assertion, adding that every time I said something he was capable of imagining perfectly—actually to "see"—the expression on my face. At that moment I understood that *his denial served the purpose of rejecting the asymmetry of the analytic relationship.* This allowed me to interpret that the supine position was so degrading for him that he simply denied it, in the conviction that we were still face to face, as in the initial interviews. After this content interpretation, Matías corrected his perception and we were able to talk about the conflict between omnipotence and impotence in which, as a rule, he felt trapped whenever he attempted to establish any type of relationship. (pp. 492–493, emphasis added)

Where Jiménez's educative interventions that relied upon reason and "facts" about reality failed, his interpretation about the function of the disavowal succeeded.[108] Jiménez began using the latter type of intervention systematically, and as a result Matías' erythrophobia began to disappear and he "started to feel calmer and less anxious with other people" (p. 493) on account of having lost his virtual conviction that others could, by looking at him, read his innermost thoughts.

The scopic drive played a significant role in Matías' virtual conviction and corresponding social anxiety. He was convinced that being the object of the gaze of others gave those others the ability to unmask him and reveal truths of which he was ashamed. Which truths? In lieu of any information from Jiménez on this matter, it is safe to assume that his anxiety at being the gaze of the Other is related to his acts of voyeurism. It might be that Matías assumed that others were looking at him for the same reasons and with the same gaze with which he looked at naked women. Matías,

---

108 In addition, Matías' virtual conviction indicated that the gaze was operative in the relational field between Matías and Jiménez. Interestingly, the two of them switched roles in accordance to which of them was speaking; when Matías was speaking, he was the subject as Other to whom Jiménez brought his gaze, and vice versa. This example also shows how the scopic drive is in some ways separate from visual perception.

as voyeur, was trying to see "the object as absence" (Lacan, 1973/1998a, p. 182)—wanting to confirm that a woman lacks a penis—and to see the Other's private jouissance. Perhaps, then, Matías imagined that others looked at him with the same intrusive and impudent gaze, wanting to unmask his veil of privacy and to discover whether he was a man or a woman. If so, it is no wonder that Matías experienced such intense shame and humiliation when he felt himself to be the object of scrutiny.

After a lengthy period of time during which Jiménez focused on Matías' "denial of differences and his swings between claustrophobic anxiety and the sensation of feeling brutally rejected as a result of his fantasy of symbiotic union and control—which he preserved by resorting to continual attribution and perverse actions—symptomatic changes resulted that surprised [Jiménez]" (Jiménez, 1993, p. 495). Matías threw away his "treasure chest" full of brassieres, stole brassieres much less often, "his masturbation ceased to be so bizarre" (p. 495), and he continued to improve his social difficulties. However, the frequency and daring of his voyeurism increased. Matías

> stopped using binoculars and started going up to the windows of his neighbors after dark and looking in through the shutters, always in the hope of catching sight of a girl masturbating. He lost interest completely if he saw a couple making love. When he occasionally came upon girls in their underwear, he became excited and masturbated in the garden. This "new" activity quickly assumed the nature of transferential acting out, which Matías carried out particularly at weekends and holidays. (p. 495)

In explaining why he committed acts of voyeurism more frequently over weekends and holidays, Matías rejected Jiménez's separation anxiety interpretations and offered the explanation that at those times he "felt out of range of [Jiménez's] power, with [Jiménez] acting as a powerful, exteriorised superego" (p. 495). This is a phenomenon I myself have observed in work with perverse patients: that the therapist can come to represent a lawgiving Other and prop up the paternal function, thereby temporarily reducing perverse enactments and symptoms.

Matías increased the audacity of his voyeuristic act to the point of forcing open closed shutters in order to gain a better view of the inside. The noise made by his opening the shutters "alerted the occupants of the house, and he had been on the point of being caught several times" (Jiménez, 1993, p. 496). Matías' audacity was a way to bolster the paternal function, as he could be reasonably certain that his chances of being caught would be amplified. Accordingly, his mother informed him that night prowlers had been spotted in the neighborhood and that the police were on the lookout for them. This news put Matías "into a state of panic and paranoia. He believed that his mother knew everything and that she was using this news to tell him indirectly to take care, and whenever he saw a police car in the village he had the certainty of being followed" (p. 496). It is interesting that Matías believed that his mother wanted to protect him from lawgiving Others rather than to turn him over to them. This is in keeping with the probable original circumstances of the inadequacy of his paternal function. His mother shielded him from his father as lawgiving Other, subverting his attempts to lay down the law and separate Matías from his mother.

Matías began implying that if he were apprehended and tried for voyeurism, Jiménez would be summoned to give evidence at the trial. If this had occurred, Jiménez' testimony would have functioned in two ways: on the one hand, Jiménez would have bolstered the case made by the law against Matías, and on the other hand, Jiménez himself would have appeared to have been guilty of complicity as a silent witness. Matías stopped engaging in acts of voyeurism only for a few days. Shortly thereafter, he asked Jiménez to forbid him to continue with his acts of voyeurism and thus directly asked Jiménez to play the role of lawgiving Other. Jiménez refused, saying that his forbidding Matías to do something would increase his already substantial sense of interpersonal claustrophobia. Jiménez "interpreted this episode as an attempt to put [Jiménez] to the test and find out how much pressure [he] could stand, how long [he] could go along with [Matías]—even under the most difficult circumstances—and how [he] could understand [Matías'] enormous difficulties and anxieties" (Jiménez, 1993, p. 496).

One of the foci of Matías' analysis was his problematic relation to women. At the beginning of analysis, Matías had only had short-term and anxiety-ridden relationships with women. In his few sexual encounters, he had had great difficulty in achieving an erection. "Whenever he had managed to overcome his initial fear and had begun a relationship with a woman, he had soon felt rejected, treated like a child, abandoned, etc. which then made him break off the relationship" (Jiménez, 1993, p. 489). After two years of analysis, Matías began a romantic relationship with Ana, a young woman who "happened" to be a close relative of someone who worked in the same analytic institute as did Jiménez.

> Matías felt extremely divided between his sexual desire for her and his fear of coming too close. The fact is that Matías oscillated very rapidly, even within the course of a single session, between acknowledging his sexual desires for Ana and his feeling that they were only impositions on [Jiménez's] part, to which he submitted. (p. 496)

Certainly, Matías' ambivalent relationship with Ana was reflective of his ambivalent relationship with his mOther.

Matías experienced significant anxiety in response to the perceived danger of being too close to and dependent upon a woman who related to him as the be-all-and-end-all of her existence. In Matías' words, *"That was why I felt reassured when I realised that she did not need me. A no-strings relationship doesn't cause anxiety. But also, during the week the relationship may disappear"* (Jiménez, 1993, p. 498). Correspondingly, Matías said, *"I often feel like a child. When I go to bed with Ana, I feel more like a child than a man. It is difficult for me to achieve an erection as well, to be really potent"* (p. 499). In his sexual encounters with Ana, he was anxious in the face of two things. One Matías spoke about through metonymy; in telling the story of his visit to the Grand Canyon, he emphasized the "overwhelming fear he had felt when faced with this massive chasm in the landscape" (p. 498) and thus betrayed his fear in the face of the female genitalia, which, for him, was terrifying in its namelessness and relation to castration. The other was interpreted by Jiménez, that when Matías slept with Ana "he felt she was stealing his penis, a vital part of his body, and he would therefore no longer be able to leave her ... The session ended with him saying, 'It is true, I have always been afraid of others taking something away from me'" (p. 497).

The Voice, Masochism, and Sadism

[I]t is the voice in the field of the Other that makes me attached to the Other.

Miller (2007, p. 145)

Lacan (2004) repeatedly emphasized that "[s]adism is not the inverse of masochism" (p. 207), that a pervert cannot alternate back and forth between sadism and masochism, and that sadism and masochism, although they have a non-symmetrical relationship with regard to the invocatory drive, are separate and distinct ontological structural diagnoses. So too has Gilles Deleuze, in *Masochism: Coldness and Cruelty* (1967/2006), questioned "the very concept of an entity known as sadomasochism" (p. 13), saying that it "is too readily assumed that the symptoms only have to be transposed and the instincts reversed for Masoch to be turned into Sade, according to the principle of the unity of opposites" (p. 13).

What masochism and sadism do have in common is a primary relation to the invocatory drive—which I explained in some detail in chapter 4. In neurosis and perversion, "the voice appears in its dimension of object when it is the Other's voice" (Miller, 2007, p. 144). Correspondingly, at the moment of the realization of the voice as object *a* in the masochistic or sadistic act, the lawgiving Other is briefly given a forceful existence. The masochist makes the voice appear in the field of the Other by getting a father substitute to embody the voice and thus temporarily serve as Other. The sadist, on the other hand, tries "to complete the Other by removing speech from him and by imposing his own voice" (Lacan, 2006b, pp. 258–259).

According to Fink (1997, p. 187), a formulation of the invocatory drive is "to command or to get oneself commanded" (*faire commander* or *se faire commander*)—the active voice is employed by the sadist and the passive reflexive voice is employed by the masochist. The goal of the perverse act is to prop up the paternal function, and the realization of the invocatory drive correspondingly involves the enunciation of a temporary law. The masochist, for example, "aims to make the Other anxious" (Lacan, 2004, p. 207), pushing him to a breaking point before he forcefully expresses his will by uttering commands. The appearance of the voice as object *a*, then, coincides with the temporary instatement of a law which sets limits to the pervert's excess in jouissance, binding his anxiety and resulting in a subjective experience of satisfaction. *Perverse subjects "get off on the enactment of castration"* (Fink, 1997, p. 192, emphasis added).

Another common misunderstanding of masochism and sadism is that their primary feature is the enjoyment of physical pain—whether it is the masochist's own pain or the sadist's enjoyment in his victim's pain. For one thing, psychological suffering, such as humiliation or intense anxiety, is often sought in addition to or in lieu of physical pain. Along these lines, Lacan (2004) said, "It's not so much the suffering of the other that is sought in the intention of the sadist, but [the other's] anxiety" (p. 123) and the masochist "aims to make the Other anxious" (p. 207). In addition, the masochist or the sadist's victim (with whom the sadist identifies) is very often humiliated and treated as an object. More importantly, however, *for the masochist and sadist physical and/or psychological suffering is merely a means to an end: the (temporary) enunciation of a law or the bolstering of the paternal function.* For the masochist, for instance, his suffering is proof that there exists an Other who is demanding a sacrifice of him.

Masochism

What [masochism] deals with is the voice. That the masochist makes the voice of the Other, for himself alone, what will give him the guarantee of responding like a dog. This is the essential part of the thing.

Lacan (2006b, p. 257)

And the voice as such emerges each time the signifier breaks down, and rejoins this object in horror.

Miller (2007, p. 145)

[The masochist] aims to make the Other anxious.

Lacan (2004, p. 207)

The masochist tries to bring something into being ... by which the Other's desire makes the law.

Lacan (2004, p. 126)

The Law and the Other's Desire

In his masochistic act, the masochist seeks to get himself commanded by a person who plays the role of a lawgiving Other. It must be remembered, however, that the pervert lacks experience with and an internalized knowledge of the lawgiving Other of the neurotic—the parental Other who imposes limits on and disciplines the child for his own good. The symbolic father provides a rational for any limit he places on the child's behavior, and he too abides by the moral law, thus practicing what he preaches.

Instead, the pervert's experience of the lawgiving Other is often restricted to a parent who sets limits on the child's behavior only when angry—in accordance with her or his whims rather than in accordance with the precepts of the law (which are beyond the parent's desire). Consequently, the child does not internalize the law but instead learns that limits are merely manifestations of his parent's desire. Furthermore, the parent of a pervert derives jouissance from blaming and punishing his or her child. In short, the parent gets off on humiliating and causing pain (physical and/or psychological) to his or her child. The

> moral law is thus inextricably associated with expressions of the Other's desire and jouissance, and the masochist seeks to elicit that jouissance in lieu of the law. Since he cannot obtain the symbolic law as such, he seeks that which he somehow understands to be associated with it. The Other's desire or will is accepted by the masochist instead of the law, in place of the law, in the absence of the law. (Fink, 1997, p. 189)

In the case of perversion, then, the Other's desire that is substituted for the law is a desire or will that eroticizes blame, punishment, humiliation, and the unequal distribution of power (originally between the child and the parent).

Roughly speaking, the masochist humiliates himself while the sadist, by contrast, humiliates his victim. Nevertheless, because "modesty is an amboceptor with respect to the circumstances of being" (Lacan, 1963/2006a, p. 772), the masochist, sadist, and each of their partners are all implicated in immodesty. Likewise, the pervert's mOther, in using her child and his body as an instrument for her jouissance, did not escape revealing the immodesty at the inmost core of her subjectivity. What is more, because the sadist identifies with his victim it can be said that he suffers humiliation by way of his identification. In sadism and masochism, excrement and feces[109] are sometimes eroticized and woven into the perverse scenario because of their utility in removing the modesty and dignity of the masochist or the sadist's victim. Excrement and feces, of course, are also related to the anal drive and the child's connection to his mother via the process of potty-training.

Recall that in "Kant with Sade," Lacan demonstrated that shame is related to the jouissance that is at "the inmost core of the subject" (1963/2006a, p. 771). The sadist's jouissance traverses and monopolizes the victim's will, humiliating him or her to the very core of his or her subjectivity. The masochistic and sadistic acts are ways of inciting this intimate shame in relation to the Other—often recreating the early relationship with the mOther but reflecting different solutions (masochistic versus sadistic) to the original traumatic situation by either getting the victim/Other, via the voice, to enunciate a law (i.e., the masochistic solution) or embodying the Other oneself and enunciating a law (i.e., the sadistic solution).

We do not experience the moral law as a set of abstract universal principles. Instead, the "voice of conscience" is transmitted to children by the voices of their parental Others and is experienced by children as "expressions of the Other's desire" (Fink, 1997, p. 189). As Lacan (2004) said, the "myth of Oedipus doesn't mean anything other than this—at the origin, desire as the desire of the father and the law are one and the same thing" (p. 126). Stereotypically it is the father who, in a particular tone of voice, enunciates a moral principle, and children interpret the father's enunciation as having to do with his desire. The father's tone of voice indicates that he is experiencing a certain type of jouissance by making his proclamation.

Regarding the implications of the relation between the father's desire and jouissance and the moral law, Fink (1997) put it well:

> The pervert seems to be cognizant, at some level, of the fact that there is always some jouissance related to the enunciation of the moral law. The neurotic would prefer not to see it, since it strikes him or her as indecent, obscene. The symbolic law is supposed to

---

109 See, for example, Michel De M'Uzan's (1973) case study of M., in which M. reportedly ingested a daily dose of feces and excrement. M. also tattooed on his body the phrase, "I have people shit and piss in my mouth and I swallow it all with pleasure" (p. 456).

be free of invocations of this kind. Indeed, it would seem that the pervert accepts the invocations in lieu of the symbolic law itself, unable as he is to obtain the latter. (p. 190)

The masochist's act in particular makes it clear that he has accepted the Other's/father-figure's desire in lieu of the symbolic law. Lacan (2004) said, "When desire and law are found together, what the masochist is determined to bring out—and, let me add, on his little stage [scène] for that dimension must never be neglected—is that the Other's desire lays down the law" (p. 126). In his act, the masochist sets the stage such that his partner, acting as Other, enunciates (i.e., brings to the fore the voice as object *a*) a temporary symbolic law.

Not All the World Is a Stage

To know oneself as the object of desire, that's always the masochist. But the masochist does it only onstage, and you shall see what happens when he can no longer remain on that stage. Not all the world is a stage, even if the stage extends quite far, even into the realm of our dreams. When we are not onstage, when we remain shy of it and we try to read in the Other what it's all about, we find nothing but a lack in *x*.

Lacan (2004, p. 127)

The masochist knows himself as an object *a* when he is on stage, so to speak, in the scene that he has authored. Correspondingly, the masochist appears to be nothing but the Other's object *a* who passively devotes himself to fulfilling the desires of his partner who plays the role of Other. At first glance, the masochist is supremely self-abnegating, letting the Other derive jouissance from him in any way that pleases the Other. This is the version of the masochistic act that is consciously endorsed by the masochist himself. For example, in Michel De M'Uzan's (1973) instructive case of the masochist M., he said, "Expressions like 'removal of the will,' 'total annihilation of the will,' 'the will doesn't exist any longer,' 'abolishment of the will,' etc., repeatedly appeared in [M.'s] conversation" (p. 460). Listening psychoanalytically, De M'Uzan noted "There was, however, something a little excessive in the way in which he spoke of the renunciation of his own will 'in favor of the one who commanded'" (p. 460). M.'s going to excess belied his assertions regarding his submission to a total annihilation of his will.

Looking beyond the manifest content of the masochist's scenario, however, reveals a different set of truths. At the level of the latent content, or the levels of the unconscious and preconscious, we see for one thing that the masochist, far from being stripped of his own will and desire, is the one whose desire pulls the strings. Not only is it often the masochist rather

162

than his "master" who determines in what ways he will serve and suffer, but it is also the masochist's desire that pushes the master/father substitute to lay down the law.

The masochist's problem is that the paternal function has been only partially instated (i.e., the pervert has undergone the process of alienation but not separation), and he attempts to solve this problem by authoring a scenario in which his partner, playing the role of Other, enunciates a law and sets limits to the masochist's excessive jouissance. "The masochist tries to bring something into being ... by which the Other's desire makes the law" (Lacan, 2004, p. 126). The masochist pretends that it is the Other who is pronouncing the law, when it would be more true to say that his "own desire takes the place of the Other's desire as law, staging or enacting it, as it were, and propping it up" (Fink, 1997, p. 187).

The masochist seeks proof that there is an Other who has agreed to play the role of lawgiving Other and impose limits or punishments upon him. Pain, humiliation, and restrictions of his freedom provide such evidence. Paradoxically, then, punishments grant relief to the masochist because they prove that the lawgiving Other exists and is setting limits upon his jouissance. The masochist gets his partner to say, "You're a bad boy" or something similar and then to exact a punishment upon him, but the paternal function bolstering effects are only temporary; it is too late for the masochist to undergo separation, and so he remains stuck at the sexual service of his mother with little symbolic space for his own. And so the masochist is drawn again and again to find relief from various substitute forms of symbolic castration. As odd as it may seem, perverse subjects sometimes even seek out, at some level, incarceration. As Lacan (2004) said, "Recourse to the very image of castration can come as a relieving, salutary solution to [issue à] anxiety for the masochist" (p. 239).

It is as an instrument of the Other's jouissance that the masochist is able to enact castration and bolster the paternal function, and so it should come as no surprise that when acting on his stage (at the conscious level), the masochist's

> declared goal is to turn himself into an object—whether it be a dog under the table or a commodity, the kind of thing one nego-tiates contracts about, selling it among other objects on the open market. In short, what he is seeking is to be identified with an everyday object, an exchangeable object. It remains impossible for him to grasp that, like everyone else, he is an *a*. (Lacan, 2004, p. 124)

By making himself into an exchangeable object, the masochist attempts to remove himself of his own will and desire—will and desire being primary features of what makes us human instead of objects—and to give it to the Other while pretending that it is the Other's will and desire rather than his own. In turning himself into a commodity, the masochist strips himself of his human dignity and thus humiliates himself for the sake of the Other who uses him. Also, the masochist desires to become an exchangeable object because such objects are subject to quasi-universal *laws* of exchange; commodities are treated equally and fairly according to the laws that govern commerce because they are all objects which can be sold and exchanged and used by an Other. Now *that* is a symbolic law that the masochist can believe in.

By believing in his own fiction, that is, that he is but a commodity to be used for the pleasure of the Other, the masochist gets himself commanded by the enunciation of the Other. Accordingly, the masochist will resist the analyst's attempts to divest him of his fiction. It is important to note that the masochist does not entirely believe in his fiction, however, because it is the result of disavowal. *The masochist's disavowal could be worded as follows: "I know very well that I am running the show and that the 'master' is really my puppet, but all the same I prefer to believe that I am but an exchangeable object who is devoted to pleasuring the Other."*

Another way in which the scene set by the masochist hides a deeper truth has to do with the fact that the masochist must often push his partner "to a breaking point, to a point of intense anxiety, before he explosively expresses his will in the form of commands ('Stop!' for example)" (Fink, 1997, p. 187). In this vein, Lacan (2004) said,

> People say that the masochist aims to give the Other jouissance. I have shown you that what is hidden by this idea is that, in the final analysis, he aims to make the Other anxious. This is what allows one to defeat his strategy. Analogously for the sadist. What is clear is that the sadist seeks to make the Other anxious. What is masked thereby is the Other's jouissance. (p. 207)

Even though the masochist would like to believe that he "aims to give the Other jouissance" (p. 207) and is devoted to providing pure enjoyment to the Other, actually the masochist "aims to make the Other anxious" (p. 207). The masochist aims to make the Other anxious—by turning himself into the instrument of the Other's jouissance—in pursuit of his higher goal of getting the Other to enunciate the law.

This is the purpose of the common masochistic strategy of "escalation," whereby the masochist demands to be given increasingly severe punishments until his partner/Other (who is not perverse) cannot bear the anxiety and utters a cry of objection. It is this realization of the voice of the lawgiving Other that is ultimately sought by the masochist. Take, for example, De M'Uzan's (1973) case of M.:

We can find in M. the characteristic attitude of the masochist who keeps demanding an increase in torture from the sadist. M. spoke willingly of this process of "escalation." At the crucial moment he did not fear anything and it was the sadist who hesitated before the extreme demand would be carried out. "In the end the sadist always chickens out." (p. 459)

The masochist reliably got himself commanded by his partner by way of this process of escalation.

Suffering as Verification of the Existence of a Lawgiving Other

As I have highlighted, the masochist derives satisfaction and relief from being punished, humiliated, and restricted in freedom because these experiences serve as proofs of the existence of a strong lawgiving Other in relation to the masochist. Suffering and humiliation are therefore means to an end rather than the primary goals of masochism. The masochist often places great focus on his sufferings, and if there are marks left on his body as the result of the Other's physical "punishments," they please the masochist to some extent because they confirm the existence of a lawgiving Other.

De M'Uzan (1973) described the tattoos on M.'s body, which served as permanent proof of his identity as object a in relation to the lawgiving Other.[110]

---

110 Detailing the mutilations done to M.'s body in the course of his masochistic acts, De M'Uzan said, "The right breast had virtually disappeared. It had been burned with a red-hot iron, had had some pointed objects put through it, and had been torn away. The navel had been transformed into a kind of crater. Some molten lead had been introduced into it and had been kept from falling out (because of perspiration) by means of a metallic stem fused to the lead. Some strips of skin had been cut in M.'s back to receive hooks so that he could be suspended while being penetrated by a man. The little toe of his right foot was missing. M. said that he had amputated it himself with a hacksaw, at the order of a partner, and had evened out the irregularities at the end of the bone with a rasp. Needles had been introduced almost everywhere, even into his thorax. His rectum had been enlarged 'to be more like a vagina.' Some photographs had been taken during that operation. It is of special interest that none of the wounds resulting from these acts had been followed by any infection or suppuration, even when foreign bodies such as needles, nails, pieces of glass, etc., had been introduced. Similarly, M. had been able to withstand perfectly the daily ingestion of urine and excrement over a period of many years. At the request of the physician who had seen him, M. had demonstrated a variety of instruments of torture: for example, small boards fitted with hundreds of spikes, a small wheel with gramophone needles attached (mounted on a handle) which was used to beat him. Finally, it is worthy of note that his genitals had not escaped the practices described above.
There was radiological evidence that many gramophone needles had even been driven into Monsieur M.'s testicles. His penis was entirely blue, perhaps as a result of an injection of ink into a blood vessel. The end of his penis had been cut open with a razor blade to make the

I shall begin with a precise list of the tattoos which covered prac-
tically his whole body (except the face). A tattoo (posterior), "Au
rendez-vous des belles queues" ("To the meeting place of the
beautiful pricks"); laterally with an arrow, "Entrée des belles
pines" ("Entrance for beautiful cocks"); in front, in addition to
some penises tattooed on his thighs, an impressive set: "Je suis
une salope," "Je suis un enculé," "Vive le masochisme," "Je ne
suis ni homme ni femme, mais une salope, mais une putain,
mais une chair à plaisir," "Je suis une chiote vivante," "Je me fais
pisser et chier dans la bouche et j'avale tout avec plaisir," "J'aime
recevoir des coups sur tout le corps, frappez fort," "Je suis une
salope, enculez-moi," "Je suis une putain, servez-vous de moi
comme d'une femelle, vous jouirez bien," "Je suis le roi des cons,
ma bouche et mes fesses s'offrent aux belles pines" ("I'm a dirty
whore," "I'm fucked," "Long live masochism," "I am neither man
nor woman but a dirty bitch, a whore just for fucking," "I'm a living shit," "I have people shit and piss in my mouth and I swallow
it all with pleasure," "My body loves to be hit, hit me hard," "I'm a
whore, fuck me," "I'm a prostitute, help yourself to me like a she-
animal, you'll really enjoy it," "I am the king of the arse-holes, my
mouth and my arse are waiting for nice pricks"). (p. 456)

Clearly, the signifiers M. wrote upon his body were the enunciations of his
desire—of his desire to be a disparaged and humiliated object whose value
is confined to causing the enjoyment of the Other.

Correspondingly, Lacan (2004) said,

the masochist himself serves the function of what I would call
dejection [or deformity; *déjet*]. This is our object *a*, but in the
guise of what is discarded [*déjeté*], thrown to the dogs, in the gar-
bage, on the scrapheap like everyday objects, since we can't put it
anywhere else. (p. 126)

By way of his masochistic acts and tattoos, M. turned himself into an
object *a* disguised as a deformed sexual deviant. According to M.,

---

orifice larger. A steel ring, several centimeters in diameter, had been placed permanently at the
end of the penis, after which the foreskin had been made into a sort of cushion filled with wax.
A magnetized needle had been driven into the body of the penis. This seemed like a piece of
perverse humor, for he said, 'The penis has the power to divert the needle of a compass, thus
demonstrating its potency.' A second ring, which was removable, encircled the attachment of
the scrotum at the base of the penis" (pp. 456–457).

what he desired was "above all an abasement of his personality." Everything that helped him to realize this "veritable moral suicide" was experienced by him as good, from the moment that M. and his wife were truly slaves of the two torturing lovers; this included everything in addition to the tortures—the banal slap or the order to eat excrement—which seemed capable of prolonging the "psychic pleasure" after the ejaculation. (De M'Uzan, 1973, p. 460)

M., then, desired to be humiliated and denigrated to the level of an object, thus removing his will and desire. M. desired to get himself commanded (e.g., to eat excrement) because it prolonged his "psychic pleasure" (p. 460) and propped up his paternal function. Rather than being understood as sexual satisfaction, the psychic pleasure or satisfaction that the pervert derives from his enactment of separation is another way of stating that the enunciation of a law binds the anxiety of the pervert and lowers his level of tension in accordance with the law of the pleasure principle.

According to De M'Uzan (1973), "M. depicted himself as motivated by a powerful need to be humiliated, a need for which homosexuality appeared to have been only an instrument, and a need to see his own will annihilated" (p. 460). Along these lines, M. himself said, "'I gave the impression of being an invert, but I wasn't one for pleasure, but for humiliation. I get no physical satisfaction from it; it was *moral* satisfaction'" (p. 460, emphasis added). M.'s use of the word *moral* here is one of many indications that his playing the role of dejected object served to make him feel as though there existed a moral law and that he, by humiliating himself, was carrying it out.

There were numerous ways in which M. regarded himself as both a man and a woman. For instance, M.'s rectum had been enlarged, according to M., in order "to be more like a vagina" (De M'Uzan, 1973, p. 456). When he was a schoolboy, "in his sexual games he adopted an exclusively feminine role. 'I was, in no uncertain terms, the "public woman" and that satisfied me'" (p. 458). Furthermore, in his tattoos, M. often referred to himself as a woman; also relevant is the phrase, "'I am neither man nor woman but a dirty bitch, a whore just for fucking'" (p. 456). In addition to humiliating him, M.'s homosexual acts and sometimes feminine identifications, of course, are indications that M. lacked the signifier for sexual difference.

The Masochist's Derision of the Other

The masochist's dual position, as object *a* and as stage manager, in his scenario also functions to give him a certain sense of control—an experience which was lacking in the masochist's early traumatic relationship with his mOther. Along these lines, the masochist often betrays an underlying derisive attitude toward the father figure's impotence. As Lacan (2006b) said,

> In the way in which we have seen the exhibitionist *jouit*, the axis of gravity of the masochist revolves at the level of the Other and of the giving the voice back to him as supplement, not without the possibility of a certain derision, which appears in the margins of the masochistic functioning. (p. 258)

What is written in the margins of the masochistic act is that the masochist is running the show and that his partner, playing the role of Other, is nothing but a marionette.

M. said and did numerous things that betrayed his derision of the Other, including his aforementioned statement, "In the end the sadist always chickens out" (De M'Uzan, 1973, p. 459). De M'Uzan noted that M. "let through a mocking a provocative attitude toward [him], his questioner" (p. 455) and that "M.'s relations with others consisted primarily of pride, contempt, challenge and a feeling of superiority" (p. 461). Nevertheless, at the same time M. "found the idea of having a supervisory position, or of exercising authority, particularly repugnant" (p. 456) and so avoided taking on such a position even though he was well-qualified to do so.

Specifically with regard to M.'s derision of his partner/lawgiving Other, De M'Uzan (1973) said that

> the "other" is, above all, the sadistic partner, i.e., a person destined to be held in contempt, someone who is devalued as he is reduced to the role of being a specific instrument. The sadistic student who shared the life of M. and his wife was ostensibly all-powerful, giving the orders, but he was considered to be essentially worth nothing and treated like feces … the quality of being all-powerful conferred by M. upon his partner was really a mockery. (p. 461)

Furthermore, it is worth noting that "M. no longer remembered the names of the sadistic partners who had shared his life for many years" (pp. 462–463). Off of the stage, then, it was apparent that M.'s partners were instruments for his desire and will rather than the other way around. As Lacan (2006b) put it, "there is a jouissance in this giving back the function of the voice to the Other, and even more so when this Other is less valued, when it has less authority" (p. 258).

"What [masochism] deals with is the voice. That the masochist makes the voice of the Other, for himself alone, what will give him the guarantee of responding like a dog. This is the essential part of the thing" (Lacan,

2006b, p. 257). Via disavowal, the masochist knows that he is obeying like a dog, and at the same time that he is the one pushing the Other to enunciate the commandment. Hence, the masochist's derision of the Other.

Sadism

> What is hidden behind the attempt to make the Other anxious in sadism is the attempt to bring out object *a*.
>
> Lacan (2004, p. 207)

> I will ask you to look at my article *Kant avec Sade*, where you will see that the sadist himself occupies the place of the object, but without knowing it, to the benefit of another, for whose *jouissance* he exercises his action as sadistic pervert. You see, then, several possibilities here for the function of the *objet a*, which is never found in the position of being the aim of desire. It is either pre-subjective, or the foundation of an identification disavowed by the subject. In this sense, sadism is merely the disavowal of masochism. This formula will make it possible to illuminate many things concerning the true nature of sadism.
>
> Lacan (1973/1998a, pp. 185–186)

> What the agent of sadistic desire does not know in carrying out his action or ritual…is what he is looking for. And what he is looking for is to make himself appear—to whom, one might ask, since this revelation can only remain obscure to himself—as a pure object, a black fetish.
>
> Lacan (2004, p. 124)

In the sadist's fantasy as well as in his sadistic enactment of separation, he views his victim's anxiety as a crucial component for providing him satisfaction. Recall, however, that the masochist constructs a fantasy scene in which he believes that he is an object who acts only for the sake of the Other's jouissance, and that the masochist's belief puts a veil over the truth: The masochist aims to make the Other anxious. Nevertheless, because "sadism is not the inverse of masochism" (Lacan, 2004, p. 207) there is no cause to simply reverse the masochist's formulation and conclude that, apparently seeking to arouse anxiety, the sadist is actually attempting to give jouissance. Instead, what "is hidden behind the attempt to make the Other anxious in sadism is the attempt to bring out object *a*" (p. 207).

In the sadist's enactment of castration, he seeks to isolate that which is most precious to his victim and to threaten his victim with its loss; in so doing he reveals that precious object as object *a*, and he uncovers its relation to a law or prohibition that he himself enunciates (the voice). Object *a* is of supreme importance in the sadistic scenario because it is something that comes into being in response to the law (or in the sadist's case, the

Other's desire or will which is substituted for the law). When the parental Other enunciates the law and makes demands upon the child related to his socialization (e.g., "Don't touch your penis in public!"), s/he reveals that object (e.g., the penis) as separate and important. At the moment at which the Other threatens the subject with the loss of the satisfaction s/he derives from an object, that object is transformed into object *a*, the cause of the subject's desire (see the section "Object *a*: The Vital Remainder" in chapter 2 for a review of the lost object).

According to Freud's 1926 definition of anxiety in "Inhibitions, Symptoms, and Anxiety," anxiety is a signal indicating danger. The danger that brings on anxiety in relation to the current discussion is that the object is about to be lost. As Lacan (1956) said, "anxiety, as we know, is always connected with a loss" (p. 273). In contrast with fantasy, which veils deeper truths, the wisdom of anxiety can be trusted "because in effect anxiety is that which does not deceive" (1973/1998a, p. 41). Anxiety is always a signal that the subject is about to lose the jouissance s/he derives from an object (castration anxiety, for instance), and the experience of anxiety brings out the identity of that object as object *a*. Consequently, *we may view the sadist's aim as isolating object* a *by enunciating a prohibition, law, or threat. The anxiety the sadist elicits is merely a means to this end.*

The victim's anxiety over the sadist's uncovering the object about to be lost primarily functions as proof of the enunciation of a law. It is for this reason that the sadist derives satisfaction from the victim's anxiety. In other words, the victim's anxiety proves that a law has been enunciated (one that mimics the operation of separation) and that the paternal function has been bolstered (albeit temporarily); correspondingly, the sadist's jouissance/anxiety is bound and reduced, producing a subjective sense of satisfaction.

Unlike the masochist, who pushes the Other to enunciate a law, it is more directly from the sadist's own will and desire that he himself enunciates a law. In Fink's (1997) words,

> The sadist believes that it would be the symbolic Other's will to wrest the object from him, to take away his jouissance, if only the Other really existed. The sadist, for whom the law has not operated, plays the part of the Other in his scenario *in order to make the Other exist*, and seeks to isolate for his victim the object to which the law applies. (p. 191)

The sadist unconsciously identifies with his victim, and so at the same time that he plays the role of lawgiving Other, so too does he experience himself as the subject upon whom the limit or loss is imposed.

Villains in movies are often portrayed as sadistic, and commonly place the hero in conundrums in which the hero faces the imminent loss of object *a*.

> What does [the villain] do to the hero when he captures him? The villain ties him up in such a way that if he tries to free himself, his beloved falls into a pool of boiling acid. In this way, the hero is forced to contemplate the imminent loss of what is most precious to him: his cause of desire, the woman who for him embodies object *a*. In certain cases, the hero is not even aware that this woman is what is most important to him in the world until he sees her dangling by a thread over the boiling cauldron. (Fink, 1997, pp. 190–191)

In this example, the villain/Other presents the hero/subject with a choice reminiscent of the choice in alienation (i.e., "Your money or your life!"): lose your life or lose object *a*—either way you lose something, and if you lose your life you also lose object *a* (your relationship with the woman). The villain is not interested in killing the hero right away (or perhaps, at all), but is instead concerned with isolating object *a*. Likewise, Harvey Dent/Two-Face in Christopher Nolan's *The Dark Knight* wants revenge against Lt. Gordon and so he points a gun at each of Lt. Gordon's family members in turn, trying to discern which of them Lt. Gordon values the most (i.e., which of them embodies object *a* for Gordon). Interestingly, it is very common for sadistic individuals to watch B movies and horror movies—movies in which such sadistic scenarios tend to arise.

Sadistic Impudence

The sadist's attempt to isolate object *a* for someone can be as comparatively (to murder) benign as instances of verbal impudence.[111] By ascertaining what is most valuable to someone's self-image, the sadist attacks someone to the core of her existence through his impudence. For example, a sadist whose case I am familiar with attended a Catholic elementary school as a boy and was involved in a class skit. The first rehearsal of the skit was supervised by his teacher, a nun. During the rehearsal, he improvised a crude joke about adults having premarital sex. The nun became visibly upset, and sharply warned him not to tell that joke when the class performed in front of the priest. Not surprisingly, he told the joke in front of the priest anyway, and he enjoyed arousing the priest's displeasure.

---

111 One sadist said of himself, "I'm the mean, sadistic guy who makes people uncomfortable and gets a rush out of it."

Through his impudent words, he isolated what was precious to the lives of the nun and the priest—namely, Catholic propriety with regard to sexual matters—and called it into question.

Sadists are sometimes verbally impudent under the guise of honesty. It is no accident that their so-called honesty is usually offensive. Of this kind of honesty's tendency to provoke shame, Jacques-Alain Miller (2006d) said, "The honest person is evidently one who ... would like it to be the case that shame did not exist—one who enrobes and veils the real of which this shame is the affect ... This is what psychoanalysis is able to point out, that the shameless are shameful" (pp. 25-26). Sadists reliably have poor relationships with others as a result of their brutal honesty which induces the shame which is related to the jouissance that is at "the inmost core of the subject" (Lacan, 1963/2006a, p. 771).

When working with sadists, it is important to remember that they can and will, at times, use the rule of free association for sadistic purposes. In other words, they will use their speech to enact separation by striving to arouse the anxiety of the therapist and to bring out object *a*. For instance, the aforementioned sadist (who attended Catholic school), whom I will refer to as "Louis," in the beginning stages of his therapy often uttered provocative transference wishes. For example, he said he knew he could not and would not do so, but he wished he could "trap [his therapist] in a dungeon and make her love him" or that he was fantasizing about walking across the session room and kissing the therapist. Such comments were designed to isolate object *a* and arouse the anxiety of the therapist. When the therapist, according to Louis, "did not seem fazed" by his words, he was disappointed.

Louis had daydreams in which he "tased" people using a "taser" like the police use, and he shared one earlier one of these daydreams in the session in which he noted that the therapist "did not seem fazed." The therapist asked the patient to associate to the word "fazed," and "tased" and "shocked" were his associations. The therapist made some interpretations to the effect that Louis wanted to take the place of a police officer and enunciate a law while enjoying the anxiety of the victim threatened with violence. Furthermore, the therapist commented that a taser has the effect of *stunning* or temporarily incapacitating a person, and that it is typically used in the context of making a physically resistant person submissive or obedient. The therapist then asked, "Who is the resistant person, and how is he or she being resistant?" Louis first answered that the therapist was resistant to his attempts to make her shocked (i.e., anxious) and also to his attempts to "cross the professional boundary" by getting her to self-disclose. Then, Louis added that he was more truly the resistant one because he was supposed to be obedient as a patient, but instead he was trying to get off on "ruffling the feathers" of the therapist and sometimes refusing to answer her questions, calling them "irrelevant." The therapist ended the session at that point, Louis being the one who desired to be castrated or tased.

As a result, in the sessions that followed Louis was more traditionally cooperative with the therapeutic process and did not verbalize any impudent transference wishes. Prior to that interpretation, Louis had escalated his threatening transference fantasies in response to the therapist's "blank screen." While neurotic patients tend to respond favorably to the therapist's lack of anxiety or worry over a symptomatic manifestation,[112] perverse patients often act out or act in all the more. Consequently, *perverse patients sometimes require the therapist to lay down a law*. For instance, a therapist might find it necessary to prohibit a patient from engaging in certain dangerous masochistic or sadistic practices.

The Sadist's Identification with His Victim

> It is clear that the sadist is only the instrument of the supplement given to the Other, but which, in this case, the Other does not want it. It does not want it, but it obeys nevertheless.
>
> Lacan (2006b, p. 259)

Whereas the masochist prefers to experience suffering himself, "the sadist discharges the pain of existence into [*rejette dans*] the Other, but without seeing that he himself thereby turns into an 'eternal object'" (Lacan, 1963/2006a, p. 778). In other words, on the one hand the sadist forces subjective division (the loss of object *a*) upon his victim, who correspondingly suffers "the pain of existence" (p. 778). In forcing the victim to undergo the loss of object *a*, the sadist can, by comparison, consider himself whole and lacking in nothing. On the other hand, he is blind to the fact that his enactment carries with it his identification with his victim. Rather than having overcome and risen above the impasse of castration, the sadist is stuck staging separation over and over again.

Although case studies of sadists are extremely rare—many authors claim to be writing about cases of sadism but misdiagnose their patient—neurotic individuals with sadistic traits provide ample examples of identifying with the victim. Such men and women derive satisfaction from informing their victims of what they stand to lose (valuables, their lives,

---

112 In her excellent autobiographical book, entitled *The Words to Say It* (1984), Marie Cardinal described her psychoanalysis. The problems she initially presented to her analyst included psychosomatic and very troubling hemorrhages. Her analyst did not respond with anxiety as had her husband and the many medical professionals she had consulted over the years, but instead advised her to stop taking her medications and to engage in the process of psychoanalysis. After her second session her bleeding had stopped for good.

or, in the case of the "victims" of police officers, their liberty) but at the same time believe that they are similar to their victims. "Police officers, military commanders, and politicians are very often depicted as considering themselves 'above the law,' yet they generally very much identify with those they squash, even as they squash them (as if to say, "This is what I myself deserve")" (Fink, 1997, p. 274).

For example, a neurotic who was a patient of mine in a forensic context had a long history of bullying which he first explained by saying "Beating kids up and stealing from them made me feel powerful." He had targeted particular boys who were "scrawny-looking" and "loners." In the next session, he described himself as a "loner," and I pointed out that he had used that word to describe his victims. At first jumping a little with surprise, the patient then elaborated upon the many ways in which he felt similar to his victims.

A Little Chanticleer or A Chicken Is Being Killed: Ferenczi's Case of the Sadistic Árpád

One of the best clinical examples of sadism is Sándor Ferenczi's (1916) case of Árpád ("A Little Chanticleer"), who was five at the time of his consultation with Ferenczi. Árpád was a sadist, and his "fundamental fetish" (Lacan, 1961/2006a, p. 610) was for poultry—in particular for cocks with long beaks. Of course, because Árpád was only five, his perverse structure was not yet fixed; Árpád may have become neurotic with the help of Ferenczi. Árpád delighted in watching poultry in the hen house for hours on end, and imitated their movements and sounds even after he was forcibly removed from the hen house. After Árpád's family moved away from the hen house, he continued his imitations and his excessive and near-exclusive interest in poultry. His favorite game, which he

> repeated endlessly every day, was as follows: He crumpled up newspaper into the shape of cocks and hens, and offered them for sale; then he would take some object (generally a small flat brush), call it a knife, carry his "fowl" to the sink (where the cook really used to kill the poultry), and cut the throat of his paper hen. He shewed how the fowl bled, and with his voice and gestures gave an excellent imitation of its death agony. Whenever fowls were offered for sale in the courtyard little Árpád got restless, ran in and out of the door, and gave no peace until his mother bought some. He wanted to witness their slaughter. (Ferenczi, 1916, p. 205)

Part of Árpád's sadistic game, then, involved imitating the fowl's death as if he were the fowl/his victim. Árpád played simultaneously at being the lawgiving Other or executioner and the victim who is castrated or killed.

174

Árpád was afraid of cocks, and he clearly enjoyed their executions—whether by his own hand in play or by his (female) cook's hand (on his orders). These symptoms began when he was three-and-a-half years old while he was on vacation in Austria and discovered a hen house. A symptom, as we know, forms as a solution to solve a problem and serves as a way of symbolizing the traumatic real. When his parents asked him to explain his strange behaviors, Árpád related an event that had happened to him at age two-and-a-half. He had gone out to the hen house with a servant, and when he urinated in it a cock bit his penis and the servant dressed his wound. Then someone cut the cock's throat.

So why did Árpád's symptom form only after his second encounter with a hen house and chickens, instead of in response to his first such encounter? The reason for this is suggested in the description of the year in between the two events, during which time Árpád began frequently "playing with his member, for which he often got punished" (Ferenczi, 1916, p. 206) and that someone had threatened to cut it off in response. Ferenczi noted that Árpád was "very defiant whenever he was reprimanded or beaten" (p. 208). In other words, having encountered sexuality and castration threats, Árpád's second encounter retroactively gave a new meaning to the first encounter. Consequently, Árpád's game functioned as an enactment of castration with the cock as the victim.

Dominique Miller (1996) presented an illuminating commentary on "A Little Chanticleer." She noted that Árpád's perversion is evident in the fact "that Árpád can no longer speak when he approaches the hen house. This encounter stirs up something real which was latent until then … This encounter with the real strikes him dumb and triggers the perversion" (p. 296). The chicken, rather than representing the lawgiving Other, is for Árpád merely an imaginary other. Árpád imitates the cock but also inflicts castration upon the cock (cutting its throat, plucking it, and even gouging out its eyes once it is already dead) just as his penis had been threatened with castration the year before. Árpád's fascination with chickens and with killing them was obvious from his games, his behavior, and his speech; he even often dreamt of "killed" cocks (Ferenczi, 1916, pp. 208–209). As Miller (1996) said, "Árpád's fascination with the object, the fact that he has no choice but to gaze at a scene in which the chicken bears the bar of his own subjective division, suggests that he has become the object" (p. 296).

On a certain occasion, Árpád was playing with a

> fowl that had just been slaughtered by the cook. All of a sudden he went into the next room, fetched a curling-tong out of a drawer, and cried: "Now I will stick this dead fowl's blind eyes"… Someone, pointing to the slaughtered fowl, asked him: "Would you like to wake it again?" "The devil I would; I would knock it down again at once myself." (Ferenczi, 1916, p. 209)

The suggestion that Árpád could awaken a dead chicken and then "knock it down again" (p. 209) evokes the curious logic of disavowal that is the constitutive mechanism of perversion. In Árpád's assertion and in his gouging out the eyes of the dead chicken, Árpád was, for one thing, denying the limits imposed by death. This is reminiscent of Sade's desire to omit his name from his grave, thus denying death.

Miller (1996) analyzed this event very well:

> What is the point of gouging out the eyes of a dead chicken? It is explained by the fact that Arpad cannot acknowledge castration. The dead chicken, representing the lack in the Other, blinds Arpad. The blind eyes reveal the Other's lack or desire. This gaze which cannot see becomes both the object as gaze in the Other and his own gaze, the object of his fantasy. Being blind, this gaze leads to the superimposing of two lacks: the maternal Other's lack and the lack in the subject who identifies with the other, that is, with the object. This double castration is unbearable and leads the subject to intensify his denial: he blinds the eyes of a dead chicken, and in so doing blinds eyes that are already blind. (p. 298)

In keeping with Freud's finding that perverse individuals experience both "[a]ffection and hostility" (1927/1961, p. 157) toward their fetishes, Árpád manifested "plainly ambivalent" (Ferenczi, 1916, p. 209) feelings toward chicken-objects. "Very often [Árpád] would kiss and stroke the slaughtered animal, or he would 'feed' his wooden goose with maize, as he had seen the cook do; in doing this he clucked and peeped continuously" (p. 209). On one occasion Árpád threw a chicken-doll into the oven but immediately took it out and caressed it.

Árpád's sadism extended, of course, to his relations to others. On several occasions Árpád threatened to harm someone's genital region. To an older boy he said, "'I'll give you one in the feces, in your behind,'" (Ferenczi, 1916, p. 211). On another occasion he said, "'I'll cut your middle out'" (p. 211). Árpád's words for male or female genitalia were remarkably ambiguous (i.e., lacking in gender-specificity), indicating his lack of the signifier for sexual difference. Along those lines, Árpád was "highly interested in the genitals of poultry. With every fowl that was slaughtered they had to enlighten him about the sex" (p. 211).

Significantly, Árpád once said the following about his mother:

> "I should like to eat a potted mother (by analogy: potted fowl); my mother must be put in a pot and cooked, then there would be a potted mother and I could eat her." (He grunted and danced the while). "I would cut her head off and eat it this way" (making

movements as if eating something with a knife and fork). (Ferenczi, 1916, p. 211)

For Árpád, cutting someone's head off was analogous to cutting off the head of a chicken, and was an enactment of castration. Note that Árpád did not differentiate between castrating women and castrating men in this manner. By saying he would like to cut his mother' head off and eat her, Árpád was perhaps indicating, for one thing, that he experienced his mother's presence as somehow posing a danger to him and that he would like to triumph over her.

However, Árpád's wish was followed by

an attack of remorse, in which he masochistically yearned for cruel punishments. "I want to be burnt," he would then call out: "Break off my foot and put it in the fire." "I'll cut my head off. I should like to cut my mouth up so that I didn't have any." (Ferenczi, 1916, p. 211)

In his discourse, Árpád made phallic objects out of his foot and head by indicating that they can be cut off or removed. Clearly, then, Árpád desired to be castrated and undergo the process of separation.

Árpád enunciated a lineage of sorts whereby his "father is the cock" (Ferenczi, 1916, p. 211)—thus attempting to give the Name-of-the-Father an important role—and his mother is the fowl. On one occasion, Árpád said,

"Now I am small, now I am a chicken. When I get bigger I shall be a fowl. When I am bigger still I shall be a cock. When I am biggest of all I shall be a coachman." (The coachman who drove their carriage seemed to impress him even more than did his father). (pp. 211–212)

Genealogies of this sort are commonly devised by children, who, having undergone alienation, attempt to prop up the paternal function (e.g., Little Hans) and enact separation. In this one, Árpád denied sexual difference by claiming that he can turn into a creature like his mother and then become like his father. Árpád planned on growing up to be a coachman, that is, to be more impressive than his father. Creating a phallic figure more powerful than his father (i.e., the coachman) was Árpád's perverse strategy to bolster the paternal function. Presumably, Árpád had seen a coachman whip horses in order to get them to do the coachman's bidding (and go faster). The coachman is therefore a figure who enacts castration upon someone (i.e., a horse), but who forces limits upon the jouissance of that someone in the name of his personal will rather than in the name of the moral law.

Furthermore, if it is true that Árpád's "father is the cock" (Ferenczi, 1916, p. 211), then it is significant that Árpád's mother, the female cook, and Árpád all have actual and symbolic roles in killing or castrating the cock. This indicates the mOther's triumph over the lawgiving Other as well as Árpád's triumph. From his original traumatic scene, Árpád learned that if a cock/father tries to castrate him, a mOther figure will simply intervene and undermine the authority of the father (i.e., slit the throat of the cock). However, insofar as Árpád identified with the cock who was being killed/who was castrated, Árpád propped up his paternal function with a sadistic solution, thus enacting a temporary separation.

Schadenfreude

There is a German word which is clinically useful and applicable to citizens of primarily English-speaking countries despite there being no English equivalent: *Schadenfreude*, meaning pleasure or joy (i.e., jouissance), in witnessing someone else's pain or misfortune. *Schadenfreude* is a common emotional state for individuals in many cultures and can be experienced by psychotic, perverse, and neurotic individuals. *Schadenfreude* often goes hand in hand with imaginary-order conflicts involving rivalry. It is commonly thought that *schadenfreude* is the defining characteristic of the sadist, but, as I have detailed, the sadist's enjoyment of the suffering/anxiety of the victim reflects an indirect relation rather than a direct one. That is to say that the sadist enjoys and takes satisfaction in the successful (temporary) enunciation of a law of which the victim's suffering/anxiety is only a sign. Correspondingly, the masochist takes pleasure in his own pain only insofar as his suffering proves that an Other is imposing limits upon him. *Schadenfreude*, then, should be understood within the context of the individual's relation to the Other. In perversion, *schadenfreude* is present in the form of jouissance in the pain/suffering that testifies to the enactment of castration.

All this being said, recall (from chapter 3) Freud's observation regarding the "divided attitude of fetishists to the question of the castration of women" (1927/1961, p. 156). The fetishist experiences both "[a]ffection and hostility" (p. 157) toward his fetish, "mixed in unequal proportions in different cases, so that the one or the other is more clearly recognizable" (p. 157). We can substitute "pervert" for "fetishist" because of Lacan's (1961/2006a, p. 610) claim that object *a* as fetish is present at the foundations of every perversion. In the section "Defiling the Other in the Perverse Act" earlier in this chapter, I discussed how the pervert expresses hostility toward his mOther in the fetish and in the perverse act. From this perspective, the sadist's *schadenfreude* has to do with his hostile attitude toward the lack in the Other—the nameless lack (related to the mOther's demand rather than her desire) which is so threatening to the pervert.

Schadenfreude *in Glover's Case of Fetishism*

The fetishist in James Glover's (1927) "Notes on an Unusual Form of Perversion" experienced *schadenfreude* regularly as part of his perverse enactment. Glover's fetishist selected as his partner a woman who wore high-heeled shoes (i.e., the fetish object representing the "maternal phallus") and who had never taken alcohol to excess. He would take her out to dinner and get her to drink quite a bit of wine. He "awaited what he called the proofs of her intoxication, especially a slackness of the mouth which made it look spoiled, any derangement of hair or dress and any increased redness of her nose" (p. 10). He enjoyed these signs that he had defiled the Other who had previously been innocent in the way of taking alcohol to excess, and thus lacking. What is more properly *schadenfreude*, however, was his pleasure in afterward keeping the woman "walking till she was on the point of falling and collapsing" (p. 10) and that on the following "morning he liked to imagine that his partner felt very sick and ill as the result of her dissipation with him" (p. 11).

Alcohol correspondingly served a fetishistic function, because he filled the lack in the Other with alcohol (instead of himself or his penis), perhaps having originally reasoned (as a child): "What she wants is not me but alcohol, which my father provides." In fact, his mOther was an alcoholic, and died of complications from alcoholism when he was seven years old. Also, alcohol represented the sexual relation because as a child, "after exclusion from [his parent's] room [at night], which he bitterly resented … he believed that they were drinking secretly together when he was not there" (Glover, 1927, p. 12).

Concerning the fetish object, he would take the woman's shoes "which, as the result of this proceeding, had become sexually attractive because the drinking of alcohol by the woman had changed them in some way, and because they had been dirtied and spoiled during the walk" (Glover, 1927, p. 10). While recalling the details of the night, he would masturbate, "after which he would throw the shoes angrily away [and say] 'Now go to Hell! I've finished'" (p. 11). It is quite possible that he had heard his father say this to his mother after he had been excluded from their bedroom. Furthermore, his father had sanctioned his interest in his mother's shoes, for instance by asking him to fetch his mother's slippers, which, to his delight, were hidden in a box (as genitalia are hidden).

Indeed, just as high-heeled shoes were at that time hidden under the woman's long skirt (Glover, 1927, p. 15), so too were her genitalia concealed. Likewise, Glover noted that his patient's strong scoptophilic impulses were centered on the idea of a hidden penis in the woman which would reappear. The idea of any hidden phallic object reappearing in connection with a woman took many forms and caused him either pleasure or anxiety. As a small child he was pleasurably excited when little girls put out their tongues at him. The shoe itself, appearing from under the woman's skirt, was the principal representation of this idea, but an interesting refinement of it was his intense pleasure when he saw a high heel on a woman's shoe for the first time. He felt it had been there all the time, but hidden. Part of this pleasure was no doubt a castration reassurance, as was indeed the shoe-fetishism itself. (pp. 15–16)

High-heeled shoes represented the maternal phallus such that ruining the shoes represented castrating the mOther.

Glover (1927) noted that his patient "vividly identifies himself with the woman" (p. 19), such that we may say that his enactment of castration upon the symbol of the woman served the dual function of castrating himself (i.e., enacting separation). He exhibited various symptoms of the lack of the signifier for sexual difference, including a belief in the maternal phallus, wearing only women's shoes until he was 19, and "his conscious wish to fantasy himself a woman" (p. 20). It is further notable that after "his mother's death he occupied her place in his father's bed, and received his affectionate caresses with ambivalent feelings of resentment and shamed pleasure" (p. 12).

Returning more specifically to this fetishist's *schadenfreude*, when the patient was a

child he took delight in catching unwary cats asleep and in urinating on them. As an adult he had the fantasy of retaining his urine and urinating into the woman in order to cause her pain. During unsuccessful attempts at coitus he was satisfied if some of his semen entered her vagina, even if his penis did not. It would burn her inside. One purpose in introducing alcohol into the woman's body was that it would burn her inside!... Drinking, he said, was the greatest crime next to murder. (Glover, 1927, pp. 17, 19)

Providing evidence of the operation of disavowal, Glover continued on to say that the "realization of his sadistic wishes was brought about in a quasimagical manner as if by the omnipotence of thought—an association which was particularly strong in the patient's mind and, indeed, almost a conscious one" (p. 17). In other words, although the patient knew on one level that his thoughts about the painful effects of semen and alcohol did not have the power to harm a woman, at the same time he preferred to believe that he could harm a woman by thinking in this manner. Furthermore, one of his favorite thoughts was "that of 'killing with a glance'" (p. 18). Obviously, the gaze is mixed in this instance with *schadenfreude*. "Moreover," said Glover, "in a magical sense the desired results were brought about by looking. If he could not alcoholize the woman he could 'look' her into that state" (p. 18). Via the magical thinking involved in disavowal, he imagined he could fill the lack in the Other, defiling and hurting her simply with the power of his gaze.

Schadenfreude *as an Existential Potentiality*

Schadenfreude, then, commonly appears in perversion in two major ways. The first is jouissance in the pain/suffering of the partner because it proves that castration/separation has been enacted, and the second is jouissance in expressing hostility toward the fetish-object. However, despite *schadenfreude*'s absence in the English language, it is folly to think that it can only be experienced by perverts. Neurotics can be extremely cruel and get off on being so—oftentimes more so than perverts (especially perverts from any of the four substructures other than sadism).

Individuals cause others mental or physical anguish, as Lacan (2006b) suggested in Seminar XVI, because their jouissance is bound up with such actions.

> The sadistic games: this is not simply interesting in the dreams of neurotics. One can see what is there where this is produced. It is nice to always have reasons to do this or that, we know very well what to think of reasons. They are secondary to what happens in practice. It always has to do with something in which it is about peeling away a subject—of what? Of what constitutes it in its fidelity, its speech [*parole*]. (p. 257)

Even though police officers and military personnel may believe themselves to have good reasons for humiliating or torturing others, the fact remains that they get off on causing others suffering.

From my knowledge of forensic literature as well as my experience working with convicted criminals at both the outpatient and "inpatient" levels of care, I hypothesize that the vast majority of individuals who commit crimes are neurotic. Many violent and "sadistic" crimes are perpetrated by neurotics—even neurotics from "good" neighborhoods and families. Moreover, it is not uncommon for the contents of a neurotic's ego-ideal to be filled with ideals that promote *schadenfreude*, such as in family or societal contexts permeated by racial or religious prejudice. I worked with numerous patients who "came up" (their slang for "brought up") in families that promoted selling illegal drugs and/or stealing even to the point of being prideful about such endeavors.[113]

---

113 In that subculture, people found ways to think of themselves as basically good people while doing things that were illegal and harmed others. For those individuals, the law of the lawgiving Other was not made up of moral standards like "abide by the law," "don't steal" or "treat others as you want to be treated yourself" but instead of moral standards like "don't rat out your fellow gang members," "you owe unquestioned allegiance to your gang," "don't cross into enemy territory," and "do what you have to do to take care of your family." These are the kinds of things that are burned early on into the psyches of the individuals who live in such environments—even if many of them come to reject those standards in favor of a US law-abiding life as they get older. Even though such moral codes are unusual and can promote acts of cruelty, I have found that most of the individuals who grow up in such environments are neurotic.

6

ANALYSIS OF A CASE
OF (PERVERSE) EXHIBITIONISM

Introduction

This case study demonstrates one way in which the theoretical suppositions and questions regarding the perverse structure (found in the preceding chapters) can be put to use in the clinic. First, I provide ample case material and observations from which to understand how "Ray"[114]—who was not mandated to participate in individual therapy—arrived at his request for psychotherapy. Likewise, I focus on the conditions that made it possible for Ray to experience himself as lacking and to consequently engage in symbolic transference. Although Ray frequently played the role of object-cause of the Other's jouissance outside of therapy and sometimes even inside the session room, at the level of desire he was still able to put himself and his life into question; thus he remarked, "I keep seeing myself in new ways."

The reader will notice that Ray's focus in psychotherapy was often on his mother and, less frequently, on his father. Ray's ambivalent relation to his mOther and to being tied to her apron strings is elaborated upon in this case study, as are the symptomatic effects of this relation to the Other including enuresis, depression, acts of exhibitionism, and problems in his romantic relationship. Ray's father is described as insufficiently filling the shoes of the lawgiving Other. This case study also tracks Ray's various creative attempts to bolster the inadequate paternal function and manage his excessive jouissance. The role of the gaze is highlighted in these temporary solutions. Correspondingly, I formulate a type of symbolic transference that is specific to the perverse structure: the subject-supposed-to-No!

---

114 All names used in this case study are pseudonyms, and I have altered identifying information.

The patient, Ray, was a Caucasian exhibitionist in his late 20s with whom I worked individually for about a year,[115] providing weekly variable-length sessions from a Lacanian psychoanalytic clinical perspective. In addition, for a year and a half he was a participant in one of the weekly 90-minute psychotherapy groups I co-led for male sexual offenders. The group employed a mixture of psychodynamic, relapse prevention, and "process" techniques.

Ray was referred by his parole officer (PO) to the outpatient forensic psychotherapy practice of Dr. Smith at which I worked. Ray's participation in individual psychotherapy was purely voluntary, but his participation in group psychotherapy was "recommended" by his PO. From conversations with Ray's PO, Dr. Smith ascertained that she (the PO) would not file a warrant for Ray's arrest were Ray to quit psychotherapy altogether. Ray met with his PO monthly, and seemed to have noticed her assessment of the situation but disavowed it in favor of the belief that she, the representative of the law, was forcing him to seek out treatment that he needed; Ray believed his PO would send him back to jail if he terminated his psychotherapy.

Because I worked in a forensic psychotherapeutic role, my individual and group patients did not have full confidentiality rights. The degree to which each patient had confidentiality rights depends upon which institution of the law was involved in his case: the federal government, the state government, the county government, and Children Youth and Family Services (CYFS). Ray's confidentiality was compromised only by state parole, which demands only occasional communication with a psychotherapy practitioner—communication which can be as vague as "he attends therapy consistently and, as far as we know, has not committed any new crimes." That being said, the office policy of Dr. Smith included the requirement that each sexual offender take an initial history polygraph and subsequent annual maintenance polygraphs.[116] These results were shared with probation and parole officers, albeit with communications regarding the limitations of the polygraph's validity.

Although Dr. Smith spoke to Ray's PO on several occasions, I never had occasion to do so. Of course, because of my role as forensic clinician, the transference was also necessarily affected because of the obligation to

---

115 After a year, I had to transfer the case to another clinician because I had to move in order to finish my graduate education. Although in instances such as these—when the therapist or patient moves away and wishes to continue the therapeutic relationship—I practice psychotherapy over the phone, I did not do so with Ray because Dr. Smith and I thought it best to keep Ray in both individual and group treatment at his practice.

116 Maintenance polygraphs are generally designed to ascertain whether or not the patient has committed any new criminal offenses since a certain date (such as the beginning of his treatment).

communicate, albeit selectively, with POs. Based on my experience working under such conditions, I found that effective psychoanalytic psychotherapy is possible in a forensic setting with many individuals.

Offense History and Prior Treatment

Prior to beginning treatment at Dr. Smith's office, Ray exposed his genitals to women on thousands of occasions, and was incarcerated in state prison on two occasions for a total of about four years for multiple convictions of indecent exposure and indecent exposure to minors. The convictions of indecent exposure to minors had resulted from Ray's strategy of selecting girls under the age of 18 as victims because he thought they were less likely to notify the police. Not only did that strategy not work, but it resulted in a more severe penalty for indecent exposure. Ray twice served probation terms, and was imprisoned for violating the conditions of his probation and going on the run (AWOL). When Ray went AWOL, he travelled across the country to stay with a friend who was a drug dealer. After using a good deal of marijuana and cocaine, Ray turned himself in. Ray had reasoned that he would be unable to get employment and would eventually be apprehended. That being said, if Ray had not been AWOL, he may have been able to avoid incarceration for that set of convictions altogether. Ray's actions seem to have been motivated by a desire to prop up his paternal function—to be in relation to an authority figure whom he was forced to obey—rather than by his consciously avowed intentions to get away with crime.

Shortly before starting therapy at the office of Dr. Smith, Ray had been kicked out of a mandated sexual offender outpatient treatment program because he missed an individual session. Ray had gone through about two years of group and individual treatment at that program which he reportedly found to be "useless." Ray's treatment there was interrupted by serving a year in prison due to a conviction for indecent exposure he got while in treatment. Ray said he was consistently dishonest with the staff at the treatment program, participated minimally in group therapy, and that he was committing acts of indecent exposure almost every day during the course of his treatment. In comparison to his treatment at Dr. Smith's office, Ray described his treatment at the former program as completely lacking in confidentiality such that he could be certain that anything he said would be reported to his PO and potentially used against him. Furthermore, Ray said that neither his group nor his individual therapist seemed adequately educated in the way of psychotherapy in general or in sexual offender treatment specifically. Ray complained that they did not offer him helpful knowledge or hope that he could stop committing acts of indecent exposure. Ray said that his group therapist had told his mother and girlfriend, "people like him don't stop."

Ray's Request for Psychotherapy

At Dr. Smith's outpatient forensic practice, Ray initially participated in about 10 individual and assessment sessions with Dr. Smith.[117] Ray complained of symptoms of depression and anxiety[118] and also wanted to work on improving his relationship with his girlfriend. According to Ray, his first session with Dr. Smith marked the last time he committed an act of exhibitionism. Prior to that and excepting his time being incarcerated, the longest he had ever gone without exposing his genitals to women had been 10 days. Among other clinical interventions, Dr. Smith taught Ray some individualized techniques for ceasing to commit acts of exhibitionism. One such technique involved Ray tape-recording (at home) a description of his exhibitionistic act and later listening to his own description. Then, Dr. Smith asked Ray to record an altered description of the scenario, in which Ray stopped himself short of the act by imagining an alternative "healthy" and legal act that afforded him intense pleasure. Instead of doing the required assignment, Ray—very unusually—chose to stop himself short of the act of exhibitionism by making disparaging remarks about himself. Dr. Smith made it clear that their work together would be temporary, because he thought it best for Ray to join a psychotherapeutic group and to do psychoanalytically-oriented individual therapy with a clinician at his practice. In addition, given what Dr. Smith identified to Ray as Ray's "issues with women," he recommended that Ray choose a female psychotherapist.

Where previous clinicians had failed completely, Dr. Smith was able to gain Ray's trust and respect in their first session. Not only that, but Dr. Smith served as a substitute lawgiving Other, temporarily propping up Ray's paternal function and enabling him to cease engaging in acts of exhibitionism. Dr. Smith was able to embody a lawgiving Other for Ray because Dr. Smith gave Ray significantly more confidentiality rights, seemed to possess useful knowledge, to care about Ray, and to believe Ray could stop his acts of exhibitionism.

After six months of participating in the psychotherapy group that I co-led, Ray approached me after a session and asked if he could begin to have individual psychotherapy sessions with me. When I inquired further about the reasons behind his request, he said that he "liked the kind of

---

117 On a self-report personality style questionnaire, Ray was found to most closely resemble a psychopathic and histrionic personality style. In that vein, also instructive is his answer on the sentence completion stem "When I was growing up I spent my time ..." Ray finished the sentence with "lighting things on fire." In a histrionic fashion, he highlighted one of the most shocking things he did as a child. When asked about this, Ray said that, although he had lit things on fire frequently, this was by no means an everyday event and he never hurt anyone.

118 One manifestation of his anxiety was his high blood pressure.

questions [I] asked," and he thought I understood him. Ray referenced the times I directed my gaze at him during group sessions "with a look that bored through [his] head" as if I knew what he wanted to say. I recall what may have been a few such instances, in which a group participant was talking about something to which I imagined Ray had a response, and so I looked over at Ray. When I did so, Ray jumped in his chair, making articulations of surprise. Clearly, object *a* in the form of the gaze was operative in these moments, but in a significantly different manner than that involved in his exhibitionistic act. Instead of Ray causing my jouissance, my gaze caused his jouissance (in the form of surprise) and desire (in the form of his desire to begin individual psychotherapy). What is more, Ray's surprise at such moments indicated that he had placed me in the role of a kind of mind-reader subject-supposed-to-know—a desirable position for the psychotherapist at the outset of therapy.[119]

On a related note, it is of interest to wonder why Ray requested individual psychotherapy at that particular time rather than at an earlier or later date. (Again, Ray's participation in individual psychotherapy in addition to group psychotherapy was purely voluntary, although suggested by Dr. Smith, and Ray's sessions with Dr. Smith ended shortly after he began group work.) Investigating the sessions prior to Ray's request will prove informative. The session before Ray requested to begin individual psychotherapy with me, I had informed the group that one of the eight group

---

119 A common and very significant type of symbolic transference projection is what Lacan called the "subject-supposed-to-know" (Lacan, 1973/1998a, p. 233). Because the analysand has repressed unconscious material, s/he can see (or be brought to see) that there is a lot about himself that s/he does not know. Either at the outset of analysis or shortly thereafter, the analysand begins to suppose that her or his analyst possesses the knowledge about her- or himself that s/he lacks. Lacan said that this signals the start of symbolic transference, and the analysand's transference love for the analyst as knowledgeable Other is associated with it.

Although, of course, the analyst does know something significant in the way of technique, the most helpful knowledge about the analysand resides in the analysand's own unconscious. Consequently, an analyst, as an Other who is supposed to know, functions as a kind of place-holder for the analysand's unconscious by allowing her or him to project onto her and by calling the analysand's attention to possible Other, unconscious meanings of her or his speech. Moving on from the position of the subject-supposed-to-know, the analyst then becomes "object *a*" or the cause of the analysand's desire to do the work of analysis.

Lacan said it is a mistake for the therapist, motivated by her own narcissism, to accept the transference projection of the subject who knows and give the analysand advice or make early or frequent interpretations. For one thing, if the analysand finds a teacher in her or his analyst, s/he will put the responsibility of the work of analysis on her and cease to be curious about her- or himself on her or his own steam. This fosters dependency on the analyst. For another, the analyst's advice will necessarily entail making judgments about the way a person should live that may not be right for the analysand. Finally, the analysand, afraid of being judged negatively by her or his analyst, might avoid speaking about certain topics that may be crucial to the success of the analysis.

participants had been arrested and put back in jail for violating the conditions of his probation. A man I will refer to as David, who had raped an elderly woman while under the influence of alcohol—for which he served almost 20 years in jail—violated his probation terms by having consumed alcohol. (David was arrested by the police for public intoxication.) The group was aware that David had been my individual patient for a short time. The group participants expressed surprise at the news that David had been drinking. The group concluded that David should have disclosed his drinking to us before it got out of hand and got him arrested because we could have helped him stop drinking and prevented his imprisonment.

In the next week's group session, Ray was visibly agitated, and so I asked him to speak. Ray reported that, when driving home from the prior week's group session, he had a "slip" and exposed himself to a woman. Ray had been driving through a bad neighborhood, was stopped at a light, and saw a woman standing by the street. She seemed to be prostituting herself. Thinking that such a woman would not be likely to tell the police, Ray decided to expose himself to her. He drove around the block, anticipating the moment of pleasure, stopped in front of the woman, and rolled down his car window. She saw him and said, "Do you want some help with that?" (referring to his erect penis). Ray immediately lost his erection and drove away from her.

When Ray reflected upon the event, he noted that he had had similar previous experiences with women he later assumed were prostituting themselves in terms of his victim not expressing shock or disgust but instead approaching him and suggesting they engage in a sexual act. On each of those occasions, Ray lost his erection, became anxious, and fled the scene. Ray said that each woman's consent, lack of surprise, and desire to touch his penis were the elements of the situation that took the pleasure out of his act of exhibitionism and elicited feelings of not being in control. It seems to me that because Ray related to his victims as to his mOther—in rigidly repetitive acts of exhibitionism that were both recreations of his relation to the Other and temporary solutions to the inadequacy of his paternal function—Ray experienced his victims' desire just as he experienced the overwhelming and suffocating desire of his mOther. Faced with the Other's exclusive demand for him and his penis and without the assistance of a lawgiving Other (otherwise supplied by the victim's lack of consent), Ray experienced anxiety and fled the traumatic scene.

Ray said he had a difficult time in deciding to disclose the news of his "offense" to the group, but that he believed that, by observing him, I would know what he had done. Also, Ray ultimately thought telling the group would be best because it would help prevent him from engaging in exhibitionistic acts in the future. This is clearly reminiscent of the group's expression of regret the former week that David had not disclosed the news of his drinking to them. Ray said he felt shaken by the experience, because he had recently become confident in his ability to abstain from acting on his exhibitionistic urges. Ray was surprised and dismayed to find that "making the choice to offend" was still a possibility for him. Furthermore, Ray was perturbed that there was seemingly no cause for his behavior, because his life was going well.

The other group participants highlighted that his offense differed from his other offenses because not only had Ray lost his erection and drove away, but he also regretted having committed an act of exhibitionism. In psychoanalytic terminology, committing acts of exhibitionism was now clearly in opposition with Ray's ego-ideal. Nevertheless, Ray said he did not take comfort in this fact, and insisted on focusing on the fact that he had committed a new offense and that he now saw himself as needing more help than before in managing his exhibitionistic urges.

In the group session, I suggested the possibility that Ray's parole violation was connected to that of David. Ray did not take up this suggestion, even though others in the group did so. Ray persisted in thinking that there must be some mysterious reason for his "offense" that he would have to continue to ponder. Then, after group, Ray asked me to begin working with him individually.

In committing an act of indecent exposure and informing me about it, Ray created a situation in which he felt that he needed to explore the motivations and desires behind his actions that were opaque to him, and that I, as a subject-supposed-to-know something about them, could help him do so via psychotherapy. Ray desired to cease committing acts of exhibitionism not only in order to avoid be re-incarcerated but also because he felt ashamed. According to Ray, indecent exposure was a "dirty and desperate act" that he would prefer he not feel compelled to do. Insofar as Ray presented with this lack of satisfaction in his life, he enabled his desire to be hystericized for genuine analytically-oriented work. In addition, Ray expected that participating in psychotherapy would enable him to respect the law and cease committing acts of exhibitionism. Ray's act of exhibitionism inaugurated his analytic relationship with me as Other—both as subject-supposed-to-know and as lawgiving Other.

Nevertheless, through Ray's offensive behavior, so to speak, he became an unruly patient in need of learning how to control himself (according to Ray's ideas of his presenting problem) just like he, as a child in relation to his mOther, could not help but wet his bed every night until he was 11. Ray's inability to control his penis and to make it behave properly was, in both cases, the cause of a closer relationship to the Other. Ray may have wished that I, as his therapist, would try, as futilely as his mOther had, to figure him out and set him straight—all the while the both of us deriving jouissance from that relation. It follows that Ray's offense and related request for individual psychotherapy inaugurated his positioning me as a first Other as well as a lawgiving Other and subject-supposed-to-know.[120]

Ray lived with his two cats and his girlfriend of four years, Susan, who was in her mid-20s. Ray was an apprentice in the construction field. Ray's appearance strongly suggested that he was not a representative of mainstream cultural values. Ray wore muscle shirts, baggy pants, and long, metal chain necklaces to sessions, and usually slouched very low in his chair with his legs spread open or stretched far out in front of him. Ray shaved his head, and this revealed the large tattoo of a spider web on the back of his head. Ray had about 15 tattoos and piercings on his tongue, lips, eyebrows, nipples, penis, earlobes, and ear cartilage. During the course of our individual psychotherapy, Ray got three tattoos and a tongue piercing.

Ray's Exhibitionism

Ray began committing acts of indecent exposure when he was 12 years old. At that time, he regularly raced home from school, went upstairs to his attic bedroom, and, in front of an uncovered window, fondled his erect penis while he watched girls walking home from school on the sidewalk in front of his house. Sometimes, as an alternative, Ray undressed, waited by the front door until a car drove by, and then opened the door and pretended he was only getting the mail out of the mailbox. Once Ray left his parental home at 15 to live with an older friend, he spent numerous hours at a time repeating his exhibitionistic scenario.

Ray took care to expose himself in situations from which he could quickly and easily escape if the police were notified—such as being in his car or hiding in choice spots in familiar parks. For instance, one of his favorite situations was to park his car in a particular parking lot downtown which afforded him a view of a woman walking along a street before she could see him. Ray masturbated while imaginatively anticipating a woman's approach. Then, if the woman walking by was alone, at least somewhat physically attractive to him, and seemed to be under the age of 50, he coughed or made another natural-seeming noise to get her attention as she walked by his car. The woman's gaze was then fixed upon his "playing with himself."

Seeing the woman's gaze upon him is what Ray described as his primary moment of enjoyment. The moment when she realized what he was doing, when she experienced the ethical boundary being broken, was the moment that Ray anticipated reading in her facial expression. Ray said

---

120 Alternatively, perhaps Ray wanted to replace David, to be the patient he imagined I wished David had been. In this instance, Ray would have wished to be object *a* for the Other.

his pleasure in the act was about the moment of the victim's "surprise and recognition." Ray said he liked inciting facial expressions of shock that corresponded to the woman's thinking "Oh, my god! I can't believe he's doing that!" In describing his pleasure in seeing the gaze of the woman on his penis, he said, "It's like: 'take that!'" Not only is this an aggressively charged phrase, but it also quite literally suggests that Ray is offering up the sight of his penis for the woman's jouissance. Ray said he liked "pretty much any expression except one of horror" because the horrified expression meant a greater likelihood of her calling the police. Ray said that he sometimes preferred it if a woman laughed when she saw him masturbate. In psychotherapy, Ray realized that the moment of the woman's gaze, full of the knowledge of his transgression, was also a moment when he felt a brief "little connection" with her, which was a main part of his enjoyment. Ray, as object *a*, made the gaze appear in the Other, making her temporarily whole.

Then, after the woman walked away, Ray would, more often than not, stay there and masturbate while thinking about her and anticipating the next woman's arrival. Ray said that he liked feeling as though he were in "absolute control of the situation." The only things left to chance were the particulars of the woman's reaction and whether or not she notified the authorities. Ray usually committed acts of exhibitionism in this manner for hours until he got too tired or until he knew or suspected that a woman had called the police.

Ray was apprehended by the police while on the scene of his offense on three occasions. Ray said he felt "some strange relief" on each occasion. He recalled sitting in the back of a police car on the way to the police station, feeling "strangely relieved" and "submissive—not putting up a fight." Ray understood that feeling of relief in terms of his desire to stop his indecent exposure, which was "exhausting." Ray was "tired of all the lies" he had to tell to those in his life to explain his absences from work and social commitments.

Ray said he did not feel he could stop his exhibitionistic acts on his own, but that he needed the "interference" of some other person or of legal consequences. Furthermore, Ray said that he did not feel guilty about his exhibitionism, because—despite what he had learned in psycho-educational group therapy—he could not imagine that his victims were very much disturbed by their experience. (It is no wonder that the dominant forensic methods of treatment are largely ineffective in treating perverse sexual offenders, because they focus on utilizing and increasing the patient's feelings of guilt in order to motivate the patient to cease re-offending.) Ray said that he daily felt the "urge" to expose himself, but developed an increasing pride in being able to resist what he called the "exhibitionistic drive." Using the techniques Dr. Smith taught him, Ray also tried to avoid fantasizing about acts of indecent exposure, but he was usually unsuccessful.

In the realm of sexual fantasy, Ray preferred looking at what he called "blow job porn." In pornographic movies he found on the Internet, he described "the usual scenario" of the heterosexual couple beginning with a blow job, progressing to having sex, and then "the big finale of their orgasms." Ray said he really liked the blow job part, skipped the sexual intercourse part entirely, and then enjoyed watching the orgasms. Ray wondered why watching people having sex interested him so little, and why watching a man get a blow job interested him so much. When I asked him to associate to "getting a blow job," he said, "In your face" and then laughed. Ray said the woman "is right up there in the scene and has to look at his penis when she is giving him a blow job." Ray liked that the woman gets off on seeing and putting her mouth on the man's penis. I said, "'In your face' is also an aggressively charged phrase." Ray responded by comparing "in your face" to the words "take that" that he had used to describe his jouissance at the moment his victim's gaze alights on his penis.

Ray said that he got much more enjoyment from his acts of exhibitionism than from sexual intercourse. Ray had difficulty in getting and maintaining an erection for the purposes of sexual intercourse. Ray felt embarrassed and like less of a man because he did not enjoy sex as much as most men seemed to enjoy it. Ray reported that Susan wanted to have sex more often than he did, and that they usually had sex once or twice a week. On his intake form, Ray reported that he "loves extremely graphic sexual talk" and that he used online video sex chat rooms.

Family Context and Personal History

Ray grew up in a lower middle-class family in the suburbs of a small city. He was the youngest of four children, and had two sisters and a brother. All of his siblings were married and had children, and his parents were still married. Sarah, the oldest, was six years older than Ray. Ray was four years younger than Mandy and two years younger than Dave. Ray recalled witnessing, as a young child, his mother sometimes getting into a rage and throwing household items at one or the other of his sisters. Ray said that his mother "physically and verbally abused" his sisters, but for some unknown reason, only "verbally abused" him and Dave. On one occasion when Ray had misbehaved, his mother gave his toys away to the children who lived next door. As the youngest boy, Ray spent much of his younger years at his mother's side.

Ray's father had a career doing skilled manual labor for an industry that suffered a dramatic decrease in demand during Ray's childhood. Ray's father's job was to set type at a printing press. Ray's father did not make very much money and there was little room for advancement in his career. Ray's father lost his job when Ray was 9, when his workplace went out of business. The family moved to another state where Ray's father had found a job, only to move back again a year later after the new workplace went out of business. Then, for almost a year—until they bought a new house—the whole family stayed with Ray's maternal grandmother who had only a one-story, two-bedroom house. All four children slept on the living room floor. Ray was told that his mother particularly disliked living with her mother, whom she felt had been "crazy" and "abusive" to her as a child.

Ray often heard his mother "put down [his] father," whom she did not seem to love or desire at all. One of her chief complaints about Ray's father was that he did not make enough money. (Ray himself was embarrassed about being poor, and was an object of derision at school on this account.) Ray said his parents never kissed, embraced, or said "I love you" to each other. Ray recalled seeing on several occasions his father try to kiss his mother. His mother always responded by laughing derisively and refusing the kiss.

Ray said that, even though his mother was a housewife, it was clear that she was the head of the household. Ray described his mother as cruel and demanding of his father, and that his father "always let her have her way" without putting up any resistance. Ray wished his father had "grown a backbone." Ray's mother was the one who punished him and his siblings, except for a few instances in which his father spanked them at her bidding. Of those instances, Ray said, "We all tried not to laugh when dad spanked us, because he spanked us so lightly that it didn't hurt at all. When mom spanked us, she was much more thorough." Ray told me that he had made it his mission to have "a backbone" in his relationships with women, even to a fault, being too much like his mother—demanding, controlling, and dissatisfied with his romantic partner.

Ray described his mother as "a crazy bitch" who readily identified herself as psychologically ill and talked to all willing and unwilling ears about her symptoms of anxiety, depression, and panic attacks. Ray felt that she wanted all her children to have psychological problems, too, because it validated her identity as "fucked up." Ray's mother was fond of saying that, because of her genes, her children would inevitably become psychologically "sick." Ray disbelieved her rationale in favor of his hypothesis that her mothering was what mostly caused their problems.

Not for the first time, Ray's mother spent a few days in an inpatient psychiatric ward—presumably for suicidality. Ray saw her at a family party shortly after her release, and did not speak to her except to say "hello." Ray imagined that she "must have left the party wondering why [he] didn't ask her how she was doing," given that she must have just gotten out of inpatient psychiatric hospitalization. Ray fantasized about the event several times, imagining his mother's hurt feelings. Since puberty, Ray's desired relation to his mOther had been one of being a bad son and of not doing what she asked of him. However, Ray's identification with his mother was also apparent, as we will see. For instance, when Ray was in the military, he spent some time in an inpatient psychiatric ward for what Ray referred to as his "breakdown."

Ray's parents were Catholic, although they never consistently attended religious services. Corresponding to his parents' Catholicism, Ray sensed that sex, which was not spoken about, was a taboo subject. Ray said his mother "thinks sex is sick"[121] and that his exhibitionism is sicker. Furthermore, physical affection of any kind was a rarity in his family. When Ray was an adolescent, he noticed that his friends' family members hugged and kissed each other and that his family in comparison seemed to avoid touching one another at all—even when sitting on the living room couch watching television together. In addition, the words, "I love you" were seldom uttered. Ray felt anxious if someone got within a few feet of him, and he felt very uncomfortable saying "I love you" to his girlfriend.

As a child, Ray shared a room with his brother, Dave. From his toddlerhood until he was about five years old, Ray showered with his father. On one occasion in the shower with his father, Ray noticed that his father's penis was "in between hard and not hard."[122] Soon afterward, Ray began taking baths with his brother Dave. For the most part, Ray's parents were careful to segregate the girls from the boys in matters of the naked body; however, there was one notable exception: When Ray wet his bed, which he frequently did, his mother took off his clothes, washed off his penis and the rest of his body, dressed him again, and washed the urine-soaked bed sheets. (Also, another early memory Ray recalled was of his mother changing his diapers.) When Ray turned five or six years of age, he began cleaning and dressing himself, but his mother still cleaned his sheets. After each time he urinated during his sleep, Ray's mother would thoroughly scold him. Ostensibly, she tried to cure him of his enuresis. She often proclaimed, "We're gonna have to get you tested!" (The implication was that Ray had something wrong with him that warranted a professional evaluation, although she never followed through with this.) Ray's enuresis functioned to prevent him from sleeping over at friends' houses, which is something his siblings often did. Ray had to stay home with his mOther. Ray wet his bed until he was about 11 years old. It is notable, of course, that he started committing acts of indecent exposure as soon as he stopped wetting the bed.

At age 13, Ray's mother found out about Ray's exhibitionism. One afternoon, after Ray had masturbated in front of the attic window for

---

121 Recall that Ray's mother also used the signifier "sick" to describe the family's mental health problems, thus implying that their problems have something to do with sexuality.
122 This phrase is evocative of the both/and logic of disavowal.

several hours, a police officer came to his house along with the mother of a girl who had seen Ray exposing himself. The police officer spoke to Ray's mother and to Ray. The officer did not file charges because Ray denied his guilt, but Ray was certain that his mother knew he was guilty. Ray's mother had been "really shocked and embarrassed." She took Ray to a psychotherapist, but Ray refused to admit that he had committed indecent exposure, and so he did not see the therapist again. After Ray moved out of his parents' house, his mother "made [his] dad move from that house because she felt embarrassed to be in the neighborhood ever since that day with the cop." Also, each time Ray was charged for indecent exposure, he was on the news, and his mother was publicly embarrassed. When Ray told me about this, I said, "Take that?" Ray agreed, saying he enjoyed making his mother squirm.

Beginning when he was eight years old, Ray frequently skipped school, committed acts of vandalism, trespassed, started fires, lied, stole, carried weapons, got into fights, broke into cars, and abused drugs. (Marijuana, cocaine, and LSD were his drugs of choice, although he also used mushrooms, codeine, aerosol sprays, GHB, nitrous oxide, ecstasy, mescaline, peyote, and ketamine. At the time of his psychotherapy, Ray did not use any of those substances but he drank 3–5 units of alcohol about once a week and was a tobacco smoker.) Once, he "peeped" into a girls' locker room. Ray was caught in his delinquent acts fairly frequently, and these actions caused his school and the police to lodge complaints about him to his mother, who would then yell at him or unsuccessfully try to punish him. For example, when Ray was eight, he was caught starting fires by the police, and had to take fire safety classes as a result. Ray was also apprehended at age 13 and 16 for trespassing, and was fined on the former occasion. (Unlike many neurotic patients who have criminal histories, Ray made several comments over the course of his psychotherapeutic treatment that suggested that he felt relieved when apprehended by the police.) Ray's response to his mother was to yell back at her and tell her she had "no right to tell [him] what to [do.]" Ray mentioned that Dave, who "did all the same shit with [him]," always managed to avoid getting caught. Ray said his problem seemed to be that he "didn't know when to stop," and it occurred to him that he had on some level wanted to get caught.

When Ray was a teenager, he "wore all black, a trench coat, listened to Nine Inch Nails, and dropped a lot of acid." Ray liked that self-presentation because he "was looking for a reaction—to shock people." After Ray graduated from high school, he followed the example of an older cousin and joined the army "because [he] didn't know what else to do with [himself]," and was stationed for several years in another state. Ray greatly enjoyed being in the army. He was a part of the armed forces for about three years, and liked the "camaraderie and respect" that he got while there. During that time, he occasionally got blow jobs from prostitutes, and he regularly committed acts of indecent exposure.

Tattoos

The tattoo certainly has the function of being for the Other, of situating the subject in it, marking his place in the field of the group's relations, between each individual and all the others. And, at the same time, it obviously has an erotic function, which all those who have approached it in reality have perceived.

Lacan (1973/1998a, p. 206)

Ray got his first tattoo at 19 when he was in the army. Ray and all the guys in his unit each got the same tattoo: a POW insignia. Ray greatly enjoyed getting a tattoo, and most enjoyed the pain involved in the process. Soon thereafter, Ray went to a tattoo parlor on an impulse, without any preconceived notion of what tattoo design he wanted. When asked by the tattoo artist what he wanted, Ray, impromptu, drew his own design. Ray designed a woman's face, and got it tattooed just below his shoulder on his arm. It was no accident that a woman's face was an object of extreme interest to Ray in his exhibitionistic scenario.

Getting tattoos was one major way in which Ray propped up the paternal function. Ray himself compared his exhibitionism to his tattoos and piercings. Ray's father was a printing press ink setter who was often out of work, and his trade was a main source of Ray's mother's lack of respect for his symbolic role as lawgiving Other. Ray's mother complained that his father was an inadequate man, husband, and father because he was a poor provider, and so his symbolic status, earned through ink, did not amount to much. By inscribing ink into his skin Ray created a new medium (i.e., his body) in which his father's work continued to be in demand, profitable, and having symbolic importance. In addition, perhaps the ink holes that comprise a tattoo function as significations of the lack in the Other $(S(\cancel{A}))$. The ink holes thus served a fetishistic function for Ray, creating presence out of absence.

Ray derived satisfaction from the pain of being tattooed not because he felt pleasure in pain but instead because the act of being tattooed metonymically relates to the instatement of the paternal function via the imagined pain of castration and via the articulation of the mOther's desire. In terms of castration, getting a tattoo involves the painful process of giving up a part of one's body (an area of the skin instead of the jouissance associated with the imaginary phallus) and allowing it to be permanently altered from its natural state and re-inscribed by that which is Other than the self. What is more, when Ray got tattooed, he was naming and fulfilling his mOther's desire in relation to his father: His mother desired that his father's skills be in constant demand and profitable. In the form of the ink of his tattoos, Ray creatively wrote on his body a better marriage between his mother and his father (his first and second Others)—one in which his mOther respected the symbolic status of his father and desired his father rather than only Ray himself.

Over the course of a decade, Ray got about 15 tattoos. Among them were tattoos of a spider (placed over his heart), a spider web (placed on his head), and several fire-breathing dragons (placed on his arms). Ray, like spiders and dragons, evoked jouissance from the Other—often in the form of surprise, disgust, and anxiety. Furthermore, the simple fact of his having so many large tattoos on readily visible parts of his body was a bit shocking. Ray's tattoos, then, were also symbolic inscriptions of his identity at the level of jouissance: Ray was the object-cause of the Other's jouissance.

During the course of Ray's psychotherapy, he got three tattoos. In the second month of psychotherapy, Ray got a tattoo which said "devil" on the back of his neck. When viewed from above, however, the same text read "angel." Ray found the design for this tattoo on the Internet and altered it slightly. The original Internet design read "angel" from the more commonly viewed angle and "devil" from the less commonly viewed angle. Correspondingly, Ray felt that only a few people knew about his "angelic" side and his good heart, but that most people know about his "tough guy" image. Two months later, Ray got a tattoo of flames going up his right hand and ice going down his arm "with an empty band in between." Ray designed that tattoo himself. When I asked for his associations, his only response was that he "set fires as a kid."

Two months before the end of our work together, Ray expressed the desire that his next tattoo be more bright, colorful, and happy. One such possibility was a large tattoo, perhaps over his leg, of "an aquarium or ocean scene." Ray said that his personality was "already like that"— already bright and colorful, but that he had not yet inscribed that part of his personality on his body. Two weeks before the planned termination of our work together, Ray got a tattoo that was bright and colorful, but was not an aquarium or ocean scene. Instead, Ray said that he had been inspired by the prior week's session to design the particular tattoo he got.

The prior session began by Ray saying, "I fucked up this weekend" and then describing how he had communicated and had sex with Susan, with whom he at that time was not officially in a relationship. Afterwards, Susan said "all the right things" to try to get him back together with her. Ray said, "Susan was saying 'All I ever wanted was love' and got me to pity her." In the session, Ray said he felt that "being independent" and not being in a relationship with Susan was a good thing for him, and that he should not let himself get drawn back into the relationship because he realized he's "never really had a space of [his] own." First, he shared a space with his mother, then the army, and then Susan. Without those things in

197

his life and without his exhibitionism, Ray said he lacked a stable identity of his own. Ray emphasized that he did not know who he was because he was so used to thinking of himself in relation to others. I stopped the session after Ray said, "Maybe who I am is the person who likes to say shocking things to people." (With neurotic and perverse patients, I practice variable-length sessions, a Lacanian technique in which the termination point of the session is determined not by the clock but by something the therapist deems as a particularly important verbalization. The scansion of the session thus functions as an intervention that aims to provoke the patient's curiosity about the possible unconscious meanings of what was last said.)[123]

Ray's tattoo was on the far left side of his face by his hair line and consisted of two sets of two bright green intertwined twisting vines. One set of vines spanned the distance between the bottom of his temple and his forehead, and the other spanned the distance between his chin and his cheekbone. There was a space in between the two sets of vines that read, in Japanese characters, "emptiness."[124] Ray had considered just having an empty space there, but decided the significance of the empty space would not be obvious to people and that he would have to write "emptiness" there to call attention to it. Ray said the vines represented his getting wrapped up with people and things and falsely identifying with them, and that emptiness is who he is without those people and things. Ray's tattoo was inspired by his realization in the previous session that his being was equivalent to emptiness, an idea he seemed to like. In addition, because Ray's tattoo was bright in color and boldly positioned on his face, Ray's tattoo also signified that his jouissance was fixed in bringing the gaze as object *a* to the Other. Ray was the person who liked to show shocking things to people.

Loving the Other

One definition Lacan gave of love is that to love is to give to the Other what one lacks—namely, desire. Ray, being less subjected to the symbolic order, had less access to desire than a neurotic subject, and therefore less ability to love. Furthermore, Ray often experienced being loved not in terms of being desired but in terms of being the object of the Other's

---

123 In contrast, the ending of the more common fixed-length session is not used as an intervention to further the therapy but instead is arbitrarily determined by 50 or 45 minutes having passed in accordance with a capitalistic "time equals money" logic. See Fink (1997, pp. 15–19) for more information on the practice of variable-length sessions.

124 Writing the word *emptiness* instead of leaving an empty space there may be another way that Ray had of turning emptiness or lack into presence.

demand. As a child, being the sole object of his mOther's demand was traumatizing; consequently, as an adult, Ray was both drawn to and repelled by the Other's love which was at the same time attractive and dangerous. The moments in which Ray did succeed in loving the Other enabled him to feel more desire than usual and thus limited his excessive jouissance, pulling him temporarily further into the symbolic order. Correspondingly, one of the aims of psychotherapy with perverse patients should be on behalf of Eros.

A major focus in Ray's psychotherapy was his relationship with his girlfriend, Susan. Susan was Ray's first girlfriend. They began their relationship in Ray's mid-20s, soon after he returned to his home town from being incarcerated. Ray met Susan at the restaurant at which they worked. Susan was three years younger than Ray. Ray described her as attractive with a slender physique and brown hair. At the time, Susan was in a relationship, and Ray, never having been interested in a committed or long-term romantic relationship, intended to have only a brief sexual relationship with her. After a few weeks, however, Susan broke up with her boyfriend, whom she described as being verbally abusive, and persistently pursued a romantic relationship with Ray. After several months of spending a good deal of time with her, Ray fell in love and finally relented to be monogamous with her—with the arguable exception of his indecent exposure victims.

Ray had told Susan about his exhibitionism a few months into their relationship. Ray appreciated that Susan knew about his sexual offense history and accepted him in spite of that. He felt that, over the years, she became the only person, other than a childhood friend who moved overseas, with whom he felt close. Ray's acts of indecent exposure got him reincarcerated during his relationship with Susan. While he was in prison, his Christmas present to Susan was to tattoo a ring on his ring finger that said "Susan."

Ray disliked a number of things about Susan, which he described as her "low self-esteem," her "dependency, clinginess, and constant demands for proof of [his] love and [his] desire for her," her "lack of self-reliance," and her being so "self-conscious and unadventurous" that she did not derive much pleasure from their sexual acts. Ray found one way to increase Susan's jouissance in sexual intercourse: He bought some toy handcuffs and "played rape with her," which "really [got] her going."

Ray frequently complained about Susan. Often, he lamented that she never bothered to get her driver's license, which results in him having to drive her around. At his insistence, Susan took the test to get her driver's license permit twice, and failed each time. Ray said that it took him several years to convince Susan to quit her job at the restaurant and get a more rewarding job. Ray felt pleased that she finally did so and much preferred her office desk job to her former position.

In Ray's relationship with Susan, he often adopted characteristics of his mother and related to Susan as to his father. Identifying with his mother, Ray described Susan as his mother might have described his father: in particular, he characterized her by "low self-esteem ... dependency, clinginess, and [makes] constant demands for proof of [his] love and [his] desire for her." Furthermore, Ray's complaint that Susan was content to stay at a low-paying grunt-work job echoed his mother's complaint against his father with regard to his job. However, Ray's efforts to get Susan to obtain a better job and get her driver's license may in part have been reflective of his desire to improve what he saw as her deficiencies and not simply to complain. In this vein, Ray was trying to turn Susan into a better Other, just as he wished he could have turned his father into a worthy lawgiving Other.

Ray and Susan dated for three years before they moved in together. Four months after that, Ray broke up with Susan and she moved back in with her parents. Ray did so because he found himself too frequently annoyed and angered by her presence and by her demands for love and affection. They got into fights almost every day, and Ray felt "angry and suffocated." To the psychotherapeutic group, Ray remarked that he felt that Susan's only ambition in life was to be his wife, and he wished that she wanted other things or other people. Another very common complaint of Ray's was that Susan did not want anything in life but him, and this was a complaint Ray also had against his mOther. Ray became anxious when Susan's demands, like his mOther's, seemed fixated on him, leaving no room for him to desire.

Only a few days after their breakup, the two of them resumed their relationship, but in a different form. Ray described the shift in their relationship as resulting from his "setting some firm ground rules" and "laying down the law." Mostly, he became "strict about not letting Susan spend any time with [him] or spend the night on weekdays." This enabled Ray to keep to a very regular schedule during the workweek and to get enough sleep. Even so, Ray said, "she knows the rules, but still asks during the week anyway if she can sleep over." When she did so, he often became angry at her, yelled, and hung up the phone. Then, Susan called repeatedly until he turned off his cell phone. In contrast, the two of them almost always spent the entirety of every weekend together. By Saturday evening or Sunday, Ray felt annoyed by her, and was ready for her to leave.

Ray knew it was unfair for him to "be dangling Susan on a string," and he wished "she'd grow some balls, say she's had enough, and leave." This statement metonymically related Susan to his father. Ray wished his father would have and could have become a "real" man by growing some balls, standing up to his mOther, and leaving her. At the same time, Ray's "firm ground rules" and "laying down the law" were indicative of Ray's efforts to be what his father was not—a lawgiving Other capable of being respected by the first Other. In that sense, Ray was in the position of his father and Susan in the role of his mother.

Soon after Susan moved out of their apartment, Ray began using a video chat Internet site. He found a circle of "cool people around the world to talk to" and also used the adult chat rooms to engage in sexual acts with women. On this site, Ray began frequently talking to and masturbating with Abby, a woman in her late 30s who lived in another state. Ray exclusively spoke with her on weeknights, and enjoyed the fact that, if he wanted to stop interacting with her, he could simply "click the x at the corner of the screen." However, Ray developed a kind of intimate relationship with her over the course of six months to the point of Abby booking a plane ticket to meet and visit Ray for five days. A few days prior to her trip, she drunkenly told him over the phone, "you don't even know how much I like you; if all goes well when I visit, there will be no holding me back." Her statement made Ray feel anxious, and so he ended their relationship two days prior to her scheduled departure, offering to pay for her plane ticket.

After the first time that Ray broke up with Susan during psychotherapy, he said he felt "hollow." In the following week's session, Ray said he had "filled [his] weekend" by getting his tongue pierced—something he anticipated would increase the pleasure of his future sexual partners. The hole created by Ray's piercing may have signified his own hollowness or lack of being. Likewise, the tongue stud, in covering over the hole/lack, served a fetishistic function for Ray. Also, quite literally, Ray planned that the tongue stud would cause the jouissance of future Others. Notably and unusually for Ray, he also spent an entire day during the weekend with his mother. When Susan did not play the role of Other, Ray sought out his mOther.

Ray said that without Susan and without committing acts of indecent exposure, he felt lost and hollow. For Ray, Susan and his exhibitionism were similar insofar as they both could serve to prop up his paternal function as well as to provide opportunities for him to be the object-cause of the Other's jouissance. Further drawing a parallel between Susan and his exhibitionism, Ray said that in relation to Susan he is "a controlling prick." Ray said that being a controlling prick helps prevent him from committing acts of indecent exposure—from being an uncontrolled prick.

After Susan moved out, Ray refused to say that they were boyfriend and girlfriend—labels he found oppressive and restricting—despite Susan's pleas to the contrary. In addition, although Ray wanted to be romantically involved with Susan for the foreseeable future, he was loath to make any promises of commitment to her beyond the following week. Ray felt angry whenever Susan "test[ed] [his] love" and asked him to say "I love you" or make promises of fidelity or commitment. When Susan asked for a proof of love during the workweek, Ray usually denied it to her, responded angrily, and then did not speak to her until the weekend. Ray thought that picking her up at her house on Friday night served as sufficient apology for having lost his temper and was also sufficient proof of love.[125]

In individual therapy, Ray wondered about his difficulty in saying "I'm sorry" or "I love you." Ray said his "actions should speak for themselves," by which he meant that his spending time with her every weekend, never getting involved with other women, and doing things like buying her presents communicated a clear message of love, fidelity, and commitment. I pointed out, though, that his actions, such as his refusal to see her five days out of the week, also communicated a contrary message. Ray realized that it was easier for him to say he loved Susan if he did not feel that Susan, like his mOther, was demanding it. Ray said, "If she would just give me the space to say 'I love you,' I'd get around to saying it." Alternatively, it may have been that Ray was rejecting Susan so as to incite her jouissance.

It may be that Ray could not express his love for Susan when he experienced her demands as divesting him of what little symbolic space he had. In addition, their relationship was often conflict-ridden because Ray was a pervert and Susan was an hysteric. Both Susan and Ray wanted the other person to play the role of Other, and both wanted to occupy the position of object *a*. It was therefore rare that one of them offered the other what she or he desired. What is more, Susan operated primarily on the level of desire, and Ray operated primarily on the level of demand.

As an example of the interpersonal conflicts produced by their different ontological structures, consider one of Ray and Susan's fights. The fight began when Susan asked Ray, "Would you come after me if I left you?" Susan's intended meaning was to ask Ray if he would ardently attempt to get her back into a relationship with him if she were to break up with him. She wanted to know that she was important to Ray—that he loved her and would miss her so much if she left that he would seek her out. However, her question, "Would you come after me" also reflects her wondering if Ray would "come" or enjoy himself anymore after having lost Susan and his opportunity to "come with her." In addition, "coming after someone" refers to someone seeking a fight with another who was in the wrong and who aroused passionate anger. Consequently, Susan's request revealed her possible desires to be loved, to be the exclusive object-cause

---

125 Predictably, Ray got back together with Susan a few weeks later, resuming his "ground rules" with her. A few months afterward, Ray decided "to let" Susan move back in with him. As a condition of his permitting her to live with him again, though, he told her she had to get her driver's license permit first. Susan jumped at the opportunity to move in with him, but said, "I'm moving in and I'll get my license whenever I get around to it!" Ray was surprised at just how pleased he was that Susan stood up for herself and asserted her own desire.

of desire and jouissance, to be at fault, and to be harmed by the Other in the name of love.

At a conscious level, Ray did not hear any of those meanings. Ray said that Susan frequently addresses this sort of question to him, and he described always answering at face value. In this instance, Ray answered, "No. If things were at a point at which you wanted to leave, I wouldn't stop you." Ray said he had "an *inkling* that what Susan really wants to hear was 'yes'" and that he loved and needed her. Ray said, "She should just say what she really means." Sometimes, after Susan asked such a question, Ray recognized a desire behind her demand, felt angry that she did not say what she really meant, and chose to answer at face value, making her upset until she made explicit her demand for love. Susan's explicit demands for love, however, fared no better.

Ray's use of the signifier "inkling" suggested that he was speaking not only about Susan but also about his father. Ray's father wanted but did not receive the love and desire of Ray's mother. Perhaps Ray's mother lodged the same complaint against Ray's father that Ray lodged against Susan; his mother may have wished that her husband would stop "beating around the bush" and just say what he wanted. Ink, furthermore, connected Susan to Ray's father insofar as Ray tattooed her name into a tattoo of a wedding ring on his ring finger. Signifying the strength and permanence of their relationship, the tattoo represented the marriage Ray wished his parents had. In addition, it was not a coincidence that Ray got that tattoo in prison, a place that forced him to respect the law.

Recall that to Susan's question, "Would you come after me if I left you?" Ray replied, "No. If things were at a point at which you wanted to leave, I wouldn't stop you." Because Ray's "No" accurately described what Ray intended to do in the event that Susan left him, Ray may have disavowed Susan's desire, mishearing Susan's speech at the level of demand $(S(A))$ rather than at the level of desire $(S(\bar{A}))$. At the same time, however, Ray's speech constituted Susan's desire as a desire to leave him, rather than as a desire for his love. In this sense, Ray heard what he wanted to hear: Susan wanted something other than him, something that he could not provide for her. Heard in this way, Susan's articulation of her desire (for something or someone other than Ray) temporarily opened up a small space for Ray's desire and subjectivity. In the same vein, when Susan occasionally temporarily moved back in with her parents (of her own accord), Ray could breathe easier, having the subjective space to want her or something else. Consequently, what Ray disavowed in instances such as these was his knowledge that Susan loved and wanted to be close with him as well as his own love and desire for Susan.

Furthermore, Ray's answer to Susan effectively functioned to cause her jouissance. Ray's response made Susan feel unsettled, distressed, and devalued. Although Susan was not my patient, I imagine that, on some level, these are all feelings that Susan wanted (because she had stayed in an ostensibly unsatisfying relationship with Ray for five years). Ray ensured that she experienced such jouissance frequently. In making Susan upset, Ray's response to Susan's query perpetuated his position as object-cause of the Other's jouissance.

Ray's mother, like Susan, was most likely a hysterical subject with masochistic tendencies. Ray, as object *a*, was joined at the hip to his mOther: He was her offensive little object, her incurably unruly son, her uncontrollable "controlling prick." Even if, at face value, Ray's mother said she wanted Ray to behave, that she wanted his prick to behave, Ray knew better.

In his relationship with Susan, there was sometimes love. More often, however, Ray experienced Susan's presence and demands for love as a recreation of the traumatic relationship between himself and his mOther. Susan, like his mOther, only seemed to want him. Susan did not want another man, did not want a better job, and did not want to spend time away from Ray. Feeling suffocated and overwhelmed with the anxiety caused by her overproximity, Ray tried to set "firm ground rules" and to "lay down the law" in order to prop up the paternal function and gain some symbolic space for himself. Lacking a blueprint for a loving relationship to the Other that is mediated by the signifier of the Other's desire, Ray was mostly stuck at the level of demand and jouissance. The only methods at his disposal of creating space between himself and the Other were anger, refusing to fulfill the demands of the Other, and creating a temporary lawgiving Other.

Group Therapy

Ray participated in weekly group psychotherapy sessions for a year and a half, and never missed a session. The other individuals in the group were neurotically structured. Ray was always an active part of the group process, and seemed to be an expert at discerning lies and omissions in matters of jouissance. Ray frequently made jokes and provocative comments. For instance, when the group became a little dull, Ray introduced the following new topic: "So, who thinks sex offenders are treated unfairly? Because I don't!" Of course, Ray knew very well that all the group participants felt themselves to be the objects of discrimination. In addition, Ray was sitting next to a man who was an ardent sexual offender rights activist and from whom Ray, predictably, elicited a strongly affect-laden response. On this occasion and others, Ray admitted to enjoying saying "rude or offensive things."

On another occasion, Ray said, "No one ever talks about sexual fantasies here! This is a group for people with deviant sexual problems, but people rarely speak about sex. If they do, they talk about it as if it were an issue in the past. Am I the only one who has an active problem?" Then, Ray tried to encourage people to talk about the enjoyment they got from their offenses. To a particularly closed-mouthed new person in the group, in trouble for attempting to meet a 14-year-old girl and have sex with her, Ray said the following: "It's okay! I saw a girl walking down the street the other day and she couldn't have been more than 14, but she had a nice ass on her! If you're attracted to underage girls, it's okay, just admit it!" Clearly, then, Ray played object-cause of the jouissance and anxiety of the others in the group.

Individual Therapy

Analytic Technique and Aims

My Lacanian approach to working with Ray in psychotherapy involved encouraging him to put himself and his life into question. Toward this end, I encouraged Ray to speak about and associate to dreams, fantasies, and parapraxes (e.g., slips of the tongue and bungled actions) and to complete sentences he began but did not seem to want to finish. Also, in prolonged moments of silence, I asked Ray to tell me what he was thinking. I listened for negations and suggested that they were ways of denying a possibly unsettling truth—an unconscious truth that warranted exploration. Likewise, in the transference I aimed to serve as placeholder for his unconscious. In other words, I attempted to get Ray to talk about aspects of his experience that he deemed unacceptable. What is more, I accepted Ray's transference projections without confirming or denying them, and this acceptance allowed Ray to begin working through his issues with his first and second Others. These techniques and guiding principles are as applicable in work with perverts as with neurotics.

I tried to keep my own personality, opinions, and feelings out of Ray's psychotherapy as much as possible and correspondingly avoided self-disclosure and adopted somewhat of a "blank screen" facial expression. When I did speak, it was to make analytic punctuations and interpretations or to encourage him to continue speaking and doing the work of psychotherapy. I have found that listening carefully and speaking primarily to make interventions (including asking questions) are more than adequate to build what psychotherapists of other orientations call the "therapeutic alliance." Patients are often touched by my ability to recollect what they have told me, especially exact words they used in earlier sessions.

Because I had to move to a different city, after only about 50 sessions I transferred Ray's case to another psychoanalytically-oriented psychotherapist. From a psychoanalytic framework, 50 sessions placed Ray in about the fourth month of analysis, and analysis with neurotic analysands often lasts between 5 and 10 years. There are very few documented cases of psychoanalytic work with perverse analysands, but those that are available support the idea that analysis with perverse analysands should be at least as long as analysis with neurotic analysands. In general, analytic work with perverts should be conducted with the same aforementioned techniques and guiding principles that are used with neurotics. Of course, the clinician's interventions will be informed by a knowledge of the perverse structure. More specific considerations of the challenges faced by the clinician in work with perverts are discussed in the last chapter of this book.

Because Ray's psychotherapy was so short, the amount and degree of therapeutic benefits evident at the time of transferring his case were not reflective of the therapeutic benefits Ray could have achieved were he to continue his analytically-oriented work. Initially, Ray desired for psychotherapy to help him cease committing acts of indecent exposure and improve his relationship with Susan. At the end of our analytic work, Ray reported improvements in both of those areas that he attributed to psychotherapy. Ray said therapy helped him stop committing acts of indecent exposure and become a better and more loving partner to Susan. Soon after beginning psychotherapy, Ray added to his therapeutic goals a desire to learn about himself and to discover how his exhibitionism is still manifest in his personality regardless of whether or not he commits acts of indecent exposure. In his psychotherapy, Ray began to be curious about himself at a level beyond that of the ego.

Ray said, "I like your technique, it's helped me more than any of my other therapists. Like that way you stare at me makes me think of things to say. And how you've trained me to say whatever comes to mind rather than planning what to say first. I keep seeing myself in new ways." Additionally, variable-length sessions worked well for Ray such that Ray often began a session by speaking more about the questions raised for him by the prior week's session. The question of who he was, of his identity at the level of being, had taken root in Ray. Ray was finding, in psychotherapy, a way to be something other than object *a* for someone—namely, me.

Relationship with the Mother and Father

Ray's relationship with his mother was one marked by avoidance and anger. Even though they lived within a 10-minute drive of one another, Ray spoke to her and visited her very little. When he did communicate with her, he found himself becoming easily annoyed and mad at her. For instance, when he saw her at a family birthday party, the only thing he said to her was "hello." Later, when she asked him for a ride home, he felt very annoyed at her demand, although he agreed to drive her home. In the car, his mother complained, as she often did, about her psychological "ailments," for which Ray had "no sympathy."

Ray told me about a daydream he had after a friend's mother died. That friend had said she wished she had had the chance to tell her mother how much she loved her before she died. In Ray's fantasy, his mother was "on the brink of death," and he was yelling at her in protest of her "mistreatment" of him as a child. Ray said that he "has an enormous amount of anger at [his] mother," but that he did not know why. After a few seconds, he said, "I don't like her facial expressions!" I punctuated this, and Ray responded that he was imagining his mother's facial expression of "irritation and disgust whenever [his] dad said anything." I commented on the link between the facial expressions of his mother and those of his victims. Ray probably was the object-cause of his mother's facial expressions of "irritation and disgust" when she discovered his bed-wetting, delinquent activities, and indecent exposure.

When he committed an act of indecent exposure, Ray provoked his female victim to display a facial expression of "irritation and disgust." In so doing, he was recreating and solidifying the affective link between his mother and father. Ray's mother's facial expressions of "irritation and disgust" were proof that his father mattered to her and had symbolic importance at least at the level of getting under her skin, if not at the level of inspiring respect and love.

Correspondingly, Ray pitied his father. Several years ago, Ray's father lost another job and was struggling financially. In response, Ray pretended he needed a vehicle and bought his father's old truck so as to stop some of his mother's complaints about their lack of money. Ray did so despite having just bought a new car. Because Ray could not afford both vehicles, he returned the new car to the dealership, incurring a heavy fine and significantly lowering his credit score. In pretending he needed something from his father and in giving his father money, Ray attempted to make his father into a more powerful phallic figure for his mother.

Lack of a Signifier for Sexual Difference

Because of the brevity of Ray's analytically-oriented psychotherapy, he did not explore the ambiguity around sexual difference that is the hallmark of perverse individuals. Nevertheless, Ray talked about two dreams in which homosexual feelings and ambiguous sexual identity were at issue. The first dream occurred in the middle of the fourth month of psychotherapy, and is as follows:

Ray had special powers and could switch back and forth between being himself and being a fly or a small bug. There was an alien invasion, and a huge alien who was in the form of a tank was slowly going down the street. There was a smaller alien "dude" who was walking in front of the tank. Ray was afraid they would find him, and so tried to hide behind the microwave, attempting to turn into a fly. Ray was unable to do so, and so the aliens caught him. Then, he was being held captive in the living room of a regular-looking house. Ray felt that he had to stroke the "dude's" hair until the dude fell asleep so that he could escape. Ray did so and was able to escape.

In recounting the dream, Ray had paused before saying that he had stroked the "dude's" hair until the dude fell asleep. Before he continued recounting the dream, Ray laughed nervously and said he was embarrassed by the last part because it "was kind of gay." Ray's laughter, embarrassment, and minimizing (i.e., "kind of") of the "gay" aspect of his relation to the "dude," all highlight that Ray repressed homosexual inclinations.

Among Ray's associations to the dream, the house reminded him of the house of his childhood friend Greg. When they were 13 years old, they spent a lot of time together at Greg's house—often using drugs (mostly smoking marijuana). Ray also remarked that it was odd that he felt trapped in the living room because there was nothing tying him down and there were no weapons. Together, these associations pointed to the conclusion that Ray was captivated, so to speak, by Greg. Ray stroked the dude's/Greg's hair as if stroking the hair of a woman. This dream, therefore, had to do with Ray's homosexual feelings for Greg.

In the seventh month of psychotherapy, Ray discussed a dream that had to do with the ambiguity around sexual difference. The dream was as follows:

> Ray was with a group of people. Someone had a "girl gecko," and it became known that the person was going to have to give it up. Ray did not want this to happen, so he gave the person his "boy gecko so the two geckos could be together" and the girl gecko wouldn't have to be released. The geckos were green and larger than usual "like the gecko on the Geico car commercial." Also, the girl gecko had a wider neck than the boy gecko, and on the underside of her neck there was a strip of brown.

In the process of associating to the dream, Ray said that geckos were everywhere in the prison where he served three years. Ray used to catch them and keep them as pets in a cage he constructed out of torn-apart cigarettes boxes. Unlike in the dream, the geckos had been mostly pinkish in hue or matched the color of the wall.

The Geico (pronounced "guy-co") gecko was personified as a man (a guy), and so the geckos in Ray's dream represented human beings. The boy and girl geckos looked almost exactly the same except for a difference in the size of their necks and the color of the underside of their necks. Because Ray lacked a signifier for sexual difference, sexual difference for him was a matter of a small difference in appearances (the female gecko's neck was a different color) and of quantitative (the female gecko's neck was wider) rather than qualitative difference (as in men have penises and women have vaginas). In reality, it is difficult to distinguish between male and female geckos, and the differences between the two amount to the presence of pores and bulges in certain places on the underside of the male, and the absence of those pores and bulges on the female. In Ray's dream, however, it was the girl who was distinguished by the presence versus the absence of additional characteristics found on her "underside"—an ambiguous term used to refer to genitalia without announcing sexual difference. Through Ray's childhood disavowal of the "maternal phallus," Ray knew that his mother did not have a penis but nevertheless persisted in believing that she had one.

In the session, I said, "On the surface, the boy and girl are alike, but the girl is different underneath?" In response, Ray said he's always thought of women as different sorts of creatures parading as the same. Later in the session, Ray said something which suggested the inverse meaning: that he thinks of women as the same sort of creatures parading as different (e.g., their makeup). This inversion is suggestive of the logic of disavowal. Ray knew very well that women are different from men, but nevertheless he could not help but believe that women are the same.

Ray said that geckos blend in with their background and all look alike, but that he had painted his identity in opposition to "blending in." Indeed, from Ray's perspective that men and women are alike, his defense against homosexuality and femininity involved standing out as different. In exposing his penis to women, he paraded and made a show of his masculinity.

Via condensation, the geckos in Ray's dream also represented Ray's pet geckos who were doubly imprisoned in the prison and in the cigarette box cage. Ray identified with the boy gecko in the dream. Geckos are one of the few lizards who talk to each other, and Ray was rather talkative. Also, Ray's identification with the boy gecko was informative insofar as geckos lack eyelids; the gaze, therefore, is always operative. Ray sacrificed his boy gecko (i.e., himself) for the sake of the girl gecko such that the geckos were caged together, and this suggests that Ray felt he must always be connected to a woman because of her need for him. Ray perceived that both his mother and Susan seemed to need him.

Interestingly, both male and female geckos, when frightened, will drop off their tails. (Ray did not talk about this, but his three years around geckos must have made him aware of this fact.) Transferring this fact to the human register, the process of giving up one's tail to potentially save one's life translates to the process of castration, in which an outside threat causes the subject to relinquish the jouissance associated with the imaginary phallus in exchange for the relative safety of life as a subject in the symbolic order. Both male and female geckos, of course, have the tails which are related to the human penis. Here, then, is another representation of men and women being the same.

Ray's Relationship with Susan

Susan was a frequent focus in Ray's psychotherapy. In the eighth month of psychotherapy, Ray shared the following dream with me:

> Susan and I were driving in a flashy red sports car. I was driving really fast down a curvy country road. All of a sudden, I saw a cliff, and it was too late to stay on the road. We were in the air crashing, and I knew we would probably die. I tucked my head in (he showed me the gesture, touching his chin to his chest) so it wouldn't hurt as much. Then, we crashed and I woke up.

In the process of association, Ray first said that he and Susan crashing might either represent their ending their relationship altogether or starting anew. Ray said, "the idea of being connected to Susan for the rest of my life is a lot scarier than the idea of us being finished." (Recall that Ray used the word "mini-connection" in describing the moment of the realization of the gaze in his exhibitionistic act.) Then, Ray said that a few days prior to the session Susan had thought she was pregnant. Susan had expressed a mixture of apprehension and pleasure at the possibility of having a child with Ray. Although her impression turned out to be mistaken, Ray spent an entire day thinking otherwise. (Ray told me that they did not and had never used "protection" of any sort, because Susan's medical issues prevented her from taking a birth control pill and Ray did not want to suffer the loss of pleasure involved in using a condom.)

In response to Susan's possible pregnancy, Ray was surprised that he had spent the day fantasizing about having a child with Susan. In his fantasies, the child was a boy. Ray had made up his mind that, were Susan pregnant, they would immediately go down to city hall and "make it official" by getting a marriage license. This idea was represented in Ray's dream in terms of the "'til death do us part" spoken in marriage vows. In the dream, only their death would put an end to their relationship.

For Ray, cars were highly cathexed with jouissance because he has often used them to commit acts of "flashing." The flashy red sports car was on a crash course, and even though Ray knew he "would probably die" he still tried to protect his head. The phrase "I tucked my head in" suggests that he tucked in the head of his penis in the attempt to make the pain of castration less painful. In becoming a father, Ray imagined he would finally be forced to give up his excessive jouissance.

In the next two sessions, Ray continued to speak about his desire to have a son with Susan. Ray said that "the right way to do things" would be to make sure he wanted to spend the rest of his life with Susan and to get married before thinking about getting her pregnant. Nevertheless, Ray's fantasy was a compromise between the "right way" and his desire to make Susan pregnant as soon as possible: Ray fantasized about getting a marriage license "so Susan could be taken care of [in terms of health insurance], getting pregnant, and then doing a ceremony later." However, Ray noted that he had difficulty going through with his compromise fantasy because he kept thinking that Susan's parents would disapprove of the plan.

Ray imagined Susan's parents would see through the plan and realize that he intended to marry Susan just so he could have a child. Ray said that the approval of Susan's parents mattered to him because they had considerable influence over Susan and would be in their lives for a long time. In contrast, the approval of his parents did not matter to him. Ray's concerns with "mak[ing] it official," "the right way to do things," and the authority of Susan's parents reflected attempts to bolster the paternal function. In desiring to be a more legitimate symbolic authority than his father, Ray thought it best to mimic Susan's parents because Susan clearly respected their authority.

Somehow, then, the idea of having a baby boy with Susan turned the anxiety-provoking idea of being connected to Susan for the rest of his life into the acceptable idea of being married and having a family with her. The baby boy would be the third term in his relationship with the Other, effecting a separation. For Ray, Susan's desire to have a child signified her lack (S (A̶)) in a manner that Ray was able to recognize and embrace, making his relationship to the Other more bearable.

Ray's Polygraph

In considering Ray's transference to me and to Dr. Smith, it is important to note that we were, in actuality, representatives of the law because of our association and communication with his parole officer. One way in which we put ourselves in the role of the law is to request that patients take annual maintenance polygraph examinations after an initial history polygraph examination. When Dr. Smith initially broached the subject with Ray, Ray said that not only did he think taking the polygraph was a good idea, but that he should have two or three a year instead of just one. After almost a year of participating in therapy at Dr. Smith's office, Ray was administered a maintenance polygraph examination.

On the day of the polygraph, the examiner, as usual, had travelled to Dr. Smith's office to administer the exam. Ray was aware that Dr. Smith had a professional rapport with the polygraph examiner, who often gave polygraphs to Dr. Smith's patients. In accordance with protocol, the examiner gave Ray a pre-test, and the results suggested that Ray was a near-perfect test subject; in other words, the results of the polygraph were likely to be valid. The examiner informed Ray of the four "yes" or "no" questions he would be asked during the polygraph, and then gave Ray the polygraph examination. The questions were as follows:

1. "Regarding you exposing yourself, do you intend to answer truthfully each question about that?"
2. "Not including the incident this summer [when Ray exposed himself to the woman who asked "Do you want some help with that?"], did you expose yourself this year?"
3. "Not including the incident this summer, did you deviantly expose yourself this year?"
4. "Other than the incident this summer, have you exposed yourself to someone without their consent this year?"

Ray answered "yes" to the first question and "no" to the remaining three questions—all of which are essentially the same question with variations in wording.

Ray failed all of the questions at a "strong deception indicated" level. I attended the results meeting with Ray, Dr. Smith, and the polygrapher, during which time the polygrapher shared his opinion that the results may have been due to Ray's webcam activity in sexual chat rooms, although Ray said that that activity had been consensual. When we wondered about the possibility of gray areas that had influenced Ray's results, such as the question of whether or not his Internet sexual activity counted as exhibitionism, Ray was dismissive. Ray said there were no gray areas in his mind, and no "what if?-type thoughts flashed through [his] mind while [he] was answering the questions." Ray said, "This would be a lot easier if there were a simple reason for why I failed the polygraph, like if I had been out there exposing myself every other day." Ray said he felt "guilty for not passing" and that he let us down. Clearly, Ray was relating to us as lawgiving Others.

After the meeting, Ray and I had an individual session. At the beginning of the session, Ray cried (for the first time in treatment). Prior to the examination, Ray had been very confident and relaxed, and his fellow group participants also had faith in his ability to pass the polygraph. Ray had taken pride in his ability to cease engaging in exhibitionistic acts. After the polygraph, Ray said, "My words don't mean shit anymore. I lost the ground I really needed! I really needed you guys to believe me."

Ray noted that the fact of his failure put him in an impossible position: He had to defend himself despite the fact that his very words of defense must now be called into question and heard with suspicion. Ray said he assumed from our position that we would trust the polygraph results over what he says. This is not necessarily true, but it is interesting that Ray said so. At some Other level, this is exactly what Ray desired; Ray wanted us, as lawgiving Others, to keep a close watch on him, insist that he continue therapy, and to hear his words with suspicion. Correspondingly, Ray said that, rather than defend himself, his best tactic was simply to continue with the therapeutic process and schedule another polygraph as soon as possible to clear his name.

A few days later, at our next session, Ray said he had just had a daydream while he was in the waiting room. Looking at Dr. Smith through the office window, he thought Dr. Smith looked "cynical." Ray imagined a scenario in which Dr. Smith spoke to him, saying, "Well? Come out with it! [referring to the truth that Dr. Smith thought Ray was holding back]" Ray responded, angrily, saying "I can't, because I have nothing to tell! And if you don't believe me I'll go somewhere else!" The daydream ended there, and Ray said he had immediately thought that he did not want to go anywhere else for therapy. "This place has changed me," he said. "I stopped exposing myself when I came here." (This last sentence has a meaningful double entendre, suggesting Ray got some kind of substitute jouissance from his treatment.) Ray wanted Dr. Smith to be a cynical representative of the law who forcefully demanded the truth from Ray.

In that vein, Ray wondered whether he had somehow wanted to fail the polygraph. Ray said, "This would fit into the pattern of everything else in my life if I somehow made myself fail the polygraph, taking away the ground I was standing on." From my perspective, Ray certainly did have unconscious motivations for failing the polygraph. Ray's failing the polygraph served to bolster his paternal function.

In this regard, there is some additional background information to consider. Recently, two other group participants had taken polygraph examinations. One man passed his examination, requested to end treatment and probation early, and we granted his request. In contrast, a man who failed his polygraph continued his treatment involvement beyond the required term of his probation. Ray may have been anxious that his success in treatment so far, paired with passing the exam, would have caused us to let down our guard or to terminate our therapeutic relationship with him. Ray's unconscious orchestrated his failing the polygraph and communicated that termination was not what he wanted or needed—that the best position for him in relation to us was as someone we mandated to be in therapy, listening "cynically" to his discourse and limiting his jouissance by propping up his paternal function.

Transference Relationship

Transference is the enactment of the reality of the unconscious.

Lacan (1973/1998a, p. 149)

At many times, Ray thought of me as the object-cause (object *a*) of his desire to do the work of psychotherapy. For example, I was positioned as the cause of Ray's desire to remember his dreams and daydreams and associate to them. Ray also had several "transference dreams" that he explored in the course of his psychotherapy.

At other times, Ray thought of me as a subject-supposed-to-know things about him of which he remained unaware. On occasion, Ray referred to me as "teaching him" something about himself. Especially at the beginning of our work together, Ray sometimes asked me what an aspect of his dream meant—as if I rather than he were the expert on his unconscious.

As is very common with perverse patients, there were also occasions upon which Ray tried to position himself as object-cause (object *a*) of my jouissance. For example, Ray often joked and sometimes succeeded in getting me to laugh, which he seemed to enjoy. As another example, in our last session Ray said, "You get a smiley face on your chart because I only flashed one person since we started or maybe that makes it a winking smiling face or something." (Actually, as discussed, Ray flashed a woman before we began our individual sessions.) A "smiley face" is something grade school teachers often give the children in their class, and a chart is something patients have. By using the words "you get a smiley face on your chart," Ray put himself in the position of an evaluator or teacher who might, through a positive evaluation, cause my jouissance.

As a final example of Ray's desire to serve as object *a* for me, Ray said that he wanted me to see him as someone who had "attractive qualities." Ray said, "Like I'm the male peacock lifting his feathers. You know, like there are some male peacocks with broken feathers and I don't want to be like that." With these words, Ray revealed his desire to be positioned as the object-cause of my gaze, as an impressive and healthy (versus broken) pea*cock*. When Ray was in the shower with his father, he had perhaps felt as though his penis was the size of a pea in comparison to his father's penis.

Ray's transference projections very often placed me in the role of a lawgiving Other or of being associated with his father. Frequently, Ray related to me as a combination of the subject-supposed-to-know and a lawgiving Other—as a *subject-supposed-to-No!* if you will. Magical thinking and disavowal were usually involved in such transference formulations. For instance, after Ray told me about numerous fantasies he had of badly "beating up" a co-worker who had spread gossip about him, Ray fantasized that were he to commit that violence I would see it on the local news and identify him to the police. (The logic of disavowal might be phrased in the following way: "I know very well that if I were to beat up my co-worker that it might not end up on the news and Stephanie might not see the news, but all the same I believe that Stephanie would find out about my transgression and report me to the police.") Ray said that belief prevented him from hurting his coworker. Of course, I did not mention that I did not own a television.

Another example was when Ray admitted to the group that he had committed an act of indecent exposure; Ray did so because he believed that I was able to read his mind and would have known about his offence. Ray's operation of disavowal in this instance was, "I know very well that Stephanie can't read my mind (and wouldn't necessarily have known about my offence), but all the same I prefer to believe that she can (and definitely knows about my offence)." Ray's disavowal led him to an admission that made him appear to need individual psychotherapy and brought him under suspicion by the law. In both of these examples, Ray bolstered his paternal function through transferentially placing me in the positions of omniscient subject-supposed-to-know and lawgiving Other.

I also functioned as subject-supposed-to-No! in the situation I recounted in chapter 4: Ray said that when he was driving to his appointment and was close to the office building, he was stopped at a light and saw what he thought might have been my car behind him. Then, he saw a woman crossing the street and he thought to himself, "Don't even look at her because if that's Stephanie, Stephanie will see and will wonder what I was thinking." Ray said that he knew that I was probably not in the car behind him and he knew that I could neither see his gaze (from my vantage point) nor read his mind, but all the same he could not help but believe that I was there and would know if he thought about exposing himself to the woman crossing the street. Despite what Ray knew about my limitations, he nevertheless preferred to believe that I would know were he to look at and consider exposing himself to a woman. This belief, facilitated by disavowal, enabled him to prop up the paternal function. In addition, Ray imagined himself in this scenario to be the object of my gaze—a gaze associated with the lawgiving Other instead of with the mOther.

At times, Ray struggled between his desire to be object *a* for me and his desire to do the work of psychotherapy. Ray produced several dreams having to do with this theme.

> In one dream, Ray and I were having a session. Via condensation, we were both in our session room and on his bed. I was sitting on the far corner of his bed and he was laying on his back under the covers with his head on the pillow. Ray felt himself falling asleep, and tried to "fight off" his sleepiness, thinking "Oh, shit! Stephanie's never going to let me get away with this." Ray, however, did fall asleep, and awoke to me saying, "We only have 20 minutes."

The setting of the dream was both the locus of psychotherapeutic work and the site of Ray's jouissance. Ray was "falling asleep on the job" and hoping I would play the role of subject-supposed-to-No! to return him to the work of "trying to figure himself out." Ray's association to my saying "We only have 20 minutes" was both to our sometimes short sessions, which he wished were longer in duration, and to our only having five remaining sessions. Three weeks prior to the dream, I had informed Ray about the necessity to transfer his case to a colleague. Ray received the news by saying, "So, I've got a month and a half. How are we going to fit in all the work we were going to do in the next two years in the next month and a half?" Not only was the remainder of the length of our treatment insufficient for Ray, but he also desired to sabotage the treatment by being a bad patient (i.e., by falling asleep) and by letting his jouissance get in the way of the work of psychotherapy. It is also noteworthy in terms of transference that I was sitting on the corner of Ray's bed, much like his mother had sat on the corner of his bed when he was a boy.

Consider also a dream Ray presented in the fifth month of psychotherapy:

> You discharged or discontinued me from therapy. You were telling me there was something I wasn't doing, like not allowing the process of therapy to work, and that I would have to be discharged from therapy because of it. You told me I was untreatable. I forget why, exactly. I think, in my defense, I was telling you about the thing that's been pointed out to me twice in group about my defensiveness, about how when people tell me things about myself that I disagree with, I'm defensive. I was saying that if I disagreed with something, I wasn't just not going to say anything about it. I was going to try to show them how I thought of it. So, my response to you in the dream was to be defensive.

In the session, I said, "You wanted me to discharge or discontinue you from therapy?"

Discharge" was associated with a release in tension, with sexual discharge, and Ray's having been discharged from the military and "discontinue" with discontinuing a product. Then, Ray remembered that there was more to the dream. At the end of the dream, Ray said he "came onto [me]." In the dream, because I was no longer his therapist, Ray felt free to pursue me sexually.

Ray told me that soon after I became his therapist and I asked him to tell me his dreams, Ray "hoped [he] would not have a sex dream about [me], because then [he] would have to tell [me] and that would be weird" and he "feared it would ruin [his] therapy." The negation and fear/wish Ray articulated pointed to his unconscious wish to sabotage his psychotherapy by way of jouissance—even though at another level that was not what he wanted to do.

Correspondingly, via Ray's dream he unconsciously expressed the wish that I would discharge or discontinue him from therapy and tell him he was untreatable because he was defensive. Ray said he could not help but be defensive, and therefore he could not help but be untreatable. Likewise, Ray's mother wanted him to be untreatable; his boyhood bad behavior, enuresis, and exhibitionism all positioned him as constitutionally ill in relation to his mother. Unconsciously, Ray wished I would discharge him (as from the military) from the burden of doing the work of psychotherapy. In this respect, instead of having to explore the question of his identity, I relieved him of that anxiety and told him: he was my untreatable object *a*. I had had enough of him and was discontinuing him as if he were a product (as if I had produced him somehow in psychotherapy). This dream exemplified Ray's conscious and unconscious struggle to desire to continue the work of psychotherapy instead of letting his jouissance get in the way.

Concluding Statements

Ray positioned himself as the object-cause of the Other's jouissance, plugging up the lack in the Other with himself for lack of a signifier for the Other's desire. Ray's exhibitionism can be understood as his attempt to signify the Other's desire and bolster his inadequate paternal function. When Ray was a young boy, his mother did not articulate her desire for people or things other than Ray. Clearly, she did not desire Ray's father, complaining that he was not a real man. Instead, Ray was the sole object of her interest and of her demands.

Ray's penis was a frequent object-cause of her jouissance (e.g., his enuresis). Even though Ray's mother protested that Ray's enuresis was a nuisance, Ray perceived that behind the façade of her excessive protests lay her jouissance. Ray's mother enjoyed his symptom. In attending to the offensive, immoral organ, Ray's mother got to see it. Ray's mother made a show out of trying to get Ray's penis to behave. Ray's mother was both upset and pleased by her unruly son. She wanted him to be a "bad boy."

Without a signifier for her sexual difference or her desire and without the intervention of a lawgiving Other, Ray was led to believe the worst: His mother wanted his penis for her own. Disavowing this horrible truth, Ray arrived at the belief that what his mother really wanted was to gaze at his penis. Ray reasoned that his mother wanted him to violate her modesty. Ray was the object-cause of his mother's jouissance—shameless, shocking, dirty, offensive, embarrassing, unruly, sick, and untreatable. In the act of exhibitionism, Ray's cough functioned to surprise the Other and bring out object *a* in the form of the Other's gaze at his immodesty. Ray coughed because his mother wanted him to be sick. Contrary to his conscious beliefs, Ray's "take that!" and "in your face!" only perpetuated his position as object *a*.

The name of Ray's father, his family name, was literally associated with something dirty and unwanted. Ray's exhibitionism was one major way in which he bolstered his inadequate paternal function. In his exhibitionistic act, Ray caused the jouissance of unconsenting women (representing his mOther) by making himself appear "dirty." And the women put a stop to his jouissance when they either fled the scene or called a police officer (a lawgiving Other). Being incarcerated as a result of his indecent exposure was another way in which Ray's actions forced him to respect the authority of a lawgiving Other.

Prior to and in the course of his psychotherapy, Ray created alternative solutions to propping up his paternal function—namely, body piercings and tattoos. The holes created by his piercings and the ink holes (bolstering the importance of his father's work) in his tattoos functioned like a fetish as significations of the Other's lack. Because Ray was structurally forced to attempt to signify something (the lack in the Other) that was not signified at the crucial time of his structural development, the work of signification was much more difficult and only yielded temporary results. The materiality and permanence of the holes created by his piercings and tattoos were one fashion in which Ray signified the lack in the Other. Ray used piercings and tattoos, then, in a similar way as exhibitionism.

Within his treatment, Ray also constructed numerous creative solutions to the problems of the perverse structure. Via the mechanism of disavowal, I often came to function in the transference as a subject-supposed-to-No!, knowledgeably putting a stop to Ray's excessive jouissance. In psychotherapy, Ray was beginning to find a way to be something other than object *a* for the Other.

7

ANALYSIS OF A CASE OF OBSESSIVE NEUROSIS AND PEDOPHILIC SEXUAL INTEREST

Introduction

What follows is a case study of my Lacanian-oriented clinical work with a neurotic patient in the context of outpatient sex offender treatment. Many of the prominent features of this case stand in stark contrast to the case of perversion presented in the previous chapter. These include the neurotic patient's inhibited desires, concern with symbolic success, desiring in relation to the Law (such that prohibition increased his desire), guilt, anxiety, and avoidance of the gaze of the Other who judges. My interventions were thus focused on these features of neurosis insofar as they presented concerns and questions for the patient.

The patient, John, was a Caucasian male in his mid-30s with a Ph.D. in a research-related field, with whom I worked individually for about four months. John had recently finished serving a year in prison for possession of about 75 images of child pornography. (All names used in this case study are pseudonyms, and I have altered identifying information.) John was referred to Dr. Smith's office by the probation system for mandated group and individual psychotherapy. I provided weekly sessions from a Lacanian psychoanalytic clinical perspective, and John also participated in weekly group psychotherapy sessions at Dr. Smith's office, although I was not one of the co-leaders of his group. The work was prematurely terminated when John moved to another state in order to live with his girlfriend and finish out his probation term and treatment at that location.

I assisted Dr. Smith in conducting John's initial assessment by administering and scoring a Rorschach and presenting my findings collaboratively to John.[126] John's assessment included a Rorschach, a MCMI-III (Millon Clinical Multiaxial Inventory), an Abel Assessment for Sexual Interest, and a Brief Symptom Inventory. John's MCMI-III results indicated

---

126 I have been trained by Constance Fischer, Ph.D., ABPP, in her method of collaborative assessment. This method is presented in Fischer's book *Individualizing Psychological Assessment: A Collaborative and Therapeutic Approach* (1994).

avoidant and dependent personality traits and dysthymia. On the Abel Visual Reaction Test, John's results indicated his sustained significant sexual interest in the following types of individuals, in order from greatest to least interest: 8- to 10-year-old girls, 2- to 4-year-old girls, adolescent girls, and adult women. John's Cognitive Distortion Score on the Abel was 10%, which means that John did not openly espouse the types of rationalizations that child molesters are known to utilize to justify their actions.

Presenting Problems

John was diagnosed, in *DSM-IV-TR* (2000) terms, with pedophilia, non-exclusive type—meaning he is also attracted to adults. Pedophilia is a diagnosis that would suggest to sex offender treatment professionals and parole and probation authorities that John might not only be at risk for future child pornography usage, but also for a "hands-on offense" with an actual child. In Lacan's diagnostic system, John was an obsessive (neurotic). When taking into consideration Lacanian diagnostics and the fact that John's only criminal conviction was possession of child pornography, the likelihood of John's recidivism (either by committing the same type of offense again or of committing a "hands-on offense") is an interesting question beyond the scope of this book. Aside from questions of risk assessment, John's obsessive structure necessitates a different treatment approach than that suitable with perverse patients. Although my work with John was limited to about 20 sessions, it was sufficient to outline the major components of a case formulation, including my position in the transference and how his diagnosis informed the direction of the treatment. This case formulation should be compared with that of the perverse patient Ray presented in chapter 6 in terms of differential diagnosis and the course of the treatment.

Prior to serving his prison sentence and after his criminal charges, John participated in individual psychotherapy for over a year with a psychologist who treated sexual offenders. John described his former therapist as supportive and as someone who gave him "tidbits of advice." John found the experience to be mostly unhelpful, especially because he "went crazy" and went to strip clubs every day for two months prior to his incarceration and did not tell his therapist, who did not suspect anything. In our first session, John noted that I looked "very perceptive" and he imagined that he "could not get away with that sort of thing with [me]."

Even though John was mandated to participate in psychotherapy, he himself wanted to pursue psychotherapeutic treatment. John's initial complaints included symptoms of anxiety, insomnia, and feelings of inadequacy and guilt. Furthermore, John wanted to question his sexuality due to his interest in underage girls.

220

John's Sexual Interest in Minors and Sexual History

John began looking at (online) child pornography in his early 20s, and did so until he was criminally charged six years later. In general, John's pornographic tastes led him to seek out novelty, socially prohibited images or acts, and pictures of girls or women who looked like girls. In the latter category, John liked pictures in which the girls were bending over so that he could see their underwear. He preferred the underwear to be shiny, sheer, and see-through. John also liked the girls to be wearing pigtails tied with large ribbons.

Prior to his criminal conviction, John "led a model life in public," excelling in graduate school and working long hours at a research lab. John's colleagues and superiors liked him and asked him to attend outside social events, but he usually refused. During this period of his life, John spent several of his free hours each day looking at child and adult pornography online, an activity which he kept secret and which felt like "some other John were doing it." Via pornography and strip clubs, John felt he had "a smörgåsbord of women." John initially went to strip clubs with friends, and felt embarrassed to be there, but progressed to going alone and feeling much less shame and guilt. John described the pleasure he got from "a click here, a click there" in the privacy of his home as "completely guttural, base, and free." "Lower-brain John," he said, "could have an orgasm that's a '10' with only a few clicks versus an average orgasm that's a '5' or '6'" with a woman."

In contrast to perverts, who depend upon the presence of the gaze of the Other, it is typical of neurotics to prefer to avoid the gaze of the Other when acting upon their perverse traits, and the Internet provides one common way to achieve this end. The Other's gaze is, "by Oedipal definition, an unmasking gaze, even an accusing gaze. The neurotic has to skirt around, to bypass the authority of the father, which means of course that he endorses this authority in a massive way" (Verhaeghe, 2001b, pp. 90–91). For the neurotic, fantasy provides a safe haven from the Other's unmasking gaze (which provokes both shame and guilt), and so it should come as no surprise that many visually-oriented masculine neurotics enjoy looking at and masturbating to online pornographic material that they would not dream of making a reality.[127]

John also participated in online sexual chat rooms where he spoke with adult women who liked to play the role of girls. What John desired in the plot structure of the fantasy in the chat was the following: The woman uses child-like words indicating her interest—a "naïve curiosity"—in John's penis, John protests mildly, and the girl insists, calling him things like "daddy." "Daddy" is a word that John found highly arousing. Then,

---

127 This is not to rule out the likely possibility that there are a significant number of masculine neurotics who do act out their perverse traits with another person.

they touch each other's genitals and John penetrates the girl, who enjoys herself all the while. John noted a strong connection between his preferred sexual chat scenario and his "original experience" with Sally.

The first time John remembered feeling sexually interested in a child was when he was 14 and babysitting four young girls. The youngest was three or four and the oldest, Sally, was seven. John had babysat for them on several prior occasions before the time when Sally said to him, "Show us your pee-pee." John was shocked and hesitated for a few seconds while thinking how to respond. In the meantime, she said, "I bet you have a big one." John said, "That's not okay. That's private and we don't ask people to do that." Nevertheless, John was secretly pleased when Sally's next words were "We'll show you ours!" When John refused to comply and told Sally that they should not undress, Sally "tried to rally the other girls" to help her, but only the second oldest girl showed any interest.

Soon afterwards, John masturbated while fantasizing about that event with Sally. In his masturbation fantasy, the same words were spoken, but he and Sally actually did engage in exposing their genitals to one another. John continued to fantasize about this, but "kept pushing the fantasy farther" to the point of ending with his achieving orgasm with his penis inside her vagina. John said he enjoyed a number of aspects of that fantasy. One was that Sally was "curious" and assertively spoke about her sexual interest in him. Sally's interest let him feel that he "was the pursued rather than the pursuer." (Not only did John enjoy feeling desirable, but his status as the pursued person was the condition for the possibility of the fantasy. Without it, John's guilt would get in the way.) Sally's saying she thought his "pee-pee was a big one" "was a very big compliment," and that, in addition to their discrepancy in size and age, made him feel like a large, sexually potent and experienced male.

In terms of his fixation on shiny sheer underwear, John said he "slowly replaced [his girlfriend's] entire collection of underwear with shiny, satiny underwear." John believed his preference for such underwear began when he was on the school bus in fourth or fifth grade and saw a girl's "shiny blue underwear" because she was sitting with her legs open near him. She was "like the third most sought-after girl" in the school and he had already had a crush on her. John said "it never would have worked because she was popular and I was a nerd." John found it "gratifying, verifying, and validating" that "she knew [he] was looking, didn't close her legs, and even smiled." John recalled another such memory of a girl with "shiny white underwear" that he caught sight of during a study hall in the seventh grade (although the girl was unaware of his gaze). Correspondingly, John sought out "up the skirt pornography"—pornography that showed girls "posing and pretending they didn't know their skirts were being looked up." John also liked that "underwear is the last barrier," and preferred "sheer underwear because it's like you're almost there but not quite."

John noted that he has "always been attracted to the forbidden." This is, in fact, quite typical of neurotics, because the desire of neurotics is structured in relation to the moral law (as well as to the Other's desire). Correspondingly, Lacan said, "Law and repressed desire are one and the same thing" (1963/2006a, p. 782). In other words, prohibition has an eroticizing function. In Fink's words (1997), when pleasure is

> prohibited by the parents, [it] takes on a further meaning, a meaning that involves the parents and the parents' desire. "Naïve," "simple" bodily pleasure is transformed into jouissance—something far more erotic, dirty, bad, and evil, something *really* exciting—thanks to prohibition … The stronger the prohibition, the more erotically charged the act becomes. (p. 67)

As we will see in the next section, John's parents played a key role in the organization of John's jouissance and desire.

Family Context and Personal History

John grew up in an upper-middle-class family and is the eldest of three siblings. Rachel is three years younger than John, and he described her as "very smart and successful." Rachel also had "a temper and some emotional problems" such that she "splits people into all good or all bad categories." John said he felt lucky to have been in the all good category for most of his life—especially after she learned about his child pornography viewing. Comparatively speaking, John said Rachel "has always been the screw-up" and he has always "been momma's little golden boy." John's other sibling, Theresa, is seven years his junior. John said that they were not very close and that Theresa was "not as smart and successful as me and Rachel."

John's parents "have always had extremely high expectations for [him]." John always received top grades in school. John's mother said he was "destined by God to become a doctor." John credits his father for giving him his "drive to be top-performing." As an undergraduate student, John chose between pursuing a Ph.D. in the research-related field and pursuing a career in creative writing. John wanted to choose creative writing, but neither of his parents supported this plan. John's father did not even think that creative writing deserved to be called a career. As usual, John chose the path in line with his parents' desires. John's father used to brag to friends about John's latest achievements. After his release from prison, John noticed that his father has ceased talking about John at all to friends, "as if [John] were nothing without a career."

John recounted a memory of having just told his father about his child pornography charges. The two of them were standing in front of the window in the living room of John's parents' house. The neighbors walked by, and John's father immediately shoved John out of sight. John said that his father's actions "were totally irrational, because the neighbors couldn't possibly have known what had happened," but that it indicated how his father felt about him and what he had done.

John described his parents' relationship in terms of his father's dependency on his mother. John's father, he said, "is the breadwinner, but he is completely helpless—silly helpless—around the house; he even wants her to help him pick out his clothes in the morning!" John said his mother "runs the household and keeps everything clean" and that his father is "completely dependent upon her and she loves it." John did not wish to be as dependent upon his future wife as his father is on his mother.

John grew up attending a conservative Protestant church service every week with his family. John mentioned that the most "pallorful" person— he meant "powerful" but slipped—in his church had been the "one with the least skeletons in his closet." In exploring the meaning of his slip, John equated religious power with a moral uprightness imbued with "pallor" or a "sickly whiteness." John said his parents "chose to associate themselves with very conservative people." John's parents taught him that sex is immoral when outside of the bonds of marriage. John rationalized having sex for the first time—a time when he was unmarried—by telling himself that he was going to marry the girl later, so that "in the eyes of God" they would have always been married.

John's road to making masturbation morally and religiously permissible was given to him by his mother. She gave him a book when he was 12 by James Dobson, an evangelistic Christian writer, called *Preparing for Adolescence*. John thought his mother had intended it as a religious guide for him to use in his upcoming years. John recalled "flipping right to the section on sex and discovering with delight and relief that Dobson said masturbation was normal and permissible." John did not look at any other section of the book.

John also remembered watching an Oprah episode on masturbation and asphyxiation with his mother when he was 14 or so and deciding to directly ask her if she thought masturbation was acceptable. She said, "Of course, *that's* not normal! [referring to asphyxiation] But masturbation is a normal part of a boy's life." John noted that she had said it was normal for a boy, but did not mention that it was normal for a girl. John then recalled that, when his sister Rachel was nine, his mother saw her touching herself under the sheets and said, "Nice girls don't do that!" It seems likely that this event (which occurred prior to the babysitting event with Sally) had something to do with John's desire for a girl—nice or not—who *did* do that.

In high school, John was only allowed to date "nice girls." John's mother expressly forbade him to date a particular girl, Laura, who had a "bad reputation" and had expressed interest in him. John regretted not having been allowed to date Laura, because he knew "she would have wanted to have sex" with him. None of the "nice girls" he dated were objects of his desire, but instead were "kind and sweet." Much to his embarrassment at the time, it was not until he was 18 and in college that he lost his virginity.

John said his sexuality was at first a "kernel" which then became a larger "ball" of himself that was "secret," "pleasure-seeking," and "shameful." John recalled having always thought he was more interested in sex and seeing pornography than other boys his age. Initially, though, he was "the good boy who occasionally hung out with the bad boys." John thought of himself as different and good because he had higher career aspirations, even as a pre-teen. Between the ages of 10 and 13, John and his friends would often go to the bookstore in the mall. His friends flipped through dirty magazines while he stood behind them, pretending to read "something like *Popular Mechanics*" and looking over their shoulders—hoping they would turn the pages at his pace. In psychotherapy, John often spoke in terms of what he calls his "higher brain" in juxtaposition with his "lower brain"—the latter being responsible for all of his sexual desires, and which he wished he "could push down and turn off with [his] higher brain."

Course of Treatment

John began psychotherapy in the midst of a jouissance crisis in which he saw himself as lacking in jouissance and in solutions to his suffering. As is typical for the beginning stage of psychotherapy with neurotics, John also thought of me as a subject-supposed-to-know—as an Other who possessed knowledge about his unconscious and his suffering. John often positioned me in the transference as the object-cause (object *a*) of his desire to do the work of psychotherapy. For example, I was positioned as the cause of John's desire to recall his dreams and daydreams and associate to them.

The only significant people in John's life upon release from prison were Rachel, his parents, and his girlfriend of seven years, Cassie. John said Cassie is "intelligent, successful, and very detailed and organized." John liked for Cassie to make "big picture decisions" for them, like where they would go on vacation. John described Cassie as being "very warm, caring, and stable" and he intended to marry her. Physically, he said she is "a little overweight" and a "bit matronly." John's descriptions of Cassie were quite similar to his descriptions of his mother.

John said he "never want[s] to have sex with *just* Cassie" but desires her to wear something special or role play with him to make her more sexually appealing. Cassie, however, did not like to role play, and would engage in it very infrequently and not very convincingly. John usually desired her to play the part of a prostitute or a virginal young girl—although he had ceased asking her to play the part of the latter since his criminal conviction.

John had a dream in which Cassie said, "You need to pull your weight! I can't support both of us." In interpreting this dream, John talked about feeling guilty and ashamed with regard to the current state of his career in comparison to Cassie's career. John was preparing to move in with Cassie, and he anticipated being a significant financial burden to her for the foreseeable future. John said he was afraid of relying too heavily on Cassie and that she might get tired of him. John said he already felt like he was turning into his father, whom he said was too dependent upon his mother.

While in psychotherapy with me, John worked for minimum wage at his father's company. Due to his felony and Megan's law status, John had very little success in his job search. John frequently worried about this, and felt "directionless and despondent." John said he felt like "a moocher" who was "out of place" residing with his sister and staying occasionally with his parents. John said he was able to "throw [him]self into work during the day" and "compartmentalize [his] anxieties" but that "the second the lights turn off" he stayed awake thinking about his "ruined career," his "inadequacy" in terms of his professional and income level, and his fears of himself and his family being socially ostracized or publicly shamed.

John avoided telling any of his friends about his criminal charges, and consequently avoided communicating with them for years. While in psychotherapy, John decided to get back in contact with a former close friend, and he was anxious about his friend's judgments of his child pornography conviction. John said his family was very supportive—especially Rachel and his mother. The past several years had been difficult for John and his family. John told me that his "family has decided to keep [his] sex offense a secret." John said that he had no part in making that decision but that he "tend[s] to take a passive role in relationships so [he] just was happy to go along with whatever [his] family wanted." John concluded that his family wanting to keep his criminal conviction a secret perpetuated the sense that who he is and what he has done is shameful and unspeakable; however, John recognized that keeping his sex offense a secret from his friends was his own contribution to the situation.

John recounted a dream in which he was in his bed at his parents' house calling for his mother, but she turned her back on him and walked away, leaving him to "feel shunned." During the process of interpretation, John came to realize that he felt "needy and dependent"—the very traits he wished he had not inherited from his father. Furthermore, John said it would be "a relief, in a way" if she did turn her back on him because he felt he deserved her disapproval for having "*sullied* her name" [my emphasis] by going against her "code of morality." John said he "cannot bear either [his parents'] disapproval or their support" and wished he could move away and "bear the burden on [his] own."

A week prior to his first major job interview, John reported a dream in which he was interviewing for a job.

In the dream, John was in a windowless room being interviewed by a panel of 12 women. The women were sitting behind three high wooden desks that were all in a row at the front of the room. Four women sat behind each desk. The women were "matronly and unattractive" looking. They all had very severe facial expressions. John was sitting on a very small chair in the middle of the room behind a desk that was comparatively huge. The desk obstructed everything but his eyes such that he was "peeping over it to see." The women noticed his predicament, and offered to get him another chair. John insisted, however, that he was fine and did not need another chair.

Via condensation, the 12 female job interviewers stood for the 12 disciples and the 12 jurors in a traditional jury. The word *matronly* also connected them to John's mother and to Cassie. As a "panel" they were also positioned as experts, as in a panel discussion. The women were expert judges on John's worthiness. Matronly and severe, they were figures of religious righteousness and morality, and John was clearly guilty and unworthy in their eyes. Furthermore, they were women because it is against women that John committed his crimes; not only did John feel that his looking at child pornography was a crime, but John also felt guilty about sexualizing women by going to strip clubs, using pornography, and even just thinking about women as sexual objects. The 12 women were in roles of Others who judge,[128] and they outnumbered and overpowered John.

John was a pathetic figure who was sitting in a tiny chair as if he were a young boy—perhaps hearkening back to a time when he felt similarly in relation to his mOther as a boy. This dream symbolism represented how inadequate and small John felt in his life, as well as how he would prefer to remain hidden (he refused a bigger chair) from the gazes of Others who judge him. John's body and crotch were hidden from the women so as to hide that which was associated with his sexual desires. In addition, John said he was sustaining his position as a sinner in his relationship to Cassie and his mother. The women in his dream, like his mother and Cassie, offered him a chance to be seen and sit in his proper place as a grown man, but John refused their offer. John felt he deserved and at some level even wanted the scorn and punishment of his mOther.

Like many neurotics, John's desires were inhibited. For example, it was rare that John directly expressed anger at or frustration with someone. John said that he usually showed his anger to others only by gritting his

---

128 This dream and the previous dream, in dealing with Others who judge, stand in stark contrast to the phenomena made present in Ray's psychotherapy. Ray, comparatively speaking, was not anxious about where he stood in the eyes of the Other who judges.

teeth. As a teenager and young man, for instance, John was so loath to cause possible feelings of rejection or hurt that he tried to make girlfriends break up with him so that he did not have to do it himself. During psychotherapy, John spoke about his feelings of anger and frustration at having so many aspects of his life controlled on account of his sex offense. Correspondingly, John said he had daydreams about being pulled over by a cop and venting his anger at the cop by yelling obscenities at him. Although John found such daydreams cathartic, he said, "They are silly; it's absurd that I would ever throw a tantrum like that."

One way in which John's aggression escaped was in the privacy of his car. Beginning when he was a boy, John invested some of his libido in cars, associating them with power and sexual desirability. At the beginning of psychotherapy, John told me about his efforts to drive at the speed limit rather than over it as part of his "new John" efforts. Prior to his incarceration, John sometimes got "road rage" and regularly exceeded the speed limit and sometimes got pulled over by cops and got speeding tickets. John's "new John" efforts also included his not downloading child pornography and not going to strip clubs. By extension, through the way he talked about what he hoped were "old John" activities, John drew a connection between aggression and sex.

When John told his family about his child pornography charges, Rachel placed more blame on their father than on John. Rachel said that, at the very least, their father was responsible for transmitting a low opinion of women to John. (It should be noted that John's father's name was also John.) Soon afterwards, Rachel called John and told him that she felt a strong conviction that she had been molested as a child, and that she suspected their father, although she could not recall any memory of being sexually victimized by their father.

In this vein, John remembered from multiple occasions of "people-watching" with his father that his father was clearly more interested in young teenage girls than in the other sorts of people who passed by. John also remembered his father saying, the day after John was criminally charged with possession of child pornography, "Maybe this is all my fault." In addition, later in the judicial process, his father said, "Maybe they could take me to jail instead of you." John's father did not elaborate on either of these comments, but they stuck in John's mind as possibly corroborating his father's sexual interest in minors.

John found further evidence for this hypothesis in the occasion upon which his father shoved him out of view of the neighbors. John felt that his father had vicariously experienced John's guilt and shame for his crime so strongly that it seemed John's father did take some responsibility for John's crime. John felt that, at an unconscious level, his father had wanted to shove out of sight that part of himself that he felt was guilty of the crime of sexual interest in minors.

Case Formulation

John's desire, then, was fixated on the sexually desirous women and children portrayed in pornography. Because of his assumptions about his father's sexual interest in minors, *John desired like his father desired*. Furthermore, John loved like his father loved, because both of them chose maternal (matronly) women upon whom they felt dependent.

Unprovoked, John said, "The idea of touching an actual child and especially of incest is revolting." This statement, alongside his obtaining jouissance by being called "daddy," suggests that John repressed his desire to touch a young girl, and perhaps more notably that he repressed his desire for his sister or mother. Recall that his mother told Rachel, "Nice girls don't do that!"—Rachel was, perhaps, the original "nice girl" who wanted to do dirty things—and that Theresa (his youngest sister) was the same age as Sally (the oldest girl he babysat) at the time of John's "original experience." (It is not uncommon—indeed, it is perhaps universal—for neurotic individuals to have incestuous desires.) In this sense, John desired to be his father in relation to his mother or sister—desirable as "an experienced man with a large penis." John's fantasy about Sally or another young girl (who perhaps stands in for one of his sisters) allowed him to imagine that he is a subject in "control" who, as "daddy" with his big "pee-pee," was never castrated.

John's ego-ideal was clearly at odds with many of his sexual desires. For one thing, John said that he did not wish to be an aggressive person (and his negation indicated a desire to be aggressive), but his aggression and sexuality sometimes went hand in hand. For another, his mother wanted his desire to be for a "nice girl" (who, by extension, was highly sexually inhibited). Believing "naughty" girls to be prohibited by his parents, such girls became highly eroticized for John. However, John made a compromise: he desired girls who appeared to be "nice" but were really "naughty"—in other words, "innocent," naïve girls who were curious and adventurous in matters of sexuality. John's desire became fixated on this type of forbidden girl.

John attempted to ascertain the demands behind his parents' desires and, for the most part, had spent his life acting in accordance with them. John interpreted his parents' desire as demands for him to get a Ph.D. and to have a successful intellectual career and to date and marry a "nice" girl relatively devoid of sexual curiosity and desire. John was on his way to achieving both, and was thus able to see himself as approaching his ego-ideal. In Freudian terms, John loved Cassie both anaclitically, insofar as she was similar to his mother, and narcissistically, insofar as she resembled his own ego-ideal.

As a boy, John learned to hide his "lower brain" urges from the outside world, and he felt guilty for having his "ball" of sexuality that was not in accordance with who he thought he should be. When he got caught with child pornography, it became public knowledge that he had failed to live up to his internalized symbolic standards. Feeling that he had lost, to some degree, the approval and love of his parents, John began to have depressive symptoms.

John preferred (legal) online pornography and going to strip clubs to having sex with Cassie. This is likely due to some extent to the fact that when John was online or at a strip club, he was able to partially hide from the judgment of the Other. Guilt, shame, and anxiety were prominent features of John's case, as well as desiring in relation to the law and desiring symbolic success. A perverse patient might feel some shame and anxiety, but would not share the experiences of guilt, desiring in relation to the law, and desiring symbolic success.

Unsurprisingly, after being told (not by me) he should not frequent strip clubs or masturbate to online pornography, John told me that his impulses to go to a strip club or to look at pornography had increased. There is a strip club near the office where John attended group psychotherapy sessions, and after group one week John said he "drove there just to see where it was" but did not go inside. In work with neurotics, prohibition only increases the strength of their desires. The proper role of the psychotherapist, therefore, is not one of judgment, but as the placeholder for the patient's unconscious and as the object-cause of the patient's desire to continue the work of psychotherapy.[129]

---

129 Nearly three years after our last session, John sent me the following letter, which he consented to be published in this book:

> As an update on my progress, I did indeed continue therapy. I am still in treatment, in fact. I am working with Dr. A's group. I also see a psychiatrist, mainly for depression medication management. The therapy has been extremely helpful on many fronts. I have become more independent of my parents, established a much stronger self-identity, and have learned how to approach interpersonal communication in an assertive (rather than passive or aggressive) manner. I still struggle with an intense pull towards sexually charged material but have rather easily abstained from underage material (much to my own surprise).
>
> I am now married to the same woman that we had discussed in therapy ... Finding it essentially impossible to find traditional employment, I started my own ... company. I am happy to say that it is flourishing ... It has been extraordinarily difficult to build this business but even more rewarding than my previous educational pursuits. I control the destiny of the business and, for the first time in my life, I feel that I control my own destiny as well ...
>
> There have been numerous hardships as well, but they have been weathered and are not as important now. They are essentially the same struggles that any registered SO [sex offender] must go through post-incarceration ...
>
> Thank you for the time that we were able to spend together in therapy and for helping me through an exceptionally challenging period of my life.

8

TREATMENT RECOMMENDATIONS FOR CLINICAL WORK WITH NEUROTIC AND PERVERSE PATIENTS

The success of treatment hinges upon making a differential diagnosis between neurosis, perversion, and psychosis and orienting the treatment accordingly. In the preceding chapters, I compared and contrasted with neurosis my elucidation of the etiology of perversion and the pervert's relation to language, the Other, and the drives. In my case studies, I showed how those theoretical understandings of the differences between the neurotic and perverse structures informed the direction of the treatment. In this concluding chapter, I will discuss the clinical implications of my findings and correspondingly make recommendations to clinicians both in and outside of a forensic context.

Mandated Treatment for Sex Offenders

Compromised Confidentiality

In many cases, work with sex offenders is mandated or "suggested" by the government, and in those cases the confidentiality of the patient is compromised to varying degrees. In general, individual treatment (regardless of theoretical orientation) will be maximally effective in situations in which the greatest possible amount of confidentiality and respect for the patient's privacy can be maintained. When individual psychotherapy is conducted in a forensic context, the necessity to communicate the patient's involvement and attendance in treatment to the parole or probation officer (PO) is one basic way in which standard confidentiality rights must be decreased. Beyond that basic compromise of standard confidentiality rights, it is largely up to the judgment of the PO and the clinician to decide to what further degree the standard rights to confidentiality and to privacy will be compromised. Clinicians should be reflective about this decision and speculate how their communications with POs might affect the treatment.

In situations in which the clinician and PO grant no rights to confidentiality or to privacy to the treatment participant, the patient's rights as a citizen are violated. Essentially, the message to the patient is the following: "Everything you say can and will be used against you; you must speak, but you do not have the right to have a lawyer present." When the patient is afraid to speak his or her mind, no real psychotherapeutic progress can be made. The patient will be motivated to lie and to say what s/he thinks the therapist and the law want her or him to say. It will also be difficult for the patient to trust that the therapist is on his side, so to speak. Uncensored speech and trust in the therapist are two of the fundamental elements of a successful psychotherapy. If the patient knows that his speech will be shared with his PO, then he will be unable to thoroughly question his identity and choices and therefore largely unable to benefit from individual therapy.

The forensic rationale for compromised confidentiality and privacy is that the patient has committed a criminal offense and that, in order to best protect the public (from the risk of recidivism), (a) the patient needs treatment and (b) the PO has a right to know about the patient's "treatment progress" related to his or her offense in order to assess the patient's level of risk for a future offense or to take action if the patient reveals to the therapist that s/he has violated the terms of her or his probation or parole. It is my contention that for the benefit of the patient's treatment goals in addition to those of the government, standard confidentiality and privacy rights should only be compromised in two ways: One, that the therapist inform the PO about the patient's attendance to sessions, and two, that the therapist inform the PO if and when the patient admits to re-offending.

The relapse prevention treatment model is the only model whose goals of treatment are not almost completely destroyed by full disclosure to the PO about the patient's speech and participation in treatment. This is because the relapse prevention model is an educational model that aims to teach sex offenders coping skills for the prevention of committing another crime. However, as I argued in the first chapter of this book, the relapse prevention model has only a small to moderate effect on preventing recidivism, and there is inevitably a subset of each treatment group for whom treatment fails entirely. A significant number of individuals in these subsets are likely to be perversely structured.

Treatment efficacy for work with both perverse and neurotic sex offenders would be improved if the following conditions were met:

1. Deviating from standard patient rights to privacy and to confidentiality for the purpose of communicating with POs should be kept to a minimum (i.e., informing a PO that the patient is continuing her or his treatment and if she or he has committed a new offense)

232

and clearly shared with the patient at the outset of treatment. There is often a significant amount of discretion left to forensic clinicians as to what degree of confidentiality to give to the patient's treatment, but in cases in which the PO demands more information, every effort should be made to collaboratively inform the PO about the benefits of confidential treatment that respects the privacy of the patient.

2. POs should not incarcerate their patients for things like missing a few sessions or failing a polygraph. Instead, POs should consider the benefits of letting the clinician handle such things within the treatment itself. As another option, in certain cases the PO might consider extending the probation or parole sentence of the patient as an alternative to incarceration. From the perspective of a cost/benefit analysis, treatment and probation are much less costly than incarceration and much more likely to result in the prevention of recidivism.

Prevention of Recidivism: The Primary Goal of Forensic Individual Psychotherapy?

Somewhat paradoxically, I argue that if prevention of recidivism was not viewed as the primary goal of *individual* treatment[130]—pride of place being given, instead, to the goals the patient makes him- or herself (including the larger goal of completing psychotherapy)—then treatment would be more effective in preventing recidivism. Clinicians should consider that sex offenses are very often symptomatic behaviors. And a symptom—for both neurotic and perverse individuals—is the subject's attempt at a solution to a problem. Exclusive focus on avoidance of recidivism means that the clinician tries to remove the patient's attempt at a solution without addressing the underlying problems. Each person's symptom—no matter how much resemblance it may bear to that of others—is highly individual and grows out of a particular family and social context. In exploring the symbolic and real order determinants of the patient's symptom, the patient can be assisted in the process of calling his whole self into question and finding alternative (hopefully legal) ways of being in the world. In this way, relapse prevention will be an effect or benefit of treatment rather than the primary aim.

What is more, if the clinician demands that prevention of recidivism be the focus of the patient's individual treatment, then the patient may feel that other—probably related—problems in his life are unworthy of discussion. For example, if I had insisted to Ray (chapter 6) that his

---

130 The patient's individual psychotherapy in which avoidance of recidivism is not the primary goal will not get in the way of the patient's participation in group treatment in which avoidance of recidivism is the primary stated goal.

relationships with his parents were secondary to and separate from his exhibitionism, then he may not have spoken about his parents as much and he may not have realized the many ways in which his relationships with his parents were intimately related to his acts of indecent exposure. Finally, if the patient is able to choose his own issues to work on in psychotherapy, he is more likely to continue his therapy (and take personal responsibility for working on his problems) after it ceases to be mandated.

Group Psychotherapy with Sex Offenders

Group psychotherapy without individual psychotherapy is much less effective than the two in conjunction. Group treatment leaders and participants tend to assume homogeneity amongst participants' problems and correspondingly to view all participants as neurotic. In some psycho-educational-based (relapse prevention or dialectical behavior therapy) groups, the unstated (often erroneous) assumption is that if participants had learned better empathy, coping, and communication skills before their offenses they would have never committed sex offenses at all. Individual psychotherapy that is informed by a structural diagnosis is essential to giving sex offenders the chance to explore their individual identities and histories as they relate to their offenses without having to censor their speech on account of the presence of other group participants.

Nevertheless, analytically- or process-oriented group psychotherapy with sex offenders can be very effective, nuanced, and individualized. Rosen (1996) is one excellent resource on analytic group therapy for sex offenders, and Welldon (1996) wrote an instructive chapter entitled, "Group-Analytic Psychotherapy in an Out-Patient Setting." Furthermore, in this book as well as in an article in *GROUP* (Swales, 2010), I have given examples of analytically-oriented group psychotherapy with perverse and neurotic sex offenders. I have found such groups to be a very helpful part of analytically-oriented psychotherapy for sex offenders.

Psychotropic Medication

Regardless of how much government and even patients themselves would like treatment for psychological problems that result in criminal offenses to be as quick and clearly defined as is most Western medical treatment, it is not. There is no substitute for intensive long-term individual psychotherapeutic work. There is no quick fix. Psychotropic drugs are only temporary solutions, but may sometimes be useful in enabling the patient to begin the work of psychotherapy and build an alliance with the psychotherapist. On the other hand, psychotropic medications can sometimes be barriers to effective psychotherapeutic treatment. For example, feelings of anxiety or sadness are human experiences that need not necessarily be shied away from or deemed pathological; if anything, the success of working through one's suffering (which includes combinations of thoughts and affects) depends upon having an affective experience within the therapeutic setting.[131] Ultimately, the decision of whether or not to take psychotropic medication should be left up to the patient.

Guilt-based Treatment Interventions

As I elucidated in chapters 4 and 5, perverse individuals experience significantly less guilt and have significantly less capacity for guilt than do neurotic individuals, and this is a permanent structural fact. Therefore, forensic treatment interventions that are based on increasing the patient's sense of guilt (in the hope that guilt will prevent them from re-offending) will most likely be ineffective in work with perverse sex offenders. Repeated efforts to appeal to the pervert's sense of guilt are likely to cause the pervert to lose faith in the therapist and will undermine the therapy.

On the other hand, in work with neurotic offenders, it will probably be somewhat effective to increase "victim awareness"—empathy for the victim—so as to increase guilt. Even so, increased feelings of guilt do not necessarily translate to the prevention of recidivism, and the possible causal link between the two is beyond the scope of this book. Furthermore, if there is a proper place for provoking guilt in patients it is in group work—not in individual psychotherapy. No matter how abhorrent the crimes committed by the sex offender, the individual psychotherapist should not play the role of judge or priest. This is because providing judgments is likely to have a detrimental effect on individual psychotherapy. When an individual therapist tells patients that certain behaviors or fantasies are bad or abnormal—that what patients thought or did was morally reprehensible (even if, by common ethical standards, this is the case), those patients are likely to stop talking about them in psychotherapy even though those behaviors and fantasies persist in their lives. Because speech is the primary vehicle of psychotherapy, when a patient stops talking about

---

131 In long-term work with a sadistic patient, psychotherapy had seemed "stuck" for a period of a few months during which the patient recalled very few dreams, lacked curiosity about himself, and presented with much less anxiety and discontent than he had previously. He revealed that he had been taking (without the knowledge of his psychiatrist) twice his usual dose (400mg) of Seroquel, an anti-psychotic drug with a sedating effect. The patient had a previous (mis) diagnosis of bipolar disorder with psychotic features, given to him by the psychiatrist who continued to prescribe him Seroquel. The patient thought beneficial the sedating effect of the drug, and had gradually increased his dosage in his attempt to feel content and to decrease his sexual desires and feelings of anger. The patient decided, however, that 800mg was too much, and so he informed his psychiatrist of his current dosage and weaned himself back down to 400mg a day. The progression of the psychotherapy improved as a result.

something the therapist will be unable to foster any change in that area of the patient's life. Certainly, there will be no shortage of people in the sex offender's life who will castigate him, as sex offenders are often hated and feared members of a community and/or family.

Prohibitions as Treatment Interventions

Furthermore, when a therapist prohibits something to a neurotic patient it often increases the patient's desire to do the forbidden thing. For example, after John was advised to avoid looking at online pornography for a while, his desire to do so amplified (see chapter 7). Because of the strength of the transferential bond between patient and individual therapist, this effect is potentially magnified when an individual therapist prohibits something to his or her patient. Nevertheless, the duty of the psycho-educational group therapist and the PO is to place prohibitions on certain of the patient's activities; fears of re-incarceration, the desire to be a good person, and the desire to avoid future social and personal repercussions should, in the vast majority of cases, suffice to outweigh the potential increase in the patient's desires to re-offend.

In contrast, prohibition has no such desire-increasing effect on a perverse patient. A perverse patient will be especially likely to heed prohibitions if they are given by a trusted group psychotherapist whom the patient has put in the position of symbolic Other. In many cases, perverse patients are looking for ways to bolster their paternal functions, and a group therapist whom the pervert "elects" to the position of symbolic Other can have a good deal of influence on the patient as the subject-supposed-to-No! This will only be possible, however, if the patient puts the therapist in the position of symbolic Other; if the patient relates to the therapist on the imaginary plane—as an other like himself—then the group therapist's prohibitions will have no therapeutic effect. Consequently, the therapist should look for signs that the patient is speaking to her or him as a symbolic Other before advising the patient to abstain from doing something. Such signs often include the patient's admissions that there is some kind of knowledge—namely, unconscious knowledge—that is at work in her or him of which s/he her- or himself is ignorant, but about which the therapist is a knowledgeable authority. So too is symbolic transference evident when the patient thinks of the therapist as being the cause of her or his desire to be curious about himself and put his understandings of his life into question. It is also best if the patient expresses the desire to stop doing that activity on his own before the group therapist enunciates her or his prohibition. That way, the patient takes what is considered in the forensic field to be personal responsibility for the desire to stop doing something.

In contrast to an individual psychotherapist, then, a group psychotherapist may accept the position of the subject-supposed-to-No! and occasionally give individualized advice to a perverse patient. It is best, however, that the group therapist mainly facilitate the patient's work in group (perhaps highlighting manifestations of the patient's unconscious) so that s/he does not diminish the authority of her or his symbolic position and so that the patient also feels encouraged to question his own thoughts, feelings, and behaviors. In other words, the group therapist can make the majority of her or his helpful interventions for the sake of the perverse patient from the position of someone encouraging the patient to do the work of group psychotherapy.

The paternal function-bolstering effects of the interventions of the group therapist, however, will only last as long as the perverse patient has a therapeutic relationship with the therapist. For that reason, the group should be long-term in nature, and the patient should be encouraged to continue attending group sessions well beyond the duration of his probation or parole sentence. Because relapse prevention is a finite subject, long-term groups should be psychodynamic or process-oriented in nature, for they may consequently assist patients in a more individualized manner by attuning to more than superficial behaviors and thoughts.

Analysis with Perverts: Possible or Impossible? Terminable or Interminable?

You are in analysis as soon as you no longer know what words mean. You are in analysis as soon as lexical meaning is progressively undone by new meaning surging forth from actual speech, new meaning constructed in analysis step by step or rather mistake by mistake.

Miller (1996b, p. 309)

As I have said, it is indeed possible to do successful analytic or therapeutic work with perverts. That possibility hinges upon the pervert's ability to see himself as lacking at some level and to correspondingly position his therapist as a subject-supposed-to-know. In 1967 (when Clavreul's 1980 article "The Perverse Couple" was first published), however, Clavreul maintained that it is impossible for a pervert to place the analyst in the symbolic transference position of the subject-supposed-to-know. Why did he do so?

One of the reasons is hinted at in his use of the word "desire" in this quote from Clavreul's (1980) article: it "is impossible for the pervert to take the position of the one 'who does not know' before a 'supposed subject of knowing,' a position of 'avowal' [aveu], where one can recognize oneself as the 'solicitor' [avoué] of the one who knows something about the object of one's own desire that one cannot know oneself" (p. 228). Clavreul's mistake here is in indicating that it is at the level of desire instead of the level of jouissance that the pervert is not lacking. The pervert, as a subject who is not certain of his desires, can position his therapist as a subject-supposed-to-know because a lack of knowledge in the register of desire is a condition for the possibility of that transference relation. Desire always implies a structural lack, and because perverts are subjects in the symbolic order, they can be brought to recognize their own lack.

What the pervert is certain of, what he has a full knowledge of, are his ways and means of obtaining jouissance. Miller (1996b) gave an excellent explanation of the apparent paradox of the analyzability of the pervert:

> Perhaps [the pervert] is suffering from that certainty [concerning jouissance] and at the same time raising the question of his desire, as if at another level he were not satisfied with his satisfaction. This fact forces us to distinguish jouissance and desire: on the one hand, we have jouissance characterized by its inertia—and Freud himself speaks of the inertia of libido during the years and years of true analysis—and on the other hand, desire as a question, metonymic desire, that is to say free desire, hidden, fulgurating or inhibited desire that is fundamentally perplexed. *That is the paradox of the perverse analysand: he is someone who has a sure answer but is nevertheless perplexed.* (p. 310, emphasis added)

The necessary condition for true analytic or psychodynamic work is the patient's having a question about himself that he addresses to an Other (the analyst or therapist) with the expectation that the Other (as subject-supposed-to-know) knows something about the answer that eludes the patient himself. In my work with Ray, that question was "Why am I an exhibitionist, and how can I prevent committing future acts of exhibitionism?" Even though we understand the "constancy of [the pervert's] jouissance as an answer, an answer which is already there" (Miller 1996b, p. 310) the pervert's desire enables him to have a question that drives the progress of the analysis or therapy.

Another possible reason why Clavreul concluded that a pervert cannot place his analyst in the role of subject-supposed-to-know and correspondingly cannot undergo analysis as we know it (but only an altered form whose success is doubtful) has to do with his hypotheses regarding the pervert's demands and the status of the analyst in the transference. In this vein, Clavreul (1980) asked,

> Does the pervert seek from us protection against eventual medicolegal troubles, thus reducing us to the role of accomplice or protector? Or does he seek to prove his good will in the eyes of a third party? Does he come into analysis to seek scabrous images that will aid him in ameliorating his perverse practices? Or better yet, does he want to get rid of some minor problem while remaining firmly decided to modify nothing of the essential? (p. 230)

Clavreul said that it is the tendency of the neurotic analyst to respond to these perceived demands in one of two ways. One route ends up moralizing the analysis by "taking refuge in such familiar terrain as alliance with the sane part of the ego, refusal of acting out, and so forth" (p. 230). The other route results in the reduction of the analyst to the role of impotent voyeur by way of going along with the pervert's strange demands for analysis. Clavreul thus supposed that "the analyst finds himself reduced to a position that is either moralizing or perverse, capable of passing from one to the other very easily ... [This is an] impossible role" (pp. 230–231).

Accordingly, Clavreul's error stemmed from assuming that the pervert does not suffer on account of his subject position and excessive jouissance. While the pervert may seem to want to get away with murder, what he really desires is to bolster the lawgiving Other's existence. In his article, Clavreul made no mention of the pervert's suffering due to the inadequacy of the paternal function. When the pervert's subject position is seen as an attempt to prop up the paternal function, one can no longer maintain that the pervert cannot undergo traditional Lacanian analysis and that the only two positions available to the analyst of a pervert are those of moralizer and impotent voyeur.

Certainly, it is difficult to do analytic work with perverts. This is largely because the pervert prefers to play the role of object a (object-cause of the Other's jouissance) in relation to the therapist, causing her anxiety and jouissance. Analytic work with a pervert requires that the therapist maneuver the pervert into the role of split subject (as someone who sees himself as lacking at a certain level) so that the therapist can take up the role of object a as object-cause of the patient's desire to do therapeutic work. In working with a pervert, the therapist must be alert to ways to get the patient intrigued by his own unconscious manifestations when the pervert occasionally lapses back into the role of object a.

Individual Psychotherapy with Perverse Patients

Given that disavowal is the constitutive mechanism of the perverse structure, a clinician should listen for the operation of disavowal in the pervert's discourse and punctuate it. Just as an unprovoked denial in the speech of a neurotic indicates a negation of something of clinical significance, so too does disavowal as it manifests itself in the discourse of the pervert as both; and logic, magical thinking, and avowals of virtual belief/certainty indicate a negation deserving of further exploration. In each case it is worth asking, what is the difficult unconscious truth(s) that is being defended against?

In individual therapy with a perverse patient (sex offender or not, mandated to treatment or not), the therapist should take care to neither accept nor reject the position of subject-supposed-to-No! or the subject-supposed-to-know. The patient's projections that the therapist is a subject-supposed-to-No! will suffice to engender a temporary therapeutic effect (i.e., the propping up of the paternal function). If the individual therapist accepts either of these positions, s/he will run the risk of keeping the therapy of the pervert stuck at that level—the level of demand rather than desire. Being stuck at the level of the Other's demand was what engendered the pervert's structural position. Working at the level of demand results in the patient remaining very closely tied to the Other rather than moving toward separation.

Because the pervert is to some extent a subject in the symbolic realm, every effort should be made to work on behalf of the patient's Eros. In other words, the therapist should situate the therapeutic work at the level of desire, striving to increase the pervert's ability to desire so as to limit the pervert's excessive jouissance and enable the pervert to reclaim his body and subjectivity from the Other. In practice, this means that the therapist will strive to orient the treatment in much the same way as s/he does with neurotic patients. The treatment will bear the most similarity to work with hysterics because of the structural similarities between the pervert's and the hysteric's position in relation to the Other as object a. Dreams, fantasies, free association, parapraxes, repetition, and talking about the past are the fundamentals of psychodynamic psychotherapy with both neurotic and perverse patients.

Situating the work at the symbolic level of desire means, for one thing, that the therapist should avoid responding to the patient's requests for advice and interpretation. Although it is common for a patient at the beginning stages of his psychotherapy to see his psychotherapist as a subject-supposed-to-know, the psychotherapist should not fall prey to the trap of believing that s/he holds privileged knowledge about the patient and what is good for him (or that if s/he does not give him advice, no one else in the patient's life will do so; in the vast majority of cases, the patient gets plenty of advice from his PO, his group therapist and fellow participants, and his friends and family). Interpreting from the position of subject-supposed-to-know incites an imaginary order relationship of rivalry with the patient in which the patient sooner or later tries to disprove the therapist's theories and interpretations. Working at the level of demand means giving knowledge to the patient and fostering a relationship which is based on the patient's dependency on that knowledge. In providing the patient with ready-made interpretations, the therapist puts words into the patient's mouth and stymies the patient's own curiosity about himself.

Working at the symbolic level of desire, however, involves the therapist's expressions of desire that the patient do the work of psychotherapy. Correspondingly, the therapist should aim to be positioned in the transference as the object-cause of the perverse patient's desire to participate in psychotherapy and as the placeholder for the patient's unconscious. This transferential position enables the patient to work through (via emotive speech) his issues with the Other.

Another way in which Lacan described the analytic progress of a subject is "the constant culmination of the subject's assumption of his own mirages" (1953/2006a, p. 251). One of the functions of the analytic method is to enable the subject to discover something about his unconscious, realizing that what he took to be his own individual thoughts and desires are actually ones he appropriated from the Other. The subject calls who he thinks he is—the sum total of his ego misidentifications—radically into question. The therapist aims to get the patient to speak about his experiences, fantasies, and dreams, to associate to them, and to be interested in possible Other, unconscious meanings of his utterances.

A difficult and delicate stage of the pervert's treatment is the beginning stage. It is more difficult to get a perverse patient than a neurotic patient to question who he is and why he has become who he is.[132] This is the question that psychoanalysis and psychodynamic psychotherapy aims to answer. This question, when unanswered, is what drives the patient to undergo psychotherapy.

Jouissance Crisis: Inscribing Lack into the Perverse Patient

Individuals usually request to begin psychotherapy when they are in the middle of what Fink (1997) called a "jouissance crisis" (p. 9). In other words, a person's symptom has ceased to provide him with the amount of jouissance to which he was accustomed, and he wants therapy to help him repair his symptom to its former functionality. The person who requests therapy is suffering and wants to feel better. He is lacking in something and usually wants the therapist to help him "fill the void." Instead of giving the patient what he thinks he wants (which is to return to the way things were before), the therapist's job is to increase the patient's curiosity about himself and to show him that his current answers to the question of being (of identity) are inadequate. In so doing, the therapist offers the patient a substitute satisfaction derived from the transference relationship

---

132 Encountering a patient who in the initial sessions does not see himself as lacking is by no means an uncommon event. Most often, this type of patient is obsessive, and his difficulty in seeing himself as lacking in relation to the therapist can be attributed to his structural reasons for negating the Other and attempting to neutralize the Other's desire. Correspondingly, the obsessive often fears seeing himself as dependent (even in terms of knowledge) upon the therapist Other. The obsessive prefers not to see himself as desiring because it threatens him with *aphanisis* and reveals to him that he is a subject lacking in being. The process of getting the obsessive to face his own lack in the process of analysis is referred to as hystericizing his desire, and this involves regularly reminding the obsessive of the Other's presence and desire.

and from deciphering manifestations of the unconscious. A jouissance crisis, then, opens the door for the patient to begin asking the question of who he is.

Perverse individuals request therapy significantly less often than do neurotic individuals because they tend to experience subjective state of satisfaction associated with their greater amount of jouissance. It is comparatively rare that perverts undergo a jouissance crisis, although it does happen. Mandated treatment is one common way in which a pervert finds his way into a consultation room. The therapist must help inscribe this lack in the perverse patient in the form of a complaint or a question of being.

Usually, the patient's seeing himself as lacking in satisfaction or jouissance is his impetus to begin the work of psychotherapy. Correspondingly, the therapist should punctuate the various areas of the pervert's life that he describes as problematic or less than satisfactory. However, the perverse patient, as mentioned above, can have a sure answer to the question of identity at the level of jouissance while remaining perplexed at the level of desire. The therapist, then, should foster the perverse patient's curiosity in himself. Why does he desire what and how he desires? It is thus important for the therapist to highlight manifestations of the pervert's putting himself into question, for instance by ending a session when a pervert says, "I don't know why I ..." The therapist's task of inscribing lack into the pervert will be an ongoing one throughout the process of therapy.

Without being faced with his own lack, the pervert will attempt to play his usual role with the therapist: the role of the object-cause of the Other's jouissance. In this role, the pervert effectively gains jouissance from the therapy and circumvents facing his own subjective lack. The role of object-cause of the Other's jouissance might take "innocuous" forms, such as persistently trying to make the therapist laugh or even trying to be a model patient. The masochistic or sadistic pervert might also attempt to bring jouissance to the therapist by causing the therapist anxiety. Sometimes, the pervert might do so by reducing the therapist to a passive observer of the pervert's crimes. If at the beginning of a psychotherapy the pervert plays this role with the therapist for very long, it will likely ruin the therapist's chance of ever being placed as object a for the pervert's desire to do the work of psychotherapy. In cases in which this has occurred, the therapist should refer the patient to another therapist and advise her or him accordingly.

In clinical work with neurotics, the therapist's position in the transference as the subject-supposed-to-know commonly results from the patient's jouissance crisis. It is from the experience of suffering that the patient, half out of hope, sees the therapist as someone who is an expert on suffering and can help him. Therefore, another way of stating the difficulty involved at the beginning of the pervert's treatment is that it is harder for the individual or group psychotherapist of a pervert to be placed in the position of subject-supposed-to-know. Neither the individual nor the group psychotherapist will succeed in obtaining this position (in the eyes of the perverse patient) if s/he is found to be somehow fraudulent with respect to the law (bending the rules of therapy, for instance)[133] or if s/he appears to gain jouissance from her or his work with the perverse patient.

In terms of the latter, perverts have a keen eye for jouissance and will usually try to accentuate the jouissance of Others. (Common counter-transference reactions to perverts include anxiety, frustration, amusement, fear, and pity.) As a result, it is very important that the group therapist and individual therapist alike maintain a stance of analytic neutrality or absti-nence. In other words, *in work with perverse patients, group and individual therapists should maintain neutrality as much as possible and refrain from any position of jouissance. The therapist thus steps entirely outside of the pervert's game of providing the Other with jouissance.* Toward this end, the therapist should strive to manage her or his feelings of counter-transference and should not self-disclose at all. It will be detrimental to the work if the therapist shares personal information or thoughts and feelings s/he has about the experience of working with the perverse patient. The pervert could potentially use all of this information to ascertain how best to bring jouissance to the therapist. (What is more, the therapist's self-disclosure often leads the patient to position the therapist on the imaginary plane as an other like himself. Imaginary order work does little to help the patient.) When the pervert plays the role of object *a*, it gets in the way of the treat-ment and of letting the therapist play object *a* as cause of the patient's desire to do the work of therapy. The therapist's neutrality is a condition for the possibility of the pervert facing his own lack and relinquishing his role in the therapy as object *a*. This is not always an easy task.

Importantly, the therapist's refusal to let the patient cause her or him jouissance—whether "positive" or "negative"—(or to use the patient for her or his own enjoyment) avoids a recreation of the traumatic relationship between the patient and his mOther. When the therapist practices ana-lytic neutrality, the pervert's expectations of the Other will be subverted to some extent. The therapist who practices analytic neutrality allows and encourages the pervert to begin the long and never complete[134] process of separating from the Other. Once the therapist attains the position of sub-ject-supposed-to-know in the transference with a perverse patient, s/he will

---

133 Perverts are especially good at identifying the hypocrisies of those who pose as symbolic authorities but do not consistently adhere to well-established rules.

134 It is structurally impossible for neurotic and perverse patients to completely separate from the Other, because they are permanently subjects in the symbolic order—the order of the Other.

be able to transition to serve as cause of the pervert's desire to do therapy if s/he neither refuses nor accepts the position of subject-supposed-to-know.

In work with perverse patients who have committed crimes[135] and are mandated to treatment, it is essential that the therapist clearly define her or his relationship to the law at the outset of treatment. The therapist should define exactly what degree of confidentiality the patient has in the treatment (i.e., when and how often the individual therapist will communicate with the PO and what information will be revealed). It is crucial that the therapist avoid violating confidentiality in this regard in the course of the treatment. If the therapist goes back on her or his word, there is a danger that the perverse patient will see the therapist as fraudulent with respect to the law, and this will undermine the treatment.

Oftentimes, even after the perverse patient has begun to do the work of psychotherapy, the pervert might try to provoke the therapist to manifest jouissance. In contrast to work with typical neurotic patients, the equanimity with which the therapist responds might only lead to the escalation of the pervert's efforts. If it becomes necessary, the therapist might have to make a transference interpretation. Beyond that, the psychotherapist might have to make the continuation of the therapy contingent upon the patient's ceasing to engage in certain behaviors outside of the therapy.

It is possible, then, that within the course of a successful analysis or psychotherapy a pervert will attempt to enact his perverse scenario with the therapist. For instance, a masochistic patient who has undergone several months of therapy might escalate the dangerous practices in which he engages in the (usually unconscious) hope that the therapist's anxiety will peak and s/he will enunciate a prohibition of those activities. In this example, the masochist's actions put the therapist in somewhat of a bind: if the therapist enunciates a prohibition, s/he deviates from analytic neutrality and the therapy might suffer from the associated risks (e.g., that the pervert attribute to the therapist a lasting wish that he stop engaging in those especially dangerous masochistic practices such that the pervert will repeatedly demand via his actions that the therapist play the role of lawgiving Other and the treatment will become stuck at the levels of perverse enactment and of demand); if, on the other hand, the therapist does not prohibit the masochist's dangerous practices, at the most the masochist might end up getting a serious injury or even getting killed and the therapist might face malpractices charges. At the least, the therapist risks being put into the position (illustrated in Jiménez's 1993 case of Matías) of impotent witness of the pervert's dangerous and/or criminal activity.

---

135 It is a common occurrence that neither fetishists nor masochists become involved in the legal system.

The therapist thus faces a difficult choice in rare situations such as these. I recommend (if the therapeutic alliance is strong and the therapy is already well underway) uttering the prohibition and subsequently interpreting the therapeutic impasse so as to move the therapy back into the level of desire. When making the prohibition to the perverse patient, the therapist should provide the patient with a rationale.[136] The therapist should take care to avoid providing a rationale that reveals her or his countertransference. The best of rationales is the one in keeping with the desire of the analyst (see Katrien Libbrecht's 1999 chapter on the topic): The patient's especially dangerous perverse practices are getting in the way of or threaten to get in the way of psychotherapy. If the patient is incarcerated or seriously injured, how will the therapy continue? This is not at all to say that the therapist should prohibit all of the patient's perverse practices, but that it may become necessary to prohibit one or some of them when they dramatically increase in danger and frequency and function as a provocation to the therapist. Such provocations, if addressed appropriately, can result in long periods of successful psychoanalytically-oriented clinical work.

In contrast, the acting out of neurotic patients often signifies that the therapist has turned a deaf ear to the importance of something the patient has said. It follows that neurotic acting out (unbeknownst to the patient) is an encrypted message to the therapist which in most cases need only be put back into the register of the symbolic by way of the therapist's interpretation.

Common Countertransference Reactions

Perversion requires the analyst to suppress all countertransference in favor of the analyst's desire, that desire which operates through the suspension of all beliefs and knowledge, through the introduction of a question mark in the place of the signified. It does so to split the master signifier in its nonsensical nakedness from the constant crystallization of enjoyed meaning, which Lacan called object *a*.

Miller (1996b, p. 308)

Sex offenders—whether neurotic or perverse—are an almost universally hated and feared population. The homogenizing effect of prejudice does not escape them, as people tend to view sex offenders as all being child

---

136 What is the rationale for providing a rationale? It has to do with the fact that the pervert's problems were originally caused by a lawgiving Other who was insufficient. The lawgiving Other of neurotics generally provides a rationale for his or her rules and prohibitions. If we, as therapists, find it wise to make a prohibition in the first place, we should be prepared to do it in a fashion in keeping with the most effective of lawgiving Others.

molesters or rapists even though a variety of offenses can cause a person to show up on the national registry for sex offenders. Corresponding to the "victim awareness" that is often taught to sex offenders in order to increase their empathy for their past and potential victims, perhaps "offender awareness" should be taught to some forensic clinicians who work with sex offenders. Of course, the crimes perpetrated by sex offenders are harmful to others, morally and legally wrong, but hatred of and moral repugnance for sex offenders should not orient the way in which psychological treatment for sex offenders is conducted. If clinicians who work with sex offenders find themselves regularly overwhelmed by feelings of disgust and hatred and notice that their treatment interventions are affected by these feelings, then measures should be taken to correct this. Those measures might range from "offender awareness" to supervision to undergoing analysis to working with different types of patients.

Another common countertransference pitfall is when neurotic clinicians become fascinated by the jouissance of perverts. Neurotics often assume or fantasize that the pervert has access to immense amounts of pleasure in comparison to their own restricted jouissance. In reality, as I have illustrated in this book, the excessive jouissance of perverts is not as good as it seems. If the perverse patient suspects that the therapist is deriving jouissance from listening to him talk about his exploits, then the therapeutic work will be compromised. A clinician should listen to and punctuate the speech of a perverse patient not with his ego, not on the imaginary plane of fascination and jealousy, but from a symbolic position of desiring the patient to do the work of therapy. If the patient talks about certain things solely to provoke the interest and jouissance of the therapist, then the therapist should indicate that s/he is not interested in such material.

The Allendale Association's Treatment Model: Managing Countertransference for the Team

The Allendale Association,[137] located in Illinois and Wisconsin, utilizes Masterson's structural diagnoses to inform its agency-wide treatment approach (i.e., the Relational Re-Enactment Systems Approach to Treatment or REStArT model). At Allendale's residential sites for youth with conduct disorder and/or other problems with aggression toward others (in addition to other "mental health" problems), the majority of the youth are given Masterson's structural Antisocial Personality Disorder diagnosis which was renamed "control sensitive" and described in "The Circle of

---

137 I completed my postdoctoral fellowship in clinical psychology at the residential site of the Allendale Association in Lake Villa, Illinois.

Security Intervention: Differential diagnosis and differential treatment" (Cooper, Hoffman, Powell, & Marvin, 2005). Masterson's Antisocial Personality Disorder diagnosis is one which bears some important resemblances to perversion.

Control sensitive youth, within Masterson's theoretical framework, are thought to lack the ability to internalize moral lessons or experience guilt. It follows that in order to function "adaptively" or "healthily" and in lieu of an internal superego, control sensitive individuals will always need some type(s) of "structure" or a stable and consistent externalized network of expectations, limits, and activities.[138] A crucial part of treatment at Allendale for control sensitive youth consists in assisting the youth in recognizing this about himself such that he can take on the role of choosing and implementing his own structure after discharge.

At its residential treatment sites, Allendale institutes its own structure in the form of quasi-universal rules and expectations and predictable and consistent behavioral consequences for not acting in compliance with those rules and expectations. This institution-wide structure is supposed to function as a kind of perfect lawgiving Other. This structure reduces the opportunity that a staff person may otherwise have to enunciate a limit, complaint, prohibition, or punishment in accordance with her whims or when she is angry—as did the pervert's parental lawgiving Other. Instead, the rules and consequences for breaking the rules are supposed to be for the youth's own good.

Importantly for our discussion of treating perversion, treatment at Allendale, amongst other things, consists of an agency-wide effort on the part of all types of direct care staff (e.g., psychotherapists, group therapists, mental health technicians, teachers, teacher's aides, etc.) to manage feelings of countertransference. In Lacanian terms, this serves to circumvent the pervert's efforts to play the role of the object-cause of the Other's jouissance. For example, a "control sensitive" or perverse boy I worked with was expected, like all residential patients, to attend weekly individual psychotherapy sessions—although he did not have to say anything during the sessions if he did not wish to do so. If he did not attend his therapy session, certain privileges would have been taken away from him temporarily. One day early in our work together, I was walking outside and passed by the patient in question. As I did so, he said, "I'm going to refuse therapy later today!" Instead of trying to convince the patient that that would be a poor choice and/or responding with a display of jouissance, I said, in an even tone of voice, "Okay, that's your choice. You know what the consequences will be" and continued on my way. Later in the day, when

---

138 This framework is blind to the possibilities for the pervert to undergo analysis and for him to prop up his paternal function through sublimation.

I arrived for our session, the patient did not refuse the session as he had indicated he would do earlier.

Instead of taking the client at his word, I understood the patient to be attempting to provoke my jouissance. After all, if the patient's desire had been restricted to refusing therapy that day, why would he have sought that interaction earlier in the day with me at all, and why would he have subsequently attended our session? My response circumvented this attempt of the patient's to play the role of object *a*, and consequently the patient's psychotherapeutic work was able to continue.

Treatment Outcomes in Work with Perverts

Long-term psychotherapy or psychoanalysis, perhaps in combination with long-term group therapy, will yield the most benefits to the perverse patient. In that regard, psychoanalysts and psychodynamic psychotherapists should consider doing contract work with state parole and federal probation so as to provide improved treatment for perverse sex offenders. Many patients are likely to continue their psychotherapy beyond their parole or probation sentence. Lacan's various definitions of the endpoint of analysis would warrant a book-length study, and so I will restrict myself here to making a few key points with regard to the benefits of undergoing psychoanalysis. These benefits are much the same for the pervert as they are for the neurotic.

The process of analysis allows the analysand to further separate from the Other and, as much as possible, to live his life in accordance with his desires instead of those of the Other.[139] Dialectization of the subject's desire decreases anxiety and fixations, and, in the case of the pervert, limits his jouissance. In general, the analysand's suffering is decreased as an effect of the analysis and he feels able to fully enjoy and derive meaning from life. The endpoint of analysis for neurotics also entails a kind of ultimate assumption of responsibility for one's life. Analytic work with perverts is likely to be significantly longer in duration than analytic work with neurotics.

Analytic work with a pervert involves helping him question, discover, and elaborate upon the signifying relations, desires, anxieties, and symbolic determinants that constitute his symptoms and perverse structure. The analyst must encourage and facilitate the pervert's position of

---

139 In terms of the Borromean clinic, it may be that attunement in analysis to operations of disavowal and elaborating upon the imaginary and symbolic determinants of the symptom (which point toward the real of the symptom and the subject's relation to jouissance) will facilitate a reconfiguration of the Borromean knot as well as the place it allows the perverse subject.

perplexity and questioning and correspondingly avoid, as much as possible, letting the pervert play the role of object-cause of the Other's jouissance. Although a permanent enactment of separation and the attainment of a neurotic structure are impossible for the pervert, the process of analysis can result in the pervert's creating and recreating ways of bolstering his inadequate paternal function and can greatly reduce the pervert's suffering.

Psychoanalysis with a perverse analysand will involve assisting the analysand in creating solutions to bolster his paternal function. In that vein, through the process of psychoanalysis the pervert will find signifiers and ways of sublimating that will temporarily function to signify the Other's desire and bolster his paternal function. Likewise, psychoanalysis can help the pervert actualize his capacity for sublimation. For example, André Gide and Leopold von Sacher-Masoch sublimated their perverse activities to some degree by creating literature. Writing is just one of the methods at the pervert's disposal to prop up the paternal function by way of sublimation instead of by perverse enactment. The enthusiasm with which Chris energetically devoted himself to researching his family history indicates one such alternative sublimation. Correspondingly, clinical work with perverse analysands can not only result in vast improvements in diverse areas of the subject's life but can also result in the prevention of recidivism.

Successful psychotherapeutic or psychoanalytic work with a pervert involves getting the pervert to partially relinquish his position as object *a*. In psychoanalysis, at least, the pervert can adopt the position of split subject in relation to the psychoanalyst who plays the role of object *a* as the cause of the pervert's desire to do the work of analysis. In Fink's (1997) words,

> In certain cases that I myself have supervised, I have seen a gradual shift on the part of genuinely perverse subjects from positions in which they engaged in no wondering of any kind about their own actions, feelings, and thoughts—court orders or the hope of getting a rise out of their therapist seeming to be their only motive for showing up to therapy—to positions of true questioning. If there is never a loss of certainty about where jouissance comes from, there is at least a lessening of certainty about motives. (p. 186)

The pervert, like the neurotic, can use psychoanalysis or psychotherapy to put himself and his life into question. Resulting from the pervert's engagement in psychoanalysis and his partial relinquishing of the role of object *a*, the analyst can expect that the pervert's anxiety and suffering will decrease and his relationships and quality of life will improve.

REFERENCES

American Psychiatric Association (2000). *Diagnostic and statistical manual of mental disorders* (4th ed., text revision). Washington, DC: American Psychiatric Publishing.

André, S. (2006). The structure of perversion: A Lacanian perspective. In D. Nobus & L. Downing (Eds.), *Perversion: Psychoanalytic perspectives/perspectives on psychoanalysis* (pp. 109–125). London: Karnac.

Bak, R. (1968). The phallic woman: The ubiquitous fantasy in perversions. *Psychoanalytic Study of the Child, 23*, 15–36.

Bickley, J., & Beech, A.R. (2003). Implications for treatment of sexual offenders of the Ward and Hudson model of relapse. *Sexual Abuse: A Journal of Research and Treatment, 15*, 121–134.

Bond, H. (2009). *Lacan at the scene*. Cambridge, MA: MIT Press.

Brousse, M.-H. (1995). The drive (II). In R. Feldstein, B. Fink, & M. Jaanus (Eds.), *Reading seminar XI: Lacan's four fundamental concepts of psychoanalysis* (pp. 109–118). Albany: State University of New York Press.

Calef, V., Weinshel, E., Renik, O., & Lloyd Mayer, E. (1980). Enuresis: A functional equivalent of a fetish. *International Journal of Psychoanalysis, 61*, 295–305.

Cardinal, M. (1984). *The words to say it*. Cambridge, MA: Van Vactor & Goodheart.

Cavendish, M. (2009). *Sex and society, volume 1*. Tarrytown, NY: Marshall Cavendish Reference.

Chasseguet-Smirgel, J. (1974). Perversion, idealization and sublimation. *International Journal of Psychoanalysis, 55*, 349–357.

Chasseguet-Smirgel, J. (1978). Reflexions on the connexions between perversion and sadism. *International Journal of Psychoanalysis, 59*, 27–35.

Clavreul, J. (1980). The perverse couple. In S. Schneiderman (Ed.), *How Lacan's ideas are used in clinical practice* (pp. 215–233). Northvale, NJ: Jason Aronson.

Coen, E., Coen, J., Diliberto, D., Graf, R., Roybal, M., & Rudin, S. (Producers), & Coen, E. & Coen, J. (Directors). (2007). *No country for old men* [Motion picture]. United States: Paramount.

Cooper, G., Hoffman, K., Powell, B., & Marvin, R. (2005). The circle of security intervention: Differential diagnosis and differential treatment. In L. J. Berlin, Y. Ziv, L. Amaya-Jackson, & M. T. Greenberg (Eds.), *Enhancing early attachments: Theory, research, intervention, and policy* (pp. 127–149). New York: Guilford Press.

Cordess, C., & Cox, M. (Eds.). (1996). *Forensic psychotherapy: Crime, psychodynamics and the offender patient*. London: Jessica Kingsley Publishers.

REFERENCES

Deleuze, G. (1967/2006). *Masochism: Coldness and cruelty.* New York: Zone Books.

Derrida, J. (1998). *Monolingualism of the other or the prosthesis of origin* (P. Mensah, Trans.). Stanford, CA: Stanford University Press. (Original work published 1996)

De M'Uzan, M. (1973). A case of masochistic perversion and an outline of a theory. *The International Journal of Psycho-Analysis, 54,* 455–467.

Ferenczi, S. (1916). *Contributions to Psycho-Analysis.* Boston: The Gorham Press.

Fink, B. (1995). *The Lacanian subject: Between language and jouissance.* Princeton, NJ: Princeton University Press.

Fink, B. (1996). The nature of unconscious thought or why no one ever reads Lacan's postface to the "seminar on 'the purloined letter.'" In R. Feldstein, B. Fink, & M. Jaanus (Eds.), *Reading seminars I and II: Lacan's return to Freud* (pp. 173–191). Albany: State University of New York Press.

Fink, B. (1997). *A clinical introduction to Lacanian psychoanalysis: Theory and practice.* Cambridge, MA: Harvard University Press.

Fink, B. (2003). The use of Lacanian psychoanalysis in a case of fetishism. *Clinical Case Studies, 2*(1), 50–69.

Fink, B. (2007). *Fundamentals of psychoanalytic technique: A Lacanian approach for practitioners.* New York: W. W. Norton & Co.

Fischer, C. (1994). *Individualizing psychological assessment: A collaborative and therapeutic approach.* Hillsdale, NJ: Erlbaum.

Foucault, M. (1990). *The history of sexuality volume I: An introduction* (R. Hurley, Trans.). New York: Vintage Books. (Original work published 1976)

Freud, S. (1950). Project for a scientific psychology. In J. Strachey (Ed. & Trans.), *The standard edition of the complete psychological works of Sigmund Freud* (Vol. 1, pp. 281–391). London: Hogarth Press. (Original work published 1895)

Freud, S. (1953a). Three essays on sexuality: I: The sexual aberrations. In J. Strachey (Ed. & Trans.), *The standard edition of the complete psychological works of Sigmund Freud* (Vol. 7, pp. 135–172). London: Hogarth Press. (Original work published 1905)

Freud, S. (1953b). Three essays on sexuality: II: Infantile sexuality. In J. Strachey (Ed. & Trans.), *The standard edition of the complete psychological works of Sigmund Freud* (Vol. 7, pp. 173–206). London: Hogarth Press. (Original work published 1905)

Freud, S. (1955). Analysis of a phobia in a five-year-old boy. In J. Strachey (Ed. & Trans.), *The standard edition of the complete psychological works of Sigmund Freud* (Vol. 10, pp. 3–149). London: Hogarth Press. (Original work published 1909)

Freud, S. (1958). Psycho-analytic notes on an autobiographical account of a case of paranoia (dementia paranoides). In J. Strachey (Ed. & Trans.), *The standard edition of the complete psychological works of Sigmund Freud* (Vol. 12, pp. 1–82). London: Hogarth Press. (Original work published 1911)

Freud, S. (1958). Recommendations to physicians practicing psycho-analysis. In J. Strachey (Ed. & Trans.), *The standard edition of the complete psychological works of Sigmund Freud* (Vol. 12, pp. 111–120). London: Hogarth Press. (Original work published 1912)

Freud, S. (1959). Inhibitions, symptoms and anxiety. In J. Strachey (Ed. & Trans.), *The standard edition of the complete psychological works of Sigmund Freud* (Vol. 20, pp. 75–176). London: Hogarth Press. (Original work published 1926)

Freud, S. (1961). Fetishism. In J. Strachey (Ed. & Trans.), *The standard edition of the complete psychological works of Sigmund Freud* (Vol. 21, p. 147–158). London: Hogarth Press. (Original work published 1927)

Freud, S. (1964). Splitting of the ego in the process of defense. In J. Strachey (Ed. & Trans.), *The standard edition of the complete psychological works of Sigmund Freud* (Vol. 23, p. 271–278). London: Hogarth Press. (Original work published 1940)

Geertz, C. (1977). *The interpretation of cultures.* New York: Basic Books Classics.

Glasser, M. (1996). Aggression and sadism in the perversions. In I. Rosen (Ed.), *Sexual deviation* (3rd ed.) (pp. 279–299). Oxford, UK: Oxford University Press.

Glover, J. (1927). Notes on an unusual form of perversion. *International Journal of Psychoanalysis, 8,* 10–24.

Good, M. (2000). Perverse defenses: A clinical vignette. *Modern Psychoanalysis, 25*(2), 199–205.

Greenacre, P. (1968). Perversions: General considerations regarding their genetic and dynamic background. *Psychoanalytic Study of the Child, 23,* 47–62.

Habermas, J. (1972). *Knowledge and human interests* (J. Shapiro, Trans.). Boston: Beacon.

Hall, G. C. N. (1995). Sexual offender recidivism revisited: A meta-analysis of recent treatment studies. *Journal of Consulting and Clinical Psychology, 63,* 802–809.

Hanson, R. K., Gordon, A., Harris, A. J. R., Marques, J. K., Murphy, W., Quinsey, V. L., & Seto, M. C. (2002). First report of the collaborative outcome data project on the effectiveness of psychological treatment for sex offenders. *Sexual Abuse: A Journal of Research and Treatment, 14,* 169–194.

Hanson, K. R., & Morton-Bourgon, K. E. (2005). The characteristics of persistent sexual offenders: A meta-analysis of recidivism studies. *Journal of Consulting and Clinical Psychology, 73*(6), 1154–1163.

Hare, R. D. (2003). *Manual for the revised Psychopathy checklist* (2nd ed.). Toronto, ON, Canada: Multi-Health Systems.

Hudson, S. M., & Ward, T. (2000). Clinical implications of the self-regulation model. In D. R. Laws, S. M. Hudson, & T. Ward (Eds.), *Remaking relapse prevention with sex offenders: A sourcebook* (pp. 102–122). Thousand Oaks, CA: Sage.

Irigaray, L. (1977). *This sex which is not one* (C. Porter with C. Burke, Trans.). Ithaca, NY: Cornell University Press.

Jakobson, R., & Halle, M. (1971). *Fundamentals of language* (2nd ed.). The Hague: Mouton. (Original work published 1956)

Jiménez, J. P. (1993). A fundamental dilemma of psychoanalytic technique: Reflections on the analysis of a perverse paranoid patient. *International Journal of Psychoanalysis, 74,* 487–504.

Jiménez, J. P. (2004). A psychoanalytical phenomenology of perversion. *International Journal of Psychoanalysis, 85,* 65–81.

Jiménez, J. P., & Moguillansky, R. (Eds.). (2011). *Clinical and theoretical aspects of perversion: The illusory bond.* London: Karnac.

Kinsey, A. (1998). *Sexual behavior in the human male.* Bloomington: Indiana University Press. (Original work published 1948)

Krafft-Ebing, R. (1922). *Psychopathia sexualis* (F. Rebman, Trans.). New York: Physicians and Surgeons Book Co. (Original work published 1886)

Kvale, S. (2003). The psychoanalytical interview as inspiration for qualitative research. In P. Camic, J. Rhodes, & L. Yardley (Eds.), *Qualitative research in psychology: Expanding perspectives in methodology and design* (pp. 275–297). Washington, DC: American Psychological Association.

Lacan, J. (1959). Le séminaire VI, le désir et son interprétation, unpublished.

Lacan, J. (1975). Le séminaire livre XXII: R. S. I., 1974–1975. (J.-A. Miller, Ed.). *Orni-car?*, *2*, 104.

Lacan, J. (1977). Desire and the interpretation of desire in Hamlet. *Yale French Studies*, 55–56.

Lacan, J. (1991a). *The seminar of Jacques Lacan, book I: Freud's papers on technique, 1953–1954* (J.-A. Miller, Ed.: J. Forrester, Trans.). New York: W. W. Norton & Co. (Original work published 1975)

Lacan, J. (1991b). *The seminar of Jacques Lacan, book II: The ego in Freud's theory and in the technique of psychoanalysis, 1954–1955* (J.-A. Miller, Ed.; S. Tomaselli, Trans.). New York: W. W. Norton & Co. (Original work published 1978)

Lacan, J. (1994). *Le séminaire livre IV: La relation d'objet, 1956–1957*. Paris: Seuil.

Lacan, J. (1997a). *The seminar of Jacques Lacan, book III: The psychoses, 1955–1956*. (J.-A. Miller, Ed.; R. Grigg, Trans.). New York: W. W. Norton & Co. (Original work published 1981)

Lacan, J. (1997b). *The seminar of Jacques Lacan, book VII: The ethics of psychoanalysis, 1959–1960*. (J.-A. Miller, Ed.; D. Porter, Trans.). New York: W. W. Norton & Co. (Original work published 1986)

Lacan, J. (1998a). *The seminar of Jacques Lacan, book XI: The four fundamental concepts of psychoanalysis* (J.-A. Miller, Ed.; A. Sheridan, Trans.). New York: W. W. Norton & Co. (Original work published 1973)

Lacan, J. (1998b). *The seminar of Jacques Lacan, book XX: On feminine sexuality, the limits of love and knowledge: Encore, 1972–1973* (J.-A. Miller, Ed.; B. Fink, Trans.). New York: W. W. Norton & Co. (Original work published 1975)

Lacan, J. (2001). *Le séminaire livre VIII: Le transfert, 1960–1961*. Paris: Seuil.

Lacan, J. (2004). *Le séminaire livre X: L'angoisse, 1962–1963*. Paris: Seuil.

Lacan, J. (2006a). The mirror stage as formative of the I function as revealed in psychoanalytic experience. In J. Lacan, *Écrits: The first complete edition in English* (B. Fink, Trans.). New York: W. W. Norton & Co. (Original work published 1949)

Lacan, J. (2006a). The function and field of speech and language in psychoanalysis. In J. Lacan, *Écrits: The first complete edition in English* (B. Fink, Trans.). New York: W. W. Norton & Co. (Original work published 1956)

Lacan, J. (2006a). The situation of psychoanalysis and the training of psychoanalysts in 1956. In J. Lacan, *Écrits: The first complete edition in English* (B. Fink, Trans.). New York: W. W. Norton & Co. (Original work published 1956)

Lacan, J. (2006a). The instance of the letter in the unconscious or reason since Freud. In J. Lacan, *Écrits: The first complete edition in English* (B. Fink, Trans.). New York: W. W. Norton & Co. (Original work published 1957)

Lacan, J. (2006a). The signification of the phallus. In J. Lacan, *Écrits: The first complete edition in English* (B. Fink, Trans.). New York: W. W. Norton & Co. (Original work published 1958)

Lacan, J. (2006a). Science and truth. In Lacan, J., *Écrits: the first complete edition in English*. (B. Fink, Trans.). New York: W.W. Norton & Co. (Original work published 1956)

Lacan, J. (2006a). On a question prior to any possible treatment of psychosis. In J. Lacan, *Écrits: The first complete edition in English* (B. Fink, Trans.). New York: W. W. Norton & Co. (Original work published 1959)

Lacan, J. (2006a). The subversion of the subject and the dialectic of desire in the Freudian unconscious In J. Lacan, *Écrits: The first complete edition in English* (B. Fink, Trans.). New York: W. W. Norton & Co. (Original work published 1960)

Lacan, J. (2006a). The direction of the treatment and the principles of its power. In J. Lacan, *Écrits: The first complete edition in English* (B. Fink, Trans.). New York: W. W. Norton & Co. (Original work published 1961)

Lacan, J. (2006a). Kant with Sade. In J. Lacan, *Écrits: The first complete edition in English* (B. Fink, Trans.). New York: W. W. Norton & Co. (Original work published 1963)

Lacan, J. (2006a). On Freud's 'trieb' and the psychoanalyst's desire. In J. Lacan, *Écrits: The first complete edition in English* (B. Fink, Trans.). New York: W. W. Norton & Co. (Original work published 1964)

Lacan, J. (2006a). Position of the unconscious. In J. Lacan, *Écrits: The first complete edition in English* (B. Fink, Trans.). New York: W. W. Norton & Co. (Original work published 1966)

Lacan, J. (2006b). *Le séminaire livre XVI: D'un Autre à l'autre, 1968–1969.* Paris: Seuil.

Lacan, J. (2007). *The seminar of Jacques Lacan, book XVII: The other side of psychoanalysis, 1969–1970.* (J.-A. Miller, Ed.; R. Grigg, Trans.). New York: W. W. Norton & Co. (Original work published 1991)

Lacan, J. & Granoff, W. (1956). Fetishism: The symbolic, the imaginary and the real. In S. Lorand & M. Balint (Eds.), *Perversions: Psychodynamics and therapy* (pp. 265–276). New York: Gramercy Publishing Company.

Le Brun, A. (1990). *Sade: A sudden abyss.* San Francisco, CA: City Lights.

Leonoff, A. (1997). Destruo ergo sum: Towards a psychoanalytic understanding of sadism. *Canadian Journal of Psychoanalysis, 5*(1), 95–112.

Libbrecht, K. (1999). The original sin of psychoanalysis: On the desire of the analyst. In D. Nobus (Ed.), *Key concepts of Lacanian psychoanalysis* (pp. 75–100). New York: Other Press.

Lihn, H. (1970). Fetishism: A case report. *International Journal of Psychoanalysis, 51,* 351–358.

Marlatt, G., & Gordon, J. (1985). *Relapse prevention: Maintenance strategies in the treatment of addictive behaviors.* New York: Guilford.

Marques, J. K., Wiederanders, M., Day, D. M., Nelson, C., & van Ommeren, A. (2005). Effects of a relapse prevention program on sexual recidivism: Final results from California's Sex Offender Treatment and Evaluation Project (SOTEP). *Sexual Abuse: A Journal of Research and Treatment, 17,* 79–107.

McDougall, J. (1970). Homosexuality in women. In J. Chasseguet-Smirgel (Ed.) *Female sexuality: New psychoanalytic views.* Ann Arbor: University of Michigan Press.

McDougall, J. (1972). Primal scene and sexual perversion. *International Journal of Psychoanalysis, 53,* 371–384.

McDougall, J. (1995). *The many faces of Eros: A psychoanalytic exploration of human sexuality.* New York: W. W. Norton & Co.

Merleau-Ponty, M. (1968). *The visible and the invisible: Followed by working notes* (A. Lingis, Trans.). Chicago, IL: Northwestern University Press.

Miller, J.-A. (1993–1994). Donc. Unpublished course.

Miller, D. (1996). A case of childhood perversion. In R. Feldstein, B. Fink, & M. Jaanus (Eds.), *Reading seminars I and II: Lacan's return to Freud* (pp. 294–300). Albany: State University of New York Press.

Miller, J.-A. (1996a). A discussion of Lacan's "Kant with Sade." In R. Feldstein, B. Fink, & M. Jaanus (Eds.), *Reading seminars I and II: Lacan's return to Freud* (pp. 212–237). Albany: State University of New York Press.

Miller, J.-A. (1996b). On perversion. In R. Feldstein, B. Fink, & M. Jaanus (Eds.), *Reading seminars I and II: Lacan's return to Freud* (pp. 306–320). Albany: State University of New York Press.

Miller, J.-A. (2006a). Introduction to reading Jacques Lacan's seminar on anxiety II (B. Fulks, Trans.). *Lacanian Ink, 27*, 8–63.

Miller, J.-A. (2006b). The names-of-the-father (B. Fulks, Trans.). *Lacanian Ink, 27*, 64–79.

Miller, J.-A. (2006c). A reading of the seminar from an Other to the other (B. Fulks, Trans.). *Lacanian Ink, 29*, 8–61.

Miller, J.-A. (2006d). On shame. In J. Clemens & R. Grigg (Eds.), *Jacques Lacan and the other side of psychoanalysis* (pp. 11–28). Durham, NC: Duke University Press.

Miller, J.-A. (2007). Jacques Lacan and the voice. In V. Voruz & B. Wolf (Eds.), *The later Lacan: An introduction* (pp. 137–146). Albany: State University of New York Press.

Miller, J.-A. (2009a). The phallus and perversion (B. Fulks, Trans.). *Lacanian Ink, 33*, 57–71.

Miller, J.-A. (2009b). The divine details (D. Collins, Trans.). *Lacanian Ink, 34*, 28–51.

Miller, M. (2011). *Lacanian psychotherapy: Theory and practical applications*. New York: Routledge.

Moncayo, R. (2008). *Evolving Lacanian perspectives for clinical psychoanalysis: On narcissism, sexuation, and the phases/faces of analysis in contemporary culture*. London: Karnac.

Money, J. (1988). *Gay, straight and in-between: The sexology of erotic orientation*. New York: Oxford University Press.

Nobus, D. (1999). Life and death in the glass: A new look at the mirror stage. In D. Nobus (Ed.), *Key concepts of Lacanian psychoanalysis* (pp. 101–138). New York: Other Press.

Nobus, D. (2000). *Jacques Lacan and the Freudian practice of psychoanalysis*. London: Routledge.

Penney, J. (2003). Confessions of a medieval sodomite. In M. A. Rothenberg, D. Foster, & S. Žižek (Eds.), *Perversion and the social relation* (pp. 126–158). Durham, NC: Duke University Press.

Nobus, D. (2006). Locating perversion, dislocating psychoanalysis. In D. Nobus & L. Downing (Eds.), *Perversion: Psychoanalytic perspectives/perspectives on psychoanalysis* (pp. 3–18). Karnac: London.

Pithers, W., Marques, J., Gibat, C., & Marlatt, G. (1983). Relapse prevention: A self-control model of treatment and maintenance of change for sexual aggressive. In J. Greer & I. Stuart (Eds.), *The sexual aggressor: Current perspectives on treatment* (pp. 292–310). New York: Van Nostrand Reinhold.

Proctor, E. (1996). A five-year outcome evaluation of a community-based *treatment* program for convicted sexual *offenders* run by the probation service. *Journal of Sexual Aggression, 2*, 3–16.

Proust, M. (1952). *The Guermantes way*. Retrieved from http://ebooks.adelaide.edu.au/p/proust/marcel/p96g/chapter1.html

Rosario, V. (1997). *The erotic imagination: French histories of perversity*. New York: Oxford University Press.

Rosen, I. (1996). *Sexual deviation* (3rd ed.). Oxford, UK: Oxford University Press.

Saussure, F. (2005). *Course in general linguistics* (R. Harris, Trans.). La Salle, IL: Open Court. (Original work published 1916)

Schneiderman, S. (1980). *Returning to Freud: Clinical psychoanalysis in the school of Lacan.* New Haven, CT: Yale University Press.

Seto, M., Hanson, R. K., & Babchishin, K. (2011). Contact sexual offending by men with online sexual offenses. *Sexual Abuse: A Journal of Research and Treatment, 23*(1), 124–145.

Soler, C. (1995). The subject and the other (II). In R. Feldstein, B. Fink, & M. Jaanus (Eds.), *Reading seminar XI: Lacan's four fundamental concepts of psychoanalysis* (pp. 45–53). Albany: State University of New York Press.

Stekel, W. (1964). *Peculiarities of behavior; wandering mania, dipsomania, kleptomania, pyromania and allied impulsive acts* (J. Van Teslaar, Trans.). New York: Grove Press. (Original work published 1924)

Stoller, R. L. (1976). *Perversion: The erotic form of hatred.* Hassocks, Sussex, UK: Harvester Press.

Stoller, R. (1991). The term "perversion." In G. Fogel & W. Myers (Eds.), *Perversions and near perversions in clinical practice: New psychoanalytic perspectives* (pp. 36–56). New Haven, CT: Yale University Press.

Swales, S. (2010). Psychosis or neurosis? Lacanian diagnosis and group therapists. *GROUP, 34*(2), 129–144.

Swales, S. (2011). S/he stole my jouissance! A Lacanian approach to gender in the group. *GROUP, 35*(3), 221–234.

Tostain, R. (1993). Fetishization of a phobic object. In S. Schneiderman (Ed.), *How Lacan's ideas are used in clinical practice* (pp. 247–260). Northvale, NJ: Jason Aronson.

Verhaeghe, P. (2001a). Perversion I: Perverse traits. *The Letter, 22,* 59–75.

Verhaeghe, P. (2001b). Perversion II: The perverse structure. *The Letter, 23,* 77–95.

Verhaeghe, P. (2004). *On being normal and other disorders: A manual for clinical psychodiagnostics.* New York: Other Press.

Ward, T., Bickley, J., Webster, S. D., Fisher, D., Beech, A., & Eldridge, H. (2004). *The self-regulation model of the offense and relapse process: A manual. Volume 1: Assessment.* Victoria, BC, Canada: Trafford Publishing.

Welldon, E. (1992). *Mother, madonna, whore: The idealization and denigration of motherhood.* New York: Guilford Press.

Welldon, E. (1996). Group-analytic psychotherapy in an out-patient setting. In C. Cordess & M. Cox (Eds.), *Forensic psychotherapy: Crime, psychodynamics and the offender patient* (pp. 63–82). London: Jessica Kingsley Publishers.

Willemsen, J., & Verhaeghe, P. (2009). When psychoanalysis meets law and evil: Perversion and psychopathy in the forensic clinic. In A. Hirvonen & J. Porttikivi (Eds.), *Law and evil: Philosophy, politics, psychoanalysis* (pp. 237–259). New York: Routledge.

Žižek, S. (1996). "I hear you with my eyes": Or, the invisible master. In R. Salecl & S. Žižek (Eds.), *Gaze and voice as love objects* (pp. 89–126). Durham, NC: Duke University Press.

INDEX

Made in the USA
Lexington, KY
28 November 2019

57815452R00155